Richard Tomlinson was born in 1958 and educated at Cambridge University, where he took first-class honours in history. After completing a doctorate in Paris, he spent two years at Columbia University in New York as a Harkness Fellow. Since 1985 he has been a television and newspaper journalist with London Weekend Television, Channel Four and *The Independent*. He has written regularly on the monarchy for *The Independent* and *The Independent on Sunday*.

DIVINE RIGHT

The Inglorious Survival of British Royalty

RICHARD TOMLINSON

LITTLE, BROWN AND COMPANY
Boston New York Toronto London

Extract on page 132 from 'Ballade Tragique à Double Refrain'
by Max Beerbohm was previously quoted in *Conversation with Max*
by S. N. Behrman (Hamish Hamilton, 1960).

Lyrics on page 177 from 'Lizzie Borden' by Michael Brown
© 1952 Unichappell Music Inc. (Renewed).
All rights reserved. Used by permission.
For UK & Eire: reproduced by permission of Campbell Connelly
& Co. Ltd., 8/9 Frith St., London W1V 5TZ

ISBN 0–316–85126–4

10 9 8 7 6 5 4 3 2 1

Printed in England

For Tess

'Kings are gods'
James I, 1610

'I am quite an ordinary sort of fellow'
George V, 1935

Contents

* References:
To avoid defacing the text with figures, the source notes have been listed at the back according to their line number on the page, with a brief citation from the passage in question: for example, page 74, line 11, 'looked so nice'. Nicolson, *George V*, p. 148. Occasionally an asterisk has been inserted in the text, to indicate that the subject is discussed at greater length in the notes.

The British Royal Family Since Victoria

Anyone who writes about the British royal family is immediately confronted by the problem of what to call the principal figures. Like other dynasties, the Windsors have the annoying royal habit of changing their names according to circumstances. For instance, the late Duke of Windsor was known in previous incarnations as the Prince of Wales (1910–1936) and King Edward VIII (1936), while his family always called him David – even though that was the last of his seven Christian names.

The problem is not simply one of nomenclature. Because the Windsors placed great importance on their titles, what they are called affects how they are seen. The present Queen's father is known to posterity as King George VI, but to his family he was always Bertie. The former title envelops him in the mystique of his office; the second suggests a rather less august personage.

As a general rule, I have departed from common practice and called them by their familial names. Here, too, lurks potential confusion, for both George VI and his grandfather Edward VII were called Bertie, while the present Queen and her mother share the name Elizabeth. But on balance, it seems to me that the advantages of using familial names outweigh the drawbacks. Unlike their titles, these names remained constant throughout their lives.

They also make it easier to see the Windsors as people – albeit very unusual people – rather than the remote figures of royal mythology.

Occasionally I have broken my own rule for the sake of clarity: for example, the elder Elizabeth sometimes becomes the Queen Mother when mentioned in same context as her daughter. This particular difficulty would have been removed if I had called the present Queen by her familial name, 'Lilibet', throughout the book; but in her case, as in that of her grandmother Queen Mary ('May'), the familial style for once seemed inappropriate. So I have compromised: until her accession in 1952 she is Lilibet; afterwards she is always called Elizabeth.

As a guide through these thickets, the following table lists the leading members of the British royal family since Victoria, including basic biographical details, their principal titles at each stage of their lives, and their familial names. Where relevant, the dates of reigns are included in brackets after the monarch's title.

Queen Victoria (1837–1901)
Born   1819
Parents   Duke and Duchess of Kent
Married   Prince Albert of Saxe-Coburg, 1840. Nine children
Familial name   Victoria
Died   1901

King Edward VII (1901–1910)
Born   1841
Parents   Queen Victoria (qv) and Prince Albert
Married   Princess Alexandra of Schleswig-Holstein, 1863. Five children (and one deceased)
Other titles   Prince of Wales, 1841–1901
Familial name   Bertie
Died   1910

Queen Alexandra

Born   1844
Parents   King Christian IX and Queen
Louise of Denmark
Married   Prince of Wales, later Edward
VII (qv), 1863. Five children (and one
deceased)
Other titles   Princess of Wales,
1863–1901
Familial name   Alix
Died   1925

King George V (1910–1936)

Born   1865
Parents   King Edward VII (qv) and
Queen Alexandra (qv)
Married   Princess May of Teck, later
Queen Mary (qv), 1893. Six children
Other titles   Duke of York, 1892–1901;
Duke of Cornwall, 1901; Prince of
Wales, 1901–1910
Familial name   George (Georgie to his mother)
Died   1936

Queen Mary

Born   1867
Parents   Duke and Duchess of Teck
Married   Duke of York, later George V
(qv), 1893. Six children
Other titles   Duchess of York,
1893–1901; Duchess of Cornwall, 1901;
Princess of Wales, 1901–1910; Queen
Consort, 1910–1936; Queen Mother,
1936–1953
Familial name   May
Died   1953

King Edward VIII (1936)
Born   1894
Parents   King George V (qv) and Queen
Mary (qv)
Married   Wallis Simpson, 1937. No
children
Other titles   Prince of Wales, 1910–1936;
Duke of Windsor, 1936–1972
Familial name   David
Died   1972

King George VI (1936–1952)
Born   1895
Parents   King George V (qv) and Queen
Mary (qv)
Married   Lady Elizabeth Bowes-Lyon,
later Queen Mother (qv), 1923. Two
children
Other titles   Duke of York, 1920–1936
Familial name   Bertie
Died   1952

Queen Elizabeth the Queen Mother
Born   1900
Parents   Earl and Countess of
Strathmore
Married   Duke of York, later George VI
(qv), 1923. Two children
Other titles   Duchess of York,
1923–1936; Queen Consort,
1936–1952; Queen Mother, 1952–
Familial name   Elizabeth

Queen Elizabeth II (1952–)
Born 1926
Parents King George VI (qv) and
Queen Elizabeth the Queen Mother (qv)
Married Prince Philip of Greece (qv),
1947. Four children
Other titles Duchess of Edinburgh,
1947–52
Familial name Lilibet

Prince Philip
Born 1921
Parents Prince Andrew and Princess
Alice of Greece
Married Princess Elizabeth, later
Queen Elizabeth II (qv), 1947. Four
children
Other titles Duke of Edinburgh, 1947–
Familial name Philip

Princess Margaret
Born 1930
Parents King George VI (qv) and
Queen Elizabeth the Queen Mother (qv)
Married Antony Armstrong-Jones
(Lord Snowdon), 1960 (marriage
dissolved, 1978). Two children
Other titles Countess of Snowdon 1960–
Familial name Margaret Rose (as a girl)

Prince Charles
Born   1948
Parents   Queen Elizabeth II (qv) and
Prince Philip (qv)
Married   Lady Diana Spencer (qv), 1981
(separated, 1992). Two children
Other titles   Duke of Cornwall,
1952–58; Prince of Wales, 1958–
Familial name   Charles

Princess Diana
Born   1961
Parents   Earl and Countess Spencer
Married   Prince Charles (qv), 1981
(separated, 1992). Two children
Other titles   Princess of Wales, 1981–
Familial name   Diana

British Royalty in the Twentieth Century: Chronology

1901   Death of Victoria. Accession of Edward VII.

1902   Coronation of Edward VII.

1906   Attempted assassination of King Alfonso and Queen Ena of Spain.

1910   Death of Edward VII. Accession of George V.
        Overthrow of King Manuel of Portugal, who settles in England.

1913   Assassination of King George I of Greece.

1914   Assassination of Archduke Franz Ferdinand in Sarajevo. Outbreak of First World War.

1917   Overthrow of Tsar Nicholas of Russia. George V obstructs British government's proposed offer of asylum to Tsar and his family.
        H.G. Wells writes to *The Times*, deploring Britain's 'alien and uninspiring court'.
        British dynasty adopts the family name of Windsor.

1918   End of First World War.
        Abdication of Kaiser Wilhelm II of Germany and King Ferdinand of Bulgaria. Collapse of Austro-Hungarian empire. Monarchies disappear in Germany and Austro-Hungary.

1919   Prince of Wales (later Edward VIII) embarks on a series
          of triumphal tours around the British empire.

1922–3   Collapse of Greek monarchy. The Greek royal family is
          forced into exile, including the infant Prince Philip
          (later Duke of Edinburgh).

1923   Marriage of Prince Albert (later George VI) to Lady
          Elizabeth Bowes-Lyon (later the Queen Mother).

1925   Death of Queen Alexandra, widow of Edward VII.

1928   Ahmed Zogu declares himself King Zog of the
          Albanians. He is the only reigning European monarch
          not related by blood or marriage to the British royal
          family.

1931   Collapse of Spanish monarchy. King Alfonso goes into
          exile.

1932   First royal Christmas broadcast, delivered by George V
          from Sandringham.

1934   Marriage of the Duke of Kent to Princess Marina of
          Greece.

1935   Silver Jubilee of George V.
          Restoration of Greek monarchy.

1936   The year of three kings. Death of George V and acces-
          sion of Edward VIII (January). Abdication of Edward
          VIII and accession of George VI (December).

1937   Coronation of George VI.
          Marriage of Duke of Windsor (formerly Edward VIII)
          to Mrs Wallis Simpson. Duke and Duchess of Windsor
          visit Germany at invitation of Nazis, and meet Hitler.

1939   Overthrow of King Zog of the Albanians, after Italian
          invasion.
          Outbreak of Second World War. As an austerity mea-
          sure, court ceremonial is drastically reduced.

1940   Buckingham Palace bombed for the first time. Queen
          Elizabeth reportedly says she can now look the East
          End in the face.
          Hitler invades Western Europe. Queen Wilhemina of
          the Netherlands and King Haakon of Norway flee to

Britain. King Zog of the Albanians also arrives in Britain, but is not recognised as an exiled head of state. Appointment of Duke of Windsor as governor of the Bahamas, after Germans hatch a plan to restore him to the British throne as a Nazi puppet.

1941   Hitler invades Balkans. Yugoslav and Greek monarchies overthrown. King Peter of Yugoslavia joins the other royal exiles in Britain.

1945   End of Second World War. Stalin occupies eastern Europe. Monarchies disappear in Yugoslavia, Bulgaria, and Albania.

1946   Plebiscites restore the Greek monarchy and abolish the Italian monarchy.

1947   Marriage of Princess Elizabeth to Prince Philip of Greece.

Communists overthrow King Michael of Romania.

1948   Birth of Prince Charles (later Prince of Wales).

1950   Publication of *The Little Princesses* by Marion Crawford, formerly governess to Elizabeth and Margaret. The first modern serve-and-tell memoirs are an international bestseller.

1951   Duke of Windsor publishes his memoirs, justifying his conduct in the abdication crisis.

1952   Death of George VI. Accession of Elizabeth II.

1953   Coronation of Elizabeth II, the first royal pageant to be broadcast live on television.

The Queen offends Scottish royalists by not wearing her state robes when she receives the honours of Scotland in Edinburgh.

1955   Princess Margaret declares she will not marry Peter Townsend.

1956   First 'informal' lunch held at Buckingham Palace, devised so that the Queen can meet a broader range of her subjects.

Prince Philip embarks on a five-month world tour, fuelling rumours that his marriage is in trouble.

1957   Lord Altrincham provokes a controversy by criticising the Queen's entourage as too 'tweedy'.

1958   Last presentation of débutantes at court.

1960   Marriage of Princess Margaret to Antony Armstrong-Jones (Lord Snowdon).

1969   Investiture of Prince of Wales at Caernarvon Castle, linked to broadcast of the specially commissioned film, *Royal Family*. Buckingham Palace denies that the two events are designed to relaunch the monarchy.

1973   Marriage of Princess Anne to Captain Mark Phillips. Lady Jane Wellesley becomes the first of many girls to be tipped as Charles's future bride.

1976   Princess Margaret and Lord Snowdon formally separate.

1977   Silver Jubilee of Elizabeth II. In a speech to both Houses of Parliament, she defends the United Kingdom against plans for devolution.

1978   Princess Margaret's *annus horribilis*. The press pursue her and Roddy Llewellyn to the Caribbean island of Mustique. On her return to England she is hospitalised with lung and liver ailments. Her divorce from Snowdon is announced.

1981   Marriage of Prince of Wales and Lady Diana Spencer.

1982   Birth of Prince William.

1984   Birth of Prince Harry.

1985   Charles and Diana give interview to Alastair Burnet of ITN to quash criticism that they lead superficial lives. Rumours grow that their marriage is in trouble.

1986   Marriage of Prince Andrew and Sarah Ferguson (the Duke and Duchess of York).

1987   Prince Edward, Princess Anne, and the Duke and Duchess of York appear in a televised knockout contest at Alton Towers. The Queen vetoes similar royal jamborees in future.

1989   Charles publishes *A Vision of Britain*, his polemic against modern architecture.

Princess Anne and Mark Phillips formally separate.

1990   Duke and Duchess of York photographed at home with their children by *Hello!* magazine for an undisclosed fee.

1992   *Annus horribilis*:

Divorce of Princess Anne and Mark Phillips. She marries Timothy Laurence later in the year.

Separation of Duke and Duchess of York. Photographs of the Duchess cavorting topless with her 'financial adviser' are published by *Paris Match*.

Separation of Charles and Diana.

Fire at Windsor Castle, followed by criticism of government's announcement that taxpayer will foot the bill for repairs.

Mounting criticism of Queen's exemption from income tax.

1993   New fiscal arrangements for Queen are announced, including the payment of income tax.

Buckingham Palace opened to public for limited summer period to help pay for damage to Windsor Castle.

Australian Prime Minister Paul Keating visits Queen at Balmoral to explain why he wishes to lead his country towards a republic. Republican movements in other Commonwealth countries become more vocal.

Princess Diana announces she is radically reducing her public engagements, and pleads for more privacy.

Archdeacon of York questions whether Charles, having broken his wedding vows, is fit to be future King.

1994   Twenty-fifth anniversary of Charles's investiture as Prince of Wales.

Charles is reported to have ended his friendship with Camilla Parker Bowles.

Introduction:
Elizabeth in Hull

In the spring of 1993 it was time once again for the Queen to travel to Hull. On her last visit to Humberside in 1987 she had admired the skills of local firemen as they rescued a young woman called Julie Mitchell from a burning chemical factory. Julie was not in any great danger from the fire, which was staged for the benefit of Her Majesty in the training tower of the brigade's new headquarters; and shortly after a hydraulic lift had plucked her to safety, it gave Elizabeth great pleasure to declare the headquarters open.

Now, on 19 May 1993, it was the turn of the Francis Askew Primary School and the Humberside British Red Cross Centre to welcome the Queen to the city. In preparing her schedule, Elizabeth's press office had left nothing to chance. They knew that earlier in the day – at 10.28 a.m., to be precise – she would be observing the preparation of high-purity gases for the semi-conductor industry at the British Oxygen Company's plant outside Grimsby.

They knew that by 12.05 p.m. she would be on the first-floor landing above the main entrance to Scunthorpe General Hospital, listening to 'an informal brief on the scope of the overall redevelopment of the hospital facilities'. They knew that exactly an hour later she would enter the Sheffield Lounge of Normanby Hall in Scunthorpe where, enigmatically, she would 'retire' for ten minutes.

And they knew that at 3.20 p.m. Her Majesty, accompanied by her consort (Prince Philip), her Mistress of the Robes (the Duchess of Grafton), her Deputy Private Secretary (Sir Kenneth Scott), her Assistant Press Secretary (John Haslam), her Equerry (Major James Patrick) – not to mention Philip's Private Secretary, the Chief Constable of Humberside, and nameless detectives – would sweep in a five-car convoy through the front gates of the Francis Askew Primary School. Exactly forty-five minutes later she would leave the school and make the short journey to the Red Cross Centre a couple of miles away which, at 4.22 p.m., it would give her great pleasure to open.

Elizabeth's many hosts in Hull that day were understandably anxious about how to behave in the presence of majesty. At the start of her reign, *Royalty Annual* pronounced on this important question. 'There is no code of conduct set down in black and white. Members of the Royal Household, if pressed, will perhaps suggest that you should speak when spoken to, not unless, and that you should reply saying "Your Majesty" – but that then "Ma'am" would be quite proper. It would be courteous to step away from the Queen without turning your back on her. You would best, if you are a lady – and indeed if you can – make a curtsy; if a man, make a short bow of the head perhaps – a brief inclination from the neck and not a bend from the waist like a waiter.'

Not so, courtiers insist today, as they travel around the kingdom organising Elizabeth's visits. She actually likes people to speak first; it saves her from having to start the conversation. She does not mind whether or not you curtsy or bow, nor is she particular about being addressed as 'Your Majesty'. One simply follows the common rules of courtesy. And yet, however much Elizabeth would prefer people to be 'natural' with her, the courtiers' advice usually falls on deaf ears.

David Whincup, the director of the Humberside British Red

Cross, was one of the few that day to keep a sense of proportion. His colleagues were worried about the pen Elizabeth would use at 4.52 p.m. to sign the visitors' book and an official portrait of herself. 'My president said, "You'll need a script pen, she always uses a script pen." And I said, "You must be crazy." I was just going to give her a black biro. But the president said, "No, no, ring the Lord Lieutenant's office. She will require it." And I rang the Lord Lieutenant's office and said to them, "You know, a biro's fine, she'll be relaxed with that"; and they said, "Remember, although it is a very important visit to you, it is an informal visit." And I thought that was nice, because we're still getting the pomp and circumstance with it, but it is an informal and relaxed visit.'

Mr Whincup understands the ambivalence of Elizabeth's monarchy. In the fifth decade of her reign she remains the most queenly of sovereigns, hedged around with enough divinity to make otherwise sane adults fret about her attitude to biros. Here she is, though, able and actually willing to use a biro. Who knows, in these informal times she may even disdain the script pens of yore. By such acts of grace Elizabeth encourages the fantasy that deep down she is just like us – an ordinary woman at ease with her corgis, her horses, and the jigsaw puzzles a manufacturer sends to her each Christmas.

Elizabeth knows she is not like us; and certainly not in Humberside or countless other provincial centres she has visited, where she observes the antics of her subjects as she moves among them. On her last-but-one visit to Hull in 1981, after it had given her great pleasure to open the Humber Bridge, a boy scout broke away from his pack and tried to give her a bunch of flowers. The scoutmaster was so appalled by this act of *lèse-majesté* that the boy's shirt was removed and he was sent home in disgrace.

It needed a statement from Elizabeth's Private Secretary, Sir Philip Moore, to calm things down in the Humberside scouting community. 'The Queen was delighted on this occasion,' Sir Philip said, 'and was sorry the boy got into trouble afterwards.

She realises there was sensitivity about security, but children by and large are not a security threat.'

None the less, the task of Elizabeth's advisers on these visits is to ensure there are no nasty surprises – or indeed any surprises at all: hence the meticulous schedule prepared in advance, which locks her hosts into a preordained pattern of conduct more efficiently than any behavioural drug.

The evening before her 1993 visit, as the royal yacht *Britannia* anchored off the Humberside coast, Elizabeth probably asked her staff to remind her why she was visiting the Francis Askew Primary School, and the Rita Pearlman Youth Centre which uses its premises. They may have spared her some of the incidental details about the school – its position on a windswept site between the local football stadium and the railway line which runs towards Doncaster, the life and times of the city councillor after whom the school is named, the fact that the late Rita Pearlman was the actress Maureen Lipman's aunt.

On a more general note, they would certainly have told her that the school stands in one of Hull's poorest districts, that many of the children come from broken homes, and that juvenile delinquency is a serious problem. She would not have been surprised to learn that even as *Britannia* was docking in Grimsby that morning, six 'rebel children' had been removed by the police for creating a disturbance. And if the courtiers had done their research properly, they would have told her how the school, under its energetic headmistress Anne Coombs, is working hard to raise its standards.

'When we told the parents about the visit they were absolutely delighted,' Mrs Coombs says. 'Now this is an area where, really, they can become quite niggly about teachers having jobs and cars, because they don't see any hope of their families having the same. But they see it – well *I* see it – as a real boost for the community. I mean, the children think she's going to come in full evening dress, a long cloak and a crown.' They are soon to be disillusioned, for Elizabeth chooses instead to wear an orange pastel box coat and matching hat.

It is 3.20 p.m., and the Francis Askew Primary School is ready to meet its royal destiny. To mark the occasion, two men, one wearing a hat made from Russian sable, the other in a top hat and tails, stand in the forecourt clutching a sword and a mace. They are Brian Leaman and Peter Nendick, the Senior and Junior Beadles of the city of Hull, and their task is to assist the Lord Mayor – resplendent in his robes of office – in surrendering the sword of the city to Elizabeth.

She steps from her Rolls Royce with the look of someone who has performed this ceremony five times before – which indeed she has, this being the fifth visit of her reign. A brief touch of the sword with her gloved hand (Mr Nendick's mace is in the reverse position, signifying that it poses no threat) and she is free to go about her royal business.

That business takes her firstly past the Girls' Brigade Divisional Band, which for the past hour has been entertaining the waiting VIPs and journalists with a selection of tunes. Now, as the girls play a xylophone and drum arrangement of Beethoven's 'Ode to Joy', Elizabeth moves towards a prefabricated hut, no more than thirty feet by fifteen feet square, which houses the Rita Pearlman Youth Centre.

Immediately John Haslam, Elizabeth's Assistant Press Secretary, realises there is a problem. Like a magnet, Elizabeth has gathered a retinue of at least twenty people: her husband, the rest of her party, the civic reception group, and the local MP and his wife, as well as the chairman of the Humberside Education Committee, the chairman of the Hull Area Management Committee, the Director of Education for Humberside, and the head of Humberside's Youth Service. At the back of the scrum are twenty journalists, including a German television crew which is making a documentary about the British monarchy. They too are trying to force an entry into the Rita Pearlman Youth Centre.

Just before he is sucked inside, John Haslam signals frantically to his namesake from the Central Office of Information, Rob Haslam, to take the press round to the rear. The Germans look disappointed, until they realise they will be able to film Elizabeth as she moves towards them, rather than over the considerable shoulder of Brigadier Miles Hunt-Davis, Philip's Private Secretary, who is doing his best to keep the local worthies at a respectful distance.

Inside the hut, there is scarcely room for the five groups, 'representing different aspects of work at the centre', to set out their wares for Elizabeth. The author of the schedule, fearing a stampede, has noted firmly that there will be only five or six people per group. Such is the lure of royalty that at least thirty more have deemed themselves to be indispensable. Mr Brian Collins, the city's Chief Fire Officer, would not have been amused by this breach of safety regulations. But he is not here today, for Mr Collins had his own rendezvous with majesty in 1987, when Elizabeth visited the fire brigade headquarters. As for the police, they are too preoccupied with potential assassins to worry about such petty details.

In the corner nearest to Elizabeth, the Humberside Dance Agency begins to dance. Such is the crush that at any moment it seems one of their number will be thrown through the window into the car park outside, where the beadles are busy packing their weapons. Elizabeth smiles and nods as the symbolic significance of the dance is explained to her by a local youth worker.

She and Philip make their way towards what the schedule describes as 'a lounge area'. It is in fact a windowless annexe, where nine members of the Hull Support Group for the Duke of Edinburgh's Award Initiative are slowly wilting in the heat. There is no ventilation, and oxygen must be in short supply. Elizabeth smiles as if she has been looking forward to this meeting for some time.

She emerges from the 'lounge area' before Philip, to be confronted by the Methodist Association of Youth Clubs, identifiable by their yellow sweatshirts, trailing pink and blue streamers before her. It is a pageant, a local youth worker explains, with 'accompanying narrative'. Elizabeth concentrates as the narrative is explained to her, then breaks into a warm smile and moves to the next display. Deprived of a royal audience, the Methodist

Association of Youth Clubs sees no reason to complete the pageant.

On a trestle table, a row of cakes is ready for Elizabeth's inspection. It is unclear who cooked them; by a process of elimination, the press decide it must either be the Youth Women's Group, the Unwaged Group, or the Junior Club – or a combination of all three. One of the photographers has cunningly positioned himself behind the last cake, but Elizabeth is wise to this ploy. She turns away before he is able to take the close-up picture which the press rules governing royal visits specifically forbid.

Many more events await Elizabeth before the Girls' Brigade Band bids her farewell with the theme from *The Dambusters*. In the playground, she compliments the First Aid Group on their first-aid skills, and a member of the Unity Venture Scout Unit on his juggling. She further compliments twenty boys and girls on their football dribbling skills (part of the Hull City FC 'Football in the Community Scheme'). She smiles at one hundred infants on the touchline, clutching their plastic Union Jacks, too busy cheering to notice that Elizabeth is not, after all, wearing a crown.

In the main school hall she has 'the opportunity to view displays from the Parents and Toddlers Group, the Hull Taskforce and Humberside Education Business Partnership'. She receives a posy from nine-year-old Jennifer Williamson, who is so nervous beforehand that she wants someone to support her; and she finds time, departing for once from the schedule, to conduct an all too brief walkabout among the small crowd outside the school gates, while her Rolls Royce cruises behind her.

In a trice the walkabout is over, and Elizabeth is on her way to the Red Cross Centre where – the schedule records – she is introduced at 4.35 p.m. to the Elderly Persons' Pop-In Club.

A cynic might ask why she bothers. Until she reaches the Toddlers' Group, who are too young to appreciate her importance, she is not especially relaxed – and who can blame her? Behind her lies almost two days of sword-touching, hand-shaking

and earnest discussions about hospital extension schemes. Ahead
lies a reception on board *Britannia*, where she will have the oppor-
tunity to meet, among others, the Chief Executive of the East
Riding Health Authority and the Chief Executive of Beverley
Borough Council. Another day of stupefying tedium awaits her in
Norfolk, before she retires for the weekend to Sandringham.

The answer lies somewhere between duty and self-interest. As
head of state, she is not constitutionally obliged to visit the less
picturesque corners of her kingdom. But she also sees herself as
head of the nation, reaching those parts of society which perhaps
the politicians cannot reach.

'I don't think you can stay in London all the time,' she said in
the 1992 BBC film *Elizabeth R*. 'You have to visit other parts of
the country to find out what's going on, or try and encourage
people in different areas, some of which have unemployment,
some of which have new factories; and I think the possibility of
meeting more people is important. A lot of people don't come to
London very often, so we travel to them instead.'

Self-interest comes from the fear that if she did not meet the
people, the people might decide they no longer needed her and
the institution she personifies. When she visited Hull the events
of 1992 – her *annus horribilis* – were still a vivid memory, and the
end was not yet in sight. It was still unknown if Charles and
Diana would eventually divorce. Lawyers continued to haggle
over the separation terms for Andrew and Sarah. The public had
conspicuously refused to subscribe to a fund for the restoration of
Windsor Castle, after the disastrous fire the previous November.
Only the controversy over Elizabeth's tax privileges appeared to
have been settled, with an announcement in February 1993 about
the deal her advisers had negotiated with the Inland Revenue.

Against this dismal background, her visit to the north-east was
intended to show the monarchy was back in business. 'This is
what it's all about,' one of her entourage enthused, as Elizabeth
received her posy from a trembling Jennifer Williamson. He
pointed through the window at the children who had reassem-
bled in the school forecourt for more spontaneous cheering.

Through the din wafted the title song from *Those Magnificent Men in Their Flying Machines*; the Girls' Brigade Band was steadily working through its repertoire. 'In Hartlepool yesterday the reception was just fantastic. The crowds were incredible. Not like in London, where people say "Oh, there's the Queen" and walk on.'

In the wake of 1992 he could not help sounding defensive; and yet on a spring day in Hull, it hardly seemed that Elizabeth was battling for the monarchy's survival. 'I sometimes wonder how future generations will judge the events of this tumultuous year,' she told her audience at London's Guildhall in November 1992, when she confessed it had been an *annus horribilis*. 'I dare say that history will take a slightly more moderate view than that of some contemporary commentators. Distance is well known to lend enchantment, even to the less attractive views.'

From her regal perspective this was not a complacent remark, but simply a statement of fact. In the twentieth century European royalty has been decimated by world wars, revolutions, *coups d'état* and assassinations; for Elizabeth, a fire in the castle, a little difficulty with the taxman, and a few marriage problems must seem mere footnotes to this catastrophic history.

British royalty has often been credited with wisdom, foresight and flexibility in avoiding the fate of their continental cousins. And yet from Victoria to George VI (the father of Elizabeth), British sovereigns were characterised by low intellectual ability, reactionary political views, and a conspicuous lack of that much-trumpeted royal virtue, common sense. Only Victoria's son Edward VII, who reigned from 1901 to 1910, possessed any political flair – and even his posthumous reputation as the 'statesman of Europe' was exaggerated.

The truth is that the British royal family were extremely lucky. They were lucky that Britain was not defeated by Germany in the First World War, and that Hitler failed to carry out his invasion plan in 1940. Both outcomes would probably have spelt the end of the monarchy. They were lucky too that the destruction of continental royalty left them, by default, as Europe's pre-eminent dynasty. In 1901, when Europe's royal families gathered for Victoria's funeral, the Habsburg, Hohenzollern and Romanov dynasties still reigned supreme in Vienna, Berlin and St Petersburg. Half a century later, at the coronation of Elizabeth, the Windsors' position at the summit of European royalty was undisputed.

And they were lucky to be popular with the overwhelming majority of their subjects, for they did not understand the nature of their appeal. George V was utterly bewildered when he returned from a triumphal visit to London's East End during his Silver Jubilee celebrations in 1935. He told the Archbishop of Canterbury in all sincerity that he was 'just an ordinary sort of fellow' – a remark which revealed more about George's natural modesty than his hold on reality.

The royal family's popularity was nevertheless more fragile than it seemed. When Victoria died in 1901 farm labourers knelt in the fields as the royal train bearing her coffin passed on its way to Windsor. Yet only thirty years before there had been a serious republican movement in Britain; and submerged beneath the public's acclaim for the post-Victorian monarchy lay an undercurrent of cynicism and indifference towards the dynasty which even at the height of the Windsors' prestige in the middle of the century never entirely disappeared.

In the past decade, this cynicism has been deepened by the Windsors' misdemeanours, gleefully exposed by a new breed of royal reporter. Distance will not lend enchantment to the spectacle presented by Elizabeth's children and their various consorts in the 1980s. Instead, future historians will note with amazement such horrors as *It's a Royal Knockout* and the less well-known *Three Quarters of a Royal Knockout* (Andrew was absent on naval duty).

But the same historians, sifting through the Squidgy- and Camilla-gate tapes, reading Fergie's masterpiece *Budgie the Little Helicopter*, and contemplating the public engagements of Princess Michael of Kent, will wonder how the royal family managed to survive these horrors. For in this respect at least, Elizabeth's prediction was probably correct; the *annus horribilis* will seem less momentous the further it recedes into the mists of time.

Reason tells us the royal show must end; but in Hull, Grimsby and countless other corners of Elizabeth's kingdom, her loyal subjects confound opinion polls about the monarchy and show no inclination to bring down the curtain.

It is a puzzle – and one whose solution begins not in the tumult of the *annus horribilis* but at the turn of the century, when the business of royalty involved rather less work and rather more fun than Elizabeth's day out in Humberside.

PART ONE

The Royal Club

1

Bertie's Club

In the late 1930s, Prince Christopher of Greece found himself short of money and sat down to write his memoirs. 'Somewhere near the middle of my forty-nine years is a sharp break,' he began. 'On one side of it is the past with its memories of an era of peace and opulence when Kings sat securely on their thrones and Europe contained three Empires and fourteen Monarchies.' On the other side, Christopher continued, lay revolution, assassination, exile and poverty. In general, he preferred to dwell on the earlier period.

Christopher remembered with particular affection the family reunions at Fredensborg, the summer home near Copenhagen of his grandfather the King of Denmark. Aunty Alexandra came from England, and occasionally Uncle Bertie joined her: they are better known as Edward VII and Queen Alexandra. Aunty Dagmar travelled the short distance from St Petersburg, with her amenable husband in tow: to their subjects, they were the Emperor and Empress of Russia.

Alexandra and Dagmar were sisters of Christopher's father King George of Greece, known to them as 'Willy'. Christopher's eldest brother Constantine had married the sister of another Willy, the German Kaiser: but this Willy was rarely invited to

Fredensborg because Aunty Alexandra disliked Prussians, on account of a family quarrel over Schleswig-Holstein.

The Fredensborg holiday was an endless round of royal japes and pranks. One year Uncle Alexander, the Russian Tsar, happened to be staying on his birthday, and his nephews gave him a garden sprinkler as a present. 'He was trying it out next morning,' Christopher recalled, 'when he spied King Oscar of Sweden impeccably turned out, in frock coat and top hat, coming up the park with the King of Denmark. The temptation proved too much for him, so he turned the squirt in King Oscar's direction and drenched him from head to foot, much to the amusement of the Prince of Wales, who was looking out of the window. The one person who certainly did not enjoy the joke was the King. Although the Emperor apologised, he never really forgave him.'

Oscar was not really 'family', which might explain his displeasure. He was descended instead from a Napoleonic Marshal. Elsewhere in Europe, cousins of a superior pedigree could be found in every corner, royalling away, having fun.

No one had more fun than King Ferdinand of Bulgaria, nick-named 'Foxy' on account of his overlong nose. Foxy was a Saxe-Coburg, the same dynasty which had produced Victoria and Albert and was sometimes rudely described as the royal stud farm of Europe. He had been elected Prince of Bulgaria in 1887 after his predecessor – another German prince – was ousted in a coup.

A Renaissance pope had once declared he intended to enjoy the papacy God had granted him. Foxy's attitude to his new kingdom was much the same. At his summer palace overlooking the Black Sea, he created a Japanese garden which tumbled down the cliffs. Thousands of Japanese butterfly chrysalids were imported – 'so that the flowers might not be lonely,' Foxy explained to his guests.

Trains were another passion, for Foxy fancied himself as an engine driver. Bulgaria's entire rolling stock belonged to him, and he would amuse himself by driving up and down the country's several railway lines. In the palace garages, Foxy assembled an impressive fleet of Mercedes and Packard limousines, and an equally handsome collection of chauffeurs to drive them; for despite fathering four children, his sexual tastes were eclectic. He would disappear into the mountains outside Sofia for days on end, with only a chauffeur, some bottles of champagne and a generous picnic hamper for company.

In the spacious international club to which Foxy belonged, there was room for many other royal eccentrics. There was King Leopold of the Belgians, another Saxe-Coburg, whose valet would pour four buckets of sea water over him as he sat in the bath each morning. Piano-playing was banned from the Belgian court, roast partridge was served most evenings, and the King always referred to himself in the third person. 'Wait for him,' he would tell his footman, striding towards his carriage.

There was the Empress Elizabeth of Austria, whose son had married Leopold's daughter Stephanie. The marriage was not a success and Crown Prince Rudolf had killed himself in mysterious circumstances. Elizabeth went half-mad with grief, and became obsessed with ancient Greece. A student from the University of Athens, whose task was to read aloud from the classical authors, was appointed to her suite. On her annual holiday in the south of France, he was also expected to carry her spare skirt. If the weather was hot, she would nip behind a tree and change out of her long dress while the Greek Reader – as he was known – continued the latest extract from Sophocles.

And there was Queen Elizabeth of Romania, better known under her gypsy *nom de plume* of Carmen Sylva. Elizabeth wrote romantic poetry and believed in giving spontaneous expression to her artistic temperament. On one occasion she attended a court ball in Bucharest dressed as a Watteau shepherdess and leading a white lamb on a pink ribbon. The lamb, unnerved by the novelty of its situation, broke free and ran wild in the palace ballroom.

Elizabeth's confidante was her lady-in-waiting Helene Vacarescu. 'The Queen is very fond of her,' Victoria observed ingenuously in 1890 after the couple had visited Balmoral. Elizabeth's stolid husband King Carol, yet another transplanted German prince, could bear it no more when he learned that his estranged wife wanted to include Helene in the line of succession, after hearing 'voices' at a spiritualist seance. He ordered Elizabeth to her ancestral estates for a cooling-off period while Helene was dispatched to Paris with a pension. A lady of many resources, she later wrote articles on the political situation in eastern Europe for the *Revue des Deux Mondes*.

In any club, however, there has to be a pillar of the institution who ensures that standards are maintained, whatever the foibles of certain members. The pillar was Christopher's Uncle Bertie, the eldest son of Victoria, who finally succeeded his mother at the age of fifty-nine in 1901, when he took the title of Edward VII. Stately, gracious and serene, Bertie was the last British sovereign in harmony with the age.

No monarch has ever pursued his pleasures so systematically. Each year, Bertie could be found at the same resorts, the same racecourses, the same country houses (where he would have his way with the same obliging ladies) at exactly the same time. In August he would head for the Bohemian spa of Marienbad, where he would spend a month trying to reduce his considerable girth. By late middle age Bertie's stomach bulged through his waist-coat, obliging him to leave the bottom button undone; and though the fashion was immediately adopted as the hallmark of a gentleman, his weight was perhaps the only aspect of his person which displeased him.

The size of Bertie's stomach is easily explained by the prodigious quantities of food he consumed during the rest of the year. Dinner was rarely less than a twelve-course meal. Grouse, partridge, pheasant stuffed with snipe, snipe stuffed with *foie gras*, pigeon pie, deer pudding, grilled oysters, cold quails, something called *Cotelettes de becassines à la Souvaroff* – all were grist to Bertie's mill.

Before Bertie's dinner there was another meal called 'supper', preceded (in reverse order) by tea, lunch, elevenses and breakfast. The food went down the royal hatch with astonishing speed – dinner rarely lasted more than thirty minutes – and Alexandra worried constantly about her husband's digestion. She had never seen anything like it, she told Bertie's doctors. Nor had they, the doctors replied.

Bertie, it is surprising to learn, was a moderate drinker; perhaps there was no time between mouthfuls. He compensated by smoking a small cigar and two cigarettes before breakfast, followed by twelve large cigars and twenty cigarettes during the rest of the day. Even his constitution could not withstand such a massive intake of toxin: he was the first of three Windsor kings this century to die from smoking-related diseases.

After a few days at Buckingham Palace in mid-September, recovering from his annual 'cure', Bertie would head north for the Doncaster races, a weekend in Inverness-shire with his banking friends the Sassoons, and a month's stalking and shooting at Balmoral. In late October the royal train would convey him from Scotland to Newmarket for the autumn races; accommodation was provided by the Jockey Club, where Bertie had his own suite of rooms.

From November to mid-December he was exceptionally busy, moving between Buckingham Palace, Sandringham and Windsor, entertaining or being entertained every evening. In the build-up to Christmas, Bertie went into festive overdrive. There were supper parties in his private box at Covent Garden, full-scale banquets at Buckingham Palace, and more intimate soirées for his lady friends (Bertie's Page of the Backstairs knew who they were). Then it was off to Sandringham for Christmas and the New Year – more presents (given and received), more gargantuan meals, and the added bonus of thousands of tame pheasants to be shot.

Bertie tried to be in London for two or three nights in January, when his ministers could catch him if they were lucky. He insisted, however, on joining the Duke of Devonshire at Chatsworth for his annual shoot, which lasted a week. February saw him at Buckingham Palace, dining his way through the month. Bertie's official duty at this time of year was to open Parliament – a task he found so stressful that it took him two months' holiday in France and the Mediterranean to recover.

We can pause at this point, as Bertie did, and examine his itinerary more closely through the eyes of his French detective,
Inspector Xavier Paoli of the Paris Sûreté.

According to Paoli, Bertie liked to travel light and incognito.
On board his special train, designed by the International Sleeping
Car Company, were only those members of his suite deemed
essential to his needs: Monsieur Fehr, the Swiss travel agent who
made the hotel bookings (Bertie had poached him from Thomas
Cook), Sir James Reid, the royal physician, two equerries, a post-
master to transcribe telegrams from London, and Caesar, Bertie's
fox terrier. In case Caesar lost his master, his collar carried the
proud inscription 'I am Caesar, the King's Dog'.

At the rear of the train were Bertie's servants: Wellard, the first
footman, responsible for Bertie's forty holiday suits and twenty
pairs of boots; Hoepfner, the second footman, formerly in the service of the German Kaiser, whose main duty was to open doors;
and Meidinger and Hawkins, the two valets, responsible for
Bertie's clothes once he was installed at his favourite Paris hotel,
the Bristol. Three motor cars, each with their own chauffeur,
plus Stamper, Bertie's mechanic, followed the royal train as it
chugged towards Paris.

Incredible though it seems, journalists got wind of Bertie's
movements and were waiting for him at the Bristol. 'As it
appears that I can't have my incognito respected,' the 'Duke of
Lancaster' boomed at Paoli one year, 'I shall be obliged, to my
great regret, to deprive myself of the pleasure of coming to Paris
in future.' Paoli was desperate, for Bertie was his most illustrious
client. He thought of using a double to throw reporters off the
scent. A retired detective nicknamed 'Edouard' by his colleagues
(he bore a striking resemblance to Bertie) was groomed for this
role, but it was no good: 'Edouard's' mannerisms were all
wrong.

'I then hit upon a simpler solution,' Paoli remembered.
'Calling together the journalists whose daily task it was to report
on the King's movements, I made an appeal to their sense of
courtesy and patriotism and besought them to be more discreet

in the performance of their duties. Lastly, I offered myself to hand them, every evening, a written account of "the King's day".' Paoli's proposal was good enough for the Edwardian rat-pack, who would have been ashamed of their disrespectful successors.

'The King's day' was the usual round of theatre visits (Bertie preferred light musicals with a bit of leg on show); encounters with former mistresses (usually in cafés, for Bertie's sexual appetite was beginning to wane); and colossal feasts every evening. None of this was reported by Paoli, who merely referred to Edward's courtesy call (with Caesar) on whichever obscure president happened to reside at the Elysée Palace – conveniently close to the smart shops on the Rue de Rivoli.

After a week, Bertie travelled south to Biarritz for the rest of March, followed by his spring cruise in the Mediterranean on the royal yacht *Victoria and Albert*. Alexandra, having missed the early part of the holiday, would usually join him on board.

Travelling across France by train, Bertie was back in England by early May for the start of the social season (it could not, in truth, start without him). His weekday headquarters was Buckingham Palace, from where he would venture forth for yet more lunching, dining, theatre-going and dancing. Weekends would find him in a variety of country houses, honouring the company (and especially the ladies) with his presence.

Ascot Week was in June, a reminder to Bertie that it was time to move to Windsor, before a brief visit to the Duke of Richmond for the Goodwood races. Like his great-granddaughter Elizabeth, Bertie was a successful racehorse owner; his stud at Sandringham produced two Derby winners, Persimmon in 1896 and Diamond Jubilee (Persimmon's brother) in 1900.

He was a less successful sailor, even though in early August he would always head for Cowes and the Regatta. For several years in the 1890s he and his nephew Willy (the German Kaiser) conducted their own personal naval battle at Cowes. Bertie's racing boat *Britannia* was fast; Willy's boat *Meteor II* was faster still – which was not surprising, since Willy had pinched *Britannia*'s designer and offered him more money to improve the original model.

'Willy is a bully, and most bullies, when tackled, are cowards,' Bertie wrote hopefully to his sister in 1891 – but Willy continued to misbehave. 'Your handicaps are perfectly appalling,' the Kaiser wrote to the Commodore of the Royal Yacht Squadron (Bertie) in 1899, two years after Bertie had given up racing in despair at Willy's one-upmanship. It was some consolation to Bertie that in Willy's other competition, to see which Navy could build the most battleships, the British held the upper hand.

As Prince of Wales, Bertie's way of life had earned him much disapproval – not least from his mother. '*Any encouragement* of his constant love of running about, and not keeping at home near the Queen, is *earnestly* and *seriously* to be deprecated,' she wrote in 1868 of a proposal to give Bertie an Irish holiday residence.

Two years later he was called as a witness in the divorce case of Sir Charles and Lady Mordaunt, and had to defend himself against the charge of adultery with the plaintiff's wife.* And in 1890 Bertie's fortunes reached their lowest ebb when he became embroiled in a gambling scandal. Sir William Gordon-Cumming was accused of cheating at baccarat during a house party at Tranby Croft in Yorkshire; among the other players was Bertie.

When Gordon-Cumming brought a civil action against his accusers, Bertie again found himself called as a witness in court; and as far as the public was concerned, it was *his* reputation, not Gordon-Cumming's, which was at stake. In Berlin, Willy had already made his own judgement. A prince should not gamble with men half his age, he wrote to his grandmother Victoria, especially one who (like Bertie) happened to be an honorary colonel of the Prussian Hussars.

Gordon-Cumming lost his case, but to restore his image Bertie was persuaded to condemn gambling in a letter to the Archbishop of Canterbury. The letter was a masterpiece of royal hypocrisy. 'I have a horror of gambling,' Bertie wrote, 'and should always do my utmost to discourage others who have an inclination for it, as

I consider that gambling, like intemperance, is one of the greatest curses that a country can be afflicted with.' None the less, Bertie made it clear that he did not regard a wager between gentlemen as gambling; like drunkenness, it was a working-class vice.

Bertie's ability to rise above his misfortunes owed nothing to improvements in his character. Morally he was incorrigible, even if his physical ability to behave immorally declined with age. The reason he proved such a successful king was because he had the ideal temperament for a European monarch at the turn of the century.

So long as he was merely heir to the throne – and it was a very long time indeed – Bertie was vulnerable to the charge of self-indulgence. 'The Prince cannot help feeling that you are a little hard and unjust upon him . . .' Bertie's Private Secretary Francis Knollys wrote to one critic shortly before his accession. 'There are many things which he is obliged to do which the outside world would call pleasures and amusements; they are, however, often anything but a source of amusement to him, though his position demands that he should every year go through a certain round of social duties which bore him to death.' Like Bertie's letter to the Archbishop (also drafted by Knollys) the case for the defence was singularly unconvincing.

As King, however, these vices were mysteriously transformed into royal virtues. In the first place, Bertie knew how to behave like a monarch. 'I never quite understood why he made people so frightened of him,' his Assistant Private Secretary Sir Frederick Ponsonby said after his death, 'but there can be no doubt that even his most intimate friends were terrified of him.'

Ponsonby was unusual in not sharing this fear – for Bertie's tantrums were dreadful to behold. At Marienbad one year, Ponsonby had even tried to beat the King at croquet, explaining to his petrified partner that the convention which held that royalty must always win was 'out of date'. Bertie won by a whisker, and so enjoyed himself that he challenged Ponsonby to a return match the next day.

Bertie also looked the part of a monarch, unlike his mother, who had spent the last forty years of her life dressed in widow's weeds. '*Mon métier à moi est d'être roi,*' he was fond of saying in impeccable French; and the highlight of his year was probably the state opening of Parliament, when he could wear the full regalia of his office, ride in a glittering carriage and (best of all) sit on a throne.

These were not trivial accomplishments, for the appearance of majesty mattered far more than the kingly wisdom which was supposed to reside between Bertie's ears. Bertie's attitude to the daily grind of state business was well illustrated in 1908, when the Liberal Prime Minister Campbell-Bannerman resigned because of ill-health. Rather than interrupt his holiday in Biarritz, Bertie insisted that Campbell-Bannerman's deputy Asquith should travel to France to kiss hands as the new Prime Minister.

Yet no European sovereign understood better the charismatic power of his office; not even Willy (the Kaiser), who with his waxed moustache, his ludicrous uniforms and his unfortunate withered arm (the result of an accident during his birth) cut a ridiculous figure on parade.

Bertie's finest hour was undoubtedly his visit to Paris in May 1903, which helped secure the *Entente Cordiale* between Britain and France. The British wanted the treaty to stabilise the situation in North Africa, where the European powers were competing for influence, and to prevent the French negotiating a similar pact with the Germans. But French public opinion was extremely hostile to Britain following the skirmish at Fashoda in 1898, where British troops had blocked French colonial expansion up the River Nile. Even Bertie found himself lampooned in the Paris press as a tyrant, a murderer and worse.

Against this background, Bertie's offer to smooth the path of diplomacy was an act of some courage. On 1 May, the day he arrived in Paris, the crowds were sullen as he drove with President Loubet to the British Embassy. A few voices could be heard shouting '*Vive Fashoda!*' and '*Vive Jeanne d'Arc!*' Two days later, as he left the Paris Opera following a command performance, the crowds were in an ecstasy of anglophilia. Bertie's carriage was nearly mobbed, and he left for London to the sound of '*Vive Edouard!*' and '*Notre bon Edouard!*' ringing in his ears.

What had Bertie done to deserve it? Essentially, he had combined majesty with *bonhomie*. To the crowds who came to abuse him and stayed to cheer, he smiled and doffed his top hat in acknowledgement. To the civic dignitaries who assembled at the Hôtel de Ville, he spoke in French of his long-standing affection for the city of Paris (and its women, he might have added).

Even an awkward evening at the Théâtre Français, where he and President Loubet watched a play with the ominous title *L'Autre Danger*, was turned by Bertie to his advantage. Seeing an actress he knew during the interval, he kissed her hand and proclaimed: 'Mademoiselle, I remember applauding you in London where you represented all the grace and spirit of France.' *Le tout Paris* swooned at this carefully rehearsed compliment.

In such a heady atmosphere, the British ambassador to Paris, Sir Edmund Monson, can be forgiven his breathless prose as he reported to London on Bertie's visit. '. . . The reappearance of the frequent visitor of former years, the well known and popular Prince of Wales coming back to his old friends as King of England, returning to the capital for which he has never concealed his predilection, aroused a feeling of gratification only equalled by the satisfaction of that large body of politicians who, from motives of reason, reflection and clear comprehension of this country's interests, have always systematically favoured the *Entente Cordiale.*'

Bertie's diplomatic duties were not finished, however. Two months later President Loubet, a true *sans-culotte*, was received by Bertie at Buckingham Palace having eschewed the regulation knee-breeches for presentation at court. 'I presume that you have come in the suite of the American ambassador,' Bertie had sarcastically remarked to Lord Rosebery when he committed the same sartorial lapse at a Buckingham Palace soirée. Loubet escaped Bertie's censure; in the higher national interest, even Bertie could excuse a man his trousers.

The *Entente Cordiale* was duly signed in April 1904. Despite the plaudits of diplomats like Monson, it would probably have been signed anyway; in relation to German rearmament, British and French interests naturally converged. Who was Bertie, though, to deny himself the title of 'statesman of Europe'?

Bertie was now at the height of his fame. Supremely assured in his royal vocation, he was inclined to patronise his more careworn European relatives. His cousin the Tsar, Bertie decided in 1905, was a trifle weak. If only Nicky would 'remain firm and stick by his promises' all his troubles with revolutionaries would be over. Alas, Bertie expected the worst of such a chinless character.

As for Willy, he did not improve with the years. In 1908, during an interview with the *Daily Telegraph*, Willy described the English as 'mad as March hares'. He also claimed personal responsibility for Britain's victory in the Boer War (Willy, it seemed, had a secret plan which had been adopted by the British commander Lord Roberts).

When he read the interview, Bertie could scarcely contain himself – with rage or glee, it is no longer clear. Even 'light-hearted and non-serious racing and society men', he told the diplomat Lord Hardinge, excluding himself from this category, had been struck by the Kaiser's folly. 'Of all the political gaffes which H.I.M. [His Imperial Majesty] has made, this is the greatest.'

Bertie's self-appointed task was to keep his fellow members of the royal club up to the mark. Regarding the odious Leopold of the Belgians in 1903, Bertie stated that he could not 'feel attracted towards a Sovereign, whether he is a relative or not, who, he considers, has neglected his duty towards Humanity.' The issue on this occasion was the Belgian Congo, Leopold's personal colony, where terrible atrocities had been committed. On another occasion, at the theatre in Paris, Bertie ignored Leopold because of the Belgian King's appalling manners. By coincidence, the two kings had hired adjacent boxes – and there they remained, refusing to pay each other the usual compliments.

There was another problem which Bertie could not help

noticing: an alarming number of his royal relatives were being shot. Someone had even shot at him. At the time, these assassins seemed a bit of a nuisance. With hindsight, they heralded the end of Prince Christopher's halcyon royal age, with the outbreak of the First World War in August 1914. It was Bertie's final stroke of good fortune to die four years earlier, the last British sovereign to sit comfortably on his throne. For his descendants, a new age of anxiety had begun.

2

The Siege

On 4 April 1900 Bertie set off with Alexandra to visit her
father in Copenhagen. It was a rare break in his usual schedule,
and one for which he and Alexandra nearly paid with their lives.
'Arrive at Brussels, 4.50 p.m.,' Bertie noted in his diary – for he
liked to be punctual. 'Walk about station. Just as train is leaving,
5.30, a man fires a pistol at P. of W. [Alexandra] through open
window of carriage (no harm done).'

Bertie knew that the first duty of royalty in these situations
was to keep a stiff upper lip, but it had been a very close shave.
The would-be assassin, a fifteen-year-old Belgian anarchist (such
people existed) called Sipido, had fired his revolver at point-
blank range. If the window on the far side of the carriage had not
also been open, Alexandra might well have been killed by the ric-
ochet.

Alexandra was rather less composed about the experience than
her husband. 'I felt the ball buzzing across my eyes and saw him
coming straight at us,' she wrote home melodramatically after
Sipido had been arrested.

Royalty's second duty was to be magnanimous. Bertie asked
the Belgian authorities to treat Sipido leniently, on account of his
age. Belgian justice took Bertie at his word and merely placed

Sipido on police probation until he came of age. Anxious to resume his revolutionary career, Sipido simply crossed the border into France.

Even the Kaiser was indignant on his uncle's behalf. 'The behaviour of the Belgians in the Sipido affair is simply outrageous,' he wrote to Bertie. '. . . Either their laws are ridiculous, or the jury are a set of damned, bloody scoundrels; which is the case I am unable to decide. With best love to Aunty and Cousins.'

In one sense, there was nothing new about Sipido's assault on the heir to the throne, for Victoria had been the object of at least five assassination attempts during her long reign. Most of the would-be regicides were mentally deranged; a typical example was Edward Oxford, a disturbed youth, who in 1840 fired at Victoria as she and Albert were driving up Constitution Hill from Buckingham Palace, and was immediately overwhelmed by the crowd.

Victoria's least favourite Prime Minister, William Gladstone, found the pattern of lunacy strangely reassuring. In 1882 yet another attempt ended in farce rather than tragedy when Roderick McLean, who had lost his senses, fired at Victoria's carriage outside Windsor station, as it waited to take her up to the castle. McLean was immediately set upon by two Eton boys, who beat him up with their umbrellas. Gladstone told Victoria that while foreign assassins had political motives, in England they were all madmen. Since Victoria believed Gladstone himself to be 'half-mad', she found his words unhelpful.

Nor was he entirely correct. Ten years before, an Irish Republican called Arthur O'Connor had pointed an unloaded gun at Victoria. O'Connor later said he wanted to frighten Victoria into persuading the government to release some Fenian prisoners. He too was treated leniently, and after a year in jail offered to be deported if the Home Secretary could find a country with an agreeable climate.

Nevertheless, the Sipido incident marked the moment when British royalty joined their continental cousins as targets for what they sincerely believed was an international revolutionary conspiracy. By the time Sipido struck, the rest of the royal club had already been given notice that it was under siege.

In September 1898 the Empress Elizabeth of Austria, on a visit to Switzerland, was murdered by an Italian anarchist called Luigi Lucheni as she prepared to board a ferry on Lake Geneva. Lucheni's weapon was a sharp-edged file which left such a narrow wound that at first Elizabeth believed she had been punched rather than stabbed. 'I was only frightened by that horrible man,' she told her lady-in-waiting, and staggered to her feet. A few minutes later she collapsed on deck, for Lucheni had struck her through the heart. Her body was carried back to her hotel on an improvised bier of sailing oars; she was dead on arrival.

'I am spared nothing,' her husband Franz Josef, the Austrian Emperor, exclaimed when he heard the news. He had now lost his son through suicide, his wife through assassination – and eventually he would lose his nephew and heir.

A grisly sequence of royal murders had been set in motion. In July 1900, a few months after the Sipido attack, King Umberto of Italy was shot dead at Monza while travelling to his holiday villa. The assassin was another self-styled anarchist called Gaetano Bresci, who in a previous incarnation had been a silk-weaver from Paterson, New Jersey. He was sentenced to life imprisonment.

Three years later King Alexander and Queen Draga of Serbia were killed in Belgrade by a group of rebel army officers. The medieval barbarity of their murder shocked the rest of Europe; to prove that the deed was done, the assassins threw the King and Queen's naked corpses out of the palace window into the gardens below.

When Bertie heard the news in London, he declared grandly that 'I cannot be indifferent to the assassination of a member of my profession.' The beneficiary of Alexander's murder was the head of the rival Karageorgevich dynasty, who accepted the vacant Serbian throne as Peter I. He was an anglophile who had translated John Stuart Mill's *On Liberty* into Serbian, but that cut no ice with Bertie, who had never read Mill (nor any other book).

For three years Britain broke off diplomatic relations with Serbia, until Bertie was assured that the regicides had been cashiered from the army.

The horror reached a climax in May 1906 when Europe's royal families gathered in Madrid for the wedding of Bertie's niece Victoria Eugenie (known as Ena) to King Alfonso of Spain. Bertie did not attend, sending the Prince and Princess of Wales in his stead; and he would have been proud of how the future George V preserved his sang-froid in the midst of so much blood.

On the morning of the wedding, spectators along the procession route were amused by a man on the upper balcony of an apartment building, who was dropping oranges into the street below. They thought he was playing an obscure practical joke. The man, a Spanish anarchist called Matteo Morral, was actually calculating the exact moment he would need to drop his bomb a few hours later to land in the moving carriage of Alfonso and Ena. Any other royal guests he managed to kill would be a bonus.

Morral's plan almost worked. '[The bomb] burst between the wheel-horses and the front of the carriage, killing about 20 people and wounding about 50 or 60, mostly officers and soldiers,' the Prince of Wales noted that evening in his diary.

'Thank God!' George continued, remembering his club loyalties. 'Alfonso and Ena were not touched although covered with glass from the broken windows . . . Both she and Alfonso showed great courage and presence of mind. They got into another carriage at once and drove off to the Palace amid frantic cheering. Am most sorry for poor Aunt Beatrice [the bride's mother and Bertie's sister] who feels the shock very much.'

At least the disaster gave George the chance to tell his diary what he thought about foreigners. 'Of course the bomb was thrown by an anarchist, supposed to be a Spaniard, and of course they let him escape. I believe the Spanish police and detectives are about the worst in the world. No precautions whatever had been taken, they are most happy go lucky people here.'

On 3 June, George and the rest of the club were still going through the motions of celebrating the marriage at the royal palace ('very hot affair . . . smell even worse'). 'My birthday (41),' he reminded his diary. '. . . A man in a village close to Madrid yesterday evening shot down a Garde Civile and then shot himself. He had been identified as the swine that threw the bomb.'

In February 1908 some more swine killed the King and Crown Prince of Portugal as they drove in an open landau across the Terreiro do Paco in Lisbon. Five years later, it was the turn of Alexandra's brother Willy, King George of Greece, to be shot dead in Salonika. The assassin, a Macedonian called Schinas, was thrown from a prison window before he could implicate the other conspirators.

In June 1914 the most famous assassination of the twentieth century occurred – at least till the death of President Kennedy. The Archduke Franz Ferdinand, nephew of Franz Josef and heir to the Austro-Hungarian empire, was shot with his wife by a Bosnian Serb nationalist called Gavil Princip while on a visit to Sarajevo. Franz Ferdinand had timed his visit to coincide with Serbia's national day, which, as the historian A.J.P. Taylor observed, was equivalent to a member of the British royal family visiting Dublin on St Patrick's Day at the height of the Troubles.

But the Archduke had a regal disregard for security measures. 'Precautions?' he remarked to an aide a few months before his death. '. . . I do not care the tiniest bit about this. Everywhere one is in God's hands. Look out of this bush, here at the right, some chap could jump at me.'

In the event, God almost saved Franz Ferdinand from his arrogance. Princip and his fellow assassins were so nervous that they missed at least five opportunities to shoot the Archduke as the royal convoy cruised up and down Sarajevo's Apfel Quay. It was only because one of the cars took a wrong turning, and Franz Ferdinand's chauffeur was forced to reverse, that Princip was given a last chance to enter the history books. He closed his eyes, turned his head away from his target, and fired.

'. . . A thin stream of blood spurted out of His Imperial Highness's mouth on to my right cheek,' the Archduke's aide-de-camp wrote in his deposition to the trial judge. 'With one hand

I got out my handkerchief to wipe the blood from the Archduke's face, and as I did so Her Highness called out, "In God's name, what has happened to you?" Then she collapsed, her face between the Archduke's knees . . . He turned his face a little to one side and said six or seven times, more faintly as he began to lose consciousness, "It is nothing" . . . Then the bleeding made him choke violently.'

The royal couple were dead on arrival at the Sarajevo governor's residence. A diplomatic crisis ensued, and within a few weeks the First World War had begun.

Until Princip struck, Europe's political map had scarcely been altered by this wave of royal murders. Only in Portugal did assassination lead to a change of regime. The new king, Manuel, clung to his throne until October 1910, when he was overthrown by republican officers. In exile, Manuel settled in Twickenham where he discovered a more agreeable vocation than kingship as an antiquarian book collector.

All that remained of Manuel's former majesty was his royal sense of humour. He enjoyed water fights, and once in a Harrogate hotel with his chum Prince Christopher of Greece caused mayhem among their fellow guests with a couple of soda siphons.

Elsewhere in Europe, the great powers actually tried to invent new kingdoms for obscure German princes to rule. In March 1914 Prince William of Wied was dispatched on an Italian gunboat to try his luck with the Albanians, newly independent from the Turks. In his pocket, William had a pension from his sponsors. He also had a rather splendid car, which he liked to drive up and down the streets of Durres, his new capital.

But he proved no match for the Albanians, who had offered William the crown without briefing him on their murderous tribal rivalries. As different factions fought for control of his notional kingdom, William's self-styled 'permanent' government steadily disintegrated. His fate was sealed by the outbreak of the First World War in August 1914, which brought to an end his subsidy from the great powers. By September William had fled the country, never to return. 'Wied is a void' was one Albanian nationalist's verdict on his brief reign.

William was the first casualty of a war which effectively destroyed the pre-1914 dynastic system. In Russia, Nicky resigned his membership of the royal club in March 1917 after the collapse of the Imperial army and the outbreak of revolution in St Petersburg. A little over a year later, he and the rest of his family were shot in the cellar of a merchant's house in Ekaterinberg, Siberia, where they had been imprisoned by the Bolsheviks.

'It was a foul murder,' George V told his diary after attending a memorial service for his Romanov cousins in London. 'I was devoted to Nicky, who was the kindest of men and a thorough gentleman: loved his country and his people.'

In November 1918 Willy joined Nicky on the list of retired members, when he abdicated a few days before his generals sued for peace. Willy 'did great things for his country', George remarked on hearing the news: 'but his ambition was so great that he wished to dominate the world & created his military machine for that object. No man can dominate the world, it has been tried before, & now he has utterly ruined his country & himself.'

The Kaiser retreated to Doorn in the Netherlands, where he lived to see another German leader make a more serious attempt to dominate the world. He lived quietly, writing two volumes of memoirs in which he recalled with affection his youthful visits to England. On one occasion, attending the match between Eton and Harrow at Lords, a lady had taught him the rules of cricket. Even Willy had once been a gentleman in the making – or so he imagined.

The last of the three great European dynasties to disappear at the end of the First World War were the Habsburgs. Franz Josef died in 1916 after sixty-eight years as Austro-Hungarian emperor, to be succeeded by his great-nephew Karl (the son of Franz Ferdinand). Karl survived two years before the disastrous military alliance with Germany and nationalist insurrection forced him into exile. Thus ended over six centuries of Habsburg dominion in central Europe.

Karl had tried to negotiate a separate peace in 1917, and for this reason George was inclined to treat him as a gentleman. In l919, when he heard that Karl's life might be in danger, he arranged for a British officer to be attached to the ex-Emperor's household as protection.

'*Je suis heureux de pouvoir venir remercier Votre Majesté de m'avoir envoyé le Colonel Summerhayes,*' Karl wrote in pathetic gratitude to George. Three years and two failed attempts at restoration later, Karl died ingloriously of pneumonia on the island of Madeira.

Beside these royal titans, other lesser kings lost their crowns. In Bulgaria, Foxy Ferdinand's luck finally ran out when he chose to remain faithful to his German ancestry and back cousin Willy in the family quarrel. At the end of the war, Foxy received notice from the victorious allies to quit the royal club, handing over the Bulgarian crown (or 'Czardom', as he liked to call it) to his eldest son Boris.

Foxy returned to his Saxe-Coburg estates to enjoy a splendid retirement, financed by the money he had plundered from the Bulgarian state treasury. Some years later an English acquaintance, Gerald Hamilton, bumped into Foxy at a minor royal wedding in Coburg. Hamilton recalled how Foxy was 'gaily attired in black breeches, a shimmering gold tunic and a large black beret surmounted by a gold and jewelled aigrette.' Foxy assured Hamilton this was the uniform of a Bulgarian field-marshal. 'I designed it myself for myself. I was the first Bulgarian field-marshal in the history of the world. And, my dear Gerald, the last.'

In Greece, the royal family became almost as confused by their plight as their British cousins. The assassinated George I (Willy) was succeeded by his eldest son Constantine who, as the Kaiser's brother-in-law, was suspected of not being a gentleman. Constantine tried to keep Greece out of the war, and though the British King wanted to believe the best of his cousin, George V supported the allied intervention in 1916 which ended Greek neutrality.

In 1917 Constantine was temporarily suspended from the club, forced into exile, and succeeded by his second son Alexander. The eldest son, also called George, was passed over because he had attended German military school and was thus regarded by the western allies as suspect. Alexander lasted three years, until he became the first king in history to be assassinated by a pet monkey. The monkey bit Alexander when the King tried to stop it attacking his Alsatian dog; shortly afterwards he died of blood poisoning.

Constantine was now readmitted to the club, reigned for a further two years, and then abdicated for a second time after Greece lost the war with Turkey. At last his son George was able to claim his inheritance, having wiped the stain on his military honour by acquiring the habit and manners of an English gentleman. But a year later he too was overthrown, relocating from the royal palace in Athens to an agreeable set of rooms at Brown's Hotel in London.* The Greeks – or at least the Greek army – had rediscovered their classical roots, abolishing the monarchy and declaring a republic.

There is a footnote to this phase of the Greek royal pageant (for more was to follow). Constantine's brother Andrew had served in the Greco-Turkish war, and in October 1922 he faced a court martial for allegedly 'having abandoned a position without orders when in contact with the enemy'. Andrew vigorously defended himself against the charge, and in England his aunt, the Dowager Queen Alexandra, now nearly eighty and still grieving for her assassinated brother Willy, roused herself from senility to come to his aid.

She badgered Andrew's brother-in-law Louis Mountbatten to lobby on his behalf with the government. She pestered her son 'Georgie' (George V) to do the same. As a result, the British embassy in Athens was informed that the King was 'most anxious' about Andrew. A former naval attaché at the Athens embassy, Commander Gerald Talbot, was sent to Greece to see if he could prise Andrew from his captors. And in one of the British empire's final acts of gunboat diplomacy, HMS *Calypso* was ordered to cruise menacingly off the coast near Athens.

The Greek military tribunal decided to humiliate Andrew rather than execute him. He was found guilty as charged, but his death sentence was commuted to perpetual banishment on the grounds of his 'lack of experience in commanding a large unit.' Andrew and his family, including his infant son Philip – too young to realise that he was sailing towards his destiny – were collected by the *Calypso*.

So ended the first membership crisis in the royal club. By the early 1920s, the eastern end of the club premises had received a serious battering. Russia, Germany, Austria, Czechoslovakia and Poland were all republics of different descriptions. Hungary still called itself a monarchy, but no one was fooled. The former Habsburg naval officer and dictator Nicholas Horthy, who styled himself Regent, was accurately described as an admiral without a fleet in a kingdom without a crown.

That left a Balkan rump of monarchies in Bulgaria, Romania and the newly formed kingdom of Yugoslavia. At the end of the First World War, the victorious powers made another attempt to add Albania to the list of Balkan kingdoms. Several candidates were offered the 'Eagle's Throne', including the former Sussex and England cricketer C.B. Fry.* He declined the proposal, even though he and his former batting partner K.S. Ranjitsinghi were soon to display their credentials as world leaders by publishing a guide to the League of Nations. For the time being, the Albanians lived without the benefits of monarchy – or indeed cricket, which at least was played on neighbouring Corfu.

The situation at the western end of the club was not entirely hopeless. Apart from Portugal, all the pre-war monarchies were still in place. In Italy, Victor Emmanuel III had distinguished himself as a coin collector before 1914. During the war he took up photography as a second pastime, taking endless snapshots of his troops with his portable camera. He was thus known to his subjects as 'The Photographer King'. Mussolini, who seized power in 1922, was not inclined to take him seriously.

In Spain, Alfonso was still on the throne, though increasingly under the control of his generals. His English wife Queen Ena never adjusted to her adopted country after the trauma of her wedding. Ena could not forget how her wedding dress had been splattered with the blood of a decapitated horse, directly under Morral's bomb. She was often homesick for England.

In the Low Countries, Albert of the Belgians was every inch a gentleman among kings. He had succeeded his dismal uncle Leopold in 1909, fought with the allies in France during the war, and after his occupied kingdom was restored to him, 'was frequently to be seen walking by himself in the streets of Brussels, wearing a tweed suit.' George V paid him a state visit in 1922; it was the least he could do.

Queen Wilhemina of the Netherlands was, in her way, equally splendid. She had succeeded her father at the age of ten in 1890, and she was set to become the longest-reigning monarch in Europe. 'The massive Wilhemina' was how one awestruck American journalist described her, though she was in fact extremely short. Wilhemina had that effect on people.

The club membership in Scandinavia seemed equally secure. In Denmark, kings were either called Christian or Frederick; from 1912 to 1947 it was the turn of Christian X. In Sweden the opera librettist King Oscar was succeeded in 1907 by the tennis-playing Gustav V (good enough to count the Wimbledon champion Jean Borotra among his friends).

Norway's King Haakon was better known to his English in-laws as 'Uncle Charlie'. He was born Prince Carl of Denmark, had married Bertie's daughter Maud, and was most surprised when he was offered the Norwegian crown in 1905 following the country's secession from Sweden. Carl had the peculiar idea of asking his putative subjects whether they approved of his accession. A referendum was held, and the Norwegians voted four to one in his favour.

His many royal relatives were puzzled by this gesture, and some thought Haakon – as he must now be called – had breached the club rules. 'A *revolutionary* Coronation! Such a *farce*,' the Grand Duchess of Mecklenburg-Strelitz wrote to her niece the Princess of Wales, when Haakon was installed at Trondheim.

'The whole thing seems curious,' the future Queen Mary replied weakly, 'but we live in *very* modern days.'

Too modern for Mary's husband George, who found himself thrust by the First World War into the position of senior club member. In the 1920s there were several other monarchs who had reigned for longer than George. None, however, could match the splendour of the British dynasty, seemingly unscathed by war, revolution or *coup d'état*.

A more imperious king than George might have relished the situation. Instead he was traumatised by what had happened to his cousins. In public he followed his father's example and kept a stiff upper lip; in private he feared the British monarchy might suffer the same disastrous fate – and acted accordingly.

3

The Great Escape

At the beginning of the First World War, George V's solicitude for his relatives knew no bounds. 'I went to Buckingham Palace & had an hour's chat with the King,' the Prime Minister Asquith wrote to Venetia Stanley in October 1914, two months after the outbreak of war. '. . . He & the Queen receive heaps of letters abusing them for their cousins (Albert of Sch. Holst. & the Duke of Coburg) who are actually fighting against us . . . He told me rather naively that Cousin Albert is "not really fighting on the side of the Germans": he had only been "put in charge of a camp of English prisoners" near Berlin! – a nice distinction . . .'

George was equally upset by the persecution of his cousin Prince Louis of Battenberg, born in Germany, who had pursued a career in the British navy. In 1914 Battenberg was First Sea Lord, and found himself denounced in the gutter press as a 'German spy'. 'Our poor blue-eyed German will have to go,' Asquith wrote again to Venetia Stanley.

On 28 October Battenberg resigned, telling the First Lord of the Admiralty, Winston Churchill, that he had reached 'the painful conclusion that at this juncture my birth and parentage have the effect of impairing in some respects my usefulness' – a sad end to a distinguished career. George was outraged, and made Battenberg a Privy Councillor as a consolation prize.

Even cousin Willy, the German Kaiser, escaped George's censure for the time being. In 1914 George objected strongly to the proposal that the Kaiser and his family should be deprived of their honorary commands of British regiments. He also resisted pressure to remove Willy's banner as a member of the Order of the Garter from its stall in St George's Chapel, Windsor.

'Although as a rule I never interfere,' that lifelong prussophobe Alexandra wrote to her son, 'I think the time has come when I must speak out . . . It is but right and proper for you to have down those hateful German banners in our sacred Church, St George's at Windsor.' George reluctantly obeyed his mother's command.

The irony of the situation, utterly lost on George, was that no one could have been more patriotically British. Travel, in his case, had narrowed the mind. In his youth he had sailed the world on HMS *Bacchante*, and then served as a naval officer in the Mediterranean and the North Atlantic; but home was where he left his heart.

'You will be going to Sandringham almost at once I suppose for dear Papa's birthday,' he wrote to his mother in October 1886 from Corfu. 'How I wish I was going to be there too, it almost makes me cry when I think of it. I wonder who will have that sweet little room of mine, you must go and see it sometimes & imagine that your little Georgie dear is living in it.' Little Georgie was twenty-one at the time.

After his marriage to Princess May of Teck in 1893, George settled down at Sandringham to the life of a Norfolk squire. The torpor of this period in his career drove George's official biographer Harold Nicolson to distraction. 'I fear I am getting a down on George V just now,' Nicolson told his diary in 1949, shortly after beginning research. 'He is all right as a gay young midshipman. He may be all right as a wise old King. But the intervening period when he was Duke of York, just shooting at Sandringham, is hard to manage or swallow. For seventeen years he did nothing at all but kill animals and stick in stamps.'

'Dear old Sandringham, the place I love better than anywhere else in the world,' was all George had to say on the subject. No wonder he found the business of abroad so tiresome. As for Nicky, Willy and his other continental cousins, he gleaned all he needed to know about them on the Balmoral grouse moors. It was hard to imagine these people as his enemies – for even Willy, despite his withered arm, was an excellent shot.

Yet this same patriotism, under pressure of war, caused George to be deeply embarrassed about his German ancestry. The Chancellor of the Exchequer David Lloyd George, who patronised him horribly, wondered aloud to his secretary in January 1915 'what my little German friend has got to say to me.' In April 1917 the author H.G. Wells, who was a republican, went further in a letter to *The Times*. It was time to abandon 'the ancient trappings of throne and sceptre', Wells argued, for the war effort was being undermined by the spectacle of 'an alien and uninspiring Court'.

'I may be uninspiring,' George complained to a visitor, 'but I'll be damned if I'm alien.' According to Lady Maud Warrender, however, he 'started and grew pale' when he heard about rumours that the royal family must be pro-German because they had German names.

It was in this xenophobic atmosphere that George made his extraordinary decision to rename the dynasty. The correct name of the British royal family was in any case shrouded in mystery. Following an enquiry from George's Private Secretary Lord Stamfordham, Mr Farnham Burke of the Royal College of Heralds ruled cautiously that since the name was certainly not Stuart or Guelph, it must be either Wipper or Wettin. Mr Burke was too tactful to mention that many people thought George, as the grandson of Victoria and Albert, belonged to the House of Saxe-Coburg-Gotha.

George wanted a name with a bit more roast beef in it. To this end, he summoned a committee of wise men, including two former prime ministers, Lord Rosebery and Asquith, and his uncle the Duke of Connaught, who fancied himself as a heraldry buff.

The Duke favoured 'Tudor-Stuart'; no good, Rosebery and Asquith said, it would remind people of the English Civil War. 'Plantagenet' (too ancient), 'York' (ditto), 'Lancaster' (ditto), 'England' (too general), 'Fitzroy' (too obscure), 'D'Este' (definitely too obscure) – all were tried and rejected.

At the eleventh hour (for George had decided that this was an urgent matter of state) Stamfordham discovered that in the fourteenth century Edward III had also been known as Edward of Windsor. George was delighted; he lived at Windsor – at the weekends, anyway – the town was in England, and not since the Saxon conquest had there been any connection with Germany. The fact that the castle owed its origin to William the Conqueror – a Frenchman – was of no relevance. The French, after all, were our allies in the titanic struggle against German beastliness.

'Do you realise that you have christened a dynasty?' Lord Rosebery wrote in congratulation to Stamfordham. 'There are few people in the world who have done this, none I think. It is really something to be historically proud of. I admire and envy you.'

On 18 July 1917 George published his own deed poll. 'We, of Our Royal Will and Authority, do hereby declare and announce that as from the date of this Our Royal Proclamation Our House and Family shall be styled and known as the House and Family of Windsor . . .' The Kaiser alone failed to treat the occasion with due solemnity. In a rare flash of wit, he told his courtiers he was going to see that well-known opera, *The Merry Wives of Saxe-Coburg-Gotha.*

Within the House and Family of Windsor, the German stain was entirely erased. The hapless Prince Louis of Battenberg was 'invited' to become the Marquess of Milford Haven, with the family name of Mountbatten. His brother Prince Alexander was redesigned as the Marquess of Carisbrooke. Cambridge acquired a marquess, formerly Queen Mary's brother the Duke of Teck. Her other surviving brother, Prince Alexander, became Earl of Athlone.

All that remained after this cleansing of the stable was

George's accent, inherited from his father. 'I do not know much about Arrt,' Bertie would tell his Surveyor of Pictures with a teutonic roll of his r's, 'but I think I know something about Arrr-r-angement.' George's eldest son and successor Edward VIII was the first 'Windsor' not to bear the evidence of his Saxe-Coburg ancestry. Under the influence of the Baltimore-born Mrs Simpson, he spoke instead with an American drawl.

The renaming of the dynasty was absurd; it was also symptomatic of deep anxiety about the future of the British monarchy. By 1917 what exercised George even more than his allegedly alien roots was the fear that he would be engulfed by the same revolutionary tide which had overwhelmed his cousin Nicky in Russia.

George's affection for Nicky was genuine and long-standing. 'Nicky has been kindness itself to me,' he wrote to his grandmother Victoria from St Petersburg in 1894, after attending Nicky's wedding to yet another cousin, Princess Alix of Hesse. 'He is the same dear boy he has always been to me and talks quite openly on every subject.'

Their affinity even extended to physical appearance. In 1896, when Nicky visited Balmoral, Lady Lytton decided he was 'exactly like a skinny Duke of York [George's title at the time] – the image of him.' On this occasion, Nicky proved he was a gentleman by leaving a £1000 tip to be distributed among the servants.

As has been seen, George was deeply shocked by Nicky's murder in 1918. Unfortunately for Nicky, George was also able to separate family feeling from what he now regarded as the higher interests of the British monarchy. In 1917 Nicky was in a dreadful hole; George decided to leave him there.

On 19 March, when he heard of the Tsar's abdication, George sent Nicky his condolences. 'Events of last week have deeply distressed me,' he said. 'My thoughts are constantly with you and I shall always remain your true and devoted friend, as you know I have been in the past.' The message never reached Nicky, who was now under house arrest with his family at the palace of Tsarskoe Selo outside Petrograd (the Russian capital had also been rechristened).

Meanwhile George's Prime Minister David Lloyd George had decided to respond favourably to an approach from the Provisional Government in Petrograd that the Tsar and his immediate family should be offered asylum in Britain. The interim Russian leader, Alexander Kerensky, wanted the Tsar out of the country. Lloyd George was desperate for Russia to stay in the war, and thought he could use the Tsar as a bargaining counter.

'It was generally agreed,' Stamfordham reported on 22 March, after a meeting with Lloyd George at Downing Street, 'that the proposal that we should receive the Emperor in this country (having come from the Russian Government which we are endeavouring with all our powers to support) could not be refused.' Lloyd George asked Stamfordham which of the King's houses could be offered to the Tsar. Stamfordham said that only Balmoral was available, 'which would certainly not be a suitable residence at this time of year.' A minor hitch, it seemed.

But eight days later, the Foreign Secretary Balfour received a letter from Stamfordham. 'The King has been thinking much about the Government's proposal that the Emperor Nicholas and his family should come to England,' Stamfordham began. 'As you are doubtless aware, the King has a strong personal friendship for the Emperor and therefore would be glad to do anything to help him in this crisis. But His Majesty cannot help doubting not only on account of the dangers of the voyage, but on general grounds of expediency, whether it is advisable that the Imperial Family should take up their residence in this country.'

A week later, at George's instigation, Stamfordham sent a more urgent message to Balfour:

Every day, the King is becoming more concerned about the question of the Emperor and Empress coming to this country.

His Majesty receives letters from people in all classes of life, known or unknown to him, saying how much the matter is being discussed, not only in clubs, but by

working men, and that Labour Members in the House of
Commons are expressing adverse opinions to the proposal.

As you know, from the first the King has thought the
presence of the Imperial Family (especially of the Empress
[she was German]) in this country would raise all sorts of
difficulties, and I feel sure that you appreciate how
awkward it will be for our Royal Family who are closely
connected both with the Emperor and the Empress . . .

The King desires me to ask you whether after
consulting the Prime Minister, Sir George Buchanan [the
British ambassador in Petrograd] should not be
communicated with, with a view to approaching the
Russian Government to make some other plan for the
future residence of their Imperial Majesties?

Balfour scarcely had time to digest this letter when a few hours
later a third dispatch arrived from Buckingham Palace:

He [George] must beg you to represent to the Prime
Minister that from all he reads and hears in the press, the residence in this country of the ex-Emperor and Empress would
be strongly resented by the public, and could undoubtedly
compromise the position of the King and Queen.

In case the government failed to appreciate George's anxiety, on
10 April Stamfordham was sent to lobby Lloyd George at
Downing Street. Lloyd George said he would consult the French
government about the possibility of the Tsar coming to France
instead. A further approach was made to Balfour, who had
received a telegram from the Provisional Government in
Petrograd which clearly assumed the Tsar would travel to
England. Stamfordham pointed out that after the King's intervention, the original offer of asylum was no longer binding. This
was news to Balfour, who nevertheless agreed to change his
instructions to Buchanan.

It is impossible to know whether without George's obstruction, the Tsar and his family would have gained asylum in Britain. Lloyd George soon lost interest in the project, once opinion in Petrograd turned against sending the Imperial Family abroad (it was feared the Tsar would become a rallying point for 'counter-revolutionaries'). In August the Tsar, his wife and children were moved to Siberia, from where they never returned.

On the other hand, George ensured that the Romanovs' best opportunity to escape their fate was lost. As the senior member of the royal club – in Nicky and Willy's regrettable absence – George had rewritten the rules. Like his father, he could not remain indifferent to the assassination of a member of his own profession. But in revolutionary times, his loyalty to the club extended no further than his family's immediate self-interest.

Nicky's overthrow had frightened George out of his wits. On 31 March, George heard with alarm about a rally at the Albert Hall to celebrate the fall of the Tsar, under the chairmanship of the future Labour Party leader George Lansbury ('the most lovable figure in modern politics', according to A.J.P. Taylor). In April, the future Labour Prime Minister Ramsay MacDonald told a rally in Glasgow that 'the reward of generations of suffering and martyrdom has at last been reaped.' MacDonald and other socialists announced a 'Convention' to be held in Leeds, which would 'do for this country what the Russian Revolution had accomplished in Russia.'

It was so much hot air. Less than seven years later MacDonald kissed hands with George at Buckingham Palace and embarked on a new career as an ardent royalist. 'He is an egotist, a poseur and a snob,' that guardian of socialist purity Beatrice Webb wrote of MacDonald in 1925. To prove her point, she later cut out a report about MacDonald in *The Times*: 'The Prime Minister left Dunrobin Castle yesterday, after his visit to the Duke and Duchess of Sutherland, for Loch Choire, near Lairg, where he will be the guest of the Marquess and Marchioness of Londonderry. It is understood that he will go to Lossiemouth today and will go to Balmoral tomorrow.'

Lansbury's revolutionary fervour proved less easy to dampen. In

January 1924 George was incensed by Lansbury's remarks at a meeting in east London, which implied that the King was blocking Labour's path to power. 'Some centuries ago,' Lansbury said, 'a King stood against the common people and he lost his head.' And yet Lansbury could tell the Labour conference a few months earlier that George's sons 'were just ordinary common people like themselves.' How did he know? He had sat behind them at a football match.

But at the height of the war, George was not inclined to give socialists – even British socialists – the benefit of the doubt. 'There seems to be a regular epidemic of revolutions & abdications throughout the enemy countries which certainly makes it a hard & critical time for the remaining monarchies,' his eldest son (later Edward VIII) wrote from France in November 1918.

> But of those that remain I have no hesitation in saying that ours is by far the solid [sic] tho. of course it must be kept so & I more than realise that this can only be done by keeping in the closest possible touch with the people & I can promise you this point is always at the back of my mind & that I am & always shall make every effort to carry it out as I know how vitally it will influence the future of the Empire!!

Using shorter sentences, George expressed the same sentiments to Stamfordham.

He was gradually persuaded that the world, after all, had not been turned upside down. At the first post-war Derby in 1919, George looked down from the royal box and saw the crowd make way for a group of disabled soldiers. He motioned towards them and said: 'They have paid the price for us. Without them there would be no Derby today.'

Socially responsible horse-racing had been one of George's central war aims. 'He developed at considerable length his personal views on racing and the war,' Asquith wrote to Venetia Stanley in March 1915, after another audience at Buckingham Palace. 'How he runs his horses still (to keep up the industry) but never sets foot on a racecourse; and how Ascot – if it comes off at all – is to be confined to racing in the morning [for the duration of the war] – no grandstand, enclosure, luncheons. . .'

In 1919, Ascot and Goodwood followed hot on the hooves of Epsom. Last year was a 'difficult' one, George told Stamfordham at Christmas. 'But I think we can congratulate ourselves that we have come through it better than any other country & please God 1920 will see things settle down . . .'

By the time he attended the 1921 FA Cup final, things had definitely settled down. 'There were 73,000 people,' George wrote to his mother. 'At the end they sang the National Anthem and cheered tremendously. There were no bolsheviks there! At least I never saw any.'

The country was all right, George continued; it was just a few 'extremists' who were doing the harm. The royal club, on the other hand, was in a shocking state – run down, depleted, short of funds and prestige. For the next twenty-five years, European royalty warmed themselves in the sun of the Windsor monarchy. When Hitler struck, they also turned to the Windsors for protection.

Within the limits set by George, the Windsors did their best to fulfil these club responsibilities. The results were mixed. Some European monarchies survived the two world wars, but by 1945 the British dynasty was unique in its unreconstructed splendour. From one point of view, the Windsors' lonely eminence appeared a source of strength, confirming that unlike their beleaguered cousins they were indeed divinely blessed. Yet the querulous Windsors were more inclined to see themselves as survivors of a royal holocaust. From their perspective, they no longer had the insurance of an international royal network which offered safety in numbers against the perils of war and revolution. While the British people took pride in the monarchy's enduring strength, the royal family sensed the foundations were moving beneath them. In public, they enjoyed their subjects' acclaim. In private, however, the Windsors compared their situation with those continental relatives who still clung to their thrones, and dreaded what the future might hold in store.

4

Bertie in the Balkans

There was another Bertie in the family, so christened because of Victoria's megalomaniac insistence that all her male descendants should carry her late husband Prince Albert's name. This Bertie was George's second son, born in 1895, who unexpectedly succeeded his elder brother David as King in 1936, the year of the abdication crisis.

In deference to Victoria's wishes, David's second name was Albert, but he chose to reign as Edward VIII. Bertie's first name was Albert; he decided to reign as George VI. At Windsor, in the hideous mausoleum where she lay next to the original Albert, Victoria turned in her grave.

Bertie's early career makes sorry reading. His initial mistake was to arrive in the world on the anniversary of Albert's death, a date set aside by Victoria to wallow in his memory. In the circumstances, she was magnanimous. 'Georgie's first feeling was regret that this dear child should be born on such a sad day,' she told her diary. 'I have a feeling it may be a blessing for the dear little boy and may be looked upon as a gift from God!'

But as a child the younger Bertie was cursed, not blessed. He had knock-knees, and was forced to wear splints overnight to correct the condition. 'This is an experiment!' he wrote to his mother when he was eight years old. 'I am sitting in an armchair with my legs in the new splints and on a chair. I have got an invalid table, which is splendid for reading but rather awkward for writing at present. I expect I shall get used to it.'

The knock-knees were cured; his stammer was not. According to the Countess of Airlie, a lady-in-waiting to his mother, the young Bertie was 'intensely sensitive over his stammer [and] apt to take refuge either in silence – which caused him to be thought moody – or in naughtiness.' Bertie's daughter, the present Queen, believes her father's stammer was provoked by being forced to write with his right hand, when he was in fact left-handed.

Academically, Bertie was a disaster. His final position at Osborne naval college was sixty-eighth in a class of sixty-eight. There was a slight improvement at Dartmouth, where he climbed the ladder to sixty-first.

Nevertheless, Bertie was deemed mentally fit to serve in the Navy. It was his physical condition that now became a worry. 'Prince Albert was in bed on sick list when we prepared for action,' the captain of HMS *Collingwood* reported to Bertie's father after the Battle of Jutland in 1916. '[He] got up and went to his turret, where he remained until we finally secured guns next day. Though his food that evening and night was of an unusual description, I am glad to tell Your Majesty that he has been quite well since and looks quite well again.'

The captain spoke too soon. Bertie suffered severe stomach pains, which caused him to spend more time ashore on sick leave than with his ship. In 1917 the problem was finally diagnosed as a stomach ulcer, which was removed. 'Personally I feel that I am not fit for service at sea,' Bertie told his father forlornly after the operation, 'even when I recover from this little attack.' The rest of his war was spent at a training station for future RAF pilots in Lincolnshire.

Bertie was not quite the hopeless case this catalogue of misfortune makes him seem. He was an accomplished athlete, good enough to enter the Wimbledon men's doubles tournament a few years later with his Equerry Louis Greig (they were knocked out in the first round). In a game of garden cricket, he once bowled his grandfather (Edward VII), his father (George V) and his brother (Edward VIII) with successive deliveries – a unique hat trick of kings.

At the end of the First World War, he was also anxious to do his royal duty. As president of the Industrial Welfare Society, he trudged around the country visiting factories; the press dubbed him, rather dispiritingly, the 'Industrial Prince'. In August 1921 Bertie (now Duke of York) held his first Duke of York Camp at Romney Marsh in Kent. This annual event brought four hundred working-class and public schoolboys together for a week of press-ups, campfire songs, and general ragging, aimed at breaking down class barriers.

Bertie loved his camps. 'One year we had arranged a push-ball match,' the chief organiser Robert Hyde recalled, 'and he [Bertie] was asked if he would referee the game. "Referee be damned," said he, "I'm going to play." Shortly afterwards a lusty young Harlequin was burrowing his shoulder into the ribs of the man in front of him, and shouting: "Now push like Hell!" In a flash came the Duke's retort: "I *am* pushing like Hell!"'

But Bertie needed a larger stage than Romney Marsh for his burgeoning talents; and in the early 1920s it was Queen Marie of Romania's happy mission to provide him with one.

She was the daughter of Victoria's second son Alfred ('Affie'), raised in England. The original plan was that Marie ('Missy') should marry her cousin George, later George V. Even by royal standards, they were deemed too closely related, and Marie had to settle instead for the unprepossessing Prince Ferdinand of Romania. Ferdinand's ears grew almost at right angles to his head. As a boy they had been stuck down with tape, but it had made no difference. Theirs was not to prove a happy marriage.

Since she did not love Ferdinand, Marie decided to love Romania – an entity which, prior to her engagement, she imagined was a town in Hungary. *The Country I Love* was the first of several books in which she poured out her heart for the benefit of her adopted subjects and American newspaper readers. It contained illustrations by her eldest daughter Elizabeth ('she too loves her country well!'), was translated into Romanian (Marie neither spoke nor wrote a word of the language), and during the First World War became the treasured property of every Romanian soldier.

Marie was touched by their loyalty. 'When I wandered amongst the sick and wounded, through hundreds of hospitals, they kept asking for "the Queen's little book" which each sufferer wanted to lay under his pillow as a precious possession.'

From a distance, Marie was an inspiration; at close range, she could be rather trying. 'Marie of Romania – one of the most wonderful women in the world. A woman like that is born once in a century': or so read the messages she wrote in her own hand and scattered around the royal palace in Bucharest.

George's feelings can thus be imagined when, in April 1921, he was invited by Marie to act as 'Koom' or sponsor at Prince Alexander of Serbia's marriage in Belgrade to her second daughter – also called Marie, but known to the family as 'Mignon'. George was relieved that his presence was not required; Marie explained that he could delegate the Koom's duties to one of his sons. Bertie took a deep breath and boarded the Orient Express.

'O Koom, your purse is burning,' the Serbian children chanted at Bertie, as he rode at the head of the wedding procession on a distinctly frisky Irish horse. Reaching into his knapsack, he showered the grateful urchins with silver coins.

'He did his part beautifully and his presence was most popular in Serbia,' Marie wrote afterwards to George. 'Everyone much appreciated that you sent one of your sons and were awfully pleased.'

Bertie, she decided, was required at the joint coronation she was staging with Ferdinand in September 1922. Ferdinand had been King since 1914, but the ceremony was repeatedly delayed by war and the threat of revolution. It was important to put on a good show, and Marie was not at all sure that the guest list was strong enough. The Infanta Beatrice ('Baby Bee') was coming from Spain, the Duke of Genoa from Italy (the King sent his apologies), and Marshal Foch from France. Marie would hear no excuses; Bertie must come.

With an inward groan – for the grouse season had begun – Bertie steeled himself for another Balkan extravaganza.

'I carry off the huge golden-incrusted crown and overpowering mantle splendidly,' Marie told her diary after the ceremony. The

crown was a copy by Cartier of one originally belonging to the
wife of a sixteenth-century hospodar. On her gold dress were
embroidered sheaves of wheat – 'the chief richness of our land'.
Marie changed into this 'somewhat overwhelming get-up' on the
train to the remote Transylvanian town of Alba Julia where, for
obscure political reasons, the coronation was held.

'So very picturesque,' Bertie wearily remarked, when asked for
his opinion; he was feeling rather homesick. Nevertheless, the
British embassy in Bucharest reported to Buckingham Palace
that 'the Duke's soldier-like appearance, his bearing, his good
looks, and horsemanship during the procession through the
entire town [of Bucharest], as well as in the parade at Alba Julia,
were all the subject of many flattering observations.'

A year later, in September 1923, Bertie was at last enjoying the
sport at Balmoral when a message arrived from the Foreign
Secretary Lord Curzon. He was required in Belgrade, where he
was to act as Koom at the christening of Marie's grandson Prince
Peter, the son of Alexander and Mignon.

'Curzon should be drowned for giving me such short notice,'
he told his Equerry Louis Greig. 'He must know things are different now.' Indeed they were: Bertie was now married to the
former Lady Elizabeth Bowes-Lyon, who tried to soothe him. *She*
was rather looking forward to being a Koomitsa.

'We were quite a large family party,' Bertie wrote lugubri-
ously to his father from Belgrade, '& how we all lived in one
Palace is a mystery . . . We were not too comfortable & there was
no hot water!!'

On this occasion Bertie was spared the knapsack, handed a set
of specially embroidered nappies, and told to hold the baby. 'You
can imagine what I felt like carrying the baby on a cushion. It
screamed most of the time which drowned the singing & the service altogether.' The baby's rage was caused by the Serbian
Patriarch accidentally dropping it in the font; in the nick of
time, Bertie had stepped forward and scooped his charge to safety.

Bertie was heartily sick of the Balkans, and vowed never to
return. But he was not to be free so easily of his Balkan cousins.

Between the wars, now that the imperial splendours of St Petersburg, Berlin and Vienna had vanished forever, London became by default the royal capital of the world, where minor European dynasties came to bask in the sun of Windsor monarchy. 'They all talk English amongst themselves, read the *Tatler*, barely understand Slovenian and Serb, and dream of their next visit to London.' So wrote the MP Henry 'Chips' Channon after staying with his friend Prince Paul of Serbia's family in 1937; and the Karageorgeviches were not alone in preferring the English social season to the dubious pleasures of Balkan court life.

Of these Balkan anglophiles, no one was more naturally cast for the role of honorary Englishman than the erstwhile German military cadet George II, the exiled King of Greece, who spent twelve happy years in London from 1923 to 1935. George was a favourite on the country-house circuit, insisting with English self-deprecation that he expected 'no red carpet'. 'I'm out of a job, so the less notice anybody takes of me the better pleased I am,' he told the socialite Rosita Forbes.

George found exile so agreeable that when the Greek monarchy was restored in 1935 he was reluctant to return to Athens. Only when he was assured the situation had 'stabilised' did he settle his account at Brown's Hotel.

A regular visitor to Balmoral during these years was King Boris of Bulgaria, the son of Foxy. Described unkindly by the American journalist John Gunther as 'the worst-dressed king in Europe', Boris lacked Foxy's airs and graces. 'Meet my wife,' he would say to visitors, introducing them to Queen Giovanna; and on sunny afternoons he could be seen pushing the family pram in the palace gardens.

Boris's unpretentious manner endeared him to the British royal family, and especially to Queen Mary. 'She kissed me on both cheeks,' he told a fellow guest one year at Balmoral. 'It was so charming of her. I felt for a moment as if I had refound my mother.'

In 1934 Balmoral received a more glamorous Balkan guest, Princess Marina of Greece, who was engaged to marry George's youngest surviving son, Prince George (later Duke of Kent). 'I was enchanted by one thing more than all else,' she told reporters after-wards, '– the ghillies' ball. The servants dance with the royal family without any sense of familiarity but with the utmost good friend-ship.' In private, Marina found her in-laws-to-be rather a dull lot, more interested in the grouse tally than the latest society gossip.

She was the sister of Paul of Serbia's wife Olga, and daughter of the utterly obscure Prince Nicholas of Greece. Marina's early life followed the usual pattern for a Greek princess: exile, poverty and a spell at finishing school in Paris. But she was beautiful, had terrific fashion sense, and in the mid-1920s had even been tipped for the marital jackpot, the hand of Bertie's elder brother David, Prince of Wales.

David preferred his women to be already married, and by 1934, when she was twenty-eight, spinsterhood beckoned for Marina. She was saved by Prince George, who breezed into her life one afternoon at Claridge's (Balkan royalty's favourite London hotel) and proposed to her a few months later.

Their wedding in Westminster Abbey in November 1934 was an incongruous blend of British majesty and Ruritanian farce. Bertie's eldest daughter Lilibet was a bridesmaid, the Abbey was packed with the crowned heads of Europe, and George V even rearranged his shooting schedule in order to attend the ceremony.

The stately pageant was spoiled by the haste with which the wedding procession travelled the short distance from Buckingham Palace to the Abbey. It was feared by the police that Macedonian terrorists might be lurking in the crowd, following the recent assassination in Marseilles of King Alexander of Yugoslavia (Mignon's husband). Accordingly, the royal mews was instructed to transport the carriages containing the Balkan royal guests at a brisk trot.

If there was one member of this Balkan clan nobody could stand, it was Marie's son King Carol of Romania. 'The King of Romania, as ever, looked ridiculous,' Channon remarked in January 1936, when the royal club recongregated in London for the state funeral of George V.

By any standard, royal or human, Carol was a cad. In 1918, as

Crown Prince, he dismayed his parents by eloping with his girl-friend Zizi Lambrino and marrying her in Odessa. The Romanian Supreme Court declared the marriage void, Carol renounced his rights to the throne, he and Zizi returned to Bucharest, she became pregnant – and to cut a long story short, Carol decided he was no longer in love. Zizi was despatched to Paris with the baby and a small pension.

The woman chosen to make an honest prince of Carol was Helen of Greece, the younger sister of the exiled King George. They were married with great pomp in Bucharest, and a son, Michael, was born in 1921; but already Carol's eye was wandering. It fell on Magda Lupescu, the daughter of a German immigrant, and such was his passion that for the second time he excluded himself from the succession. He and Magda departed for France, where they too settled in Paris.

Carol's first escapade on English soil was in May 1928 when, from a safe house in Godstone, Surrey, he plotted to recover his crown. The house belonged to a Romanian expatriate called Barbo Ionescu, the project was backed by the newspaper magnate Lord Rothermere, and on 28 May Carol attempted to board a plane at nearby Croydon aerodrome, bound for Bucharest. At the last minute he was arrested by police and deported to France. In Bucharest, Queen Marie was mortified, and apologised on her son's behalf to Buckingham Palace.

Two years later, with the help of the French air-ace Lalouette, Carol landed in Bucharest and overthrew his nine-year-old son Michael, who had become King on Ferdinand's death. Magda arrived next day on the Orient Express. She was installed in a cottage in the palace gardens, connected by a tunnel to the main building. Helen was sent into exile without Michael, who was told he must learn to be a prince before he could sit on a throne.

Just in case anyone doubted Carol's right to be King, an extra button for his personal use was installed in the palace's lift system. It read 'M' – for Majesty.

Bertie, like the rest of his family, loathed Carol, and there was much sympathy for Helen when she was invited to Buckingham

Palace for tea. Unfortunately, in 1938 the British government decided that Carol should be awarded a state visit, with Bertie as host. The Foreign Office had cast Carol in the unlikely role of Balkan 'strongman', capable of withstanding Hitler's menaces from the west and Stalin's from the east. Carol's anti-semitism, his admiration for Mussolini, and his past record of treachery were conveniently discounted.

Carol landed at Dover in November 1938, with Michael in tow. At Buckingham Palace, it was reported that the seventeen-year-old Michael had become 'firm friends' with Bertie's daughters Elizabeth and Margaret, then twelve and eight respectively. 'They found a great deal in common, especially when comparing notes about autographs and stamps,' a newspaper reported.

Bertie and Carol may also have discussed philately; they were both keen stamp collectors. The atmosphere, however, seems to have been thunderous. On the day of the state banquet at Buckingham Palace, Bertie flew into a rage when the details of the crinoline evening dress Norman Hartnell had designed for the Queen were leaked to the newspapers. On no account, he told her irrationally, must she wear Hartnell's creation. With his blood pressure rising by the minute, Bertie could scarcely disguise his relief when he at last bade his odious cousin farewell.

Carol's state visit was a futile attempt to revive the dynastic diplomacy of Europe before the First World War, when palaces were also power centres. By the late 1930s, the ties linking British royalty to the continental monarchies were essentially sentimental; and though Carol was a great-grandson of Victoria, in his case the reservoir of affection had long since run dry.

Sentiment, however, governed Bertie's relations with his other European cousins. He might detest Carol, but when Hitler unleashed his Blitzkrieg, his sense of family loyalty drove him to act as their patron and protector. Even as the royal club was being destroyed forever, Bertie was determined to uphold its spirit. The pity, from his point of view, was that so few of his cousins felt bound by the same code of honour.

5

Ourselves Alone

In September 1940, Carol of Romania became the first Balkan monarch to let the royal side down. Having allowed Hitler and Stalin to dismember about a third of his kingdom, Carol abdicated in favour of Michael and fled the country with Magda. On board the sealed train which took them to exile was a sizeable chunk of Romania's national art treasures – useful bargaining chips as Carol negotiated his passage into Franco's Spain. The couple eventually settled in Portugal, where Carol resumed his interest in stamp-collecting. He was last seen in Britain at an international stamp fair held at Kensington's Olympia, two years before his death in 1953.

Bertie had more faith that his other Balkan cousins would stand up to Hitler. In September 1939 he wrote to Boris in Sofia, reminding him of the excellent shooting they had enjoyed at Balmoral the previous year, and urging him to keep Bulgaria out of the war (the best option for the western allies, given their lack of influence in the Balkans). 'How good of him to remember me,' Boris told the British Minister in Bucharest, with tears in his eyes.

A year later Boris received another supportive message from Bertie, in the wake of Carol's disgrace. It seems to have escaped Bertie's attention that Boris had also helped himself to a slice of

Romania, and lacked the backbone to withstand Hitler. Soon Boris had joined the Axis powers and was making the familiar journey for Hitler's Balkan puppets to the Führer's mountain retreat at Berchtesgaden.

Boris found these meetings with Hitler extremely stressful, and in 1943, returning from another Berchtesgaden browbeating, he died of a heart attack. Bertie did not even send his condolences to Queen Giovanna, who with her son, the nine-year-old King Simeon, was expelled by the victorious communists in 1946. So ended the royal house that Simeon's grandfather Ferdinand had built.*

The Karageorgeviches in Yugoslavia also claimed Bertie's attention. In 1934, when King Alexander was assassinated, 'Chips' Channon's old friend Prince Paul was appointed Regent until Alexander's son and heir Peter came of age. With Hitler threatening Yugoslav neutrality, Bertie and his wife knew Paul would be grateful for their moral support. 'My dear Paul' he wrote to the Yugoslav Regent in November 1940, 'we have been thinking so much of you since I last wrote to you in July. So much has happened everywhere, and the situation in your part of the world has become so much more critical in [sic] this time.'

Another 'personal message of friendship' followed four months later when Bertie heard that Paul was thinking of signing the Axis pact. 'Yugoslavia owes so much to your inspired example and steadfast leadership,' he told him hopefully. 'Our two countries share so many common ideals, and we have been close personal friends for so long, that I can feel certain that we can rely upon you to make the right decision.'

Paul was an Oxford man (Christ Church, BA Hons.), but Bertie's appeal to his gentlemanly instincts cut no ice. In March 1941 Yugoslavia followed Bulgaria and Romania into Hitler's embrace. Two days later Paul was overthrown by a group of disgusted Yugoslav officers and Peter – now aged seventeen – was installed on the throne. Hitler promptly invaded, and within barely a week Peter had followed Paul to Athens.

'A weak and unfortunate prince' was Churchill's verdict on

Paul. He was sent to Kenya with Olga to reflect on his sins; soon afterwards he suffered a nervous breakdown, from which he never fully recovered. Peter was brought to London, where he and his mother ('Mignon') were invited to tea at Buckingham Palace. 'Queen Elizabeth was present also,' Peter remembered, 'and received us cordially. Like any English hostess, she poured out the tea, but we were allowed only one lump of rationed sugar. Uncle Bertie treated me very kindly.'

Privately, Uncle Bertie found Peter a callow youth and, resuming his responsibilities as Koom, he consigned the King of Yugoslavia to the care of Henry Thirkill, Master of Clare College, Cambridge. Nor did Bertie approve of Peter's louche appearance. Once, at Buckingham Palace, Peter appeared with a gold watch-chain dangling from his uniform. 'Take it off!' Bertie roared at him. 'It looks damned silly and damned sloppy!'

Peter was in reality a less than grateful godson. Like Bertie in Belgrade twenty years earlier, he was unimpressed by the domestic arrangements at Balmoral. The house was 'still quite Victorian from the point of view of plumbing; for example, there was no running water in the bedrooms; hot water was brought in in polished cans and the rooms were equipped only with big wash-bowls.'

Worse, Bertie was appalled by Peter's far-fetched schemes to regain his throne. 'I cannot renounce my people, my Army, the traditions of my ancestors,' Peter wrote grandly to Bertie in March 1944 from Cairo, where he had been sent to join his cousin, the thrice-exiled King George of Greece. 'Apart from all this,' he added plaintively, 'I don't feel happy here and am lonely . . . Please convey my best love to Aunt Elizabeth.'

Peter wanted to marry his cousin Alexandra, daughter of the Greek King who had been assassinated by a monkey. Bertie eventually agreed, and in July 1945 the couple produced a son and heir, Crown Prince Alexander. Claridge's was once again the scene for the latest episode in the Balkan royal saga. The baby was born in 'Yugoslavia', a suite of rooms designated national territory for the purposes of the Karageorgevich succession.

In the real Yugoslavia, the triumphant communists abolished the monarchy at the end of the year. Peter and Alexandra departed for America, where he sank the royal family jewels in a plastics factory and a shipping company, both of which went bust. Their marriage disintegrated, Peter became an alcoholic, and died prematurely of liver failure in Los Angeles in 1970. As a final snub to his Windsor cousins, he refused the Queen's offer of a grave in the gardens of the royal mausoleum at Frogmore.

One other Balkan monarch tried Bertie's patience, before he abandoned the region as a lost royal cause. In June 1940 King Zog of the Albanians, accompanied by his half-American wife Queen Geraldine, their baby son Prince Leka, several Albanian princesses, a royal household of thirty-six, and some army boxes filled with gold bullion, arrived in Liverpool from France, confidently expecting an invitation to stay at Buckingham Palace.

Zog was the only European sovereign unrelated to Bertie, and it was not even clear if he was entitled to call himself King. Born Ahmed Zogu, in the early 1920s he achieved a meteoric rise up the greasy pole of Albanian tribal politics as a seasoned practitioner of the blood feud. Until 1928 he was President; then, with the support of his Italian patrons, Zog decided his destiny was to ascend 'the Eagle's throne'.

His coronation in Tirana was a fearful affair. To deter assassins, the branches were cut from the trees along the procession route, and as a further precaution Zog arrived in the parliament building twenty minutes early. 'The world has understood that if the sons of the eagle [Albania's national bird] are left in peace they can build a state,' he told the assembly, before scuttling back to the royal palace.

Eleven years later Zog was usurped by Victor Emmanuel ('the Photographer King') when Mussolini invaded Albania. Zog had taken out insurance against this possibility. His account at the Chase Manhattan Bank in New York was worth $2 million; a further £50,000 was deposited with Lloyd's Bank in London; and there were the crates of treasure he and his suite lugged over the mountains into Greece, ahead of the invading Italians.

But money could not secure Zog an entrée to Buckingham Palace, when he fled to Britain after the fall of France. The British government refused to recognise him as an exiled head of state, and though Queen Mary was sympathetic, Bertie decided that a line must be drawn. The Albanian royal household had to settle for the Ritz Hotel in Piccadilly.

Barred from political activity, Zog passed the war by organising marathon poker parties with his courtiers, during which huge fortunes were won and lost. He considered whether to buy *The Times*, telling one English acquaintance: 'I won't give a penny more than ten million for it.'

In 1945, after this project collapsed, the Zog ménage departed for King Farouk's Egypt, where he set up as an arms dealer. The Egyptian authorities thought he should pay income tax. 'Kings never pay taxes,' he told them scornfully, and moved to the south of France. When he died in 1961 his son Leka was proclaimed King of the Albanians at the Hôtel Bristol in Paris – once the favourite hotel of the elder Bertie*. Albanian royalty at last sheltered under the same roof as the illustrious Windsors.

Sans Zog, Buckingham Palace became a wartime refugee centre for Bertie's west European cousins. 'I was woken by the police sergeant at 5.00 a.m.,' Bertie told his diary on 13 May 1940, 'who told me Queen Wilhemina of the Netherlands wished to speak to me. I did not believe him, but went to the telephone & it was her. She begged me to send aircraft for the defence of Holland. I passed this message on to everyone & went back to bed.

'It is not often one is rung up at that hour, and especially by a Queen,' Bertie continued. 'But in these days anything may happen, and far worse things too.'

Although distantly related, Wilhemina was virtually unknown to Bertie. On holiday in Scotland before the war, she and her daughter Juliana had not even paid a courtesy call at Balmoral. Posterity records instead that in 1936 the Deputy Chief Constable of Perthshire was made a Chevalier of the Order of Orange-Nassau – 'in appreciation of the arrangements made by the police to secure privacy and solitude'.

Now, in her country's supreme crisis, the proud Wilhemina found herself forced on Bertie's charity. When she called Buckingham Palace, Wilhemina was about to leave The Hague before it was stormed by the invading Germans. She planned to join the Dutch forces in Zeeland, but because they had been isolated, she travelled first to the Hook of Holland, where a British destroyer was waiting to collect her.

Wilhemina was disgusted when the captain told her he was sailing to England, having been forbidden to make radio contact with the Dutch ground troops (it might have revealed his position to the Germans). By mid-afternoon Wilhemina was in Harwich, where she phoned Bertie a second time. He advised her to take the train to Liverpool Street station. Bertie added that Wilhemina's daughter Juliana, her son-in-law Bernhard, and their children had already arrived at Buckingham Palace by another route.

A couple of hours later, Bertie and Elizabeth were waiting to greet Wilhemina at Liverpool Street. The indomitable Dutch Queen fully intended to catch another train to the south coast, and thence return to the Netherlands, but Bertie managed to persuade her to come to Buckingham Palace instead.

'She was naturally very upset and had brought no clothes with her,' he recalled. Elizabeth set about trying to organise Wilhemina's wardrobe. She was shown a selection of fashionable hats by a salesgirl summoned to Buckingham Palace, only to point at the one on the salesgirl's head and say firmly, 'That is the hat for me.'

A month later, in June 1940, Uncle Charles (King Haakon of Norway) arrived on Bertie's doorstep with his son Olav. After several weeks fleeing the Germans in northern Norway, they had reluctantly abandoned the struggle and boarded a British destroyer bound for Scotland.

Because of his own experience, Haakon was worried that Bertie and Elizabeth might be kidnapped by German parachutists. To reassure his uncle, Bertie showed him the Buckingham Palace security arrangements. A button was pressed and within seconds,

Bertie told Haakon, highly trained guardsmen would be swarming over the premises.

Several minutes later an equerry was sent to discover why nothing had happened. The duty policeman had decided it was a false alarm 'as he had heard nothing of it'. When the equerry insisted it was genuine, a few guards appeared in the gardens, where they thrashed around in the shrubbery looking for Germans. Bertie and Elizabeth were highly amused, Haakon less so. He soon moved out of the palace, returning once a week to deliver and collect his laundry. Such were the wartime privileges of royalty.

King Leopold of the Belgians, great-nephew of the partridge-eating Leopold, refused Bertie's invitation to join his cousins at Buckingham Palace. Instead he surrendered to the Germans, and spent the rest of the war under house arrest.

Bertie was inclined to forgive him. He told the US envoy Harry Hopkins that Leopold had 'mixed up' his duties as King and Commander-in-Chief of the Belgian army. On balance, Bertie felt his offence did not merit the ultimate royal penalty imposed on the German Kaiser during the previous war – removal from the noble order of Knights of the Garter.

But the order could not tolerate the stain on its dignity caused by the continued membership of Victor Emmanuel, Mussolini's puppet: by Bertie's command, the 'Photographer King' lost his visiting rights at St George's Chapel, Windsor. In 1946 he also lost his throne, abdicating in favour of his son Umberto, and departing with his camera to Portugal. Umberto scarcely had time to disclose his favourite hobby when his subjects abolished the Italian monarchy in a referendum.

Other monarchs were also beyond Bertie's power to help. In occupied Denmark, King Christian rode each afternoon through the streets of Copenhagen on a horse, a gesture of resistance his subjects were reported to find inspiring. In neutral Sweden, King Gustav V 'symbolised the unity of the nation'. According to the Swedish Institute, 'this means that the monarchy was rooted in the personal popularity of the King.'

King Alfonso of Spain died in exile in 1941. A broken figure, he apologised for taking so long to expire. The Spanish monarchy had collapsed ten years earlier, after the republicans claimed victory at the general elections. Notionally, General Franco restored the monarchy when he overthrew the republic; in practice the Bourbons were told to wait, pending Franco's death.

At the end of the First World War, Europe's surviving royals had tried hard to maintain the pretence that they still belonged to an extended dynastic system. Tentatively (for revolution was in the air), they resumed the pre-war round of coronations, funerals and weddings as if nothing – or nothing much – had happened. By the end of the Second World War, even an incurable royal nostalgic like Bertie had abandoned the pretence. Too many dynasties had been deposed; and those that remained were unable to revive their former glory, with the partial exception of his own family.

In eastern Europe, only Romania and Greece survived of the pre-war monarchies. King Michael of Romania clung grimly to his throne for two years until, in December 1947, the communists forced him to abdicate by threatening a massacre of 'counter-revolutionaries'. Not long afterwards Michael could be found in Hertfordshire, managing a chicken farm.*

King George of Greece died in April 1947, six months after paying his bill at Claridge's – his latest London base – and returning to an uncertain future. George was succeeded by his brother Paul, whose wife Frederica, a German princess, had been suspected during the war of pro-Nazi sympathies.

At the start of the reign, Frederica's right-wing views were less of a problem than her highly strung temperament. She recoiled from public engagements, and suffered a nervous breakdown. 'One day,' she recalled in her memoirs, 'when it was my official duty to go to church, I had my appendix taken out instead! There was nothing wrong with my appendix. After the operation Palo [Paul] said to me with a knowing smile, "Please remember you do not have a second appendix on your other side!"'

Palo helped Frederica to pull herself together, and she was

soon using her considerable charm to extract more aid for the Greek government from the US Secretary of State General Marshall. The Marshall Plan, if Frederica is to be believed, owed its existence to her meeting with the General in London, soon after Palo's accession.

Having won the Greek civil war, Frederica's mind turned to weightier matters. 'I took up nuclear physics,' she recalls. Frederica discovered that 'the material world to which I and all beings belong exists in appearance only, but in essence is the unseen power. *The Real and the True, in its last analysis, is not what I observe, but that which I do not observe, that which I truly am. The Real and the True is the Power Unseen.*'

By the late 1960s the Power Unseen had transported Frederica to India, where we shall leave her. The Greek monarchy, meanwhile, collapsed for the third time in the twentieth century when her son King Constantine was forced into exile, after staging a farcical coup attempt against the military regime of the colonels.

In Belgium, the crown was held in a regency from 1945 to 1950 by Leopold's brother Charles, while Leopold remained in disgrace in Switzerland. Charles was invited to Sandringham by Bertie, where he played a sound game of table tennis in the games room, but was suspected of drinking too much. There were also rumours about boys, and in old age Charles made no secret of his homosexuality. 'I thought people like that shot themselves,' George V had once remarked; and as his father's son, Bertie had nothing more to do with him.

Leopold returned to Belgium after a plebiscite on the monarchy in 1950, but left-wing riots forced him to abdicate in favour of his eldest son Baudouin. By 1956 Leopold had mended his fences with the Windsors, turning up at Buckingham Palace one spring afternoon to take tea with the Queen.

The 'massive' Wilhemina returned to the Netherlands in happier circumstances at the end of the war, newly appointed by Bertie to the Order of the Garter. She gave Bertie a horse in gratitude. In 1948, fifty years after reaching her majority as Queen, Wilhemina abdicated in favour of her daughter Juliana. She too became a religious mystic in old age, writing a best-selling auto-biography with the portentous title *Lonely but not Alone*.

Haakon returned to Norway in May 1945 on the same British destroyer which had deposited him in Scotland five years before. He lived long enough to celebrate the fiftieth anniversary of his reign in 1956, and to welcome his great-niece Elizabeth to Norway on a state visit.

The pageant of Swedish royalty continued undisturbed, as one Gustav succeeded another. Gustav VI (1950–73) was – we learn from his official biography – 'a respected name among archaeologists, and his knowledge in many other fields meant that even the experts found him an interesting partner in discussion.'

In Denmark the cycle of Christians and Fredericks was finally broken in 1972 when Princess Margrethe succeeded her father Frederick IX. Margrethe has many accomplishments. She has studied history, political science and economics at five of the great European universities, including Cambridge and the Sorbonne. She has illustrated the Danish edition of Tolkien's *Lord of the Rings*. With her husband Prince Henrik, she has translated Simone de Beauvoir's *Tous les hommes sont mortels*. Is it any wonder that her subjects regard Margrethe, according to the Danish Foreign Ministry, as 'the world champion among Queens'?

But only in Britain did the monarchy survive in all its pomp, a gloriously unreconstructed relic of the original royal club. 'The British Kingship . . . what a piece of work it is!' the historian G.M. Trevelyan wrote in November 1947. 'It has just weathered the storms of two world wars, in which old Empires and modern dictatorships have foundered. It has emerged from the ordeal yet stronger than before.'

Trevelyan's eulogy marked the marriage of Bertie's eldest daughter Elizabeth to Prince Philip of Greece, who had sailed for England twenty-five years before on board HMS *Calypso*. In his own words, Philip was just 'a discredited Balkan prince'; surely, the rest of his family told him, he was the luckiest man in the world to secure Elizabeth's hand in marriage.

If any event symbolised the Windsors' emergence as the world-champion dynasty, it was this first post-war royal extravaganza. Tribute was paid to Elizabeth by her future subjects in the form of 2578 wedding presents. Mr B.F. Long sent a glass marmalade jar and spoon. Mr Ronald Wilson-Smith wrote a cheque. Hundreds of women, including Mrs H. Fielding and Mrs L.R. Talbot, sent nylon stockings, a luxury during the austerity years. Mrs L.M. Cormack gave the couple a box of chocolates – 'sent by Queen Victoria to her troops in South Africa, 1900'.

More gifts were laid at the happy couple's feet by their beleaguered European relatives, who at Bertie's invitation travelled to London for the last great gathering of the royal club. Palo and Frederica could only manage copies of the Vapheio gold cups, dating from 1500 BC, which were excavated in 1888. Queen Marie of Yugoslavia ('Mignon') gave Philip a gold cigarette case with diamond motifs. Philip was too tactful to tell her he had given up smoking on his stag night.

The Grand Duchess Xenia rummaged through her few remaining Romanov heirlooms and found an 'amethystine agate and silver gilt snuff box with ruby lift'. Her declining years were passed in a grace-and-favour apartment at Hampton Court provided by the grateful recipient.

'You know, Uncle Bertie,' Philip's cousin Alexandra said after the wedding breakfast at Buckingham Palace. 'Peter and I envy Philip so much, and we know what today means to him.' Alexandra was now 'Queen' of Yugoslavia, though she had never set foot in her kingdom. Once she had hoped to marry Philip, but he was uninterested in her (she had also been the object of King Zog's predatory attentions, but that is another story).*

'We both know what it's like not to have a father, or a settled family home, and Philip knows too,' Alexandra continued meaningfully. 'He's been in the same situation for such a long time. Now he's got you and Aunt Elizabeth, as well as Lilibet, you know. He *belongs* now.'

'Yes, Sandra,' Bertie said, 'that's right, he belongs – he does belong, Sandra – come and have a drink.'

A few days later Bertie wrote Elizabeth a letter which suggests he was not entirely convinced. 'I was so proud of you & thrilled at having you so close to me on our long walk in Westminster Abbey, but when I handed your hand to the Archbishop I felt that I had lost something very precious . . . Our family, us four, the "Royal Family" must remain together with additions of course at suitable moments!!'

Philip's heart must have sunk when he read this letter. But did Bertie betray more than the anxieties of an overprotective father? 'Us four' was a defensive image in a world where 'the guild of monarchs' – to use his grandfather's phrase – had vanished forever. In future the royal family must rely on each other.

If only they could: for at heart the Windsors did not regard themselves as reliable people. On the contrary, Edward VII's successors were chronically lacking in self-esteem. Royalists like Trevelyan might talk of Bertie 'raised up aloft as the high-shining symbol of our historic and enduring unity'. For his part, Bertie remembered how he had burst into tears on his mother's shoulder when, at the age of almost forty-one, he first learned he was to be King.

Revolution, *coup d'état*, assassination – all these fates the querulous Windsors might escape, and still find the British kingship, in the words of their accession speeches, 'a heavy burden'. For Bertie, the burden was especially heavy. 'All my ancestors succeeded to the throne after their predecessors had died,' he complained to a wartime minister. 'Mine is not only alive, but very much so.'

PART TWO

The Home Front

6

David's Disgrace

In 1951, to Bertie's horror, the Duke of Windsor published his memoirs. After years of feuding with the rest of the royal family, it was an attempt by David to set the record straight about his abdication. Bertie was already wearily familiar with this version, and disputed every part of it; but if he had dared to read the book (it seems he did not), he would not have disagreed with David's account of their childhood, growing up together on the Sandringham estate at the turn of the century.

David was academically brighter than Bertie, though not much. He never learned to write English grammatically, and it was a mercy to his readers that his memoirs were produced with the help of a hired journalist. At Sandringham, the two boys were taught jointly by Henry Hansell, a mournful bachelor whose pastimes included staring across the flat Norfolk countryside and visiting churches.

'I do not wish to be critical of Mr Hansell,' David wrote, 'but, on looking back over those five curiously ineffectual years under him, I am appalled to discover how little I really learned . . . Although I was in his care on and off for more than twelve years I am today unable to recall anything brilliant or original that he ever said.'

David, soon to be followed by Bertie, was sent to Osborne Naval College on the Isle of Wight, where he was bullied horribly. On one occasion, 'an empty classroom window was raised far enough to push my head through and then banged down on my neck, a crude reminder of the sad fate of Charles I and the English method of dealing with Royalty who displeased.' Cadet's honour prevented David from sneaking on his persecutors.

In 1911, at the age of seventeen, he was invested as Prince of Wales at Caernarvon Castle. 'All Wales is a sea of song,' David declared in Welsh (he had been coached by Lloyd George). 'The dear boy did it all remarkably well, and looked so nice,' his father reported in his diary that night – virtually the only compliment George bestowed on his eldest son during their forty-two-year acquaintance.

David found the ceremony acutely embarrassing. 'When a tailor appeared to measure me for a fantastic costume designed for the occasion, consisting of white satin breeches and a mantle and surcoat of purple velvet edged with ermine, I decided things had gone too far . . . There was a family blow-up that night; but in the end my mother, as always, smoothed things over. "You mustn't take a mere ceremony so seriously," she said. "Your friends will understand that as a Prince you are obliged to do certain things that may seem a little silly."'

Less convincing is David's recollection that the investiture led to 'a painful discovery about myself . . . While I was prepared to fulfil my role in all this pomp and ritual, I recoiled from anything that tended to set me up as a person requiring homage.'

After serving in France during the First World War (to his chagrin, behind the front line), he claimed to have made another discovery. 'The idea that my birth or title should somehow or other set me apart from and above other people struck me as wrong . . . I suppose that, without quite understanding why, I was in unconscious rebellion against my position.'

His words ring hollow. David consciously rebelled against the tedium of being heir to the throne – the endless round of ribbon-cutting, tree-planting and ship-launching which Bertie performed so well. As for the privileges – the gracious living and obliging women – he was happy to keep them.

And yet, for a brief period in the early 1920s, David seemed in the words of his biographer Frances Donaldson, 'miraculously fitted for the job to which he had been born and bred.' On his father's behalf, he visited every corner of the empire in a series of triumphal tours. In Australia (but it could equally have been New Zealand, Canada, or South Africa), he recalled there was 'a mass impulse to prod some part of the Prince of Wales. Whenever I entered a crowd, it closed around me like an octopus. I can still hear the shrill, excited cry, "I touched him." If I were out of reach, then a blow on my head with a folded newspaper appeared to satisfy the impulse.'

At home, he displayed a touching consideration for his fellow war veterans and the unemployed. In February 1932, concerned about the slump, he issued 'a fresh call for service' at the Albert Hall. He even invited the Prime Minister and the Chancellor of the Exchequer to his home at Fort Belvedere on the edge of Windsor Great Park, in order to discuss a housing venture on his Duchy of Cornwall estate.

The courtiers had a rather different view of David. Soon after the First World War, he asked Sir Frederick Ponsonby, now his father's Keeper of the Privy Purse, how he was faring as Prince of Wales. 'If I may say so, Sir,' Ponsonby told him frostily, 'I think there is risk in making yourself too accessible . . . A Prince should not show himself too much. The Monarchy must remain on a pedestal.'

As someone who enjoyed thrashing Edward VII on the croquet lawn (or later, George V on the tennis court), Ponsonby's remarks seem hypocritical. Less easy to dismiss is the opinion of Alan Lascelles, David's Assistant Private Secretary until 1929, when he resigned in disgust.

Lascelles' growing frustration with David erupted in the letters he wrote home to his wife. 'I can't help thinking that the best thing that could happen to him, and to the country, would be for him to break his neck,' he told her in August 1927 during a stressful tour of Canada. Three weeks later Lascelles likened his own position to that of a jockey – 'trying to induce a race-horse to race, whose only idea is to stop in the middle of the course and perform circus tricks; or an actor manager whose Hamlet persists in interrupting the play by balancing the furniture on the end of his nose.'

Lascelles reached the point of no return a year later, during a shooting tour of Kenya with David. In London, George had fallen seriously ill with a lung infection and the Prime Minister Stanley Baldwin wanted David to return immediately. David dismissed the request as 'just some election dodge of old Baldwin's'.

'Then, for the first and only time in our association, I lost my temper with him. "Sir," I said, "the King of England is dying and if that means nothing to you, it means a great deal to us." He looked at me, went out without a word, and spent the remainder of the evening in the successful seduction of a Mrs Barnes, wife of the local Commissioner. He told me so himself next morning.'

David's interest in married women, rather than marriage, was already the despair of his parents. It was not entirely his fault. In the aftermath of the First World War and the decimation of European royalty, the ranks of eligible princesses had shrunk considerably. Yet at the Embassy Club off Bond Street which he frequented during the 1920s, David could have enjoyed himself with any number of unattached young ladies. Instead, he preferred the maternal embrace of Mrs Freda Dudley Ward.

She was the wife of a complaisant Liberal MP and had first met David in 1918, when she ran into a house he was visiting to shelter from an air raid. Other married women passed through David's life – notably Lady Thelma Furness, who joined him on the Kenyan safari – but Mrs Dudley Ward remained the royal *maîtresse en titre* until she telephoned David at St James's Palace one morning in May 1934. The palace telephonist, who was used to these calls, was extremely upset. 'I have something so terrible to tell you that I don't know how to say it,' she told Mrs Dudley Ward. 'I have orders not to put you through.'

The woman who had supplanted Mrs Dudley Ward (and Lady

Furness, who received the same treatment) was a thirty-eight-year-old American called Wallis Simpson. According to 'Chips' Channon, who affected to like her, Mrs Simpson was 'jolly, plain, intelligent, quiet, unpretentious and unprepossessing'. Channon contradicted this picture by adding, more accurately: 'She has already the air of a personage who walks into a room as though she almost expected to be curtsied to. At least she wouldn't be too surprised. She has complete power over the Prince of Wales, who is trying to launch her socially.'

Mrs Simpson was doubly married. She had divorced her first husband, a violent drunk called Earl Winfield Spencer, in 1927. The second husband, a half-American businessman called Ernest Simpson, was a more obliging character. After David had made Wallis's acquaintance at a party, Ernest would accompany his wife down to Fort Belvedere for the weekend. Later, he delegated this duty to Wallis's old friend, Mrs Katherine Rogers.

Gwendolyn Butler, a friend of the royal family, witnessed a scene between David and Wallis which spoke volumes about their relationship:

The Prince: 'Have you got a light, darling?'
Wallis: 'Have you done your duty?'
Little man gets on his haunches, puts up his hands and begs like a dog. She then lights his cigarette. Horrible to see.

So it was that when George died at Sandringham in January 1936 (having been hastened to his grave by the royal doctor Lord Dawson who, seeing the king was dying, administered an overdose of morphia and cocaine)* all the elements were in place for what became known as 'the year of three kings'.

The key events are not in dispute. David wished to marry Wallis, after her divorce from Ernest in October on the grounds of Ernest's adultery at the Café de Paris near Maidenhead with the improbably named Buttercup Kennedy. Prime Minister Stanley Baldwin, who was the bane of David's life, told him that Wallis would be unacceptable to the government, the opposition, his

British subjects, the governments of the Dominions, and – by implication – the rest of the planet. David disagreed, and wanted to go abroad for a few months (Belgium, perhaps) while the British people delivered their verdict. Baldwin pressed his case, and on 10 December announced David's abdication to the House of Commons.

At issue is the interpretation of these events, and in particular, of David's conduct. 'I reject the notion put forward by some,' David later wrote, in a thinly veiled reference to his family, 'that faced with a choice between love and duty, I chose love. I certainly married because I chose the path of love. But I abdicated because I chose the path of duty. I did not value the Crown so lightly that I gave it away hastily. I valued it so deeply that I surrendered it, rather than risk any impairment of its prestige.'

He recalled the traumatic meeting with his mother Queen Mary in November 1936, when he first told her of his intention to marry Wallis. 'The word "duty" fell between us. But there could be no question of my shirking my duty. What separated us was not a question of duty but a different concept of kingship.'

Just how different was made clear by Mary in a letter she wrote to David a year and a half later. 'You will remember how miserable I was when you informed me of your intended marriage and abdication and how I implored you not to do so for our sake and for the sake of the country. You did not seem able to take any point of view but your own . . . I do not think you have ever realised the shock which the attitude you took up caused your family and the whole Nation. It seemed inconceivable to those who had made such sacrifices during the war that you, as their King, refused a lesser sacrifice.'

If Mary was shocked, Bertie was distraught at his sudden elevation to the throne. 'He sobbed on my shoulder for a whole hour,' Mary told Harold Nicolson in 1948: 'There, upon that sofa.'

Encouraged by his wife – the 'ice-veined bitch', in David's description – every act of Bertie's reign was designed to repair the damage he imagined his brother's abdication had caused to the monarchy.

The damage, however, was remarkably slight; and in view of his subsequent misadventures, David's resignation from the royal club may have been his most valuable service to the monarchy.

Until the eleventh hour, the vast majority of David's subjects had no inkling of his domestic problems. In June, Wallis joined him for a holiday cruise off the coast of Dalmatia, which was widely reported in the European and American press. Newsreel footage showed David and Wallis clambering ashore to visit a Croatian village, enjoying a picnic on the beach, or buying souvenirs in the shops – lovers for all the world to see (even though they still kept separate cabins).

As his adoration for Wallis reached a new pitch of intensity, so David seems to have felt the need to shed his clothes in her presence. Diana Cooper, also on board, recalled David's 'spick-and-span little shorts, straw sandals and two crucifixes on a chain round his neck.' Some days, this outfit might be worn with 'a tiny blue-and-white singlet' bought in a peasant village. At other times, the King went topless. Sailing through the Corinth canal, David removed his vest before waving to the crowd which had gathered on the bridge to catch a glimpse of the King and his mistress.

None of these pictures was published in the British newspapers. Instead, the British public was treated to dreary accounts of David's meetings with the Greek Prime Minister, the Turkish President, and King Boris of Bulgaria – the last report failing to mention the argument between Boris and his brother the Grand Duke Kyril (both of whom had inherited Foxy's enthusiasm for railways) about which of them should drive the royal train back to Sofia, after it had deposited David on his homeward journey at the Yugoslav frontier.

The British press was bound by its habitual deference towards the monarchy, which encouraged rigorous self-censorship regarding the private lives of the royal family. No instructions were issued from Buckingham Palace ordering a blackout; it simply existed as a matter of course.

But it could not last: David's Private Secretary Sir Alec Hardinge told him so on 13 November, less than a month before the abdication, and on 1 December the floodgates were opened by the Bishop of Bradford, Dr Blunt. In a speech to his diocesan conference, the Bishop took as his subject the forthcoming coronation, and the need for the King to show 'faith, prayer and dedication'. 'We hope,' Dr Blunt said, 'that he is aware of this need. Some of us wish that he gave more positive signs of such awareness.'

'The storm breaks,' Harold Nicolson wrote in his diary, when the national papers – taking their lead from the provinces – used the Bishop's comments as a pretext to discuss the battle between David and Baldwin.

Within the Establishment to which Nicolson belonged, and which had known of David's infatuation for at least a year, the abdication crisis created a mood approaching hysteria. High society was divided between self-styled 'cavaliers', who backed David, and 'roundheads', who supported Baldwin.

'Chips' Channon, a cavalier (and a first-class drama queen), was at the centre of the storm. 'A day of doubt, torment and indecision,' he told his diary on 9 December. 'Towards six in the evening we knew definitely that the abdication was signed. Honor [Channon's wife] went to Kitty Brownlow's at midnight and the Buists came in, hysterical and weeping. They had a plan, a mad one, of rushing to the Fort [Belvedere] in a last final attempt, and they rang up Osbourne, the King's valet, and he said that the King refused to see them, or even speak on the telephone.'

The rest of the population was rather less agitated. 'London was outwardly quiet during the weekend', *The Times* was puzzled to report on 7 December. 'In a situation so provocative of strong opinion and profound feeling everywhere, little outward expression was given – on any significant scale – to what was occupying all minds.'

The evidence is all circumstantial, but it suggests that for the vast majority of David's subjects, the abdication crisis was a ten-day wonder. Even when the abdication was announced, on 11 December, *The Times* could find 'no demonstrations or signs of marked popular feeling'. In Parliament Square, 'there was no

change in the demeanour of the crowds after the decision to abdicate became known, and no emotion was perceptible that could
with any justice be described as a corporate reaction.'

In the provinces, the chief concern seems to have been the
effect on the souvenir business of scrapping David's projected
coronation the following May. Birmingham jewellers complained
about the 'heavy expenditure' already incurred producing effigies
of 'King Edward'. Nottingham lacemakers grumbled about the
waste in manufacturing special coronation doilies and tablecloths.
They need not have worried: the 'King Edward' items became
collectors' pieces, while even more money was to be made from
the new 'King George' souvenirs.

The muted reaction of most people to the abdication was
partly due to their ignorance of events until the very end. Even
when the crisis broke, the newspapers continued to report its
progress obliquely — referring to 'the King's affair', rather than
his infatuation with a twice-divorced American.

But it was also because the public shared the newspaper editors' belief that the royal family's privacy should be respected.
Cosmo Lang, the Archbishop of Canterbury, discovered this fact
on 13 December, two days after the abdication, when he delivered a radio broadcast of quite stupendous sanctimony on the
previous week's events.

'Strange and sad it is,' Lang observed of David, 'that he should
have sought his happiness in a manner inconsistent with the
Christian principles of marriage, and within a social circle whose
standard and way of life are alien to all the best instincts and traditions of his people.'

Lang's remarks were greeted with general outrage — though
few could match the wit of Gerald Bullett, who composed a
poem to mark the occasion:

> My Lord Archbishop, what a scold you are!
> And when your man is down how bold you are!
> Of charity how oddly scant you are!
> How Lang, O Lord, how full of Cantuar!

David, who detested Lang, would have approved of the squib. What he found far harder to accept was the idea that, in wishing to leave him in peace, his former subjects also wished him to pass into oblivion.

'I now quit altogether public affairs,' he told them in his abdication broadcast. If only it were true, Bertie must have wished, after David had phoned him yet again at Buckingham Palace with unsolicited advice. These calls were bad enough, and within a few months Bertie instructed the useful Walter Monckton (David's intermediary with Baldwin during the abdication crisis) that they must cease.

More worrying were David's 'political' activities, which in the early years of Bertie's reign posed a far graver threat to the prestige of the monarchy than the abdication. To Bertie, it seemed scarcely conceivable that David – even David – could contemplate treason. The evidence, however, was staring him in the face.

7

David and
the Germans

David's affection for Germany dated from 1913, when he was sent on an improving tour of the country by his parents. He stayed with his many German relatives, and remembered especially fondly 'Onkel Willie and Tante Charlotte' – the portly King and Queen of Württemberg.

After a large lunch at the palace, Willie and Charlotte would take David on their daily ride through the suburbs of Stuttgart. 'Onkel Willie would quickly fall asleep, only to be constantly aroused by a swift jab of the Queen's elbow to acknowledge the salute of one of his soldiers, the precise salutation of a solid Württemberger, or to straighten the Homburg hat that kept sliding rakishly to one side of his head.' Willie was so used to this treatment that he could even straighten the hat in his sleep.

As a result of this tour, David learned to speak competent German. His French, by contrast, was comically bad, despite spending five months in France the previous year. Visiting David at his home outside Paris in 1958, the writer James Pope-Hennessy was amused to discover his host speaking German with his gardeners, one of whom came from Alsace.

David's military service in France during the First World War (at his father's insistence, he was kept away from the front line) did nothing to alter this basic affinity. Like many other veterans, he fervently believed that Britain must never again go to war with Germany.

'The subjugation of a vanquished people by victorious States was no longer conceivable,' he told the German ambassador in 1935 – or so the ambassador claimed in his dispatch to Berlin. A few months later, David told the annual conference of the British Legion that he felt 'there could be no more suitable body . . . to stretch forth the hand of friendship to the Germans than we ex-service men, who fought them and have now forgotten all about it and the Great War.' For this speech, David was rebuked by his father, who warned him not to meddle in politics.

There is no doubt that David also admired the Nazis for tackling the two social problems about which he cared the most – unemployment and housing. 'You are aware from my reports that King Edward, quite generally, feels warm sympathy for Germany,' Leopold von Hoesch, the German ambassador to Britain, informed Berlin in January 1936. 'I have become convinced during frequent, often lengthy talks with him that these sympathies are deep-rooted and strong enough to withstand the contrary influences to which they are not seldom exposed.'

Another of David's German cousins, the Duke of Coburg, met the new King in the same month. Coburg was a convinced Nazi, and had been sent by Hitler to explore the possibility of an Anglo-German agreement. He reported that 'an alliance Germany–Britain is *for him* [David] an urgent necessity and a guiding principle for British foreign policy.' Furthermore, 'to my question whether a discussion between Baldwin and Hitler would be desirable, he replied in the following words: "Who is King here? Baldwin or I? I myself wish to talk to Hitler, and will do so here or in Germany. Tell him that, please."'

Hitler's understanding of the British constitution was already confused from reading too many trash novels in his youth about the English aristocracy, and he seriously believed that the King could secure his cherished agreement; its purpose being to keep Britain neutral in the event of war while he achieved the domination of continental Europe. The Duke of Coburg's report about David's state of mind was probably exaggerated, as were the dispatches from von Hoesch's replacement as ambassador to Britain, the former wine merchant Joachim von Ribbentrop. Both men, anxious to rise in the Nazi hierarchy, had their own reasons for fuelling Hitler's fantasies.

Less easily dismissed, however, is the evidence of David's British friends and acquaintances, who appear to have taken his pro-German views for granted. Duff Cooper, then Secretary of State for War, dined with David immediately after delivering a tough speech to the Great Britain–France Society in Paris, where he had described the two countries as confronting the same threat (a scarcely veiled reference to German rearmament).

'As he approached me I saw that his face was heavy with displeasure. I expected a rebuke and I think he was preparing one, but suddenly the frown fled, giving way to his delightful smile as he laughed and said: "Well, Duff, you certainly have done it this time."'

Chips Channon, who was sympathetic towards Germany, none the less remarked of David in November 1936: 'He, too, is going the dictator way, and is pro-German, against Russia, and against too much slipshod democracy. I shouldn't be surprised if he aimed at making himself a mild dictator, a difficult task enough for an English king.'

David's political views have often since been described as naive, as if this somehow excused them. They seem, on the contrary, especially inexcusable in view of the opportunities he had been given to travel the world, meet the political leaders of the day, and generally prepare himself for the role of constitutional sovereign.

If proof were needed of both his naivety and his hypocrisy, it came in September 1937, when it was announced that he and 'the Duchess' (they had been married in June) would shortly be visiting Germany and the United States 'for the purpose of studying housing and working conditions in these two countries.' David had not, after all, decided to 'quit altogether public affairs'; the lure of the political limelight, and the chance to show his wife that he still counted for something in the world, had proved too great to resist.

The Nazi leadership which had issued the invitation could scarcely believe its luck; desperate to gain respectability for the regime, a visit by the former King of England was a major propaganda coup. In the company of the Nazi Labour Minister Dr Robert Ley, an alcoholic who was later convicted at Nuremberg of war crimes, David and Wallis were rapturously welcomed at a series of housing projects, youth camps and hospitals across Germany.

David gave what the *New York Times* described as a 'modified' Nazi salute when he met Heinrich Himmler, Rudolf Hess and Joseph Goebbels at a reception. There was reportedly another salute when he inspected the guard of honour of the Death's Head Division of the Hitler Elite Guards; and again when he and Wallis were granted the supreme privilege, an audience with the Führer at Berchtesgaden.

Hitler's interpreter at this meeting, Paul Schmidt, could recall 'nothing whatever to indicate whether the Duke of Windsor really sympathised with the ideology and practices of the Third Reich, as Hitler seemed to assume he did.' On the other hand, David offered 'appreciative words for the measures taken in Germany in the field of social welfare' – which rather contradicts Schmidt's claim. Hitler was impressed by Wallis, who joined the conversation 'when any social question of special interest to women arose'. 'She would have made a good Queen,' he remarked, after the couple had departed.

It was against this background that in the summer of 1940, on Hitler's authority, the Germans conceived their extraordinary plot to kidnap David and install him on the British throne in place of Bertie. The details of the plot are not in doubt. The question is whether David connived at what would have been, in wartime, an act of high treason.

David's war was not a happy one. In September 1939, when

Hitler chose to ignore his telegram appealing for peace and invaded Poland, he and Wallis were staying at La Croe, the house they rented on the French Riviera. Walter Monckton phoned from London on the government's behalf, offering David and Wallis a plane to fly them back to England.

David rejected this proposal. He told Monckton that they would only return on condition that he and 'the Duchess' were invited to stay at Windsor as full members of the royal family. Ever since his marriage in June 1937 David had been attempting to reverse Bertie's decision that Wallis should not be entitled to the style 'Her Royal Highness'. Where David was 'HRH The Duke of Windsor', his wife was denied royal status. It was, in David's opinion, an unforgivable insult.

'You *only* think of yourselves,' David's friend Major Metcalfe, who was staying at La Croe, told him in a fury. 'You don't realise that there is at this moment a war going on, that women and children are being bombed and killed, while you talk of your pride! What you've now said to Walter has just bitched up everything.'

There was a further problem, David explained, once he had abandoned his original objection. 'It seems *she* wd rather go in a boat,' Metcalfe wrote home to his wife in despair, '*any*thing *but* a plane. She is terrified & so is *he*!' A boat commanded by David's cousin Louis Mountbatten was sent to Cherbourg, and on 12 September the Duke and Duchess of Windsor, accompanied by three pet cairn dogs, Pookie, Prisie and Dette, returned to England for the first time since the abdication.

They were soon back in France, where to his disgust (he expected to be made a general, at least) David was assigned to humdrum 'liaison duties' with the British Military Mission. The Duke 'produced a valuable report on the defence of the front line', Major-General Howard Vyse informed the War Office in October 1939. Among other details, he had noticed that the anti-tank ditches were weak, the anti-tank crews were poorly trained, and there was little attempt at concealment.

But when the Germans exploited these weaknesses seven months later – or rather, ignored them, choosing to launch their invasion through the unprotected Ardennes forest – the Duke was nowhere to be found. Without telling Vyse or his aide-de-camp, the long-suffering Metcalfe, he fled on 28 May to Biarritz and the arms of the waiting Wallis. From there they proceeded to the Cap d'Antibes; and within a few weeks, as France capitulated to Germany, he and Wallis were struggling with thousands of other refugees to cross the border into neutral Spain.

'*Je suis le Prince de Galles!*' David shouted at the hapless French veterans of the First World War who manned the checkpoints on the way to the frontier. For some reason the *anciens combattants* were impressed by this declaration. Waving aside refugees of less noble ancestry, they allowed the 'Prince and Princess of Wales' to pass. Further strings were pulled with the Spanish embassy in Paris, and on either 20 or 21 June (the dates are unclear) David and Wallis reached the relative safety of Spain.

In Madrid, the British ambassador to Spain, Sir Samuel Hoare, was expecting them. His instructions were to expedite David and Wallis's onward journey to Portugal (also neutral), where they would be collected by flying boat and returned to England.

The German ambassador to Spain, Eberhard von Stohrer, had also been tracking their movements. On 23 June he sent a telegram to Ribbentrop, now Germany's Foreign Minister. 'The Spanish Foreign Minister requests advice with regard to the treatment of the Duke and Duchess of Windsor who were to arrive in Madrid today, apparently in order to return to England by way of Lisbon. The Foreign Minister assumes . . . that we might perhaps be interested in detaining the Duke of Windsor here and possibly in establishing contact with him.'

Although Spain was neutral, its government under General Franco was friendly to the Germans. Franco owed Hitler a huge debt for the Germans' military assistance during the civil war of 1936–9. Furthermore, Franco depended on the Spanish fascist movement as a power base, and in the summer of 1940 it made sense to back what looked like the winning side in the war Hitler had started. For all these reasons, the Spanish proved willing accomplices in the plan Ribbentrop now put into action.

Replying to Stohrer, Ribbentrop asked whether it was possible 'in the first place to detain the Duke and Duchess of Windsor for a couple of weeks in Spain before they are granted an exit visa? It would be necessary at all events to be sure that it did not appear in any way that the suggestion came from Germany.'

Hoare, meanwhile, told the Foreign Secretary Lord Halifax on 26 June that he was inviting David 'from time to time to lunch and dinner in order to keep him on the rails. I am certain that somehow or other Winston must find him a job. I know how difficult this is. Nevertheless I feel that there will be a great deal of trouble unless he does.'

The 'trouble' began when David informed Churchill from Madrid that he would obey the first part of the Prime Minister's instruction and travel to Lisbon. As to the second part, returning to England 'for consultations', that depended on 'the Duchess' being accorded equal treatment with the wives of other royal brothers.

Churchill, preoccupied by the marginally more important question of imminent German invasion, threatened David with a court martial if he did not return. 'Your Royal Highness has taken active military rank and refusal to obey direct orders of competent military authority would create a serious situation. I hope it will not be necessary for such orders to be sent. I most strongly urge compliance with wishes of Government,' he wired.

This telegram, dispatched on 28 June, had been submitted by Churchill to Buckingham Palace for Bertie's approval; but at some point during the next three days, Bertie decided that he would really rather not see his elder brother back in England. On 1 July Churchill met Bertie at Buckingham Palace and it was decided to offer David the governor-generalship of the Bahamas – a posting which was both suitably obscure and remote. Churchill's friend Lord Beaverbrook thought David would find the appointment 'a great relief'. 'Not half as much as his brother will,' Churchill replied.

Was this all Hoare had meant when he warned of the need to keep David 'on the rails'? In his subsequent despatches to

Halifax, Hoare was anxious to refute the impression that the former King was not committed to the allied cause. At a reception held in David and Wallis's honour at the British embassy, 'so far from making defeatist remarks they went out of their way to show their belief in final victory.' The next day Hoare added that 'the Windsors have behaved admirably during their stay here'.

There are three reasons why Hoare's testimony should be treated with caution. Firstly, as a member of the Chamberlain government he had been closely associated with the pre-war policy of appeasement. It was Hoare, as Foreign Secretary in 1935, who negotiated the notorious plan with his French counterpart Pierre Laval (a future collaborator), which would have sanctioned Mussolini's invasion of Abyssinia.

The plan collapsed amid a storm of protests, Hoare was forced to resign, and in May 1940 – having served as a member of Chamberlain's war cabinet – he was sacked by Churchill, the incoming Prime Minister, for suspected defeatism. The suspicion was well founded, and Hoare's appointment to the Madrid embassy, like David's dispatch to the Bahamas, was intended to push him to the sidelines. Since in 1940 Hoare was highly sceptical of a 'final victory' for the allies, his comments about David's views on the subject are tainted.

Secondly, Hoare was an unctuous monarchist, proud of his contacts within the royal family. He was a regular guest of Bertie and Elizabeth at Sandringham, which was close to his home in Norfolk, and returned the compliment by sending the Queen copies of the books he periodically wrote. Among his papers in the Cambridge University Library are several letters from Elizabeth thanking Hoare for his kind thought.

It is thus possible that after his initial remark about David's unreliability, Hoare paused to consider the effect these words would have on his relationship with Bertie and Elizabeth. They would have wholeheartedly agreed with him; on the other hand, it was not an allegation they wished to see on the public record.

If Hoare changed his mind, the evidence probably lies in a box of his papers at Cambridge described as 'correspondence with

George VI, Queen Elizabeth and the Duke of Windsor and memos 1925–58'. A note in the catalogue explains that 'this file may not be seen without the permission of the Royal Librarian'.* At some point, the last seven words of this instruction have been crossed out.

Thirdly, Hoare's testimony was contradicted by other diplomats who met David in Madrid. Marcus Cheke, a junior officer at the British embassy, overheard David predicting the fall of the Churchill government. That would bring in a Labour administration, David continued, a negotiated peace with Germany would follow, his brother would abdicate, and he would be recalled to the throne.

The US ambassador in Madrid, A.W. Weddell, reported a similar conversation at his own embassy. 'The Duke of Windsor declared that the most important thing now to be done was to end the war before thousands more were killed or maimed to save the faces of a few politicians . . . In the past ten years Germany had totally reorganised the order of its society in preparation for this war. Countries which were unwilling to accept such a reorganisation of society and its concomitant sacrifices should direct their policies accordingly and thereby avoid dangerous adventures.'

Weddell, representing a neutral power (America did not enter the war until December 1941), concluded that: 'these observations have their value if any as doubtless reflecting the views of an element in England, possibly a growing one, who find in Windsor and his circle a group who are realists in world politics and who hope to come into their own in [the] event of peace.'

And yet, by agreeing to travel to Portugal, David made Ribbentrop's plan considerably more difficult to execute. Portugal was also neutral, but more strictly so than Spain; and in Berlin, Ribbentrop was forced to adjust his arrangements.

For almost the whole of July, David and Wallis stayed in Lisbon, while two dramas unfolded around them. The Germans, with the cooperation of the Franco government, were desperate to lure the couple back to Spain; the British, who almost certainly knew of the German plans, were equally desperate to extract the former King from Portugal. Caught in the middle, David's attitude to these conflicting overtures was, to say the least, ambivalent.

Their host in Portugal was a banker called Ricardo Espirito Santo e Silva, who owned a house a few miles outside Lisbon. The senior German diplomat in Lisbon, Baron von Hoyningen-Huene, reported that Espirito Santo was sympathetic to the German cause, and he was drafted into the conspiracy.

The US minister in Lisbon, Herbert Pell, had lunch with David and Wallis at Espirito Santo's house on 20 July, and sent a gloomy telegram back to Washington. 'Duke and Duchess of Windsor are indiscreet and outspoken against British Government,' he cabled. 'Consider their presence in the United States might be disturbing and confusing. They say that they intend remaining in the United States whether Churchill likes it or not and desire apparently to make propaganda for peace.'

It was now almost three weeks since their arrival in Portugal, and they were still refusing to budge. Initially, David refused to travel to England until the question of Wallis's status within the royal family was settled. When, almost immediately, Churchill offered him the Bahamas posting, a deeply resentful David accepted on three conditions: firstly that he and Wallis should be allowed to travel to Nassau via the United States ('medical reasons' for the Duchess were cited, but it seems that she wanted to catch up on her shopping); secondly that his chauffeur should be released from National Service to join him in the Bahamas; and thirdly that his valet should also be released.

Churchill, sparing a moment from his preparations for the Battle of Britain, told David that the first two demands were impossible. Meanwhile, Piper Alistair Fletcher of the Scots Guards was informed that he could best serve his country in its darkest hour by looking after the ex-King's clothes.

In Lisbon, Huene was convinced that these absurd manoeuvres were delaying tactics by David while he waited for 'a turn of events favourable to him'. 'He is convinced,' Huene continued in his 11 July dispatch to Ribbentrop, 'that if he had remained on the throne war would have been avoided, and he characterised himself as a firm supporter of a peaceful arrangement with Germany. The Duke definitely believes that continued severe bombing [of Britain] would make England ready for peace.'

Ribbentrop now sent an urgent message to Stohrer in Madrid, ordering him to enlist the Franco government in the delicate task of luring the Duke of Windsor back to Spain. If necessary, Spain could 'intern' the Duke as an English officer and treat him as a 'military fugitive . . . At a suitable occasion the Duke must be informed that Germany wants peace with the English people, that the Churchill clique stands in the way of it, and that it would be a good thing if the Duke would hold himself in readiness for further developments.'

The Spanish emissary chosen for this approach was Miguel Primo de Rivera, leader of the fascist movement in Madrid, who was certainly acquainted with David and may even have been – as Stohrer claimed – an 'old friend'. Rivera later insisted that he had no knowledge of the Germans' involvement in the plot, and believed that he was acting purely on his own government's behalf: which suggests that he was either gullible or disingenuous.

On 23 July Stohrer reported the result of Rivera's mission in a 'most urgent, top secret' telegram:

He [Rivera] had two long conversations with the Duke of Windsor; at the last one the Duchess was present also. The Duke expressed himself very freely . . . Politically he was more and more distant from the King and the present British Government. The Duke and Duchess have less fear of the King, who was quite foolish, than of the shrewd Queen, who was intriguing skilfully against the Duke and particularly against the Duchess. The Duke was considering making a public statement . . . disavowing present English policy and breaking with his brother . . . The Duke and Duchess said they very much desired to return to Spain.

A further telegram with more information from Rivera was transmitted by Stohrer to Ribbentrop on 25 July:

> When he [Rivera] gave the Duke the advice not to go to the Bahamas, but to return to Spain, since the Duke was likely to be called upon to play an important role in English policy and possibly to ascend the English throne, both the Duke and Duchess gave evidence of astonishment. Both . . . replied that according to the English constitution this would not be possible after the abdication. When the confidential emissary then expressed his expectation that the course of the war might bring about changes even in the English constitution, the Duchess especially became very pensive.

Meanwhile, Ribbentrop had sent an SS officer called Walter Schellenberg to Lisbon to achieve the same object by more direct means. A message was delivered to Wallis, warning of a conspiracy. Another anonymous message claimed that the ship which was due to convey them to the Bahamas would be sabotaged. By these and other dastardly devices Schellenberg convinced the querulous couple that they were the target of an assassination plot by the British secret services.

When he arrived in Lisbon on 30 July, sent by an utterly exasperated Churchill, it took all Walter Monckton's formidable skills as a barrister to persuade David that this was not, in fact, the case. On 2 August, David and Wallis – clutching, we hope, Pookie, Prisie and Dette – boarded the American ship that was waiting for them in Lisbon harbour, and set sail for the Bahamas.

There were two postscripts to the story. On 3 August, Stohrer wired Ribbentrop from Madrid: 'The Spanish Minister of the Interior just informed me that his confidential emissary [Rivera] had just telephoned him from Lisbon . . . that on the day of their departure he had spent a considerable time with the Duke and Duchess. The Duke had hesitated even up to the last moment. The ship had had to delay its departure on that account.'

Twelve days later, on 15 August, Huene sent a further telegram from Lisbon: 'The confidant [Espirito Santo] has just received a telegram from the Duke in Bermuda [*sic*], asking him to send a communication as soon as action was advisable. Should any answer be made?' When German Foreign Office documents were captured at the end of the war, no answer was found.

Huene's final telegram seems the surest evidence that David was prepared to commit treason. The case for the defence is that none of the main actors on the German side was a remotely reliable witness. Espirito Santo, Rivera and Stohrer all had their own careerist motives for talking up the conspiracy – as did Ribbentrop in Berlin, anxious to present Hitler with a wonderful prize. Huene himself was not a Nazi, but for that reason needed to prove his loyalty. The Lisbon embassy, staffed by professional diplomats, was regarded with suspicion by Ribbentrop.

But can David's testimony be trusted? In 1957, when the captured German diplomatic documents containing this story were published, he issued a statement through his London lawyers. Ribbentrop's communications with Stohrer and Huene were 'complete fabrications and, in part, gross distortions of the truth,' David said. He admitted that while in Lisbon he had been approached by 'certain people' trying to persuade him to return to Spain, whom he discovered to be Nazi sympathisers. 'At no time did I ever entertain any thought of complying with such a suggestion, which I treated with the contempt it deserved.'

David's official biographer Philip Ziegler is inclined to believe this protestation. 'Everything that is known of the Duke's character,' Ziegler writes, '– his obstinacy, his pride, his courage, his conviction that with all their faults the British were the best of peoples – suggests that he would never have played the traitor's part.'

It depends in the first place on the definition of treason. As Ziegler accepts, there is plenty of evidence that in the summer of 1940 David was convinced that Britain had lost the war; and, further, that he might have some future role to play after the defeat. The distinction Ziegler draws is between uttering these sentiments to neutral parties – as David undoubtedly did – and making his opinions known to the enemy. In view of Rivera's known sympathy with the Germans it seems a fine distinction, even taking into account David's invincible political naivety.

It depends secondly on a judgement about David's capacity for rational behaviour. Ziegler maintains that David would never have sent such an incriminating message to Espirito Santo from the Bahamas, knowing that it would almost certainly be read by the British and the Americans. Furthermore, if he was preparing himself for 'future action', why did he finally agree to leave Portugal, rather than stay in Lisbon at Espirito Santo's house?

David's earlier biographer, Frances Donaldson, believes the telegram was genuine – motivated by a belief that 'he had too precipitately refused an opportunity to serve his country'. Writing in 1974, only two years after David's death, she said that 'in the calmer atmosphere of today no one would attribute actual guilt in the sense of deliberate treachery to the Duke, but comparative guilt is easier to estimate, and there is no doubt that his actions would have earned fierce reprisals in the atmosphere of, for instance, the French Resistance.'

Twenty years later, even Lady Donaldson's verdict seems too charitable. The atmosphere of the Battle of Britain would have been enough to earn David fierce reprisals – whether or not he sent that last, damning telegram – if his former subjects had known the truth. Fortunately for David, they never did.

Bertie was one of the few who did know the full story. From the moment his elder brother crossed into Spain, Churchill kept him fully abreast of developments. As early as 7 July, Bertie's Private Secretary Sir Alec Hardinge wrote a memorandum, based on the intelligence reports which had been shown to the King. After his unhappy time as David's Private Secretary during the abdication crisis, Hardinge was heavily biased against the former King. But it is unlikely that he would have written the note without being briefed by Downing Street.

Germans expect assistance from Duke and Duchess of Windsor. Latter desirous at any price to become Queen. Germans have been negotiating with her since June 27th. Status quo in England except for undertaking to form anti-Russian alliance. Germans' purpose to form Opposition Government under Duke of Windsor, having first changed public opinion by propaganda. Germans think King George will abdicate during attack on London.

Here was one anxiety for Bertie at the height of the invasion scare. Another was the fear that in wartime, the monarchy had suddenly become irrelevant. Even as David 'bitched up everything' – to borrow Major Metcalfe's words – Bertie and Elizabeth were doing their best to rally the nation. Most of the nation, however, failed to return the compliment.

8

Bertie's War

Life was hard in the royal household during the Second World War. President Roosevelt's wife Eleanor, visiting Bertie and Elizabeth at Buckingham Palace in 1942, recalled how strictly the restrictions on heat, water and food were observed. 'There was a plainly marked black line in my bathtub above which I was not supposed to run the water. We were served on gold and silver plates, but our bread was the same kind of war bread every other family had to eat, and, except for the fact that occasionally game from one of the royal preserves appeared on the table, nothing was served in the way of food that was not served in any of the war canteens.'

Accustomed to American central heating, Mrs Roosevelt almost froze to death in her bedroom, and finished her visit by catching Bertie's cold.

Everyone knows that the royal family shared the nation's wartime hardship. It must therefore have been a slip of the pen when Sir Samuel Hoare, last seen in Madrid, scribbled himself an *aide-mémoire* after an especially agreeable stay at Sandringham in January 1945. 'Dinner 8.45 p.m.,' Hoare wrote. 'Three courses. Very good. King and Queen drinking champagne as usual.'

Similarly, the memoirs of Mr F.J. Corbitt, the royal household's deputy comptroller of supply during the war, can be dismissed as pure fiction. Mr Corbitt told a story about Bertie wanting some more of his special toothpicks (the Negri brand), and Elizabeth placing an order at the same time for sauce to go with her favourite wartime staple, lobster cocktail. It was 'a minor triumph', he alleges, when he took delivery of 10,000 Negri toothpicks and 'enough bottles of Tabasco sauce . . . to last for years.' Corbitt, like Bertie and Elizabeth, would have been horrified at the thought of using the black market. He was simply fortunate to have friends who worked in the leading London hotels.

Bertie's mother Queen Mary, meanwhile, had noticed the difficulty of obtaining *pâté de foie gras* in wartime – or so Corbitt claimed in *Fit for a King*, his aptly titled memoirs. Corbitt said that in 1945, when Mary was staying at Sandringham, Bertie ordered a tureen as a special surprise. Corbitt reported dolefully that a tureen would cost £5. 'Back came an urgent order. I was to get the pâté at once and send it immediately to Sandringham. When his mother's wishes were in question, nothing was too difficult or too expensive for King George VI.'

The real hardship experienced by Elizabeth was recalled by a more reliable source, her couturier Norman Hartnell. The war, in Hartnell's words, created 'a new dress problem for the Queen': 'What should she wear when visiting bombed sites? . . . How should she appear before the distressed women and children whose own kingdoms, their small homes, had been shattered and lay crumbled at her feet?' After urgent consultations with Mr Hartnell, Elizabeth decided she must never wear black – the colour of mourning – or, for some reason, green. Instead, Hartnell and his team ran up a series of combat frocks in 'the gentle colours – dusty pink, dusty blue and dusty lilac . . . She wished to convey the most comforting, encouraging and sympathetic note possible.'

At least Elizabeth knew how the distressed women and children felt. 'I'm almost glad we've been hit,' she said when Buckingham Palace was bombed for the first time in September 1940. 'I can now look the East End in the face.'*

Bertie took the outrage more personally. The bomb had clearly been dropped by the 5th Duke of Galliera, he decided – a distant Spanish cousin who was part of the plot to remove him from the throne and reinstate David. Only one other relative, Bertie thought, had the flying skills and a sufficiently detailed knowledge of London to locate Buckingham Palace. He was Prince Christopher of Hesse, now serving in the Luftwaffe.

When he had recovered from the shock, Bertie, like his wife, was strangely reassured. 'I feel that our tours of bombed areas in London are helping the people who have lost their relations & homes,' he told his diary, '& we have both found a new bond with them as Buckingham Palace has been bombed as well as their homes, & nobody is immune from it.'

The bond was sealed on a visit to Peckham and Lambeth in October 1940, with the Minister of Food Lord Woolton as their guide. 'Good luck' and 'God bless,' the crowds cheered, as the royal carriage passed through 'a very slummy district'. Elizabeth asked about morale, and Woolton told her that all these people had lost their homes. 'The Queen was so touched she couldn't speak for a moment: I saw the tears coming into her eyes and then she said, "I think they're very wonderful."'

A month later Coventry was hit by a devastating German raid, and Bertie set off for the Midlands to comfort the bereaved. Herbert Morrison, the Minister of Supply, reported to the Civil Defence Committee on the damage. 'What amused me was Morrison's almost sobbing reference to the King's visit,' another Committee member, Harold Nicolson, wrote to his wife. 'He spoke about the King as Goebbels might have spoken about Hitler. I admit that the King does his job well. But why should Morrison speak as if he were a phenomenon?'

Nicolson did not regard Bertie as a phenomenon, in contrast to Elizabeth, whom he considered 'one of the most amazing Queens since Cleopatra'. But he was right to be sceptical about the effect of these royal visits. For every bombed-out subject who cheered (according to Woolton, anyway), 'we thank Your Majesties for coming to see us', there were perhaps others who privately resented the intrusion into their ruined lives.

During a wartime visit to a provincial city, one woman gave vent to such feelings of envy. 'It's all very well for them traipsing around saying how their hearts bleed for us and they share all our sufferings, and then going home to a roaring fire in one of their six houses,' the woman was supposed to have said. Naturally her remarks were omitted from the usual laudatory report of the royal couple's descent on their bombed-out subjects.

Bertie in any case wanted to be more than a wartime cheerleader. As head of state, he felt he should play a central part in the business of licking Hitler. At Windsor, where he and Elizabeth retired each weekend to see their semi-evacuated daughters, Bertie had a room converted into a workshop. Seated at a bench, he would hand-finish gun mechanisms for the munitions industry, while cursing the way he was overlooked by his ministers and generals.

Bertie's political frustrations began even before war was declared. In August 1939, hearing of the Nazi–Soviet pact, he proposed using his royal influence with Emperor Hirohito of Japan (Hirohito had happy memories of eating bacon and eggs for breakfast when he stayed at Buckingham Palace). 'His Majesty . . . feels that, when dealing with Orientals, direct communication between Heads of State may be helpful,' Hardinge told the Foreign Office. Bertie's offer was rejected.

A few days later, Bertie wanted to deliver a personal appeal for peace to Hitler: the Pope, the American President, and, for goodness' sake, *his brother*, had all sent telegrams. The Prime Minister Neville Chamberlain was unmoved.

Bertie had recovered his equilibrium by 29 August, when he received the ambassador to Egypt, Sir Miles Lampson, at Buckingham Palace. The King, Lampson noted, was 'in admirable form' – only worried that the international crisis was causing him to miss the Balmoral grouse season. 'He had never had so many grouse up there as this year. He had got 1,600 brace in six days and had been much looking forward to this week's shoot. It was utterly damnable that the villain Hitler had upset everything. HM thought that there would now be peace and that this time Hitler's bluff had been called.'

Three days later the Führer commenced his *battue* of the Polish army.

Once war was declared, Bertie's political judgement was equally acute. He was a staunch supporter of Chamberlain, who presided over the phony war, the loss of Norway and the German invasion of France, before losing the confidence of the House of Commons in May 1940. 'It is most unfair on Chamberlain to be treated like this after all his good work,' Bertie told his diary. 'The Conservative rebels like Duff Cooper ought to be ashamed of themselves for deserting him at this moment.'

Bertie's preferred choice to succeed Chamberlain was the Foreign Secretary Lord Halifax – a politician indelibly associated with pre-war appeasement. 'I cannot yet think of Winston as PM,' Bertie told his diary the day after Churchill kissed hands. '. . . I met Halifax in the garden [of Buckingham Palace] & told him I was sorry not to have him as PM.'

Churchill was a fervent royalist, and worked hard to dispel the bad impression he had made on Bertie in the 1930s, when his belligerence persistently undermined the sterling efforts of Chamberlain and Halifax to maintain the peace. 'No Minister in modern times . . . has received more help and comfort from the King,' Churchill wrote to Bertie in November 1942, after the allied victory at El Alamein. 'It is needless to assure Your Majesty of my devotion to Yourself and Family and to our ancient and cherished Monarchy . . . but I trust I may have the pleasure of feeling a sense of personal friendship which is very keen and lively in my heart and has grown strong in these hard times of war.'

Bertie, too, came to trust Churchill, after his initial misgivings. 'Our people will one day be very thankful to you for what you have done,' he told Churchill after El Alamein – which for once, in Bertie's case, was an accurate political prediction.

And yet he and Elizabeth worried that Churchill was hogging the limelight. 'K. and Q. feel Winston puts them in the shade,' the Conservative MP Victor Cazalet recorded in June 1942, after visiting the royal confidante Mrs Greville. 'He is always sending messages for Nation that King ought to send.' Cazalet also dined at this time with Sir Alan Lascelles, now Bertie's Assistant Private Secretary, and Halifax. 'We talk of K. and how Winston quite unconsciously has put them [*sic*] in background. Who will tell him?'

Bertie's resentment of Churchill peaked in June 1944, when the Prime Minister booked himself a grandstand seat for the first day of the allied invasion of Normandy, on board the cruiser HMS *Belfast*. Not to be outdone, Bertie placed his own reservation – only to be told by the Supreme Allied Commander General Eisenhower that the largest seaborne assault in the history of warfare was not the place for either the King or his Prime Minister.

'The right thing to do is what normally falls to those at the top on such occasions,' Bertie wrote wistfully to Churchill, 'namely, to remain at home and wait.' Churchill begged to disagree. 'I am very worried over the PM's seemingly selfish way of looking at the matter,' Bertie told his diary. 'He doesn't seem to care about the future.'

'Please consider my own position,' he wrote again to Churchill. 'I am a younger man than you, I am a sailor, & as King I am the head of all three services. There is nothing I would like to do better than to go to sea but I have agreed to stop at home; is it fair that you should then do exactly what I should have liked to do myself?'

'Since Your Majesty does me the honour to be so much concerned about my personal safety on this occasion,' Churchill replied sarcastically, 'I must defer to Your Majesty's wishes, & indeed commands.' Bertie insisted he was not making a constitutional point, which was true: the dispute was entirely personal.

Bertie's rancour was increased a few months later, when Churchill refused to let him visit his 'forgotten army' in India. 'A visit from me would buck them up,' he told the Prime Minister. Churchill feared that a descent by the last King-Emperor on the subcontinent would antagonise President Roosevelt, who sympathised with the Indian independence movement. Bertie was so upset that he decided the real reason for the veto was because 'I would have got the Burma Star and Winston wouldn't.'

Very rarely, Churchill allowed Bertie to slip the leash. In the summer of 1943 Bertie inspected the victorious troops in North Africa, a visit which – rather like the rest of his war – combined general exhaustion with fleeting exhilaration.

Travelling incognito as 'General Lyon', Bertie was so tired when he reached Algiers that he refused to discuss his schedule, and promptly retired to bed. Churchill's delegate in North Africa, Harold Macmillan, was left to discuss the arrangements with Sir Alec Hardinge – 'whose attitude towards the trip [made] one wonder why he advised the King to undertake it at all.'

Macmillan found Hardinge 'idle, supercilious, without a spark of imagination or vitality'. He found Bertie, on the other hand, greatly improved by a good night's sleep. All went smoothly until it was time to review troops from Montgomery's Eighth Army – for Bertie had a secret phobia about this elementary royal duty.

'I can't, I can't . . . I'm not going to do it,' he muttered under his breath, as the troops assembled outside his tent. His Equerry Sir Piers Legh – who had perhaps witnessed the same situation before – said firmly: 'Well, Sir, I'm afraid you've got to do this. You've come all this way and you've got to.'

'No, I'm going home, I'm going home,' Bertie continued. 'Well, all right Sir, you'll have to swim,' Legh told him. Confronted by this dire prospect, Bertie grabbed his cane and strode into the desert sun to do his duty.

Bertie was not the total nincompoop such stories suggest. Within the narrow ambit he found so frustrating, he was a perfectly competent wartime King. On the same trip, for example, he met the feuding generals Giraud and de Gaulle, rivals to lead the Free French forces in North Africa. Churchill told Macmillan not to invite them to lunch with Bertie unless they were 'behaving well'. 'Are they?' Bertie asked. 'No, Sir,' Macmillan said, '. . . I can't say they are behaving well.'

Bertie insisted on holding the lunch, telling Macmillan 'it

may do good, and it can do no harm'. He sat between Giraud and de Gaulle, and according to Macmillan, 'spoke in good French to both generals' – quite an achievement considering his stammer.

A few days later, Bertie gave a garden party for British and American troops at his villa in Algiers. 'It was a *tremendous* success,' Macmillan reported. '. . . HM did very well and was most gracious to everybody. The Americans were really delighted, and letters will reach every distant part of the USA.'

But it is equally misleading to claim, as so many writers do, that Bertie and Elizabeth played a central wartime role. Their fate was to be marginalised – by the politicians and the generals, but also by their subjects, most of whom never saw the royal couple on their wartime visits, and scarcely thought about them from one week to the next.

'I should think they're quite nice people, quite harmless, but redundant,' a twenty-year-old man told the pioneering survey group Mass Observation in July 1940. 'I'm not very interested in them.'

'People simply aren't interested in them,' another man said. 'They don't dislike them or anything – they just don't think about them. I don't think I've spoken about them at the office for – oh, ever such a long time.'

In the same survey, inevitably suppressed by the censor, a working-class woman, aged forty-five, said: 'I think it's all a bit silly – kings and queens in wartime. I don't think they're wanted, All them things are all right in peacetime – we like to have ceremonies, and royal robes – but now it's up to us all – not kings and queens. That's what I think, anyway.'

Four years of earnest endeavour apparently failed to alter this perception of Bertie, at least among the people Mass Observation studied. In December 1944 Bertie made one of his happier radio broadcasts, announcing that the invasion threat was over and the Home Guard would be disbanded. A survey of twenty-four people by Mass Observation revealed that thirteen of them did not bother to listen. 'I didn't hear it,' a 'male, 40, lower-middle-class' said. 'That sort of thing doesn't appeal to me. No, I've not got a lot of feeling about the Royal Family – our Grinning Queen and all the rest. I think they've outlived any use they ever had.'

Another man ('50, working-class') also 'didn't hear it . . . I've got no use for all that'. A middle-class man, aged thirty-five, 'was with some people and we all agreed that we didn't want to hear it so we didn't listen. The Royal Family bores me.'

A woman ('40, lower-middle-class') said, 'I didn't hear it because we've got illness in the house and when anybody turns the wireless on there's a row. I *knew* we should miss something interesting if we didn't have it on.' But she was less interested in what Bertie said than in how he coped with his stammer. 'The King speaks so much better than he did, quite like anybody else now.'

That patronising view was shared by another woman ('55, working-class') who heard the broadcast. 'He's speaking much better now – much stronger – you can't help but admire him. I thought it was very nice indeed.'

Harold Nicolson disagreed. Hearing Bertie deliver a speech in the Palace of Westminster on 17 May 1945, Nicolson wrote that 'his stammer makes it almost intolerably painful to listen to him. It is as if one reads a fine piece of prose written on a typewriter the keys of which stick from time to time and mar the beauty of the whole.'

And yet only a week earlier on VE Day this uninspiring man had been the object of mass adulation as people flocked to Buckingham Palace to celebrate Hitler's defeat. Few crowds gathered at Downing Street; instead, Churchill was summoned by Bertie to join him on the palace balcony and take his share of the applause. In war, despite his best efforts, Bertie was an irrelevance. In peace, of its own accord, the symbolic power of his crown was miraculously restored.

If actors and audience had paused to reflect on this transformation, they might have been puzzled. Bertie was head of state; but like his brother, his father, his grandfather and (dare it be said) his great-grandmother Victoria, he was intellectually and temperamentally unsuited for the role of a constitutional monarch.

In a wider sense, Bertie was head of the nation; but in common with his predecessors, he barely understood the nature of his popularity. Superficially, the royal family's appeal was based on the 'ceremonies and royal robes' which were gradually being discarded by the surviving continental dynasties. At a deeper level, however, it was the contrast between the majesty of the royal spectacle and the Windsors' shortcomings as 'ordinary people' which sustained their popularity.

In the reign of the prosaic and humble George V – so unlike his father – the patronising assumption took root among his subjects that at least the royal family were just like them: modest, homely, and possessing the supreme British virtue of dullness. It was a reassuring image when set against the bombastic menace of the fascist and communist dictators; and thus the Windsors' very weaknesses became paradoxical assets which increased their appeal.

As the myth of royal ordinariness took root, the essential strangeness of British royalty was obscured. During the twentieth century, the Windsors became untypical of the remaining continental sovereigns, who were reduced to the status of monarchs on bicycles. Furthermore, they became increasingly untypical in thought, habit and feeling of the vast majority of their subjects. In the long term, as the press grew more intrusive in its coverage of royalty, myth and reality were bound to collide. In the short term, the combination of mediocre talent and obsessive personal behaviour which characterised the Windsors remained hidden to all but a few courtiers and politicians.

9

The Royal Learning Curve

'Whatever would you do if you had a ruler with brains?' Lloyd George was once asked by one of his cabinet colleagues, after he ignored a summons by the King to attend a privy council. Lloyd George had no worries on this account. 'The King is a very jolly chap,' he told his wife on another occasion 'but thank God there's not much in his head.'

'I am not a clever man,' George V remarked to the MP Victor Cazalet, 'but if I had not picked up something from all the brains I've met, I would be an idiot.'

The title of royal idiot was reserved instead for George's elder brother Eddy, who would have become King if he had not died prematurely (or not a moment too soon, in the opinion of some courtiers) in 1892. Eddy's wits were so slow as to be almost stationary. 'It is to physical causes that one must look for an explanation of the abnormally dormant condition of his mental powers,' his tutor Canon Dalton wrote in 1879, when Eddy was fifteen. Dalton, in common with other members of the royal household, suspected that Eddy had suffered brain damage during his birth.

Soon afterwards, Eddy went up to Cambridge. 'I do not think he can possibly derive much benefit from attending lectures,' his tutor reported. 'He hardly knows the meaning of the words *to read*.' Writing for Eddy was also a challenge. Part of a letter he sent to Gladstone in 1885 'admitted of no possible grammatical construction', according to the Prime Minister's secretary.

As for speaking, Victoria's Private Secretary Sir Henry Ponsonby noticed Eddy's habit of leaving his sentences unfinished, as if he had lost his train of thought. Ponsonby wondered whether Eddy had inherited his mother Alexandra's congenital deafness.

'Do you think I can *really* take this on, Mama?' the sensible and well-educated Princess May of Teck asked in 1891, when she became engaged to Eddy. Fortunately there was no need. Eddy died of pneumonia a few months later, and with unseemly haste, May was engaged to his younger brother George, now second in line to the throne,

Compared to Eddy, George was an intellectual titan. He could read (slowly), he could write (in a childish hand), and he could hold his own in a conversation. And yet, in the words of John Gore, author of an officially commissioned 'personal memoir' of George, he was for most of his life 'below the educational and perhaps intellectual standard of the ordinary public school-educated country squire.'

Canon Dalton tried hard with George – he had long since despaired of Eddy – but when the boy was eleven he felt bound to report that 'Prince George wants application, steady application. Though he is not deficient in a wish to progress, still his sense of self-approbation is almost the only motive power in him.'

Under the watchful eye of his wife, George did make painstaking efforts to improve his mind. A ledger recorded the 'books I have read since May 1890': and in between *Silver (The Life Story of an Atlantic Salmon)* and *Fifty Years and More of Sport in Scotland*, George found time to read Professor Neale's biography of Queen Elizabeth, Malcolm Muggeridge's account of Stalin's Russia, and *Uncle Tom's Cabin* by Harriet Beecher Stowe.

But the effect of this programme was severely limited. George remained an incorrigible philistine. 'Furniture, furniture, furniture,' he grumbled at May, when she was discussing the Balmoral heirlooms with a knowledgeable godson. 'I'll tell you what, Turner was *mad*,' he told the director of the National Gallery, Kenneth Clark. 'My grandmother always said so.' On a visit to the Tate Gallery, he summoned May with the news that 'here's something to make you laugh' – an exhibition of Impressionist paintings.

At least George's heart was in the right place. In 1910, when the writer Thomas Hardy reached his seventieth birthday, the King was asked to send a congratulatory telegram. 'It shall be done,' he said and the next day Thomas Hardy of Alnwick, Northumberland, who made George's fishing rods, received the royal message.

Bertie (George VI) shared many characteristics with his father, but not, it seems, a desire to rectify his disastrous educational record as a boy. In the 1920s, when he was Duke of York, the only book he ever discussed with his staff was *The Empty Tomb and the Risen Lord*, an account of the resurrection by Canon C.C. Dobson.

This was in sharp contrast to his clever wife, who read biographies of General Haig and Talleyrand, modern novelists, and in 1939 – to improve her understanding of Hitler – parts of *Mein Kampf*. She thoughtfully sent a copy to the insular Foreign Secretary Lord Halifax. 'I do not advise you to read it through, or you might go mad,' she wrote in her covering letter, 'and that would be a great pity . . . Even a skip through gives one a good idea of his mentality, ignorance and obvious sincerity.'

Bertie's official biographer Sir John Wheeler-Bennett assured his readers that the King had 'a most agile mind which, with the hovering volatility of a humming bird, would dart from subject to subject, often with bewildering rapidity.' In mere mortals, this is usually described as a low attention span.

The question is whether, as constitutional monarchs, such deficiencies mattered. Kenneth Rose, the author of a magisterial biography of George V, thinks not. 'In the end,' he writes, quoting Violet Markham, 'it is character not cleverness that counts;

goodness and simplicity, not analytical subtlety and the power to spin verbal webs.'

Yet George's character did not count for much with clever and ruthless politicians like Asquith and Lloyd George, whose contempt for his intellectual ability was transparent. 'I am going to see the King at 6,' Asquith wrote to Venetia Stanley in March 1915, 'when I suppose we shall have the usual all-round-the-place talk about things in general.' Lloyd George, then Minister of Munitions, complained the same year that the King was 'much more interested in petty personal details than in the turning out of hundreds of guns and millions of shells.'

Other politicians more sympathetic to royalty despaired of George's random chatter. Neville Chamberlain was invited to dine at Windsor in 1917 as Director-General of National Service; but George 'hardly mentioned it and talked about anything else that came into his mind, forestry, drink, food control, race horses etc . . .'

George learned by bitter experience during the constitutional crisis at the start of the reign* to distrust his ministers. In 1911 he agreed to Asquith's demand that, if the Liberals won the forthcoming general election, and if the Tory majority in the House of Lords continued to block a bill for constitutional reform, he would create enough sympathetic peers to ensure the bill's passage. Almost immediately, George regretted his decision as a beastly, underhand procedure, since he was required to keep his agreement secret from the Tory opposition.

'What right had Asquith to bring you with him to browbeat me?' he berated the former Liberal leader in the Lords, the Marquess of Crewe, twenty years later. 'I remember that after talking to him I walked over to the fireplace and I heard Asquith say to you, "I can do nothing with him. You have a go." A dirty low-down trick.'

Like the country squires they superficially resembled, George and Bertie were diehard Tories: it is a myth that they were above politics. 'The whole atmosphere reeks with Toryism,' Lloyd George wrote to his wife from Balmoral in September

1911. '. . . The King is hostile to the bone to all who are work-ing to lift the workmen out of the mire. So is the Queen.'

Forty years later, the Labour Chancellor of the Exchequer Hugh Gaitskell stayed with Bertie and Elizabeth at Windsor. They were 'extremely conservative in their views,' he told his diary, 'especially the Queen . . . [She] talked as though everybody was in a bad way nowadays, not happy, poor, dispirited etc. She did not say this in anger but implied that it could not be helped and that she hoped it would come to an end some day. I got into an argument with her then and implied that not everybody was quite so miserable and perhaps she did not see the people who were happier. I think she resented this.'

The official biographers have praised the manner in which George and Bertie put aside their political bias in dealing with socialist governments. But it was not quite that simple.

'I have been making the acquaintance of all the Ministers in turn,' George wrote to his aged mother Alexandra in February 1924, soon after Labour formed its first administration. '. . . They have different ideas to ours as they are all socialists, but they ought to be given a chance & ought to be treated fairly.'

In general, George did treat them fairly during the eleven months Labour was in power; but he was helped by the fact that Labour – without an overall majority in the Commons – enacted virtually no socialist measures. Privately, George continued to deplore the creed which had murdered poor Cousin Nicky. 'Don't ever bring that anarchist son of yours to see me again,' he told Canon Dalton. 'I don't like his views.' Anarchists and socialists were all the same to George.

'That anarchist son' was Hugh Dalton, Chancellor of the Exchequer in the 1945 Attlee government, and Bertie inherited his father's loathing of the man. He took great pleasure in imag-ining (falsely) that he had thwarted Dalton's ambition to be Foreign Secretary.

As the first King to be confronted by a government with a serious socialist project, Bertie balked. He was bemused when the Health Minister Aneurin Bevan resigned in 1951 over the proposed introduction of dental charges. 'I really don't see why people should have false teeth free any more than they have shoes free,' the King told Gaitskell. In another conversation with Gaitskell about the forthcoming budget, Bertie asked hopefully, 'Is it going to be the end?'

Bertie and George had two methods for coping with reds at Buckingham Palace, pending the welcome return of their shooting friends in the Tory party. Patrician socialists and 'intellectuals' were regarded as class traitors. In 1924 the new Education Minister C.P. Trevelyan complained that at his swearing-in George 'went through the ceremony like an automaton.'

'Why did you join them?' Bertie asked the Earl of Longford, who served in Attlee's government. Longford wanted to say, 'Because I believe that each one of us is equal in the sight of God' – but spared Bertie's feelings with a bland reply.

Genuine sons of the proletariat were patronised as if they were tenant farmers at Sandringham. In 1924 George was anxious to ensure that his new ministers wore the correct kit for presentation at court. 'In no case do I expect anyone to get more than the Levee coat; full dress is not necessary on account of the expense.' George's Private Secretary Lord Stamfordham thoughtfully told the Labour Chief Whip, Benjamin Spoor, about the excellent prices for court clothes at Moss Bros.

Jimmy Thomas, the former railwaymen's leader, was a particular favourite with George, and was summoned to Balmoral each year to tell him salty jokes. 'I was elevated by the thought that we were simple men and simple friends, speaking a simple language and meeting on simple ground,' Thomas wrote in his simple-minded memoirs.

Like Maurice Chevalier, who for career reasons learned to speak English with a French accent, Thomas deliberately dropped his aitches in the royal presence. The formidably intelligent Ernest Bevin, Attlee's Foreign Secretary, pulled the same trick more subtly. 'I like your crockery,' he once told Elizabeth, pointing at a cabinet of priceless gold plate. An equerry objected to Bevin's habit of keeping his hands in his pockets when greeting the

King. The gullible Bertie said he preferred Bevin that way, because it showed he was 'a real Englishman'.

Yet in the end, George and Bertie's handicap was less political bias than a royal incomprehension of the political process. George's rudimentary understanding of the constitution was gleaned from the writings of the Victorian journalist Walter Bagehot, which subsequently became required reading for heirs to the throne. The present Queen, for instance, was instructed in Bagehot by the Vice-Provost of Eton, while her governess, acting as chaperone, was handed *Uncle Fred in the Springtime* by P.G. Wodehouse to pass the time.

Bagehot was a curious choice, liable to confuse their shallow minds, for he was not in any sense an enthusiastic monarchist. 'On the Continent, in first-class countries,' he wrote, 'constitutional royalty has never lasted out of one generation . . . As far as experience goes, there is no reason to expect an hereditary series of useful limited monarchs.'

He deemed that monarchy was only desirable 'in a country like this, where the population is as yet uneducated . . . The common people believe that they cannot resist the Queen, and consequently obey laws which are not supported by an adequate force.'

Perhaps such passages were censored before they reached the royal classroom. George concentrated instead on Bagehot's more anodyne precepts, which shortly after the hapless Eddy's death he copied into his notebook. 'The value of the Crown in its *dignified* capacity,' he wrote, 'is that a) it makes Government *intelligible* to the masses; b) it makes Government *interesting* to the masses; and c) it *strengthens* Government with the *religious* tradition connected with the Crown.'

The trouble with these theories, as George discovered, is that they were not much use when political thugs like Asquith and Crewe had you pinned to the fireplace.

Despairing of theory, he constructed his own political fantasy world, where statesmen behaved like gentlemen and a party leader's word was his bond. So it was that in August 1931, at the height of a sterling crisis, George persuaded the Labour Prime Minister Ramsay MacDonald to form a coalition with the Liberals under Sir Herbert Samuel, and the Tories under Stanley Baldwin. After the three leaders had shaken hands at Buckingham Palace, George delivered a short homily.

> His Majesty congratulated them on the solution of this difficult problem, and pointed out that while France and other countries existed for weeks without a Government, in this country our constitution is so generous that leaders of Parties, after fighting one another for months in the House of Commons, were ready to meet together under the roof of the Sovereign and sink their differences for a common good . . .

Within a few weeks, Samuel was threatening to resign over a free trade issue, Baldwin was boasting about having stitched up MacDonald, and MacDonald had been expelled from his local Labour party.

Such was the political judgement of kings.

The King's Private Secretary was there to help him form that judgement, and the importance of this position in the history of the modern British monarchy can scarcely be exaggerated. It was not simply that the Private Secretary acted as the principal liaison between the monarch and the government of the day (as he still does). Furthermore, given the varying degrees of political ineptitude displayed by Victoria and her successors, his political advice was essential in sustaining the myth of a wise, constitutional monarchy.

The first, and greatest, modern Private Secretary was Sir Henry Ponsonby, who served Victoria from 1870 until she had literally worked him to death twenty-five years later. 'It is very difficult for me to find words to express how deeply grieved I am at the sad termination of dear Sir Henry's long & trying tho' I think & believe painless illness,' Victoria wrote to his widow. For the last

ten months of his life, Ponsonby had been speechless and paral-
ysed, following a massive stroke caused by stress.

In many ways Ponsonby, a former soldier, was not cut out to be
a courtier. The royal family deplored his dress sense. 'I appeared
in uniform,' he wrote to his wife, after attending a royal funeral.
'Prince of Wales pleased but critical. Prince Albert Victor [Eddy]
told me I had too much crape.'

He deplored their enthusiasm for blood sports. At Balmoral, if
asked to go deer-stalking, he would stuff novels and magazines
into his coat pockets to while away the hours. Ponsonby even
went into print (pseudonymously), attacking those who 'try to
kill the greatest number of pheasants in the shortest space of
time.'

Another piece by Ponsonby mocked 'the absurdity of spiritualist seances'. He was provoked by Victoria's habit of speaking to
the departed Albert through the medium of her truculent
Scottish manservant John Brown (when he was in the mood).

Ponsonby's genius was to save Victoria from her own fanatical
and irrational political views. 'She cannot and will not be the
Queen of a democratic monarchy,' Victoria raged to a minister in
1880. Nor, in the second half of her reign, did she want to share
government with the Liberals. Time and again Ponsonby, a closet
Liberal, patched up relations between Victoria and Gladstone,
described by her on the fourth occasion he became Prime
Minister as 'an old, wild incomprehensible man of eighty-two
and a half'.

Gladstone was suitably grateful to Ponsonby. After one crisis
in 1884, he wrote to Ponsonby 'to fulfil my intention and desire
to record my sense of the tact, discernment and constancy with
which you have promoted the attainment of an accord.' 'I can
assure you that Mr Gladstone felt what he wrote to you,' the
Prime Minister's secretary wrote to Ponsonby the next day. '. . . I
often have the pleasure of hearing him sing your praises.'

Ponsonby's political achievement is especially impressive
because so much of his time was wasted by Victoria on utterly
trivial questions. In 1886, for example, the painter Sir Frederick

Leighton wished to copy a portrait of the Queen by Sir Martin Archer Shee. 'It is a monstrous thing no more like me than anything in the world,' Victoria wrote to Ponsonby – leaving him to tell Leighton.

In 1892, a society lady asked permission to write an article about the Royal Mews and Kennels. 'This is a dreadful and dangerous woman,' Victoria decided. 'She [*sic*] better take the facts from the other papers.'

The Private Secretary who is most often compared with Ponsonby is his successor Sir Arthur Bigge (later Lord Stamfordham), who held the position during the last years of Victoria's reign, and from 1910 until his death in 1931. During the reign of Edward VII, he served as Private Secretary to the Prince of Wales (later George V); and from the beginning, George was almost pathetically dependent on the older man.

'I feel that I can always rely on you to tell me the truth, however disagreeable, & that you are entirely in my confidence,' he told Bigge in 1902. When Stamfordham finally died, after half a century of royal service, George said simply that 'he taught me how to be a King'.

Stamfordham paid his own fulsome tribute to Ponsonby. 'One of, if not the greatest gentlemen I have known,' he wrote; 'the entire effacement of *self*; the absolute non-existence of conceit, side or pose; the charming courtesy to strangers old, young, high, low, rich, poor.'

These were not, however, qualities Stamfordham shared with Ponsonby; on the contrary, he was a difficult colleague. In this respect Stamfordham's entry in the *Dictionary of National Biography*, written by the royal librarian Sir Owen Morshead, is a minor masterpiece of courtly discretion. Morshead noted how 'a certain austerity which he had imbibed in the north-country vicarage [his father was a prelate] mellowed in later years to a gentler tolerance, and he came to be regarded by his colleagues with a love which perhaps never wholly cast out fear.'

One person who found Stamfordham intolerable was Lord Knollys, Edward VII's former Private Secretary, who shared the top position during the first three years of the new reign. 'Quite between ourselves,' Knollys wrote to his friend Asquith in 1913 after he had been sacked by George, 'my position had become almost an impossible one, and it was made worse by the strong divergence of opinions which existed between the King and his surroundings (*not the Queen*) on one side and myself on the other, on nearly every question of a public nature.'

Stamfordham, a Tory, violently disagreed with Knollys, a Liberal, about whether George should have made his undertaking in November 1910 to Asquith and Crewe that in the event of a Liberal victory at the general election he would create enough peers to ensure passage of the Parliament bill. Whether or not Stamfordham was correct to oppose the agreement, he allowed his political feelings to colour his relations with the Liberal leadership in a manner which Ponsonby would have found unacceptable.

'I received from him today,' Asquith complained to Lord Knollys in July 1912, 'a letter which both in tone and substance is quite unexampled in my communications with the Crown.' Stamfordham was just as abusive about the Liberal Prime Minister. 'Two years ago tomorrow,' he minuted in November 1912, 'Asquith commenced his policy of intimidation and dragooning. He put a pistol to the King's head . . . [and] he is going to reap his own reward.'

If Stamfordham represented a falling-away from the standards set by Ponsonby, his successor Sir Clive (later Lord) Wigram accelerated the decline. As a former officer in the Indian Cavalry, Wigram approached the world's problems in a gung-ho spirit.

'He is a very nice fellow,' Frederick Ponsonby (son of Sir Henry) wrote patronisingly in 1915, when Wigram was an Assistant Private Secretary, 'and very hard-working and business-like, but his horizon is limited and he does not seem to be able to take a broad-minded view of the many perplexing questions that come here . . . His views are those of the ordinary officer at Aldershot.'

The BBC Director-General Sir John Reith, meeting Wigram

in 1932, also found him 'very genial, but it seems to take a good deal to make him understand things.'

Wigram was not quite as dim as he seemed. At the end of the First World War, he wanted to open up court functions to 'more classes of the community', describing those who opposed him as 'palace troglodytes' (the reactionary Stamfordham would have fallen into this category). He succeeded in appointing the first full-time press secretary at Buckingham Palace, on the principle that 'His Majesty must get out of the habit of hiding his light under a bushel.' 'We sailors never smile on duty,' had been George's response when Stamfordham made a similar entreaty.

Wigram's difficulties began when he strode briskly into the political arena, clutching a ragbag of sporting metaphors. 'The Government,' he noted in June 1931, 'look fairly firm in the saddle at the moment, and without doubt Lloyd George and his team are proving sound half-backs to the Labour forwards.'

Whether Ramsay MacDonald fell off his horse or the Liberal half-backs dropped the ball, not even Wigram could tell; for two months later, confounding his predictions, the government had collapsed and he was confronted by a major political crisis ('my first Test match'). Fortunately, 'our Captain [George] played one of our best innings with a very straight bat. He stopped the rot and saved his side. He was not-out at the end and had hardly turned a hair, or shown any sign of fatigue.' While George and MacDonald put together the National Government XI, Wigram appears to have stayed in the pavilion, making the teatime sandwiches.

Wigram's successor Sir Alec Hardinge was so traumatised by the abdication crisis that by the time Harold Macmillan met him in 1943, during Bertie's visit to North Africa, he was in the middle of a nervous breakdown. Before leaving England with Bertie, he had pinched the keys to the cabinet boxes, so preventing his colleagues at Buckingham Palace from continuing 'the King's business'. Soon after his return there was a painful interview with Bertie, and Hardinge's resignation was accepted 'for reasons of health'.

Hardinge's deputy and David's former Private Secretary, Sir Alan Lascelles, thus succeeded to the top position. It is difficult to make any judgement about Lascelles, except to say he was a very odd cove. He was a gifted speechwriter and nursed frustrated ambitions to be a novelist. Intellectually, he was the most able Private Secretary since Ponsonby.

And yet as a young man Lascelles had failed the Foreign Office entrance exam, and by his own admission he was something of a drifter. For a period after his resignation from David's service, Lascelles chose not to work at all, supporting his family on a small private income. Like Ponsonby, he was ambivalent about court life, while lacking Ponsonby's humour and detachment. On his retirement in 1953, Lascelles was appalled by the idea of a leaving party; and just to show he did not care, in old age – passed in a grace-and-favour apartment at Kensington Palace – he grew a most uncourtly shaggy beard.

Whatever Lascelles' qualities, the Private Office he ran seems to have been a sleepy place compared with Ponsonby's time. Sir Edward Ford, who joined the household as an Assistant Private Secretary in 1946, was told by Lascelles that his presence was only required at Buckingham Palace when there was work to be done. Thus Ford – who had trained as a barrister – was able to spend a week in Nuremberg, attending the Nazi war crimes trials.

At Balmoral and Sandringham, the working pace was even more leisurely – at least for Bertie. 'If there was something urgent,' Sir Edward recalls, 'you could get the King before 9.30 in the morning, or by ringing up his page and saying you would like to see him a bit early; but normally he would go out shooting at 9.30 and one would have the morning to do the work. And then, after tea, one would be able to see him.'

British royalty's retreat from politics is often described as an example of wise adaptation. 'The present position of the Crown,' G.M. Trevelyan wrote in his 1947 eulogy on the Windsors, '. . . is the most characteristic product of our national genius for affairs . . . inspired by the peculiarly British love of preserving old names, forms and loyalties, while pushing on to new distributions of power.'

But that is not how George and Bertie viewed the crown's position. They raged at their impotence, while lacking Victoria's determination – however misguided – to force her ministers to take her into account. Victoria bombarded her governments with thousands of memoranda; George and Bertie went shooting; and their hapless Private Secretaries were left to squeeze the news of the Munich agreement or the outbreak of the Second World War in between the latest grouse scores from Balmoral.

In the end, George and Bertie ordered their lives according to the domestic rhythms of the court, rather than the baffling commotion of the political arena. Like their subjects, they imagined themselves to be homely kings. If only they had realised how strange were their homely ways.

10

At Home with George and Bertie

Members of the public who visit Sandringham today are not allowed to tour the estate offices, located in a gloomy brownstone building about three hundred yards from the main house. The building is York Cottage, once the principal private residence of George V, and for over thirty years the home he loved best.

'Until you have seen York Cottage, you will never understand my father,' David told George's official biographer Harold Nicolson. When he visited the cottage in October 1949, Nicolson was astonished by what he found. 'It is almost incredible that the heir to so vast a heritage lived in this horrible little house,' he told his diary. '. . . The King and Queen's baths had lids that shut down so that when not in use they could be used as tables. His study was a monstrous little cold room with a north window shrouded by shrubberies, and the walls are covered in red cloth which he had been given while on a visit to Paris. It is the cloth from which the trousers of the French private soldiers used to be made. On the walls he had some reproductions of Royal Academy pictures.'

Visitors to the Windsors' grander private homes have been equally scathing about the royal family's taste in architecture and interior decor. Sandringham House, just up the hill from York Cottage, was purchased for the elder Bertie by Victoria in 1862. Almost immediately Bertie commissioned the architect A.J. Humbert, who had helped design the royal mausoleums at Windsor, to replace the original eighteenth-century house with a more fashionable mock-Jacobean structure.

A century later another official biographer, James Pope-Hennessy, visited Humbert's Sandringham during research for his life of Queen Mary. 'A preposterous, long, brick-and stone building,' Pope-Hennessy noted. The house was 'hotel-like – Pitlochry or Strathpeffer perhaps – tremendously vulgar and emphatically, almost defiantly hideous and gloomy.'

The interior decor of Sandringham is a legacy of the elder Bertie and Alexandra's contrasting tastes. Bertie was naturally drawn to the grandiose, and in between portraits of his parents he hung a huge tapestry depicting the life of the Emperor Constantine, flanked by a couple of haberdiers' axes. Alexandra preferred miniatures, and the cabinets are crammed with the knick-knacks she hoarded like a magpie. Three showcases in the main drawing room hold a collection of upmarket junk, including porcelain animals, birds and flowers, jars, cups and mugs, and miscellaneous ornaments in quartz, amber and rock crystal.

In the flower-bed along the west wall of the house, Alexandra left two more lasting monuments, in the form of memorials to her favourite dogs. Her great-granddaughter, the present Queen, has continued the tradition along the perimeter wall of the main garden. A plaque in the wall commemorates Sandringham Brae, 'a Gentleman among Dogs', next to Sandringham Sydney ('Sydney was an honest worker, a faithful companion and will be missed by all').

At Balmoral, the Scottish estate near Aberdeen which Albert bought on Victoria's behalf in 1852, the royal owners committed a similar act of destruction, pulling down the old house and building a new residence on a nearby site. 'The new house is up one storey, and, with its dressed granite, promises to present a noble appearance,' Albert wrote hopefully in 1853. '. . . The workers, who have to be brought here from a distance and to camp in wooden barracks, have already struck several times, which is now quite the fashion all over the country,' the royal foreman added in exasperation.

When the house was at last completed, Victoria set to work on the interior decor. The Liberal politician Lord Clarendon, an early guest at Balmoral, was especially struck by the drawing room. 'The curtains, the furniture, the carpets . . . are all of different plaids,' Clarendon noted, 'and the thistles are in such abundance that they would rejoice the heart of a donkey if they happened to look like his favourite repast, which they don't.' Another Liberal statesman, Lord Rosebery, thought Victoria's drawing room at Osborne (her house on the Isle of Wight) 'the world's ugliest until I saw the one at Balmoral.'

The first point of interest about these houses is how they belied the public's image of the royal family's domestic life. In the early 1920s the architect Sir Edwin Lutyens designed a dolls' house for Queen Mary to mark the nation's gratitude for her service during the First World War. The dolls' house was commissioned by Princess Marie Louise, one of Victoria's grandchildren, and under her beady eye, no detail was overlooked in the pursuit of verisimilitude.

Real water dripped from the tiny taps in the bathroom, real wine was stocked in the miniature wine cellar, and in the library, the finest authors of the day contributed pocket-size stories, bound in tiny one-inch volumes. The former prime minister Asquith was one of the few personages Marie-Louise approached (she wanted one of his speeches for the library) who declined to cooperate, describing the dolls' house as 'a singularly fatuous exercise'.

Asquith, like George Bernard Shaw (another non-contributor), was in a minority, and when the dolls' house was displayed at the British Empire Exhibition in 1924 spectators were left in no doubt that this was a privileged glimpse into the private life of royalty. The companion volume to the dolls' house, written by A.C. Benson, encouraged the delusion.

Victoria (1837-1901).
The Queen is amused during her Diamond Jubilee procession through London, 22 June 1897. 'No one ever, I believe, has met with such an ovation as was given to me, passing through those six miles of streets,' she wrote in her diary. '...The crowds were quite indescribable, and their enthusiasm marvellous and deeply touching.'

Edward VII (1901-1910)
'The rare, the rather awful visits of Albert Edward, Prince of Wales, to Windsor Castle. Caricature by Max Beerbohm. 1921. 'There are many things which he is obliged to do which the outside world would call pleasures and amusements,' Bertie's Private Secretary explained to a critic, who shared Victoria's disapproval of the Prince of Wales. 'They are, however, often anything but a source of amusement to him, though his position demands that he should every year go through a certain round of social duties which bore him to death.'

George V (1910-1936).
To his right, his eldest son
David (later Edward VIII); to
his left, his second son Bertie
(later George VI). The picture
was taken in 1935, George's
Silver Jubilee year, when the
King declared: 'I pray to God
that my eldest son will never
marry and have children, and
that nothing will come between
Bertie and Lilibet and the
throne.'

Edward VIII (1936).
David stands on his head while
cruising in the Mediterranean,
a few months before his
abdication. 'I suppose that,
without quite understanding
why, I was in unconscious
rebellion against my position,'
he recalled in his memoirs.

George VI (1936-1952). Bertie, according to his official biographer, had 'a most agile mind which, with the hovering volatility of a humming bird, would dart from subject to subject, often with bewildering rapidity.' In mere mortals this is usually called a low attention span. Fortunately, Bertie's clever wife made sure he did his paperwork.

Elizabeth II (1952-   ). Princess Elizabeth in front of the miniature cottage presented to her and Margaret in 1932 by the people of Wales. As a little girl Lilibet poured ink over her hair, fought with her younger sister, and vandalised the Scottish railway at Glamis. 'We had lots of time to place crossed pins stuck together with gum on the lines,' her governess recalled, 'and wait for the next train through to turn them into enchanting little scissors.' But when Lilibet realised she was going to be Queen, she began to behave herself.

COURTIERS

General Sir Henry Ponsonby, Private Secretary to Queen Victoria (1870-1895). The unsung hero of Victoria's later years, he was literally worked to death by the Queen. 'Too, too sad!' was Victoria's remark when she heard Sir Henry had suffered a massive stroke in January 1895. At his funeral ten months later, she thought the hymn 'Now the labourer's task is o'er' 'particularly applicable' to 'dear Sir Henry'.

Sir Arthur Bigge, later Lord Stamfordham (*below, standing*), Private Secretary to Queen Victoria (1895-1901) and to George V as Prince of Wales and King (1901-1931), pictured with the King in the gardens of Buckingham Palace, 1918. When Stamfordham died, George's tribute was simple: 'He taught me how to be a King'. Courtiers were more ambivalent about Stamfordham. 'He came to be regarded by his colleagues with a love which perhaps never wholly cast out fear,' the royal librarian Sir Owen Morshead recalled.

Mabell, Countess of Airlie (*right*), with Queen Mary, photographed by the Prince of Wales (later Edward VIII) in France, 10 July 1917. Lady Airlie was a lady-in-waiting to Mary for half a century, and saw a side of the Queen never vouchsafed to the public. She remembered Mary 'learning the words of "Yes, We Have No Bananas" and singing it with me at the top of our voices for the joy of shocking a particularly staid member of the Household' and 'hopping round one of the drawing rooms at Windsor to represent a grasshopper in a game of Dumb Crambo after dinner'.

Sir Clive Wigram, later Lord Wigram, Assistant Private Secretary to George V (1910-1931), Private Secretary (1931-36). 'He is always very genial, but it seems to take a good deal to make him understand things,' Sir John Reith remarked in 1932. Wigram's addiction to sporting metaphors did not help. 'The Government looks firmly in the saddle at the moment,' he wrote in June 1931, 'and without doubt Lloyd George and his team are proving sound half-backs to the Labour forwards.' Two months later the Government collapsed: 'my first test match', Wigram told the Archbishop of Canterbury.

Sir Alan ('Tommy') Lascelles, Assistant Private Secretary to the Prince of Wales (later Edward VIII) 1920-29; Assistant Private Secretary to Edward VIII and George VI 1936-43; Private Secretary to George VI and Elizabeth II 1943-53. Lascelles (*right*) with the Prince of Wales in Canada, 1924. Lascelles' contempt for Edward VIII pre-dated the abdication crisis. 'I can't help thinking that the best thing that could happen to him, and to the country, would be for him to break his neck,' he told Prime Minister Stanley Baldwin in 1927.

A Buckingham Palace garden party between the wars. 'It is quite possible, without undue shame, to arrive at Buckingham Palace in a taxi,' Harold Nicolson wrote in 1937. But before the Second World War, admission to court functions was strictly controlled, and the Lord Chamberlain published a rule book for correct behaviour in the presence of royalty. Even he could not legislate for the debutante who dislocated her knee in mid-curtsy, and was carried from the Throne Room to hospital.

DRESSING UP

Bertie (Edward VII) models his latest range of country wear. One year at Marienbad, Bertie's summer watering hole, a journalist spotted the King dressed in a green cap, a brown overcoat, a pink necktie, grey shoes, white gloves and knee-breeches. 'We sincerely hope His Majesty has not brought this outfit home!' the *Tailor and Cutter* commented.

George V's children pretend to be Scottish at Balmoral, 1911. Their great-grandfather Prince Albert designed a special 'Balmoral' tartan for the royal family (not worn in this picture). Their great-grandmother Queen Victoria affected a Scottish accent when north of the border ('pound' became 'poond'). Yet until the younger Bertie (*second from right*) married Lady Elizabeth Bowes-Lyon, daughter of the Earl of Strathmore, in 1923, scarcely a drop of Scottish blood flowed through the royal family's Hanoverian veins.

George V at Windsor in the late 1920s, dressed for the Ascot races. Among other sartorial innovations, he disliked trousers with turn-ups and front creases, and ladies' dresses that finished above the ankle. More generally, George abhorred 'Soviet Russia, painted fingernails, women who smoked in public, cocktails, frivolous hats, American jazz, and the growing habit of going away for the weekends' - or so said his eldest son David, who liked all these things.

'It is not a palace nor a ceremonious residence,' Benson declared, 'but essentially a home, a family mansion belonging to a Monarch who seeks relief from cares of state in a quiet family life and in a commodious rather than luxurius regime. It is dignified rather than magnificent, commodious without being luxurious.'

Surveying the gracious interior which lay behind Lutyens's equally elegant neo-classical façade, Benson decided that 'the inmates are people of cultivated interests and tastes. The pictures are well-selected, and the library is rich in the works of contemporary authors.' If the public who admired the dolls' house had been allowed to peek inside York Cottage – decorated throughout by the Maples furniture emporium – they might have disagreed with Benson's verdict.

Despite the artifice of the dolls' house, the royal family's domestic setting defied comparison with the wider world. Nicolson found 'nothing to differentiate [York] cottage from any of the villas at Surbiton'; but no Surrey commuter would have crammed his home with the scores of servants, equerries and ladies-in-waiting deemed essential to the needs of royalty (George once confessed not to know where the servants lived, assuming they must have slept 'in the trees').

Nor, despite the emphasis at Sandringham and Balmoral on hunting and shooting, did this lifestyle resemble more than superficially that of the landed aristocracy, which by the inter-war period had fallen on hard times. The Duchess of Beaufort, Queen Mary's niece, was astonished by the number of servants (over fifty) her aunt brought with her when she came to stay at Badminton House in Gloucestershire for the duration of the Second World War. 'Pandemonium was the least it could be called!', the Duchess wrote to Osbert Sitwell, a confidant of the old Queen, soon after Mary's arrival. 'The servants revolted, and scorned our humble home. They refused to use the excellent rooms assigned to them. Fearful rows and battle royals over my body . . . The Queen, quite unconscious of the stir, has settled in well.'

In the end, once rising taxes and falling revenues had taken their toll of the landed aristocracy, the homely ways of the Windsors were unique to themselves; and like any closed world, from boarding schools to convents, the domestic life of the court generated its own peculiar and often fractious ambience.

The courtiers, driven to distraction by the tedium, found it hard to maintain their good humour. In Victoria's time, Sir Henry Ponsonby would deliberately start arguments between ladies-in-waiting to relieve the torpor. By the reign of George V, the bickering seems to have erupted of its own accord.

Lady Airlie wryly recalled her difficulties at Windsor during Ascot week in the 1920s. Before dinner, she was expected to assemble the other ladies in the correct order of precedence to greet George and Mary. 'There was always an argument when Winifred, Duchess of Portland, was in the party, because she insisted on putting herself at the head, although the Duchess of Roxburghe was actually entitled to this place. Winnie based her claim on the fact that she had been Mistress of the Robes to Queen Alexandra, and said that Queen Victoria had made the decision that a duchess who had been Mistress of the Robes should take precedence of all other duchesses for the rest of her life.' Fortunately the Duchess of Roxburghe was 'very good-natured', and, after a brief tussle, ceded her position.

What passed for royal wit was equally childish. Lord Clarendon remarked that he never told his best jokes to royalty, since pretending to jam his fingers in the door amused them more. The earlier Bertie's favourite prank was to pour a bottle of brandy over his bachelor friend Christopher Sykes. For anecdotes, Bertie relied on the Rothschilds, who instructed their agents around Europe to cable the Prince of Wales with the latest Jewish stories – which were then repeated, verbatim, at the Sandringham dinner table.

At Balmoral, the younger Bertie (George VI) never tired of one particular jape. He would balance a book over an open door (the Reverend Dobson's work, perhaps), and watch while it fell on to the head of the next guest to enter the room. Bertie and his family found the joke unbearably funny – as did the hapless victim, who always remembered to be amused as well.

But if there was a distinctive brand of royal humour it was what they called 'chaff' – the practice of bullying their courtiers, in the knowledge that there was no right of reply. George's 'chaff' was legendary, and virtually indiscriminate. Lady Curzon, for instance, made the mistake of arriving at Windsor during the First World War, just as the court went into mourning for an obscure royal relative. She had only one black dress, which she had bought in Paris.

'It was rather short in front, and had a long pointed train. This made the King laugh very much. I was made to turn round in front of him, and he laughed and said "How ridiculous! Off the ground in front, and all that trailing behind on the floor!" However,' Lady Curzon recalled loyally, 'His Majesty was kind enough to assure me that I looked charming in it.'

The younger Bertie enjoyed himself hugely one year while shooting at Holkham, the adjacent estate to Sandringham. A member of the host's family moved the line of guns to where he thought, wrongly, the birds would fly. When the birds flew in the other direction, Bertie seized his opportunity to indulge in some 'chaff'.

'We are all very glad to know that you have some ideas,' he remarked sarcastically, 'but have you any better ideas?' As they moved to the next position, Bertie asked, 'What are your suggestions for this drive? We hope you have some ideas.' Further on: 'Where would you like us to stand here? Should we cross the hedge and face in the opposite direction?' Bertie's 'joke' still had some mileage several months later, when the anonymous victim joined him for a duck shoot, and was peppered with enquiries about the best position for the guns.

Good taste, manners, restraint – these were not the Windsors' watchwords when they retreated to their private domain. Whether shooting, stamp-collecting or descending on antique shops, they lacked any sense of proportion. It was as if, deep down, they were compensating for all the constraints they encountered on the public stage.

*

'Seven guns in four days at Sandringham killed 10,000 head,' Lord Lincolnshire noted in December 1912. 'The King one day fired 1700 cartridges and killed 1000 pheasants. Can this terrific slaughter possibly last much longer?'

It could: in December 1913, at Hall Barn in Buckinghamshire, the home of the newspaper proprietor Lord Burnham, George again shot over 1000 birds in a single day. 'He was proud of the way he had shot . . .' his eldest son David recalled, 'but I think the scale of the bag troubled even his conscience; for, as we drove back to London, he remarked, "Perhaps we went a little too far today, David."'

For George, it was a rare moment of doubt in a lifelong mission to exterminate his kingdom's wildlife. The sight of a dead sparrow on the Buckingham Palace lawn might bring tears to his eyes. At Sandringham, meanwhile, an average of 20,000 head of game per year were shot between the wars, long after other grandees had abandoned such 'sport' as too expensive and – in the aftermath of the First World War – rather distasteful.

Serious illness and near-death in 1928 failed to blunt George's enthusiasm for mass murder. Too weak to hold a gun for several months, he fretted that he was losing his marksman's eye. Hearing of the King's plight, his gunmaker Purdey constructed a replica weapon he could use indoors, with an electric light that flashed from the barrel when he pulled the trigger. Confined to a wheelchair, George was thus able to take potshots at servants, courtiers – perhaps even his wife.

The younger Bertie was marginally more balanced in his approach to shooting. Under his father and grandfather the Sandringham pheasants were so tame that one, finding its way to the west terrace, was adopted by the aged Alexandra as a pet. Instructions were sent to York Cottage that on no account must 'Georgie' shoot this particular bird.

Bertie replanted the forests so that the pheasants at least attained a diagonal lift-off, rather than the traditional horizontal trajectory. Yet if he was more of a sportsman, Bertie's enthusiasm was just as obsessive. Sir Edward Ford, who joined the household in 1946, recalls that 'the King was really a compulsive shot. At Balmoral and Sandringham he would shoot almost every week-day.'

Bertie's game book, which he kept continuously from 1907 until a few days before his death in 1952, records the tally for every shoot, plus his own observations about the weather and the quality of the sport. At Sandringham he would go out in his distinctive yellow shooting tweeds, which he had designed himself.

Like George, mere illness was no obstacle to a good day's shoot. At Balmoral in August 1948 Bertie continued to enjoy the grouse, even though his lower legs were almost completely numb. Each evening he would kick them against a table to restore the circulation. The grouse dispatched, he grudgingly agreed to see a doctor, who diagnosed arteriosclerosis, with a risk of gangrene and therefore amputation of the right leg.

Bertie continued to shoot through several operations and the onset of cancer. On 5 February 1952 he shot hares and rabbits in the company of Sandringham estate workers – an annual mopping-up operation at the end of the season. Bertie especially enjoyed his last kill, a hare he caught at full speed. A few hours later he too was dead.

Indoors, George, and to a lesser extent Bertie, liked to pore over their stamp collection. 'Did Your Royal Highness hear that some damned fool has just paid £1450 for a single stamp?' a courtier asked George in 1904, knowing of his hobby. 'I was the damned fool,' George replied.

Like shooting, George's passion for stamps was conceived on an epic scale. By the end of his life he had assembled about 250,000 specimens, making it the largest private collection in the world. George was a gentleman, but the idea of fair play in pursuing his hobby seems to have deserted him.

As Prince of Wales, he arranged to receive every new printing from the Post Office and the Crown Agents for the Colonies; the Universal Postal Union in Switzerland was further instructed, on his father's royal authority, to send him one example of all the stamps registered at its headquarters.

On his accession, ambassadors and colonial administrators were advised by Whitehall to send the most interesting overseas issues to Buckingham Palace via the diplomatic bag. A new court appointment was created, Philatelist to the King, and a room set aside at the palace for the burgeoning collection.

Sir Edward Bacon – knighted by George for his services to philately – was the first holder of this august office. Escorting George to a stamp exhibition, he would warn other collectors of 'one very human foible': George 'did not very much like seeing stamps which he did not own himself and which he could not acquire.'

Perhaps the strangest aspect of this enterprise was George's attitude towards the stamps he collected. Not only was he unimpressed by exotic designs; he actually disliked them. 'I want you to make me a promise,' he told Kenneth Clark, a member of the postage stamp committee, shortly before he died. 'Never allow them to make all those fancy issues of stamps like some ridiculous place like San Marino. We invented the postage stamp – all it had on was the sovereign's head and postage and its value. That's all we want.'

Clark honoured his promise. In the 1960s he resigned from the committee when the Postmaster-General, Anthony Wedgwood Benn, wanted to make more frequent issues of illustrative stamps, some without the Queen's head.

In the field of art – or rather, royal heirlooms – Mary matched her husband's phenomenal acquisitiveness. Clark for one had a low opinion of her taste. 'The English are not very fond of art but they are very fond of pedigrees,' he noted caustically in his memoirs, referring to his appointment by George as Surveyor of the King's Pictures. '. . . When it came to the Royal Collection this condition was intensified. I should have spent my time reading the history of the Hanoverians and working in the National Portrait Gallery.'

It was not that Mary was ignorant. In her youth, when her parents were – to use her charming expression – 'in short street', she had spent two years of genteel poverty in Florence, which ignited her interest in art history. But she lacked the priorities of the genuine connoisseur. Instead, her self-appointed mission was to 'recover' the thousands of items which had left the royal collection, especially since George IV's death in 1830. Some of these heirlooms had been sold; others had been lent; still more had gone missing. All, in Mary's opinion, were rightfully the royal family's property.

The Labour politician Margaret Bondfield, who served on committees with Mary during the First World War, remarked that she would have made an excellent factory inspector; and it was in this spirit that Mary descended, often unannounced, on the country houses and stately homes she suspected of holding royal memorabilia.

If an object seemed especially desirable, she might remark meaningfully to her hosts, 'I am caressing it with my eyes.' Perhaps they would resist this first assault on their consciences: in which case Mary would ask at the end of the tour whether she could 'say goodbye to that dear little cabinet'. If these stratagems failed, a letter of thanks would arrive a few days later from Buckingham Palace, with an enquiry about the price of the 'dear little cabinet', which the owners had foolishly imagined was not for sale.

So it was that 'with his humble duty' Lord Lincolnshire parted with a Derby porcelain group of the sons of George III for the sum of £300. Lord and Lady Lee of Fareham were less intransigent, presenting their miniature portrait of Charles II as a 'gift'. In return, Mary graciously sent them her autographed photograph.

Bertie (George VI) inherited his mother's tendency to regard art as a branch of royal genealogy. 'How many portraits are there at Buckingham Palace of Princess Caroline of Anspach?' he would ask a junior adviser on the royal collection, having already conducted his own count. 'I am afraid I do not know, Sir.' 'But you *ought* to know.'

Away from the serious business of plundering England's stately homes, Mary liked to relax by visiting antique shops. Here she would indulge a more personal hobby, the collection of miniatures and curios (the only interest she shared with her mother-in-law Alexandra). As royalty, she rarely deigned to pay for the items which took her fancy. Instead, she would seize the desired object and walk briskly out of the shop, leaving the nonplussed shopowner wondering what to do next. A lady-in-waiting would usually explain: send a bill to Buckingham Palace and payment would be made from a slush fund set aside for Mary's 'purchases'.

Despite their monstrous enthusiasms, life in the royal household under George and Mary could be unbearably tedious compared with the previous reign, and utterly remote from the spectacle of refined good living presented by the Queen's dolls' house. Max Beerbohm, who had flourished under the earlier Bertie, poked fun at the torpor of George and Mary's court in an imaginary exchange between a lord- and lady-in-waiting:

> HE: Last evening
> I found him with a rural dean
> Talking of District Visiting
> The King is duller than the Queen

> SHE: At any rate he doesn't sew
> You don't see him embellishing
> Yard after yard of calico . . .
> The Queen is duller than the King.

A.C. Benson, anxious as ever to please, referred instead to the 'quiet domesticity' of George and Mary's lives; yet both Benson's and Beerbohm's images are misleading.

By nature George, like the younger Bertie, was the most domesticated of kings, far happier dining alone with his wife than entertaining high society. From his point of view, one of the great advantages of York Cottage was that it was too small to entertain guests; and even at Buckingham Palace, he and Mary rarely extended invitations or accepted them.

On the other hand, for a quiet supper at home George would

don his garter medal, Mary would sport a tiara, and some hapless bandsman would play the national anthem. In private, George remained a king to his bones, acting out the pedantic rituals of royalty.

These rituals became ever more elaborate as George and Mary's domestic circle widened. At Windsor, while Lady Airlie struggled to get her troops into line, David recalled how the same scene – reenacted each evening – appeared to the royal family. 'A few seconds before 8.30 my father and mother with the other members of the family present would start down the corridor towards the Green Drawing Room. At the door we would be met by the Master of the Household, who, as he backed across the threshold, would bow the King and Queen in.'

On one side of the room, arranged in a crescent, would be the ladies, dressed in evening gowns and jewels; on the other, the men, dressed either in the Household uniform (known as the Windsor coat) or black tail coats and breeches. 'While my mother shook hands with the men,' David recalled with a mixture of horror and amusement, 'my father would repeat the same formality with the curtseying women. Then the man who had been commanded to sit on my mother's right would bow and, offering her his arm, escort her to the table while the strains of "God Save the King" issued from a grille in the dining room behind which was concealed a Guards string band that played during dinner.'

Like David, Bertie occasionally affected to disdain court protocol. 'There must be no more high-hat business,' he remarked euphorically to a courtier in 1939, after he and Elizabeth visited President and Mrs Roosevelt at their home in upstate New York. The President had greeted Bertie on arrival with a large cocktail, and the next day invited him to swim in his pool. Bertie, overwhelmed by this democratic gesture, plunged in.

'I hoped the Queen would feel she could relax in the same way,' Mrs Roosevelt recalled, 'but I discovered that if you were a queen you could not run the risk of looking dishevelled, so she and her lady-in-waiting sat by the side of the pool with me while the men were swimming.'

At heart, however, Bertie preferred the high-hat business. His visit to the White House was preceded by immensely detailed instructions from Buckingham Palace about protocol, including the precise interval that must elapse between the King and the Queen being served (thirty seconds). 'We will not require Fields [the White House butler] to have a stop-watch,' was the President's lofty response when a worried Mrs Roosevelt showed him the document.

Fields' counterpart in the royal household did not need a stop-watch; he already knew the royal routine. No meal was eaten (ladies' gloves could be removed), no bath was run (6.30 a.m. on the royal train, when the locomotive slowed), no newspaper arrived on the royal breakfast table (*The Times*, special edition, ironed) which did not require its own ritual. These were the signs by which the homely Windsors affirmed their majesty: firstly to themselves, secondly to the court, and only then, through the monarchy's public pageants, to the mass of their subjects.

11

Keeping Up Appearances

'Royalties in public always behave as if they were enjoying complete privacy,' 'Chips' Channon observed in 1923, after attending the marriage of Queen Mary's niece to the future Duke of Beaufort. Channon was a professional snob with the professional misfortune to be raised in America; as such, he completely misunderstood what he saw. Royalties in public might seem oblivious of the watching crowds. Even *en famille*, however, they were always on parade.

'Frock coat and epaulettes, without medals and riband, only stars,' George wrote to Bertie in 1927, before a family reunion at Victoria Station. '. . . We will not embrace at the station before so many people. When you kiss Mama take your hat off.'

Bertie understood the importance of such matters. A few months earlier, visiting the Canary Islands, he had received an angry letter from his father. 'I send you a picture of you inspecting Gd. of Honour (I don't think much of their dressing) with yr. Equerry walking on yr. right next to the Gd. & you ignoring the Officer entirely. Yr. Equerry should be outside and behind, it certainly doesn't look well.'

'I noticed the same thing about the photograph you sent me,' Bertie replied apologetically. '. . . It was an unfortunate moment for the photograph to be taken.'

David, on the other hand, was a constant worry, long before he started undressing in public to impress Wallis Simpson. 'Wear the Balmoral kilt and jacket on weekends, and green kilt and black jacket on Sundays,' George wrote to David when he was about twenty. 'Do not wear the red kilt till I come.'

In old age as the Duke of Windsor, David liked to wear a kilt (Stuart tartan) for dinner with the Duchess at their home in Paris. As a young man, his taste had veered more towards loud-check plus fours and fluorescent golfing jerseys. In rebellion against his father, he could not accept what seemed perfectly obvious to George – that incorrectly dressed princes eventually lost their thrones.

Already in 1920, touring Australia and New Zealand, David's sloppiness was endangering the monarchy. 'From various photographs of you that have appeared in the papers,' George wrote to him from Buckingham Palace, 'I see that you wear turned-down collars in white uniform, with a collar and black tie. I wonder whose idea that was, as anything more unsmart I never saw; I have worn tunics for twenty years in white, which was very smart.'

A year later David was touring India when a photographer caught him wearing blue overalls (officer's trousers) with a white tunic. 'A most extraordinarily ugly uniform,' George exploded. 'I wonder when the order was given, as white overalls have always been worn with white tunics by the Army in India.'

Small wonder that when David succeeded to the throne, he survived less than a year. How could a King who boasted of abolishing frock coats for wear at court, and told the Yeomen of the Guard they need no longer sport Tudor-style beards, expect to uphold the dignity of his position?

And yet David was not as liberated as he imagined. In his second volume of memoirs, *A Family Album*, which is little more than a personal history of fashion, he remembered taking 'a special pride in the uniform of the Brigade of Guards, whose most distinctive feature is the famous bearskin cap.'

He claimed that the secret of wearing the bearskin was to make sure it was properly 'broken-in' to the head. 'I used to keep my head "in training" for the bearskin, by wearing it in moments of leisure and privacy during weekends at the Fort.'

On one level, the hereditary obsession of Windsor men with clothes was simply the result of having too many moments of leisure, and not enough work to occupy their time. The elder Bertie (Edward VII), denied any important role as heir to the throne, spent much of the first sixty years of his life turning himself into a royal fashion plate.

'. . . He takes no interest in anything but clothes, and again clothes,' Albert complained of his eldest son when Bertie was still in his teens. 'Even when out shooting, he is more occupied with his trousers than with his game.'

Years later, a French journalist witnessed the fruit of Bertie's sartorial labours at Marienbad. The King was spotted (in truth, it was hard to miss him) wearing 'a green cap, a brown overcoat, and pink necktie, grey shoes, white gloves and knee-breeches.' 'We sincerely hope His Majesty has not brought this outfit home!' the *Tailor and Cutter* reported with an obsequious shudder.

These were Bertie's holiday clothes. At home among his subjects, no one paid more attention to the minutiae of correct form. The notoriously scruffy 8th Duke of Devonshire was a particular target for his venom. Only one thing had marred the evening, Bertie told the Duke at the end of a ball in his honour. 'What is that, Sir? the Duke asked anxiously. 'Your garter is upside down,' Bertie told his host, with a withering look.

Such outbursts, and the still more rigorous rules of dress George instilled in his sons, might seem an expression of royal insecurity. If courtiers and even princes did not wear the right clothes, how could due obeisance be paid to the throne? But the need to keep up appearances came so naturally to the Windsor men – with the partial exception of David – that it was only outsiders who found their behaviour eccentric.

Sir Edward Ford provides a good example of how the younger Bertie was able to spot details mere mortals (including himself) would miss. Shortly after the war, he remembers returning to Buckingham Palace with the King from a public engagement. 'As soon as we had arrived, the King ordered me to ring up the

Ministry of Works and find out what had happened to the cross on Victoria's orb.'

A phone call by Ford to the Ministry of Works elicited the information that the orb on Victoria's statue in the Mall had been removed the previous evening by a drunk. Most pedestrians, let alone a passenger in a car, would not have noticed the detail; but Bertie had spotted that 'something was wrong', and by royal command the Ministry was expected to put it right.

Correct form was absorbed by the royal family from their environment. At Sandringham and Balmoral, they might live out a distorted and sometimes grotesque ideal of homeliness; at Buckingham Palace and Windsor, the formality of the court was a source of constant amazement to the uninitiated.

Some rituals were self-imposed. Sir Alec Hardinge's wife, dining at Windsor in 1921, recalled the rigmarole surrounding the removal of the long white gloves which were *de rigueur* for ladies at dinner. 'When I had worn these gloves at dances in London, the usual custom, if you wanted to free a hand, was to undo some of the buttons and put your hand through the gap.' That was not good enough for George: 'When ladies wished to disentangle themselves from their gloves in his presence – which they had to do, in order to eat – they had to take them off altogether. At the end of the meal, we were to put our gloves on again, if Queen Mary herself did so.'

What gave these rituals added resonance was the knowledge that, until very recently, court ceremonial had been either non-existent or utterly chaotic. Victoria's memory was sacred to her descendants: but to understand why they placed such inordinate emphasis on correct form, it is necessary to recall the shambles of late nineteenth-century court life.

At the Great Exhibition in 1851, the novelist and republican Thackeray was one of many who watched in amazement as the Lord Chamberlain walked backwards into the Crystal Palace, heralding the arrival of Victoria and Albert.

'Shall we wonder – shall we be angry – shall we laugh at these old world ceremonies?' he wrote a few years later, recalling the spectacle. 'View them as you will, according to your mood; and with scorn or with respect, or with anger and sorrow, as your temper leads you.'

After Albert's death in 1861 Victoria's attitude towards these old-world ceremonies was rather one of dread. In 1886 she wrote a typically irrational letter to Ponsonby to justify her position, in the light of criticism in the press about her near-invisibility.

'The Queen has been very much hurt by an article . . . imputing to her the bad state of Society and making out there had been no Courts for twenty years!! Whereas excepting Balls and Parties and going to Theatres and living in Town the Queen neglected nothing . . .'

Ponsonby was used to these tirades. In 1892 he reported laconically to his cousin and fellow-courtier Sir Spencer Ponsonby-Fane that, 'Princess B[eatrice] seems to think it possible that H.M. wd. go to one Drawing Room. But H.M. in sad and mournful tones said to me she was damned if she would.'

Victoria's neglect of court life had two consequences. The courtiers, like actor-managers, forgot the art of staging ceremonial (if they had ever possessed it); and the crowds which flocked to Buckingham Palace, on the rare occasions when Victoria held a court function, risked being trampled to death in the chaos.

Lady Airlie, a débutante in the 1880s, remembered that at her presentation 'so great was the crush that [we] could hardly move forwards or backwards. The guests often numbered 3000 and the majority spent their time trying to fight a way through the crowded rooms. Many of the girls waiting to be presented had their dresses torn in the struggle, others retired weeping because the ordeal had been in vain, and they had not succeeded in reaching the Queen, who always left long before the last débutantes had passed before her.'

In 1897 a similar scene occurred in the Buckingham Palace ballroom, where Victoria had graciously agreed to receive the congratulations of MPs on her Diamond Jubilee. 'In came the House of Commons like a crowd being let on to the ground after a football match,' Frederick Ponsonby – then a junior equerry – remembered. 'There seemed to be no order and the Speaker, Prime Minister, and Leader of the Opposition were lost in the struggling mass of MPs.'

Fearing for the life of Victoria – who was too busy shouting at her Lord Chamberlain to notice the danger – Ponsonby and other able young courtiers formed a protective ring around her. After a quarter of an hour, unable to stand the pandemonium, Victoria turned on her heels and fled the battle. As a consolation prize, the disgruntled politicians and their wives were offered tea at Windsor the following week.

With the death of Victoria and the accession of the elder Bertie, who cared passionately about the theatre of monarchy, the court experienced a revival which was literally dramatic. If Bertie was a suitable majestic presence, centre stage, the *mise-en-scène* was chiefly the work of Reginald Brett, the second Viscount Esher. In 1897 Esher had been drafted by Bertie on to the committee which organised the Diamond Jubilee celebrations, and as secretary to the Office of Works and (from 1902) Deputy Constable of Windsor Castle, he became unofficial master of ceremonies at the Edwardian court.*

Despite having four children, Esher was homosexual by nature. Mothers of Eton boys would warn their sons about taking walks along the river with him, and for a time he even had an incestuous crush on his own son Maurice (unconsummated, it appears). His sexuality is not irrelevant, for he was the first in an unbroken line of homosexuals – Osbert Sitwell and Noël Coward were conspicuous later examples – whose fascination with royalty was essentially camp. They loved the theatre of monarchy; they loved even more the gossip that swirled around the throne.

Yet Esher was no dilettante. If he had wished, he could have been a cabinet minister, and among his other achievements was to chair a committee responsible for the most far-reaching military reforms since the Napoleonic wars. He brought the same formidable skills to the task of enveloping the monarchy in bogus tradition and ritual.

'The ignorance of historical precedent in men whose business it is to know is wonderful,' Esher told his diary in 1901, when the arrangements for Victoria's funeral threatened to collapse in chaos. Such was the general state of knowledge about royal pageantry that in some cases Esher simply invented 'traditions' to suit the occasion.

In 1901, only a few months after Bertie's accession, Esher advised Sir Arthur Ellis, Master of the Household, on how to stage a court drawing room. '. . . If his Majesty will stand before a Canopy – even though on the floor – at Buckingham Palace, in the Ball Room – and the Queen stands about four feet away on his left – with all the Princes and Princesses grouped *behind* them, the effect will be very fine.'

In these matters, Bertie always did as Esher told him; Alexandra was more of a problem. When the hapless Ellis, on Esher's advice, made suggestions about her dress for the coronation, he received a furious reply in the Buckingham Palace post. 'I know better than all the milliners and antiquaries,' Alexandra raged. 'I shall wear exactly what I like, and so shall all my ladies – *Basta!*'

The dazzling court which was summoned to life by Esher and Bertie remained largely unchanged until the Second World War. Thackeray would have blinked in amazement at the revival and occasional invention of supposedly ancient traditions. In addition to the Lord Chamberlain, a supporting cast of Ruritanian figures now appeared in all their splendour. As the sovereign's carriage rode out from Buckingham Palace at regular intervals, he was accompanied by Silver Stick-in-Waiting, an officer charged with protecting the King from assassination with the help of a silver truncheon. Another officer, Gold Stick, offered a second line of defence.

At least Silver Stick's title described his function. What would Thackeray have made of the Lord Great Chamberlain, first in the table of precedence, whose functions had almost entirely been delegated to the Lord Chamberlain? All that remained of this once great position was the right to carry the sovereign's crown at the state opening of Parliament, the right to exclude MPs from the Palace of Westminster at weekends, and a centuries-old dispute between the Ancaster, Carrington and Cholmondeley families about who indeed had the right to be Lord Great Chamberlain.

Further down the table of precedence were other stately relics. There was an Earl Marshal, who competed with the Lord Chamberlain for the privilege of supervising royal ceremonial. Since the task was in any case delegated to more competent courtiers like Lord Esher or the Lord Chamberlain's Comptroller, it hardly seemed to matter.

There was a Keeper of the Privy Purse – a position held by the younger Ponsonby after the First World War – who really did possess a purse, made of silk tapestry. But for advice on their vast private investments, George and Bertie relied on the more expert opinion of banker friends like Sir Edward Peacock and Lord Revelstocke. The Keeper occupied himself with more mundane tasks, such as presiding over the Board of Green Cloth – a table covered in a green cloth – where pubs were licensed within 'the Liberty of the Verge of the Palaces'.

It comes as no surprise to learn that the Master of the Horse was not master of the horse, his functions being performed by the Crown Equerry; that the Mistress of the Robes was always a duchess; that the difference between a Lady and a Woman of the Bedchamber was the difference between a peeress and the daughter of a peer; and that the Equerry, not to be confused with the Crown Equerry, wore a piece of decorative rope on the shoulder of his uniform as a reminder of his original duty, which was to tether his sovereign's horse. The word itself, taken from the French *écurie* (stable), was a further reminder: but in the age of the Daimler (George's preferred limousine) and the royal train, he was merely required to cut a dashing appearance in the presence of majesty, and act as a low-grade runner in the royal household.

In 'learning the ropes' of court life – a favourite royal expression – it helped that many of these courtiers had a military background, where arcane rules were taken for granted. The Equerry was in fact a service appointment, rotated between the army, the navy and the air force. But in addition, many senior courtiers were professional servicemen before joining the house-hold. For instance, every Private Secretary from General Grey in the 1860s to Major Hardinge in the 1930s – titles they used in correspondence – had been a career soldier, with the exception of Lord Knollys.

It helped even more that so many courtiers came from families with long traditions of royal service. This was no accident: in the first place, the royal family preferred to employ the sons and daughters of courtiers they had known, who were more likely to 'know the ropes'; moreover, forced on each other's company for weeks, even months, it was inevitable that many ladies and gen-tlemen of the court decided to marry.

The principal court families in the early twentieth century were all interrelated. They included the Ponsonbys, the Barings, the Spencers, the Lyttletons, and the Lascelles: Alan Lascelles, for instance, who retired as Private Secretary in 1953, was a cousin of the Earl of Harewood, who married George and Mary's daughter, also called Mary.

Even more striking was the existence of court dynasties. Stamfordham, the son of a Northumberland vicar, came from a family with no previous court connections. But his grandson Michael Adeane became Private Secretary to the present Queen when Lascelles retired in 1953; his great-grandson Edward Adeane was for a period Private Secretary to Prince Charles.

Lady Airlie's record in founding a court dynasty was still more impressive. Her son became Lord Chamberlain to Queen Elizabeth, now the Queen Mother; her eldest grandson, the 13th Earl of Airlie, has been Lord Chamberlain to the present Queen since 1984; his younger brother Angus Ogilvy is married to the Queen's cousin, Princess Alexandra; and his wife, the Countess of Airlie, has been a senior lady-in-waiting to the Queen for over twenty years.

These families were not necessarily wealthy. In fact service at court, with its perks in the form of free board, sumptuous liv-ing and grace-and-favour residences, was a traditional career move for impoverished younger sons. It was, nevertheless, a fine equation, because the salary was pitiful and the expense could be damnable – especially in such a clothes-conscious household.

Frederick Ponsonby, the younger son of Sir Henry, was perpetually short of cash, and dreamed up ever more fantastic schemes to pay off his debts. In 1927 he published some letters from the late Empress Frederick of Prussia to her mother Victoria; an act which outraged her son Willy, the exiled Kaiser, who threatened to sue Ponsonby for breach of copyright. Another of Ponsonby's ideas was to raise King John's treasure, allegedly buried beneath the Wash, and if so, conveniently close to Sandringham. He was unable to find partners for his enterprise.

Lady Airlie was so hard up by the end of her long life that her last weeks were spent – by her own choice and against the wishes of her children – moving between dingy hotels in Paddington. She had never been rich, and the financial demands of court life almost bankrupted her.

In her memoirs, Lady Airlie recalled with dread her expenditure on clothes during Ascot week in the 1920s. 'For the weekend before the races,' she wrote, 'the minimum equipment was an afternoon dress, with coat or short jacket, a smart suit for church on Sunday – in case we went to Eton or Wellington chapel – and two evening dresses. For the actual week there had to be two dresses to wear in the morning before the drive to the course, then four very chic ensembles – dress, coat, hat and bag – for the races, and five full evening dresses.'

What Lady Airlie possessed was breeding: by which the royal family meant not simply an ancient lineage – though that helped – but an ability to take the arcane procedures of court life in one's stride. The potential for mishaps began, both for the royal family and the courtiers, when the palace opened its gates to the outside world.

'It is quite possible, without undue shame, to arrive at Buckingham Palace in a taxi,' Harold Nicolson rejoiced in 1937, 'even though one's taxi driver (in an orgy of democracy) insists upon throwing his cigarette down upon the red carpet of the steps.' But Nicolson, off to dinner with Bertie and Elizabeth, was a royal insider who knew the ropes. For the uninitiated, who nonetheless still constituted something called 'Society', it was deemed necessary for the Lord Chamberlain to issue instruction manuals regarding correct behaviour at court.

In 1937 particular attention was paid by the Lord Chamberlain to the curtsy. The previous year, some débutantes had failed to curtsy properly at a presentation. It was not entirely their fault, since they were outdoors in the Buckingham Palace gardens, it was pouring with rain, and there was a serious danger they would slip in the mud. None the less, the Lord Chamberlain felt obliged to warn ladies about the correct procedure.

'The curtsy should be made gracefully and with an absence of stiffness; the left foot is drawn backwards, the knees are bent, and the body gradually lowered until the left knee is within a few inches of the floor; the back is kept straight and the head kept up.'

Unfortunately the manoeuvre proved too ambitious. A few years later an Australian girl, presented by her country's High Commissioner, froze in mid-curtsy, to Bertie's fury. As the girl was carried, weeping, from the throne room, it emerged that she had dislocated her knee. In future, the Lord Chamberlain decreed, the curtsy need not incur the risk of injury.

Nor did the court books prove any help to a peeress whose knicker elastic snapped in the middle of the Buckingham Palace ballroom. Surrounded by several other titled ladies, to whom she had signalled her distress, she shuffled to a settee and stuffed her lingerie between the cushions. The next day her maid was dispatched to the tradesmen's entrance to reclaim them.

The 1937 court book described a regime which was soon to be drastically modified. In May 1937 the last court ball was held, to celebrate Bertie's coronation, and in July 1939 the royal couple hosted the last evening court at Buckingham Palace. It was not that Bertie genuinely disliked the 'high-hat business'; but the outbreak of the Second World War forced him to reduce court ceremonial in the higher national interest of belt-tightening.

Bertie signalled his own commitment to the war effort by personally designing a more sober 'utility' household uniform which continued to be worn after 1945. Even so, at a time of clothes rationing, the expense for junior courtiers was considerable.

Sir Edward Ford, who joined the household on a salary of £1500 in 1946, was by his own account very lucky in this respect. 'Admiral Sir Basil Brooke, who was Treasurer to Queen Elizabeth, had died, and his widow, through the offices of the King's elderly equerry Harold Campbell, offered me his clothes. So among many other garments I got a Windsor coat, which was a marvellous break.'

At the end of the war, Bertie was inhibited from reviving full-scale court ceremonial not only by the economic crisis, but also by the advent of a socialist government. It was a defensive impulse his mother failed to appreciate. 'They won't do enough of this kind of thing now,' Queen Mary complained tactlessly to the Labour minister Hugh Gaitskell at a Buckingham Palace banquet in honour of the Shah of Iran, shortly after peace was declared.

Mary, at least, still knew how to behave like royalty on these occasions. Elizabeth Longford, whose husband was a junior minister in the Attlee government, recalls being introduced to the old Queen at another state banquet in 1945.

'After dinner the wives were brought up in turn to the distinguished people at the top table. My turn came to meet Queen Mary. She said "I hear you live in Oxford", which we did then, so I gave some sort of boring answer and the conversation flagged before it had hardly begun. And then I saw her signalling with eyes about to panic to her lady-in-waiting, who was a little way away, as if to say, "Take this lady away and bring somebody else quick!"'

But however much Mary longed for the mixture of formality and royal bad manners which characterised the pre-war household, the court's function as the focus of fashionable society collapsed in the decade after 1945. In 1958, the last débutantes were presented to Elizabeth at Buckingham Palace. Henceforth, the royal family performed their residual social duties in the more democratic setting of the garden party.

Mary's old friend Lady Airlie, always more receptive to change than her mistress, had few regrets about the passing of the old court. 'The new setting for Monarchy is far less brilliant than that of my youth,' she wrote to her daughter in 1956, a few months before her death, 'but in many ways it is more interesting.'

In one respect, Lady Airlie was wrong. While the interior life of the court had lost its pre-war lustre, the public setting for the British monarchy had never been more brilliant. The marriage of Elizabeth and Philip in 1947, the funeral of Bertie in 1952, and Elizabeth's coronation the following year re-established the external grandeur of the British monarchy, after the self-imposed economies of the Second World War. And in the vast crowds which congregated for these spectacular pageants, the Windsors found reassurance that they might, perhaps, escape the bicycle-riding fate of their surviving European cousins.

12

The Royal Variety Performance

'No one ever, I believe, has met with such an ovation as was given to me, passing through those six miles of streets,' Victoria wrote after her Diamond Jubilee procession in June 1897. '. . . The crowds were quite indescribable, and their enthusiasm truly marvellous and deeply touching. The cheering was quite deafening, and every face seemed to be filled with real joy.'

In the sixtieth year of her reign the old Queen's eyesight was failing, and it is hardly surprising that she could not describe the crowds. Over the next half-century the crowds returned in staggering numbers as, dead (funerals) or alive (jubilees, weddings and coronations), royalty was paraded before the people. But no one really knew who these people were, or what exactly they were cheering. Instead, like Victoria, they drew their own conclusion.

'There was pride,' Harold Nicolson wrote of George's Silver Jubilee celebrations in 1935: '. . . pride in the fact that, whereas the other thrones had fallen, our own monarchy, unimpaired in dignity, had survived for more than a thousand years. Reverence in the thought that in the Crown we possessed a symbol of patriotism, a focus of unison, an emblem of continuity in a rapidly dissolving world. Satisfaction in feeling that the Sovereign stood above all class animosities, all political ambitions, all sectional interests. Comfort in the realisation that here was a strong benevolent patriarch personifying the highest standards of the race. Gratitude to a man who by his probity had earned the esteem of the whole world.'

Nicolson's description could have been applied to any of the other great pageants between Victoria's Golden Jubilee in 1887 and Elizabeth's coronation in 1953. It was not untrue, but it did not reveal very much. In particular, it failed to consider how such fervour could have arisen among people who, for centuries, had regarded royalty with suspicion, irreverence, and even hostility.

Under the Hanoverians it was part of the mythology of freeborn Englishmen that in the seventeenth century Charles I had been executed and James II overthrown to advance the cause of liberty. The later Hanoverians, meanwhile, did nothing to advance the cause of monarchy.

'There never was an individual less regretted by his fellow creatures than this deceased king,' *The Times* famously observed when George IV died in 1830. 'What eye has wept for him? What heart has heaved one throb of unmercenary sorrow?' When George's younger brother and successor William IV died seven years later, the *Spectator* condemned him for his 'feebleness of purpose and littleness of mind, his ignorance and his prejudices.'

Victoria's accession temporarily abated the flow of vitriol that was poured on the throne. Who could resist an eighteen-year-old Queen, especially one so apparently self-assured? Certainly not Charles Greville, who witnessed Victoria's maiden appearance before the grizzled elder statesmen of the Privy Council. 'There never was anything like the first impression she produced, or the chorus of praise and admiration which is raised about her manner and behaviour,' he told his diary.

The honeymoon failed to last, principally because Victoria – hopelessly dependent on her Prime Minister Lord Melbourne – allowed the crown to become identified with the governing Whigs. Among Tories, she was given the contemptuous nickname 'Mrs Melbourne'.

Melbourne faded, to be replaced in Victoria's affections by her new husband Albert; and over the next twenty years, this cold German prince signally failed to establish himself in the affections of his wife's subjects. In 1854, at the start of the Crimean War, it was even rumoured that Albert faced charges of treason. Crowds gathered hopefully outside the Tower of London to enjoy his incarceration.

After Albert's death from typhoid in December 1861, Victoria withdrew almost entirely from public view for more than a decade. Each year, for example, her ministers would beseech the Queen to attend the state opening of Parliament; and each year Victoria would insist that her nerves were too 'shattered' to contemplate the ordeal. 'The Queen was *always* terribly nervous on *all* public occasions,' she wrote to the Prime Minister Lord John Russell on December 1864: 'but *especially* at the opening of Parliament, which was what she *dreaded for days* before and hardly ever went through without suffering from headache before or after the ceremony; but *then* she had the *support* of her dear husband, whose presence alone seemed a tower of strength, and by whose dear side she *felt safe* and *supported* under every trial.'

It was Victoria's self-imposed seclusion at Windsor, Balmoral and Osborne on the Isle of Wight which provided the setting for the last serious republican movement in Britain.* In March 1864 a poster appeared on the gates of Buckingham Palace, announcing 'these commanding premises to be let or sold, in consequence of the late occupant's declining business'. A few weeks later, on April Fools' Day, *The Times* sarcastically 'reported' that 'Her Majesty's loyal subjects will be very pleased to hear that their Sovereign is about to break her protracted seclusion.'

In the meantime, republican clubs were being established across the country; by the early 1870s there were at least fifty. And in the autumn of 1871 the rising Liberal politician Sir Charles Dilke decided to test the republican mood during a speaking tour of the provinces.

Dilke had already indicated his own views on the royal family by voting in Parliament against the award of a dowry of £30,000 to Victoria's daughter Princess Louise, and an annuity of £15,000 to her son Prince Arthur. On 6 November he put his case to an audience in Newcastle.

'It is said that some day a Commonwealth will be our government,' Dilke declared. '. . . Well, if you can show me a fair chance that a republic here will be free from the political corruption which hangs about the monarchy, I say, for my part – and I believe that the middle classes in general will say – let it come.'

When *The Times* reported this speech three days later, it accused him of 'a recklessness bordering on criminality'. As the outcry continued, Dilke, realising that his political survival was at stake, subtly changed his tune.

To attack corruption, he told an audience in Leeds, 'is not to condemn the monarchy, because [it is] no necessary part of the monarchy, although the opposite idea – that of promotion by merit alone and of the non-recognition of any claims founded upon birth – is commonly accepted as republican. I care not whether you call it republican or whether you do not, but I say that it is the only principle upon which, if we are to keep our place among the nations, we can for the future act.'

Three years later, writing to an elector in his Chelsea constituency, Dilke completed his climbdown. '. . . Nothing was further from my mind than to impute blame to Her Majesty,' he said, referring to his infamous Newcastle speech: '. . . I never for a moment thought my words to be so understood, [and] I am heartily sorry that they were so understood, and that the very fact that they were shows that they were wrong.'

Dilke's campaign had been sabotaged by an unfortunate coincidence. A few days after his Newcastle speech, Bertie was stricken with typhoid and for several weeks the Prince of Wales's life hung in the balance. The nation held its breath, while the future Poet Laureate Alfred Austin struggled to do justice to the telegram messages from Sandringham:

> Flash'd from his bed, the electric tidings came,
> He is not better, he is much the same.

Republicanism suddenly seemed in poor taste; especially so when a few months later Victoria graciously condescended to a service of thanksgiving for Bertie's recovery in St Paul's Cathedral.

'Everywhere troops lined the street,' she wrote in her journal, 'and there were fifteen military bands stationed at intervals along the whole route, who played "God save the Queen" and "God bless the Prince of Wales" as the carriages approached, which evoked fresh outbursts of cheering. I saw the tears in Bertie's eyes and took and pressed his hand! It is a most affecting day, and many a time I repressed my tears. Bertie was continually with his hat off' – as he would be during many more carriage rides before his own state funeral in 1910.

It was too soon to say Victoria had emerged from seclusion, and just as she refused to preside over a splendid court, so her public appearances continued to be grudgingly bestowed – and sometimes grudgingly received by her subjects. Frequently in the 1870s and 1880s she simply refused to venture forth in public. But the 1872 celebrations for Bertie's recovery set a precedent which made it harder for Victoria to refuse her courtiers' advice – warmly supported by Bertie – that the fiftieth anniversary of her accession in June 1887 demanded an appropriate public jamboree.

A Golden Jubilee had been planned for George III in 1810, but was cancelled when the king was declared insane. That seemed to Victoria a more unhappy precedent, and for months she resisted Bertie's entreaties. Even when she gave way, Victoria categorically refused to wear her state robes for the Jubilee procession, despite a painful audience with her favourite daughter-in-law Alexandra, who begged in vain for Victoria to exchange her widow's bonnet for a tiara.

The Golden Jubilee confounded Victoria's worst expectations and proved how a monarch could achieve popularity simply by living to a great age. Victoria had not changed; what had changed was her subjects' perception of a Queen who in reality remained the same dogmatic, selfish and generally impossible person she had been when she ascended the throne. Already in April, two months before the main event, an appearance by Victoria at the Albert Hall generated scenes of near hysteria. Lord Frederic Hamilton, who was sitting nearby, declared that 'no one who saw it can ever forget how the little old lady advanced to the front of her box and made two low sweeping curtsies to the right and to the left of her . . . as she smiled through her tears on the audience in acknowledgement of the thunders of applause that greeted her.'

Such was the prelude. The official celebrations began on 20 June, when Victoria was driven through cheering crowds to the station at Slough. More crowds were waiting for her when the train reached Paddington, where a carriage drove her in triumph for what she described in her journal as 'a large family dinner' at Buckingham Palace. 'The King of Denmark took me in, and Willy of Greece sat on my other side. The Princes were all in uniform, and the Princesses were all beautifully dressed. Afterwards we went into the Ball-room, where my band played.'

The next day Victoria drove in procession to Westminster Abbey for the official thanksgiving service. She was so nervous that she burst into tears before she could pluck up the courage to set off from the palace; but having stipulated to the Archbishop of Canterbury that the service should be short ('for the weather will probably be hot and the Queen feels faint if it is hot'), she was pleased with the result. In the Abbey she sat alone on the Coronation Chair ('Oh! without my beloved husband, for whom this would have been such a proud day!') while the choir sang Albert's own *Te Deum*. At the end of the service, the massed ranks of European royalty filed past her, and breaking with protocol, Victoria embraced them all. There was a special hug for her eldest daughter Vicky, the Crown Princess of Prussia, whose husband was stricken with cancer of the throat.

When the royal party returned to the palace Victoria 'felt quite exhausted and ready to faint, so I got into my rolling chair and was rolled back to my room.' There she distributed her own Jubilee presents to her adoring relatives; commemorative pins for the men and brooches for the women. 'Half dead with fatigue',

Victoria struggled through a Jubilee banquet in the evening, before being rolled back to her room to enjoy the illuminations in St James's Park.

On the following day, there was yet another lunch at Buckingham Palace for the kings of Europe, and in the afternoon a party for 26,000 deserving schoolchildren in Hyde Park, which Victoria graciously attended. Each child was given a mug bearing the Queen's portrait, a bun and a glass of milk. Six military bands entertained the huge crowd and at the end of the party, a hot-air balloon emblazoned with Victoria's name was released to float across the London sky.

From Hyde Park it was a short journey to Paddington, where more tumultuous crowds waited to greet her, and so home to Windsor. Riding up the hill from the station to the castle, Victoria passed beneath a triumphal arch constructed by the boys at Eton. 'This day will ever remain indelibly impressed on my mind,' she told her journal that evening, 'with great gratitude to that all-merciful Providence, Who has protected me so long, and to my devoted and loyal people. But how painfully do I miss the dear ones I have lost!'

Victoria's Diamond Jubilee ten years later provided further evidence of how public opinion had shifted in the old Queen's favour. The erstwhile republican Joseph Chamberlain, once a friend of Dilke but now a fervent monarchist, proposed that this second Jubilee – marking sixty years on the throne – should take as its theme the unity of the empire under one crown. So it was that Field Marshal Lord Roberts led a Jubilee procession from Buckingham Palace to St Paul's Cathedral which included the Jamaican Artillery, the Royal Nigerian Constabulary and several policemen from Borneo.

After a ten-minute pause at the end of the procession the royal party appeared, headed by Captain Oswald Ames of the Life Guards – at six feet eight inches the tallest man in the British army (and according to Victoria's waspish daughter Alice 'the stupidest'). At St Paul's, the *Daily Mail* correspondent Mr W.G. Stevens was among scores of journalists waiting to record the scene:

'Already the carriages were rolling up full of the Queen's children and her children's children. But we hardly looked at them. Down there, through an avenue of eager faces, through a storm of whitewaving handkerchiefs, through roaring volleys of cheers, there was approaching a carriage drawn by eight cream-coloured horses. The roar surged up the street keeping pace with the eight horses. The carriage passed the barrier; it entered the churchyard; it wheeled left and then right; it drew up at the very steps of the Cathedral; cheers broke into screams and enthusiasm swelled to delirium.' Sitting in the carriage, Stevens saw an old lady – 'so very quiet, so very punctual, so unmistakeably and every inch a lady and a Queen.'

Vanity Fair, in a leading article called 'The Triumph of Monarchy', concluded the next day that the Jubilee had shown 'how powerful may be a good Monarchy even in these degenerate days of what is called Democracy. The cheers that rent the air were more than hearty . . . they came from the heart – the heart of a nation that is indeed loyal to the backbone: a nation that from the beginning has held its head high in the pride of its might, and that today knows that it stands highest in the roll of the countries of the world.'

Almost by accident, the court had discovered a mass market for royal pageantry; and if Victoria, despite two Jubilees, remained a reluctant brand leader, Bertie was happy to please the customers in the next reign.

It was easy to imagine that popular antipathy to royalty had been obliterated in a frenzy of flag-waving, Jubilee parties and loyal toasts. The story was not quite that simple. After Dilke, no politician with serious ministerial ambitions dared flirt with republicanism for over a century. But beneath the surface adulation lay other, contrary emotions which recalled a less deferential past.

Journalists who covered state pageants were naturally drawn towards royalist fanatics to illustrate what they imagined to be the undifferentiated fervour of the crowd (and hence the nation). At Elizabeth's coronation in 1953, for instance, it was the turn of seventy-three-year-old Mrs Zoe Neame from Buckinghamshire, who had watched every royal parade since the First World War.

Two days before the royal procession was due to pass through Trafalgar Square, Mrs Neame had already claimed her position. She told reporters that for the past six months, whenever it rained, she had stood in her garden, allowing herself to be soaked – an essential toughening procedure for her not so lonely vigil. Her efforts were not in vain, for on the great day it poured.

Mrs Neame and her ilk made good copy, but they were not representative of popular attitudes to royalty. On 12 May 1937 Mass Observation had attempted a more ambitious exercise, when they sent anonymous eavesdroppers into the crowds which gathered for Bertie's coronation, and also commissioned reports on how the public celebrated around the country.

The survey made no claim to be scientific, and for this reason – like other Mass Observation studies – has been dismissed as unreliable. But the sheer randomness of the research, based on snatches of conversation and personal impressions, in many ways produced a more reliable snapshot of the contrary emotions stirred by royalty than did later opinion polls.

The pollsters demanded straightforward answers to straightforward questions. The mass observers, in contrast, made no attempt to rationalise their subject matter. At the very least, they demonstrated that the glib rhetoric of chroniclers like Nicolson scarcely began to fathom the often contradictory response of the people to royalty.

Confusion began with the mass observers, who illustrated that the perception of royalty was very much in the eye of the beholder. A children's nurse, who described herself as 'C. of E.', was standing between Buckingham Palace and Marlborough House on the Mall.

There was a sudden stir of excitement and the Procession began. Princess Margaret Rose looked very much a little princess from a story book, I thought, and the Queen looked really charming. There was real genuine excitement and feeling when our beloved Queen Mary passed through, also for Princess Marina and the Duke of Kent.

When the beautiful Fairy Coach came into view with the King and Queen the crowd sent up a cheer worthy of a British subject and as I gasped in admiration at the look of calm dignity on the face of the new King I recalled the words of the Duke of Windsor when he abdicated, and realised that with his charming Queen and happy children he was well chosen to be our King.

That was not how Bertie and Elizabeth seemed to another mass observer as the royal coach reached Parliament Square. He described himself as 'male, 27, married, teacher, "inactive left"', and he thought Elizabeth's hair 'looked informal and astray like a woman's who is getting up in the morning'. As for Bertie, he was 'bony, frozen, nervous, staring. He looked like a thin head on an ancient seal.'

Bertie had good reason to be frozen, nervous and staring, for what awaited him at Westminster Abbey was a catalogue of disasters which rather undermines the myth of flawless pageantry. 'Elizabeth's procession started first,' he told his diary that evening, 'but a halt was soon called, as it was discovered that one of the Presbyterian Chaplains had fainted & there was no place to which he could be taken.'

As the coronation began, so it continued – at least through Bertie's eyes. The Dean of Westminster insisted he should wear the coronation surplice inside out; his Groom of the Robes corrected the mistake. The Archbishop of Canterbury, Cosmo Lang, covered the words of Bertie's coronation oath with his thumb, and then – Bertie suspected – placed the crown on his head the wrong way round. One of the bishops trod on Bertie's coronation robe. 'I had to tell him to get off it pretty sharply as I nearly fell down.'

Since this was the pre-television theatre of monarchy, none of these mishaps was visible to Bertie's subjects. But among the crowds gathered outside the Abbey there were various remarks suggesting that the show was not exactly a smash hit. Already in the morning, before the procession began, the children's nurse 'could not help feeling that the people were like a lot of sheep and came early because others had come, as I heard one or two of the crowd remark that they had come much against their will.'

After the service, as Bertie and Elizabeth returned to Buckingham Palace, a woman in Arlington Street observed cynically that 'when the Royal Coach passed it was cheered like the others': but, 'the only sincere cheers seemed to be for Queen Mary and her granddaughters'. As a 'left-wing atheist' she was no doubt biased.

At the corner of Regent Street and Vigo Street, Bertie and Elizabeth may have heard a man shout, 'What a coach!' He was, however, ridiculing rather than admiring their fantastically ornate gold carriage.

Away from the procession, mass hysteria failed to erupt. Listening to the service on the radio, a man in south-east London confessed he felt tears coming into his eyes, especially when Queen Mary entered the Abbey. But, he continued matter-of-factly, 'anything done in unison, even children drilling, has that effect on me. After a time we became bored with the broadcast . . . We had a drink or two, then early lunch and a nap.'

At a café in Leeds, shortly after the broadcast had ended, a couple 'overheard no remarks about the Coronation although the room was full of people. We heard a waitress say that the children's costumes [for the local coronation parade] had been judged.'

In Hertford, a coronation jamboree in the grounds of the castle seems to have fallen flat. 'The first round of the Artillery Salute caught the crowd unawares. Most people "jumped", and after a short pause of surprise, the crowd broke into a general wave of laughter. Some frightened children cried, and some girls put their fingers to their ears . . . The repeated playing of the King seemed to cause some irritation, but most people stood still while it was played . . . When the salute was completed a girl said "Is it finished now?" The crowd quickly began to move off.'

As for the loyal citizens of Hastings, they tried hard to rejoice and forget their English reserve, with limited success. Part of the 'all-day Coronation sports' was to be 'an ingenious and quite decorous version of the strip-tease act . . . Couples – men and girls – wearing ordinary clothes over bathing costumes, have to undress and then dress in each other's clothes. Prizes go to those who do the change-over in the shortest time.'

Glancing through these reports, a royalist would have been consoled by the thought that the English lacked the fervour, not to mention the attention span, to start a revolution. Many people, however, far from being in awe of royalty, were positively disrespectful. A group of Belfast workmen, who appear to have been Protestant and loyalist, remarked 'that the King and Queen would be a long time without a meal today and the clerk said, amid laughter, that they would take a snack in their pockets. From this evolved facetious and imaginative remarks on the crowning ceremony.'

Such irreverence illustrates how the Windsors' relationship with their most loyal subjects was based on contradictory emotions. The grand pageants inaugurated by Victoria's Golden Jubilee placed the royal family on a pedestal. But this ceremonial projection also allowed the public to indulge its favourite fantasy about the Windsors: that here were ordinary people placed (perhaps against their will) in an extraordinary situation. Thus was born the myth of a dynasty which was both the grandest in the world, and instinctively in tune with the everyday life of the nation.

The fantasy acquired irresistible force because even the principal actors believed it; for, making a virtue of their own lack of self-esteem, the Windsors saw themselves as both a stately and a down-to-earth dynasty.

Driving through London's East End in 1935 during his Silver Jubilee festivities, George was staggered by the tumultuous reception. 'But I cannot understand it,' he remarked to the

ubiquitous Cosmo Lang. 'I am quite an ordinary sort of fellow.'
'Yes, sir, that is just it,' Lang replied.

David was one of the few members of the royal family to see
through this fallacy – at least in relation to George. 'Because my
father himself was a simple man, the legend grew that his life was
simple too,' he wrote in his memoirs. This was untrue: 'I knew no
one who liked his comforts more, save perhaps myself.
Everything about him was always of the best – his clothes, his
fine hammer guns by Purdey, his food, his stationery, his cigarette
cases by Fabergé.'

The ability of royalty to believe otherwise was encouraged by
those who should have known better. 'I have always felt that
when I knew what the Queen thought, I knew pretty certainly
what view her subjects would take,' Victoria's last Prime Minister
Lord Salisbury said on her death: 'and especially the middle class
of her subjects.'

It was a ludicrous statement, given Victoria's portfolio of monstrous prejudices, including a horror of ice hockey, electric lights
and heated rooms. Lord Salisbury's only excuse was that he was
almost as remote from the middle class of her subjects as Victoria
had been.

Asquith, who *was* middle class, could still tell Venetia Stanley
in 1915, after another 'all-round-the-houses' audience with
George, that 'I don't know a better reflection than his talk of
what one imagines to be for the moment the average opinion of
the man in the tube.'

Royalty happily swallowed such nonsense. In 1942, Bertie
complained to Lord Woolton that his Minister of Labour Ernest
Bevin, a proletarian to his chubby fingertips and founder of the
Transport and General Workers Union, 'had no understanding of
the mind of the people'. Neither had Churchill, Bertie added for
good measure. 'The King has been brought up to do the industrial side of the royal job, and he knows more about the working
man than the Minister of Labour,' Woolton was informed.

To acquire this knowledge, Bertie (the 'Industrial Prince')
found the comforts of his royal station no obstacle. At one of his

Duke of York camps before the war, a working-class boy remembered seeing Bertie's four-poster bed, specially transported from London, being wheeled into his private tent for the night.

It was a rare glimpse of how royalty really lived. Despite his many 'industrial duties', Bertie was completely unknown to the majority of his subjects when he suddenly succeeded David as King in December 1936. Cosmo Lang, ever obliging, 'introduced' Bertie to the people in an article for *The Times*; but apart from the embarrassing disclosure about the new King's stammer, Lang's piece was so sycophantic as to be meaningless. After racking his brains, the sub-editor decided that Bertie was best described as 'a practical idealist' with 'an astonishing memory'.

The advent of radio was supposed to have brought the royal family closer to the people. So suspicious were the clergy of this invention that the BBC was refused permission to broadcast Bertie and Elizabeth's wedding service in 1923 – for fear that it would be heard by people in pubs.

By 1932 times had changed to such an extent that, much against his will, George was persuaded to interrupt his Sandringham Christmas and speak to the Empire. The words, two hundred and fifty-one of them, were provided by Rudyard Kipling; the voice – gruff and resonant – was entirely his own. 'I speak now from my home and from my heart to you all; to men and women so cut off by the snows, the desert, or the sea, that only voices out of the air can reach them.' Thus was invented another royal tradition, the annual Christmas broadcast.*

But these broadcasts only created an illusion of familiarity. As if to demonstrate the gulf that separated sovereign from subject, George recorded in his diary that he had 'broadcasted' at 3.35 p.m. on Christmas Day. His subjects heard his message half an hour earlier: for there was such a thing as 'Sandringham time', ordained by the elder Bertie to maximise the hours of daylight shooting, which set the Sandringham clocks thirty minutes ahead of the nation.

The fantasy that the Windsors were just like us was in fact constantly undermined by the conflicting knowledge that this could never be so: not simply because they lived in palaces and rode in carriages, but also because (it was imagined) they possessed an inner royal grace which marked them out from the common herd.

In May 1939 Queen Mary provided an appealing example of this mysterious quality while being driven through south London, when her Daimler was hit by a lorry carrying steel tubing. According to one royal commentator, 'nothing, perhaps, that Queen Mary has done on occasions of state or at private ceremonies, has ever become her so well as the manner of her leaving the wrecked car. She joked with one of the workmen who helped her, and bent to adjust her dress before she was taken into a nearby house while doctors were informed by telephone.'

A spectator at the scene remarked that 'she climbed up and down those ladders [out of the upturned car] as if she might have been walking down the steps at the Coronation. She had not her Hat or one curl out of place . . . The only outward sign of disorder was a broken hat pin and her umbrella broken in half.'

Seventy-one years old, badly bruised, with a glass shard in the cornea of her eye, Mary knew her royal duty. It had been 'a lucky escape', she told her dumbstruck hosts at a house in Wimbledon Park Road, while she waited for the reserve Daimler to be fetched from the royal mews; and yes, she would appreciate another cup of tea.

In the same fashion, Bertie was transfigured by his premature death at the age of fifty-six. As an example of human frailty in a royal setting, his stammer lacked epic stature; it was simply a source of mutual embarrassment between subject and sovereign. His death, by contrast, invested Bertie with a dignity which in life he had so signally lacked.

'During these last months the King walked with death,' Churchill broadcast to the nation on the first day of the new reign, 'as if death were a companion, an acquaintance, whom he recognised and did not fear.' In fact, Bertie had no idea he was about to die; following an operation in the autumn, he imagined that he was on the road to recovery.

'We all saw him approach his journey's end,' Churchill continued. That was closer to the truth, for despite precautions by the royal household, Bertie was the first King whose physical condition became the subject of speculation in the press.

'Why are we proud to print this picture?' the *Sunday Pictorial* asked its readers defensively in September 1951, after Bertie was shown entering a clinic in Wimpole Street. 'Because it is news, because it is human, because it is symbolic. It is a happy and reassuring picture of a monarch about whom his people had been anxious for a long time.'

The people would have been less reassured if they had been told the result of this consultation, which revealed that Bertie had a tumour on his left lung. Even Bertie did not know the tumour was malignant: that information was reserved for his wife and his Private Secretary.

Bertie's health problems can be traced to his eighteenth birthday when, to encourage the habit, his mother gave him a cigarette case. His physical decline began in earnest during the royal family's tour of southern Africa in 1947. Bertie was worried about his absence from Britain in the middle of a very harsh winter, both meteorologically and economically; and as the royal train journeyed across the Veldt, he smoked like a chimney. According to one witness, he was also drinking too much.

By a series of accidents, the left-wing journalist James Cameron found himself covering this tour. One evening on the royal train, the press were summoned to Bertie's dining car. Cameron recalled:

We found him behind a table covered with bottles of all sorts of things, with which it would seem he had been experimenting, with some dedication. 'We must not f-forget the purpose of this t-tour,' he said, 'trade and so on. Empire co-operation. For example, South African b-brandy. I have been trying it. It is of course m-magnificent, except that it is not very nice. But,' he said triumphantly, 'there is this South African liqueur

called V-Van der Humm. Perhaps a little sweet for most.
But, now, if you mix half of brandy with half of Van der
Humm . . . Please try.'

Cameron was not overimpressed with Bertie's performance on
the tour. He noticed, for instance, how at each stop along the
royal train's route, 'the King would stand shaking at the door of
the train, dreading the inevitable encounters.' Only his wife,
looking 'radiant, or at any rate full of beans', saw Bertie through
the ordeal.

Elizabeth had more immediate worries about Bertie's condition: during the tour he lost seventeen pounds in weight. Within
a year he was suffering from persistent cramp in his legs, the first
symptom of the arteriosclerosis caused by his heavy smoking. In
the spring of 1949 he underwent an operation at Buckingham
Palace, and for a time doctors feared they might have to amputate
his left leg.

By now, Bertie's pallor was so ghostly that it was difficult to
disguise the fact that he was seriously ill. At receptions and state
banquets, he started wearing make-up – an expedient fiercely
denied by the royal family, but confirmed on close inspection by
the French ambassador René Massigli.

In May 1951 Bertie told his mother that his doctors had diagnosed 'a condition of the left lung known as pneumonitis . . . I
was X-rayed and the photographs showed a shadow.' This was the
cancer which eventually led to the removal of the lung in
September.

It was too late. By Christmas, Bertie was too weak to deliver a
live radio broadcast. Instead, with Elizabeth's help, he pre-
recorded the broadcast in short bursts. He referred in all sincerity
to how 'by the grace of God and through the faithful skill of my
doctors, surgeons and nurses have I come through my illness.' Six
weeks later he was dead, killed by a blood clot on the heart.

For three days Bertie's body lay in state in Westminster Hall,
while an estimated 300,000 of his subjects paid their last
respects – 'an utterly unbelievable cavalcade that must, somehow,

be Monarchy's gesture to all the forces of logic,' the reporter from the *Illustrated London News* decided.

'When a King dies,' the reporter also said, 'we, who have to put into words the strange grief and grievous strangeness of the time, then know how ill we have served ourselves over the years. While the King lived we spoke of him as this, and as that, endowing him with all the remote virtues of an infallible man; such men do not die. But the King died; and we found somehow a different thing: that we loved him . . . We do not find it hard, now, to salute a King who, inheriting a generation racked and anxious as no other before, did what he had to do with dignity, patience and courage.'

The reporter was James Cameron, and the last time he had seen Bertie he scarcely endowed him with all the remote virtues of an infallible man. Looking back on this piece – so unlike the rest of his journalism – almost thirty years later, Cameron claimed to be neither proud nor ashamed of what he had written. '. . . It reflected precisely the mood of the time, and that was what I was employed to do.'

For once with Cameron, that is an unsatisfactory explanation. He, too, had been seduced by the myth of ordinary grandeur; a belief that in the most personal sense, Bertie could share his people's suffering, and yet suffer more nobly. Gone was the stammering, half-drunk, querulous individual Cameron had encountered in South Africa. In his place was a figure of 'dignity, patience and courage'. Bertie's sufferings were real enough – but in the light of what Cameron knew about the deceased King, his report was a distortion.

If a journalist as lucid as Cameron could lose his way in the Windsor tapestry, what hope was there for the rest of the nation?

Midway through the century, the mutual ignorance of royalty and nation was wonderful to behold. The restyled Windsors had battled their way through fifty years of war, revolution and socialism, without beginning to understand the circumstances which had led to their survival. At every twist in the saga, they left a record not of wisdom in adapting to change, but of near-suicidal folly. George's support for his German cousins in 1914, David's determination to marry Mrs Simpson, David's 'brush' with the Germans – time and again the royal family invited their own destruction.

What saved them was a truly royal measure of luck. They were lucky that Britain escaped invasion in the First World War, and again in 1940: otherwise they would surely have suffered the fate of their cousins. They were lucky to be served by courtiers like Ponsonby and to a lesser extent Stamfordham, who saved them from their own political misjudgements. They were lucky to live in an age of deference, when the private affairs of royalty remained so.

Above all, they were lucky to stumble on a formula for their own survival which capitalised on their human shortcomings. Lord Esher and other pageantry professionals supplied the carriages; sitting in them, the Windsors offered the spectacle of homely people, doing their best in an extraordinary situation.

The only cloud on the horizon concerned whether the dynasty, unable to comprehend or even recognise its mistakes, was ever likely to learn from them. But in 1952, once due respect had been paid to Bertie, that was not a question which troubled either royalty or nation. They were too busy enjoying the 'new Elizabethan age' which the chroniclers told them had now begun.

PART THREE

Elizabeth

13

Margaret,
Getting Down To It

'Everybody is talking about this being a new Elizabethan era,' Princess Margaret told the Queen's Chaplain a few months after her sister's accession. 'Well it won't be, unless we all get down to it and do something about it.'

Even before the era had begun, Margaret was getting down to it in her own inimitable fashion. In August 1951 she could be found in Petworth, West Sussex, attending a house party at the family home of her close friend Billy Wallace. On 2 August Margaret and Billy motored over to Broadlands in Billy's red sports car to attend a dance for Lady Pamela Mountbatten. Among the other guests were Lilibet and Philip, who had spent the first days of their honeymoon at Broadlands four years before.

But tonight Margaret was the belle of the ball – as she invariably was these days. The other guests admired her stunning white gown of silver-threaded tulle, the necklace of diamonds round her neck, and the way she danced with Billy to one of her favourite tunes – yes, 'Diamonds are a Girl's Best Friend'. Into the small hours she and Billy danced, long after her sister and brother-in-law had excused themselves.

Back in Petworth, Margaret just had time to slip into a day dress before she and Billy were off to nearby Cowdray Park – star guests at a barbecue hosted by the Argentinian polo team. Eight Argentinian lambs were roasted whole on spits, while the band played a selection of Latin American tunes.

Soon it was time to bid Billy and his mother, Mrs Herbert Agar, goodbye; for Margaret was off to Balmoral, where her parents were worried she might not be getting enough sleep (she was only twenty-one). The author of the *Princess Margaret Gift Book* tells us that every day she went riding on a grey pony, 'usually . . . accompanied by the King's Equerry, Group Captain Peter Townsend'; and a photographer snapped Margaret and Peter disappearing into a field together. But for the moment, the public assumed Townsend was just a very conscientious equerry – whatever that meant.

Margaret's social duties resumed as soon as the royal family returned to London: she was a busy princess. On the evening of 29 October, during a charity performance at the Victoria Palace Theatre, she made news by smoking her first cigarette in public, through a long ivory holder. More cigarettes were smoked a few hours later at the Café de Paris, where her good friend Noël Coward was giving the first performance of his new cabaret.

Up until now, Margaret had always been chaperoned at her public appearances, usually by her mother. But on 21 November she absolutely insisted on honouring a charity ball in Paris with her presence. She chose the occasion to bid adieu to the years of austerity – years which, strangely, seemed to have passed her by – in a gown manufactured from fifty yards of white organza.

'Although Princess Margaret has no intention of setting out as a leader of fashion,' one commentator observed, 'nor has any wish to do so, inevitably, in her position, she has become one.' The New York Dress Institute, noting the same leadership qualities, voted her the fourteenth best dressed woman in the world in its end-of-year poll.

If anyone had asked in her first flowering 'What is Princess Margaret for?' – as they frequently did in the years to come – the answer would have been easy. She was sunshine, laughter, gaiety, frocks and fun – with more than a hint of sex, if the royalist press had dared to admit it. In short, she seemed to represent the opening-up of the monarchy to the modern world: a breath of fresh air blowing through the court, was one cliché that came easily to mind.

Margaret's style was cramped a little by the death of her father. She was distracted with grief, far more so than her less demonstrative sister, and for months there were rumours that she was planning to become a nun.

'The night-club phase is almost over,' the *Princess Margaret Gift Book* reported at the end of 1952. 'No longer does she think that the logical peak of an evening out is the visit to the dimly lit and throbbing club where youngsters dance and their elders drink in the belief that they are having a whale of a time.'

Those who knew Margaret better were not so sure – among them her former governess Marion Crawford, the author in 1950 of the serve-and-tell memoirs *The Little Princesses*. For her sins, Crawfie (as she was known to her employers) lost her grace-and-favour cottage in the grounds of Kensington Palace and was banished forever from the royal presence.

Crawfie's second career as a social columnist for a women's magazine also ended in disgrace. In June 1955 she wrote an article describing in gushing tones the spectacle of the royal parade at Ascot. Alas, the parade was a figment of her imagination, having been cancelled because of a rail strike. Crawfie's contract was cancelled and her career in journalism came to an abrupt end.

The cloud over Crawfie has obscured the fact that *The Little Princesses* is one of the most acute studies of modern British royalty ever written. Crawfie's prose may have been sugary, but before entering royal service she had trained to be a child psychologist. As an intelligent woman, living with the royal family and sleeping in the same room as Lilibet and Margaret, she was uniquely placed to observe the developing personalities of Bertie's daughters.

Crawfie was also writing without the benefit of hindsight. If Lilibet's destiny was assured once her father became King, that was much less true of Margaret. Her future was a blank page, which is why Crawfie's description of Margaret in the late 1940s, just as she was entering her night-club phase, seems so prescient.

The picture that emerges is of a girl who was talented, frustrated, self-centred, and a bit of a menace. 'Lilibet never took the keen interest in clothes that Margaret does,' Crawfie recalled. 'Margaret at an early age would draw little sketches of beautifully dressed ladies with sylph-like figures, and pictures of frocks she would have liked to have for herself. Excellent designs some of them were, too. There are so many things Margaret could have done with brilliance and distinction.'

Her room was a mess. 'In the centre . . . she has a large round table on which can always be found a lavish clutter. Letters, invitations, dance programmes, greetings telegrams – in short, a hoosh-mi. Her white wooden dressing-table is littered with bottles, manicure instruments, and small ornaments.'

And what was lacking, to Crawfie's disapproval, was any parental control. 'We are only young once, Crawfie. We want her [Margaret] to have a good time,' Elizabeth told the governess shortly after Lilibet's wedding in 1947, when Margaret was still only seventeen. By night, Margaret was a party princess; by day, Crawfie was expected to complete her education: something had to break, and it seems to have been the latter.

'Other girls have work to do,' Crawfie told Margaret. 'They can't stay late in bed. They have got to get up in the morning after a dance and catch a bus. They probably have to get their own breakfast.' And she said, 'Crawfie, even if I wanted to cook my breakfast, I couldn't, because there's nothing here to cook on.' 'She turns it all into a joke,' was Crawfie's despairing comment.

Margaret's congenital gaiety stood her in good stead during what is usually described as the tragedy of her life: the long-drawn-out affair with Peter Townsend, culminating in her decision in 1955, under intense pressure, not to marry him. It may have been a tragedy, or at least rather sad; but at the time, Margaret scarcely looked the part of a tragic heroine. She was too busy getting down to it.

Townsend was (and is) much older than Margaret. He was

born in 1914 and had served with distinction during the Battle of Britain as a fighter pilot. Soon afterwards he suffered a nervous breakdown – the pilot's equivalent of shell-shock – and was transferred to ground duties. In 1944, with no previous connection at court (his background was middle class), Townsend joined the household as an equerry. He was selected as part of Bertie's policy to honour the bravest officers from the three services. Like his predecessors, Townsend expected to return to the RAF after a few months.

Instead, Bertie rapidly found Townsend indispensable, and by stages his appointment became a permanent one. By early 1947, when Townsend accompanied the royal family on their southern African tour, he was a trusted member of their inner circle; more so than far more senior courtiers such as Bertie's Private Secretary Sir Alan Lascelles, who regarded Townsend with a certain suspicion. As a mark of royal favour, in 1950 Townsend was made Vice-Master of the Household – a meaningless title, except that it pushed him further up the table of precedence within the household.

Why Townsend should have won the royal family's confidence is as interesting – and ultimately unanswerable – a question as why another junior equerry, Timothy Laurence, should have achieved the same feat over thirty years later. And just as the stages by which Laurence wooed and won Princess Anne are shrouded in obscurity, so too is the way Townsend wooed and eventually lost Margaret.

In 1978 Townsend told his side of the story for the first time, when he published his autobiography. After a gradual estrangement, not helped by his prolonged attendance at court, he and his wife Rosemary separated in 1951. A year later, in December 1952, Townsend was granted a divorce on the grounds of her adultery.

It was during 1952, he says, that he and Margaret 'found increasing solace in one another's company' – Margaret because of her father's recent death, Townsend because of the collapse of his marriage. 'One afternoon at Windsor Castle, when everyone had gone to London for some ceremony, we talked in the red drawing-room, for hours – about ourselves. It was then that we made the mutual discovery of how much we meant to one another . . . It was, to us both, an immensely gladdening disclosure, but one which sorely troubled us.'

Their secret could not last, for Margaret was incapable of discretion. At Lilibet's coronation in June 1953 she was seen by a reporter flicking a speck of dust from Townsend's uniform – a gesture which spoke volumes about their relationship. After the service another reporter, Donald Edgar, was amazed by Margaret's familiarity with Townsend. 'At first I thought this slight man in RAF uniform was a member of the royal family,' he said; but then he saw 'the officer holding out his hands, Margaret almost falling into his arms, a half-embrace.'

Within a fortnight the 'scandal' of Margaret and Townsend was all over the papers. 'Stop these scandalous rumours,' the *People* screamed on its front page, allowing it to repeat the rumours at length. 'The story is of course utterly untrue!' it concluded. The *Daily Mirror* decided that the story probably was true, and asked its readers whether Margaret should be allowed to marry Townsend. 'YES' was its banner headline when *Mirror* readers signalled their almost unanimous approval.

The court failed to bow to public opinion. Instead, Townsend was dispatched to a minor diplomatic posting in Brussels and Margaret was told to wait for two years before making a final decision. This cooling-off period was not arbitrary. Under the terms of the Royal Marriage Act, which had been passed in the reign of George III, when Margaret reached the age of twenty-five in August 1955 she was free to marry without her sister's permission.

The day at last arrived, and shortly afterwards she and Townsend were reunited at the Berkshire home of the Queen's friends Mr and Mrs John Lycett Wills, with the press in hot pursuit. Still Margaret delayed her decision. Then in October 1955 there was a meeting at Lambeth Palace between Margaret and Archbishop Fisher of Canterbury, which appears to have made up her mind. A statement was issued by Margaret to the press:

I would like it to be known that I have decided not to marry Group Captain Peter Townsend. I have been aware that, subject to my renouncing my rights of succession, it might have been possible for me to contract a civil marriage. But, mindful of the Church's teaching that Christian marriage is indissoluble, and conscious of my duty to the Commonwealth, I have resolved to put these considerations before any others.

Townsend departed on a world tour to forget his sorrows, financed by articles about his travels (but not about Margaret) for the *Daily Mail.* He eventually settled in Belgium and remarried happily. So ended the official version of this unhappy tale.

The unauthorised version is rather more interesting. Townsend's memory seems to be playing tricks with him when he describes 1952 as the year when he and Margaret 'found increasing solace in one another's company'. The previous summer at Balmoral the press had certainly noticed something was afoot between Margaret and the King's Equerry; and if at the time they merely alluded to the possibility of an affair, Townsend was far less discreet in his autobiography.

He remembered in particular an incident from this holiday. 'One day, after a picnic lunch with the guns, I stretched out in the heather to doze. Then, vaguely, I was aware that someone was covering me with a coat. I opened one eye – to see Princess Margaret's lovely face, very close, looking into mine. Then I opened the other eye, and saw, behind her, the King, leaning on his stick, with a certain look, typical of him: kind, half-amused. I whispered, "You know your father is watching us?" At which she laughed, straightened up and went to his side. Then she took his arm and walked him away, leaving me to my dreams.'

The story is unimportant, except that it shows how easily the history of romance – especially one between a princess and a soon-to-be-divorced commoner – can be shaped by later events. It is taken for granted, for instance, that Margaret spent two years of agony during Townsend's exile in Brussels, and that she never fully recovered from the shock of losing him. All her later unhappiness with Snowdon and other men sprang from this trauma.

If so, she disguised her inner torment superbly. There was one momentary lapse, in the summer of 1953, when it was announced that Townsend was to report for his new duties as air attaché in the Brussels embassy on 15 July. At the time, Margaret was paying a return visit to Rhodesia and South Africa with her mother, where – among other important functions – she opened the Princess Margaret Hospital for Asian and Coloured People of Mixed Races. Hearing the news about Townsend's departure, she disappeared from public view for several days with a 'bad cold'.

Back in England she was soon behaving as if nothing – or almost nothing – was amiss. What else could she have done? There was no escaping Townsend's two-year ban, and in the meantime she found plenty to distract her.

Clothes, for instance. 'Make no mistake,' one of Britain's 'leading dress designers' told journalists, 'what Princess Margaret wears is news with a capital N.' Among the news items in 1953 were platform shoes, the initial of the Christian name on a handbag, strapless evening gowns, headscarves, a feather cap and a white wool monkey jacket.

In the summer of 1954, while Townsend continued to languish in Brussels, Margaret turned her attention to the theatre. With a little help from her aristocratic friends in 'the Princess Margaret Set', she staged an amateur production of an Edgar Wallace thriller at London's Scala Theatre. Royal protocol decreed that Margaret could not act; instead, she took on the important role of co-director.

'The whole evening was one of the most fascinating exhibitions of incompetence, conceit and bloody impertinence that I have ever seen in my life,' Noël Coward wrote in his diary, after attending the first night. '. . . In the dressing room afterwards . . . we found Princess Margaret eating *foie gras* sandwiches, sipping champagne and complaining that the audience laughed in the wrong places. We commiserated politely and left.'

In 1956, the year after Margaret renounced Townsend, the

royalist press tried once again to paint her in a more serious light. It was uphill work. 'Princess Margaret singing popular jazz and buying records from American "musicals", dancing the latest dances and reading the latest novels – that is a true picture,' the BBC royal correspondents Godfrey Talbot and Wynford Vaughan-Thomas wrote. 'So is Princess Margaret playing Chopin at her piano, using her conversational gifts in learning swiftly about the political problems of the day, reading historical biographies and the works of the Brontës,' they added, with just a hint of desperation.

They spoke, too, of Margaret's 'chronic good humour' as 'after the troublesome waters of last autumn, she sails again, serenely and bright in manner and dress, through the changing but agreeable seas of steady public duty and private pleasure.'

She was afloat on the agreeable seas of public duty in February 1956 when she paid a visit to the BBC television studios in Lime Grove. It was Margaret's kind of occasion: a rehearsal of the light entertainment hit show *Tin Pan Alley*. Margaret sang along with a delighted cast:

> You can't chop your poppa up in Massachusetts,
> Not even if it's planned as a surprise.
> No, you can't chop your poppa up in Massachusetts;
> You know how neighbours love to criticise.

Margaret was no hypocrite – or at least, she made no secret about the kind of princess she was. She would probably have winced at the laboured descriptions of her 'serious side', despite her occasional essays in social and political comment (the Queen's Chaplain, for his part, thought her remark about the new Elizabethan era showed she was 'not unaware of international economics'). But as a figure in royal history she deserves to be taken seriously for two reasons.

In the first place, she broke the modern taboo on press coverage of royalty's private affairs. During the nineteenth century far more was known about the elder Bertie's escapades than was ever revealed about David's affairs with married women in the 1920s and 1930s. The public were even treated by Victoria to two volumes of intimate memoirs of her life at Balmoral in which, among other titbits, readers were offered a first-hand account of Princess Vicky's betrothal to the Crown Prince of Prussia.

If Crawfie's memoirs opened the sluice gates after the Second World War, it was the Townsend affair which burst the dam. The story was simply too good for the press to ignore – even though, twenty years earlier, journalists had spared readers the details of David's affair with Mrs Simpson.

It helped that Margaret, in brushing that momentous speck off Townsend's shoulder, had placed their affair in the public domain. It helped too that in the joyous dawn of new Elizabethanism, there seemed no crime in reporting the happy story of a princess in love (or, like the *People*, in denying these 'scandalous rumours').

But best of all, the Townsend affair, with its drawn-out quality and its complete lack of constitutional significance, was a wonderful opportunity for the British Establishment to pontificate about moral standards. It was a pleasure they had largely been denied in 1936, because the story of 'the King's affair' had been kept a secret till the eleventh hour. As the Archbishop of Canterbury Cosmo Lang discovered after his notorious post-abdication radio broadcast, there was no point giving a sermon about immorality in high places if his congregation did not know the text.

'One is very thankful that her sense of duty has prevailed, for quite obviously this was a matter of very great importance to the moral standards of the country': thus spake the Reverend Thomas Hannay, Primus of the Episcopal Church in Scotland, after Margaret's renunciation of Townsend in October 1955.

'All the peoples of the Commonwealth will feel gratitude to her for the selfless, royal, way which in their hearts they expected of her': thus, ungrammatically, *The Times*, in a leader the following day.

It is not at all clear that the peoples of the Commonwealth – and more particularly Britain – felt any such thing. As she breezed through the first years of the 'new Elizabethan age', monogrammed handbag in one hand, cigarette holder in the other, there were quite a few of her sister's subjects who rather resented the way Margaret got down to it. This was not so much a moral judgement as a perception that, at a time when most girls could only dream of white organza, in having it all Margaret was having rather too much.

On the other hand, Margaret was interesting – and here lay her second contribution to royal history. The last member of the family to excite so much press interest was David in the 1920s, but by the end of the decade even he had retreated from public view, preferring to cultivate his garden at Fort Belvedere.

As Crawfie suspected, Margaret's 'night-club phase' never really ended. It was her natural milieu, and in the wake of the Townsend affair, journalists could depend on The Princess Margaret Set – soon to be joined by a young photographer called Tony Armstrong-Jones – for further copy.

Irresistibly, Margaret was cast in the role of the first truly modern princess, in tune with 'new Elizabethanism' even if she stayed up too late. The irony was that in private (if such a concept really existed for a trouper like Margaret), she was a surprisingly old-fashioned girl. She was, for instance, a sincere Christian, and there is no reason to doubt that she meant what she said in 1955 about being mindful of the Church's teachings.

Margaret's 'modern' image arose from the contrast between her West End lifestyle and the dogs-and-horses leisure-time activities of her elder sister. A year after the Townsend denouement the *Daily Mirror* accused Elizabeth's court of being as 'aristocratic . . . insular and – there is no more suitable word for it – as toffee-nosed as it has ever been.'

The *Mirror* stopped short of applying these adjectives to the Queen, but the comparison between the two sisters was inescapable. Margaret had been getting down to it; Elizabeth, it increasingly seemed, had not.

14

Elizabeth,
Getting On With It

No character is preordained, and as a little girl even Lilibet behaved badly. Crawfie tells us that she was 'quick with her left hook' when Margaret needed thumping. A French mistress, newly appointed, was reduced to tears by Lilibet's naughtiness. One day in the classroom, fed up with verbs, the little princess 'picked up the big ornamental silver inkpot and placed it without warning upside down on her head. She sat there, with ink trickling down her face and slowly dyeing her golden curls blue.'

'I never really got to the bottom of what had happened,' Crawfie recalled.

These acts of rebellion were gradually suppressed. The Lilibet we see through Crawfie's eyes as she reaches adolescence is earnest and conscientious – almost obsessively so. Several times a night she would hop out of bed to straighten her shoes and refold her clothes. Margaret and Crawfie soon laughed her out of that phase.

The same scrutiny was brought to bear on a detachment of Grenadier Guards, whose honorary colonel she became at the age of sixteen. 'After one inspection, at which Lilibet had made some rather pointed criticisms in her ringing voice, one of the majors said to me, laughing: "Crawfie, you should tell the Princess quietly that the first requisite of a really good officer is to be able to temper justice with mercy."'

It was not really Lilibet's fault, for she knew nothing of the world and its ways. As a girl, her upbringing had been more sheltered than any heir to the throne since Victoria. George V and his elder brother had gone away to sea for two years. David and Bertie had both mixed with their upper-class peers at the naval academies of Osborne and Dartmouth. But Lilibet and Margaret had been educated 'privately' at home by Crawfie and a few helping hands like the nameless 'Mademoiselle'.

Nor did Crawfie feel this education was adequate, especially for Lilibet, who barring the arrival of a brother would one day be Queen. 'I had often the feeling that the Duke and Duchess [Bertie and Elizabeth], most happy in their own married life, were not over-concerned in the higher education of their daughters. They wanted most for them a really happy childhood, with lots of pleasant memories stored up against the days that might come and, later, happy marriages.'

In frustration, Crawfie went to see the girls' grandmother Queen Mary with a proposed timetable. Not enough history, Mary said, a little more Bible reading, less arithmetic and plenty of poetry; and once a week an improving trip to a museum with their granny. 'Queen Mary through all the years was an immense help and comfort to me personally,' Crawfie said pointedly. Lilibet and Margaret's mother, apparently, was not.

And then, just as Lilibet reached an age when she might have expected to broaden her horizons, she was incarcerated at Windsor for the duration of the war with Crawfie and Margaret. Even though the whereabouts of the little princesses was a state secret, from time to time their mother graciously invited photographers to Windsor, to remind the public of their continuing existence. In these pictures Lilibet and Margaret are always dressed in identical smocks, pinafores and white socks. Only in 1944, it seems, when Lilibet celebrated her eighteenth birthday, was she allowed to dress in grown-up clothes.

Yet Crawfie assures us that Lilibet was mature beyond her

years. It was for Margaret's sake, and for the sake of her overprotective parents, that she tolerated her prolonged girlhood.

Towards the end of the war, in an effort to amuse the
princesses, a Girl Guides troop was organised at Windsor. Lilibet
had long outgrown such activities and, like Crawfie, disliked the
idea of sleeping in a tent. '. . . She was immensely tactful about
this, and never actually refused, but there always seemed to be
some very good reason why she should not do so. I felt much
sympathy for her. She was getting older, and had been brought
up so much alone, I could understand why she did not want to
undress before a lot of children all of a sudden, and spend the
night with them.'

It was easy to mistake this tact for a pliant nature. When she
fixed her mind on something, however, Lilibet was immovable.
In the spring of 1945, when she turned nineteen, Lilibet insisted
that like other girls her age she should do National Service. Her
parents were reluctant, but Lilibet had her way.

Each morning she was driven from Windsor to Aldershot,
where she was based as a second subaltern in the Auxiliary
Territorial Service. Among other experiences, before royal duties
reclaimed her, she was photographed in overalls underneath a
truck; part of her course in vehicle maintenance, or an early photo
opportunity, depending on the point of view.

If Lilibet was doing her duty, she must also have been grateful
for the opportunity, at last, to escape the seclusion of life in the
royal household. The same impulse played its part in the major
drama of her life before she became Queen: her struggle with her
father for permission to marry Philip.

Interviewed in 1971, Philip was cheerfully vague about when
he and Lilibet became engaged. 'I suppose one thing led to
another,' he told his semi-authorised biographer Basil Boothroyd.
'I suppose I began to think about it seriously, oh, let me think
now, when I got back in 'forty-six and went to Balmoral. It was
probably then that we, that it became, you know, that we began
to think about it seriously, and even talk about it.'

That may have been Philip's impression. Lilibet seems to have

been thinking about it for rather longer. Apart from the occasional meeting as children, their first conscious encounter was at
Dartmouth Naval College in July 1939. Philip, then seventeen
and a naval cadet, was ordered to look after the little princesses,
who were accompanying their father on a nostalgic visit to the
scene of his youthful academic failure. Between this date and the
Balmoral love tryst, the course of their romance is difficult, if not
impossible, to reconstruct, for there are too many conflicting
versions.

Already in January 1941, when Lilibet was still only fourteen,
that ubiquitous royal gossip Chips Channon mentioned matter-
of-factly that 'he [Philip] is to be our Prince Consort, and that is
why he is serving in our Navy.' Years later, when confronted with
this remark, Philip said: 'Inevitably I must have been on the list,
so to speak. But people only had to say that, for somebody like
Chips Channon to go one step further and say it's already decided,
you see what I mean?'

The question may have been undecided on Philip's side, but
Lilibet seems to have made up her mind very rapidly. Some time
in 1942 a photograph of Philip appeared on her bedside table at
Windsor. When her father saw the photograph he rebuked her for
giving the palace gossips food for thought. Lilibet dutifully
removed Philip's portrait – only to replace it with another one,
presumably supplied by him, 'disguised' by the naval beard he
had grown.

Bertie's attempts to deflect Lilibet from her target were certainly the behaviour of an over-possessive father who did not
want his daughter to grow up. But beyond that, he appears genuinely to have distrusted Philip. In Philip's own words, before his
marriage to Lilibet he was merely 'a discredited Balkan prince';
and for someone with Bertie's experience of Balkan princes – his
feckless godson King Peter of Yugoslavia comes to mind – Philip
hardly seemed like a stunning prize for Lilibet.

It is not clear if Philip ever found the same wavelength as his
highly strung prospective father-in-law. On that momentous visit
to Dartmouth in 1939 he infuriated Bertie by paddling a dinghy

right up to the royal yacht, in a misconceived farewell gesture. 'The damned young fool!' Bertie shouted in fury. Philip affected not to hear him, and kept paddling.

At Sandringham in 1947, a month after his marriage to Lilibet, Philip committed the sartorial error of arriving for Christmas without a kilt. Why kilts were obligatory for Christmas, several hundred miles south of the border, is anyone's guess, but Philip had to borrow one in Stuart tartan that had belonged to George.

Philip was tall; George had been short: the kilt ended several inches above Philip's knees. Arriving in the Sandringham dining room, where his in-laws were waiting, Philip sought to placate Bertie by dropping a mock curtsy. Everything Bertie held most dear was offended: clothes, correct form and his father's memory. According to a courtier, he berated Philip 'in a roar of quarter-deck language'.

Whatever his motives in obstructing the match, Bertie played a losing hand with comical ineptness. He was simply no match for his daughter. Towards the end of the war he abandoned his policy of locking Lilibet away like a medieval virgin. On the King's orders, dashing young officers from the Household Cavalry were rounded up and brought to Windsor for games of canasta and conga dances round the ballroom with Bertie, Margaret and – naturally – Lilibet.

'The Body Guard' was how Queen Mary sarcastically described these officers to her old friend Lady Airlie. *They* wanted Lilibet to marry nice young Philip, and that was still Lilibet's firm resolve. Philip's picture stood defiantly on her bedside table, and from time to time he would dash to Buckingham Palace from his naval base in Wiltshire.

Bertie's final, despairing tactic was to remove Lilibet to the other side of the world. At Balmoral in 1946 he made it quite clear that Philip had overstayed his welcome. 'The boy must go south,' he decreed – even though 'the boy' was now twenty-five and had tried in vain to win Bertie's consent for the marriage. Too soon, Bertie had told him, insisting that Lilibet must first accompany the rest of the royal family on the ill-fated tour of southern Africa.

In July 1947 the engagement was at last announced – 'to which union the King has gladly given his consent,' the public were told. Bertie still thought it might be best to wait till the following summer (the weather would be nicer), but Lilibet was by now implacable, and the wedding went ahead in November.

In her undemonstrative way, so unlike Margaret, Lilibet had shown formidable determination to overcome her father's objections to the marriage. It was with the same single-mindedness that she prepared herself for her inheritance.

'I will be good,' the eleven-year-old Victoria had famously remarked, when she learned that she would one day be Queen. Lilibet, too, discovering her destiny at about the same age, was determined to be good; but unlike her great-great-grandmother, she appeared to have the temperament to fulfil her promise.

Everyone who met Lilibet in the last years of Bertie's reign speaks of her almost preternatural earnestness. 'I understand you have been to see some of the homes where we are trying to rehabilitate young women offenders against the law,' she told Eleanor Roosevelt, during a visit to Windsor by the former First Lady in 1948. 'I have not yet been to see them but could you give me your opinion?' If Lilibet was going to do a job, it had to be done properly.

Lilibet's future subjects were introduced to her in April 1947, when she broadcast a message to the British people and the empire on her twenty-first birthday, during the tour of southern Africa. It is a speech she has constantly recalled in later years, and for once the words were her own – or at least her family's. According to the BBC correspondent Frank Gillard, who was covering the tour, Bertie took one look at the draft prepared by his staff and was appalled.

'Can you imagine a young person of my daughter's age uttering such pompous platitudes?' he told Gillard; and for the next two hours, on the lawn of the Falls Hotel in Victoria, Rhodesia, Gillard helped Bertie, Elizabeth and Lilibet compose a new version.

Who could forget Lilibet's ringing words of dedication? Certainly not Lilibet:

> I declare before you all that my whole life, whether it be long or short, shall be devoted to your service and the service of our great Imperial family to which we all belong. But I shall not have the strength to carry out this resolution alone unless you join in it with me as I now invite you to do. I know that your support will be unfailingly given. God help me to make good my vow and God bless all of you who are willing to share in it.

Despite its careful drafting, however, the message of the speech was not entirely clear. From where did Lilibet derive her legitimacy? From God, in whose presence she and the Archbishop of Canterbury would perform the mysterious rites of anointing six years later? Or from the people, without whom Lilibet could not fulfil her resolution?

Sitting on the hotel lawn at Victoria Falls, the royal family were unable to resolve in their own minds the central ambiguity of the British monarchy. Indeed, there is no reason to imagine that Bertie had ever considered it, since an ability to think logically was not his strong point.

But when she succeeded Bertie in 1952, Lilibet's subjects were entitled to feel confused, especially in the light of this broadcast. The rhetoric of 'new Elizabethanism' spoke of democracy and openness – a decisive break with the discredited past of hierarchy, class, and privilege. Here was a young Queen, however, who used the language of command rather than consent. An 'invitation' in Lilibet's highly structured world did not assume a refusal: 'I know that your support will be unfailingly given.'

Her transparent humility could also be misunderstood. It was the humility her father and grandfather had felt when, hopelessly ill-equipped for the task, they were confronted by the 'heavy burden' of kingship. If George and Bertie had seen themselves as ordinary chaps, Elizabeth was too intelligent – and too isolated – to swallow the same delusion.

The only occasion in her life when she had moved freely and anonymously among the people was on VE-Day in May 1945. Accompanied by an escort from the 'Body Guard', she and Margaret joined the throng that had gathered in the Mall. In the end, however, and despite the vehicle maintenance course, Elizabeth knew she was not like other girls.

She was also far more vulnerable than George and Bertie had been at the start of their reigns. 'In a way I didn't have an apprenticeship,' she said in the 1992 BBC documentary *Elizabeth R*. 'My father died much too young and so it was all a very sudden kind of taking on and making the best job you can.' Elizabeth's idea of making the best job was to carry on as her father had done: to get on with it rather than get down to it.

A symbolic moment occurred a few months into the reign, courtesy of a character called Richmond Herald. It was the Queen's wish, he announced, 'that from the beginning of the Year 1953 Knights of the Garter should, when wearing the Garter with evening dress in the presence of the Sovereign, or on any other occasion of major importance, also wear knee breeches.' This was monarchy according to the Lord Chamberlain's rule books, last published in 1937, rather than the carefree spirit of 'new Elizabethanism'.

Elizabeth was indeed as unlikely a 'new Elizabethan' as could be imagined; and that explains the sense of disappointment which gradually surrounded her during the 1950s.

'In the beginning it was fine,' says one of her closest advisers from the period, 'because the Queen was a very pretty girl – she had these wonderful dark blue eyes, you know. But then it got stuffy, or seemed to get stuffy. It suited Michael Adeane [Lascelles' successor as Private Secretary], because he was quite a stuffy sort of person; and in a way it also suited the Queen, who could be quite stuffy herself.'

Sir Edward Ford, who worked under Adeane as an Assistant Private Secretary, disagrees. 'What we were concerned about was to make sure the monarchy was not aloof from people,' he says, looking back on these early years. 'We were already arranging walkabouts, and in organising her programme we were trying to ensure she met the largest number of ordinary people. We were trying to get the stiffness out of it.'

He gives some examples of what he and his colleagues attempted. 'If she was visiting a school, we would insist that she should be taken round by the boys; and if she had a meal, that she should sit between two boys (or two girls). Similarly, if she had to go two or three hundred yards from the site of one visit in a town to another, if possible she should walk there, rather than be driven in her car. It wasn't change forced on us – but we were trying to match her own development.'

How far she was aware of these changes is hard to tell. The rhetoric of 'new Elizabethanism' made it seem as if revolution was in the air. 'The modern concept of Royalty demands that the Sovereign and her Consort shall enter fully into the ordinary life of the people with all its facets and changes of activity and outlook,' *Royalty Annual* pronounced in 1955. 'We are no longer content with the Queen as a symbol, a figure-head – nor is Her Majesty.'

And yet the underlying tension between her assigned role as a 'new Elizabethan' and her own deeply conservative nature was apparent every time she ventured forth among her subjects. In 1955, the year of the 'modern concept' of royalty, she could be seen about her business in a variety of settings. If she was trying to enter fully into the ordinary life of the people, it seemed at best a half-hearted effort.

We find Elizabeth on 3 March, sitting on her throne in the Buckingham Palace ballroom, while several hundred débutantes passed through at a rate of nine per minute. Entertainment was provided by a pianist from the Irish Guards who played a medley of tunes, including 'Lovely to look at' and 'Ain't she sweet?'

On 25 July she visited Winchester College – as she was soon to visit the fee-paying schools of Harrow, Repton and Mill Hill. 'In education there is room for the unconventional as well as the conventional; for the new as well as the old,' she rather daringly told the pupils. But, she said, returning to safer ground, 'in striving to achieve this aim, we must be careful that the new does not obscure the old and that, in times of change, traditions that have been tested by long experience should not be discarded.'

The following month she was in Wales on a whistle-stop tour of the principality. 'All people now are merrie-minded,' a children's choir sang as the royal train pulled into Brecon station. At the Brecknockshire Agricultural Show a Welsh mountain pony tried to eat Her Majesty's bouquet – a rare moment of spontaneity, significantly provided by an animal. A few hours later she was at Trecastle, opening the Swansea Corporation's new reservoir. 'A plentiful supply of pure water is a river of life to a great town,' she told the local worthies.

'We were getting dull,' says the same courtier who accuses her of stuffiness. 'We had to change because we were getting so boring.' He adds, however, that 'the Queen doesn't have to be interesting. She has to be fascinating, which is a different thing, because she is an archetype. People need to have dreams about her.'

It is an important distinction. In the 1950s Elizabeth may have seemed dull in human terms, but she retained enough divinity to fascinate her subjects. The 'crisis' which enveloped the monarchy towards the end of the decade has to be seen in this context. No matter how boring her actions and utterances, no matter how dreary she seemed compared with her sister, she was the Queen – greeted wherever she went with rapture and awe. In this respect her exalted sense of her own position was the best security against an uncertain future.

It was the rhetoric of 'new Elizabethanism' that eventually misled, rather than Lilibet's stated intentions. Firstly, it sowed the seeds of disappointment in a public which had reason to expect something more exciting. At this level, though, the disappointment was containable. If Elizabeth was not quite the Faery Queen people anticipated, her rather colourless personality could easily be accommodated in the familiar myth of royal ordinariness. 'Poor lass,' people said, 'she'd like to have some fun, but she can't.' If only they had known: Elizabeth was not that kind of queen.

More importantly, 'new Elizabethanism' created a restlessness within the court that forced even conservatively minded courtiers to speak the language of reform. A new era had dawned; therefore they had to evolve. It scarcely mattered that the opinion polls, for what they were worth, consistently showed widespread support for the monarchy. Did not these same polls show that people had wanted Margaret to marry Townsend, that the court was 'toffee-nosed', that the people, too, thought it was time for change – never mind to what degree or to what end?

For one person in particular, change could not come too soon. Philip had put up with much since his wife became Queen: ostracism by the courtiers, the sacrifice of his naval career, and those interminable presentations and balls. If anyone was bored, it was Philip.

Not long after he stood beside Elizabeth in the Buckingham Palace ballroom, gazing at all those débutantes, he appears to have reached breaking point. It was time to start getting stuck in, or as he later said, 'adapting the monarchy to changing times'. And in the cause of reform, Philip at least was going to have fun – lots of fun, within the limits imposed by his royal status.

15

Philip,
Getting Stuck In

Philip's shock at Bertie's death in February 1952 was witnessed by his Equerry Michael Parker, who broke the news to him at the Treetop Hotel in Kenya. 'He looked as if you'd dropped half the world on him,' Parker remembered. 'I never felt so sorry for anyone in my life.'

The shock lasted for some time. His elder sister Margarita recalled that after the funeral Philip disappeared to his room, refusing to speak to anyone. 'You can imagine what's going to happen now,' he said bleakly, when she finally managed to force an entry. Soon afterwards he was struck down by jaundice, and retired to bed for several weeks.

Looking back on this period almost twenty years later, Philip tried to explain his misery. At Clarence House, where he and Elizabeth had set up home, 'whatever we did, it was together. I suppose I naturally filled the principal position. People used to come to me and ask me what to do. In 1952 the whole thing changed very, very considerably.'

Apart from losing his place as head of the household, Philip had already sacrificed his naval career. In July 1951, with Bertie's health failing, he relinquished his command of the frigate HMS *Magpie* and came home on indefinite leave. Answering the call of royal duty, as Elizabeth's consort he was expected to follow her around at public engagements, always remaining several paces behind her.

'Oh, the future', Albert exclaimed in despair to his diary, soon after marrying Victoria. Philip felt much the same.

His frustration has to be seen against his background as an obscure Balkan prince. The first thirty years of Philip's life had been a long struggle to gain acceptance – as a naturalised Englishman, as a successful naval officer, and as a member of the royal family. It was not easy, but by 1952 he thought he had succeeded (even with his prickly father-in-law). Bertie's sudden death threatened not only his career prospects, but also his self-esteem.

'Constitutionally I don't exist,' he protested, as the courtiers prepared for their next audience with Elizabeth. They were happy to discount Philip as a factor in the 'modern concept' of royalty. But they were wrong to underestimate him. Once Philip had recovered from jaundice he set out to rebuild a career as his own man – in the process making their lives hell (though that was not necessarily his intention).

'He could just about handle the older courtiers by the time I arrived,' recalls a former member of his staff, who joined the household in 1957. 'They were all a bit frightened of him. I shouldn't think they'd admit it, but they were.'

What the old guard especially underestimated in Philip, beginning with Stamfordham's grandson Michael Adeane, was his willpower. As Elizabeth's husband, he insisted on being treated with respect. 'Because she's the Sovereign, everybody turns to her,' he told Basil Boothroyd in 1971, referring to these early years. '. . . She's asked to do much more than she would normally do, and it's frightfully difficult to persuade . . . many of the Household . . . The fact that they report to the Queen is important to them, and it's frightfully difficult to persuade them not to go to the Queen, but to come to me.'

They also underestimated his ambition. From Philip's point of view, there was a convergence between his own need to develop a second career as royal consort, and the need he saw to purge the household of its more arcane rituals and customs.

Whether they underestimated his ability is a more difficult question to answer. Intellectually, Philip was certainly the most capable royal prince since Albert; but then, in the age of George and the two Berties, there were not many rivals for the honour.

His own self-estimate is an incongruous and very royal blend of modesty and arrogance. 'Some people speak because they have a special knowledge of a particular subject,' he wrote, introducing a collection of his speeches in 1960. 'Others are expected to have something suitable to say on any occasion. I belong to the latter group . . .' Yet he added grandiloquently that 'these speeches embody the reflections of an unprejudiced observer on the life and some of the problems of the middle of the twentieth century.' The reader scarcely knows what to think.

His energy, on the other hand, was indisputable. Michael Parker, his Private Secretary at the start of the reign, said later that 'he pitched into it with a vigour that was absolutely staggering. I don't think he's let up.' Another member of his staff, speaking of the late 1950s, recalls that 'he'd never say no to a request. If somebody suggested something and I'd write down, "I don't think you'll have time for this," he'd say, "I'll go." He'd never spare himself an inch and after a long day of lunches and dinners and speeches, he'd just manage to climb up the stairs to his office and he'd say, "I'm going to write a speech now." I felt quite guilty going off to bed.'

The questions arise about the use to which Philip put his energy: whether, in other words, his intelligence matched his drive and ambition. For a naval officer, he seems in these early years to have been strangely deficient in any overall strategy, and at times he was literally game for anything.

On 18 February 1953, for instance, he could be found at the Land Agents' Society jubilee dinner, toasting 'the Society'. On 24 July it was the turn of the Chartered Insurance Institute annual luncheon (toast: 'the Chartered Insurance Institute'). In the midst of his responsibilities as head of the commission planning the coronation, there were several other engagements of a rotarian nature.

'He had a lightning brain, I've never known a quicker brain,' a former adviser recalls. 'I remember we were going to an engagement once, and he said, "Am I supposed to make a speech?" and I said, "Yes you are, Sir." "Oh God," he said, and grabbed the file. And literally between two sets of traffic lights he'd absorbed all he wanted to absorb, gave it back and wrote a little speech.'

But what speeches they were. 'I congratulate you on the success of your efforts to preserve this lovely part of the Highlands,' he told the North of Scotland Hydro-Electric Board on 13 October 1952. 'To suggest that the Power House alone destroys the beauty of Glen Affric is being as fastidious as the fairy tale princess who could feel a pea under fifteen mattresses.'

'In my opinion, the working formula is Happiness plus Efficiency equals High Productivity,' he told the National Union of Manufacturers a year later. To the students of University College, Cardiff, in December 1954, he offered this off-the-cuff advice: 'I would like every . . . student or graduate to be able to do three things. First, to work his way round the world on £5 – if you haven't got that much, you can do it on less. Secondly, to run a holiday camp, or possibly a boys' club. And thirdly, to report a congress or conference in your own particular subject for the journal of a learned society or institute and write an editorial.'

It would be wrong to dismiss Philip as a lightweight. For the causes which interested him, such as the National Playing Fields Association, he used his position as royal consort to become an extremely effective fundraiser and cheerleader. In some areas, like his support for better design in industry, he was well ahead of his time. But there was something random, even promiscuous about his initiatives, ranging from lofty pronouncements on the state of the planet to the expression of rotary club wisdom (sometimes to rotary clubs).

His approach to reforming the monarchy was similarly ill-defined. On a purely practical level, the results were mixed. Sir Edward Ford, who was working in the Private Office, recalls that in the 1950s 'he had a large board set up in his Comptroller's room, with pegs and colours, showing what every member of the royal family was doing at any one time; really to avoid them all being, for example, in Birmingham on the same day. It didn't make much difference. But,' Sir Edward adds, 'when it came to devising a programme ahead, he was very imaginative.'

Whether he had a coherent strategy is more doubtful. 'You might ask whether all this rushing about is to any purpose', he told Basil Boothroyd in a 1971 memorandum he had 'dashed off'. 'Am I doing it to make it look as if I'm earning my keep, or has it any national value?'

Unable to answer his own question, he offered Boothroyd some further advice. 'I think you might like to discuss the changes in "style" and "function" since the last reign, and what – if any – influence I have had on them . . . What of the Commonwealth now that the political links had gone? Had [my] own travelling any point? Did greater personal knowledge of the Sovereign mean less mystery . . .?'

The first innovation in the 'style' of the monarchy which can be directly traced to Philip was the introduction of 'informal lunches' in May 1956. 'The new-style private luncheon,' according to the royal chronicler Brigadier Stanley Clark, was 'an opportunity of feeling the pulse of the nation by contact with ordinary men and women in all walks of life in the community.'

On 11 May 1956, the day ordained for Elizabeth's first democratic lunch, no ordinary women could be found. The ordinary men included Major-General D.C. Spry, Director-General of the Boy Scouts' International Bureau; Sir William Haley, the editor of *The Times*; the Right Reverend J. Montgomery, Bishop of London; Lord Aldenham, a banker; Sir Frank Lee, a civil servant; and to make up the numbers, two members of the household.

The net was widened a little five days later when the chairman of the National Coal Board ('once a miner at the coal-face') and the managing director of Wembley Stadium were invited to represent the workers. Lord David Cecil, Sir Oliver Franks, the Headmaster of Eton, the Vicar of St Martin-in-the-Fields and Sir Arthur Bliss (Master of the Queen's Musick) ensured that there were at least a few familiar faces around the table. Not until the lunch on 27 February 1957 did a woman make the guest list – the actress Flora Robson. She reported that the subjects discussed with the Queen included beards, hypnotism and blind people.

Courtiers today might describe the relationship between acorns and oak trees. In 1956, the acorns of royal populism had scarcely taken root.

One member of the household, especially, had no sympathy for Philip's modest efforts to open up the monarchy. He was Elizabeth's Press Secretary Commander Richard Colville, inherited from Bertie, who was the scion of an old court family.

Few people today have a good word for Colville; one of them is Sir Edward Ford. 'Richard Colville got frightful stick from the press, who saw him as a "Mr No". But he wasn't really. He took great trouble to see that they should all have equal access.' Most of Sir Edward's former colleagues disagree. 'I used to call him "Sunshine" Colville,' one recalls. 'He was a sort of anti-press officer. His view was really, "Don't tell the buggers anything."'

From one point of view Colville was an excellent Press Secretary for Elizabeth and Philip, because he was a ferocious guardian of the royal family's privacy – even Margaret's, of whom he surely disapproved. Thus on 11 April 1955, when he issued a press release announcing that Charles would be educated with other children, no mention was made of the school (Hill House in Knightsbridge). Journalists were simply warned to leave Charles and his future school chums in peace.

But Colville had no understanding of public relations. 'If there comes a time when the British monarchy ever needs a *real* public relations officer,' he said with an audible shudder in 1964, 'the institution of the monarchy in this country will be in a serious decline.' The decline had hardly begun in 1956, and so long as courtiers like Colville and Sir Michael Adeane held sway in the household, Philip's reformist ambitions were bound to be sabotaged.

As Elizabeth's consort, Philip's position in relation to the old guard ought perhaps to have been stronger. It appears, however, that their marriage went through a rocky patch during the early years of the reign. In many respects, their interests were incompatible. He was bored by horse-racing; she was bored by his after-dinner speeches. He liked flying; she did not. He liked his naval friends; she preferred her dogs. Whatever the reason, they were spending quite long periods apart – sometimes weeks on end. It was unusual even for a royal couple with separate public commitments, and especially so for a husband and wife with two young children.

Commander Colville's press team, already out of their depth with the Townsend affair, were quite unable to cope with the rumours that swirled around the royal marriage. One piece of gossip linked Philip to Hélène Cordet, a childhood friend who had become a British television star, hosting a show called *Café Continental*. There was, as Commander Colville failed to say, no truth to the story – even though Hélène Cordet encouraged more speculation in *Born Bewildered*, her aptly titled memoirs.

Perhaps most damaging was the incident in 1954, when Philip assisted Elizabeth at the opening of the Victorian State Parliament in Melbourne. As they entered the chamber, it seemed to spectators that the Queen had been crying. Had there been a row with Philip? Certainly he was in a foul mood. 'What the bloody hell's that doing here?' he said, pointing at the mace which was inside the chamber – unaware that in Australia, unlike Britain, this was the correct constitutional procedure.

It was against the background of these rumours, and his own mounting frustration with the court, that Philip set off in October 1956 on his world tour. The pretext for the tour was an invitation to open the Olympic Games in Melbourne (of all places). Perhaps to upset the household, perhaps to upset his wife, perhaps simply for the hell of it, Philip had grafted on to this straightforward task a far more ambitious itinerary: to visit, over a period of five months, 'the small and out-of-the-way communities and possessions of the Crown'.

In short, he was making this sacrifice for the Commonwealth –

and he wanted no one to be in any doubt that five months on board the newly commissioned royal yacht *Britannia* was indeed a sacrifice. On Christmas Day, floating somewhere between New Zealand and Cape Horn, he linked up by radio with Elizabeth's annual broadcast to her subjects. Apologising for his own absence from the family hearth, Philip's disembodied voice crackled through the ether: 'Without absent friends to remember today there would be no Commonwealth, for we can gain nothing without some loss. We are the solid facts beneath the words and phrases, we are the solid flesh-and-blood links which draw the Commonwealth under the Crown.'

There was more of the same when he finally returned from his personal odyssey in February 1957, and was invited by the Corporation of London to report on his discoveries. 'I, for one, am prepared to sacrifice a good deal if, by so doing, I can advance [the Commonwealth's] well-being by even a small degree. This Commonwealth, of which every member is so proud, came into existence because people made sacrifices and offered their service to it. Now it has been handed down to us and if we don't make sacrifices for it, we shall have nothing to hand on to those who will follow us and the world will have lost something of much greater value than just a grand conception.'

At least between making sacrifices for the Commonwealth, Philip managed to squeeze in some fun. 'Royal occasions usually conjure up visions of speeches, banquets, pomp, and ceremony,' his shipmates Viscount Cilcennin and Michael Parker began their official tour diary. 'This story is rather different. Zest for living, a sense of humour and a strict embargo on formality conspired to make this tour something quite unique.'

'There seems not to have been a dull moment,' the brochure continues. At Penang in Malaya, 'His Royal Highness was able to watch charming girl dentists practising on the teeth of Malayan infancy most efficiently.' There is 'an interesting note' on the Kuhakuka tribe in New Guinea – 'who seemed always to have an arrow strung ready for use, and would fight at the drop of a hat. They are obviously the Irish of New Guinea.'

At a ranch in central Australia, the royal party noticed some more 'natives' – cow hands, in fact. 'Aboriginals take to this work but are inclined to go "walk about" just when they are wanted,' the tour diary remarks briskly.

There was just time to drop in on the Olympics and make a brief stopover in New Zealand, before *Britannia* entered the Antarctic Ocean. The crew were issued with 'Red Nose Certificates' by Philip, which he had designed with the help of Edward Seago, the tour's official artist.

Another nautical jape was 'the great beard-growing contest' (Philip was judge), which came to an exciting climax as *Britannia* reached Gambia, on the west coast of Africa. Waiting to greet them were further natives ('the Gambians are mostly Moslems, happy, hardworking and loyal'), but Philip had more urgent business to consider: a crocodile shoot.

'The most interesting item in the day's bag was a piece of game shot four times through the head by Lieut.-Commander Parker, given the *coup de grâce* by Prince Philip, alarmingly coming to life again some time later with snarlings and threshings of the tail, and being finally dispatched with a knife by a local villager.'

All good things have to come to an end, and as the diarists remarked of the tour – 'to its extreme value in Commonwealth terms a Governor-General had testified months before. The most cursory glance at the diary, with its regular sequence of enthusiastic welcome, confirms him [*sic*].'

Despite the rumours about his marriage which had followed him around the world, it was Michael Parker, not Philip, who returned to a domestic crisis. Like Mrs Townsend, Mrs Parker had become tired of her husband's long absences on royal service, and sued him for divorce. The story broke in the papers shortly before the *Britannia* arrived in Gibraltar, by which time Parker had resigned from the household.

With the memory of the Townsend affair still vivid, it was assumed that Lilibet had pushed him. That was not in fact true. When the story broke, she had called *Britannia* by radio telephone and urged Parker to stay. Philip's visible fury in Gibraltar, where he was reunited with Elizabeth, was not directed at her but at the press, who had forced Parker's (voluntary) resignation.

If there had been muted criticism of the cost of the tour – rather more than the £5 Philip had recommended as a global travel budget to the students at Cardiff – before the Parker débâcle the publicity for the voyage had generally been favourable. It was now submerged beneath a flood of adverse headlines; in addition, Philip had lost his best friend and firmest ally at court. His isolation had never seemed more complete.

Yet Philip's situation was not as bleak as he feared. At home, as a thoroughly modern prince, his star was in the ascendant; the burghers of London, tucking into their lunch at the Mansion House, hung on his every word.

What had he learnt from the tour? Philip asked his audience. He had learnt that 'Australia is rushing ahead with tremendous confidence and business-like energy.' In New Zealand, 'again I was impressed by its prosperity'. As for the Antarctic: '. . . The great question now is whether the Antarctic can be exploited in any way . . . If anything is found, it may be difficult to get it out; but it certainly will not be impossible.' In the meantime, Philip wondered whether the Antarctic could be converted into 'a gigantic germ-free cold store where the periodic world food surpluses might be stored against lean years and famine.'

After the adults, it was the children's turn to hear of his travels: several thousand of them packed into the Royal Festival Hall, and millions more watched a special television programme. 'Forty minutes to get round the world,' Philip began his broadcast. 'Well, it may be a bit of a rush, it may leave you a little bit muddled, but I don't think it matters very much.'

Philip's position within the royal household had also taken a turn for the better. He and Elizabeth, having missed each other rather more than they cared to admit, no longer seemed to be drifting apart. Furthermore, a few months after his return a controversy erupted which gave Philip the necessary leverage to win his battle with the old guard at court. For in August 1957 it was unofficially declared that the monarchy was in crisis.

16

The Royal
Boredom Threshold

In August 1957 an obscure magazine called the *National and English Review*, which was soon to go out of business, published a special edition on the monarchy. The magazine's owner and editor was Lord Altrincham, better known as John Grigg, a young Conservative peer and a professional journalist. What Altrincham had to say in the edition's keynote article changed the course of royal history – or so it seemed at the time.

'The Queen's entourage,' Altrincham wrote, '– those who serve her from day to day, who accompany her when she travels and sit with her when she eats – are almost without exception people of the "tweedy" sort. Such people may be shrewd, broad-minded and thoroughly suitable for positions at court, but the same is true of many who are not "tweedy"; and the fact that the Queen's personal staff represents almost exclusively a single social type creates an unfortunate impression.'

In the tradition of a loyal subject, he blamed the courtiers for Elizabeth's deficiencies. Her speaking style, Altrincham said, was 'frankly "a pain in the neck"'. Like her mother, she appears to be unable to string even a few sentences together without a written text – a defect which is particularly regrettable when she can be seen by her audience . . . The personality conveyed by the utterances which are put into her mouth is that of a priggish schoolgirl, captain of the hockey team, a prefect, and a recent candidate for confirmation.'

Altrincham's argument was not especially original; the *Daily Mirror* had made the same point the year before, when it accused the court of being toffee-nosed. But Altrincham had the advantage of being an old Etonian, a peer and a Tory, which in the snobbish climate of Harold Macmillan's Britain guaranteed that his criticisms would receive serious attention.

Diehard royalists were predictably outraged. 'What a cowardly little bully you are!' Miss M.I. Greenwood wrote to him from Bournemouth. 'I can well imagine what a beastly specimen you were at your preparatory school – the sort who hit boys smaller and weaker than yourself, no doubt.'

Mr Burbridge of the League of Empire Loyalists – a collection of flag-waving patriots – struck Altrincham in the street following a television interview on the article. 'I suppose ninety-five per cent of the population of this country were disgusted and offended by what was written,' said Sir Laurence Dunne, the Chief Metropolitan Magistrate, finding Burbridge guilty of assault.

At the other extreme were would-be republicans who jumped on Altrincham's bandwagon, like the playwright and angry young man John Osborne (much to Altrincham's embarrassment, since he had cast himself neither as an angry young man, nor as a republican). 'My objection to the royal symbol is that it is dead,' Osborne told the readers of *Encounter* in October 1957. 'It is the gold filling in a mouthful of decay.'

Inside the royal household there was consternation. An unfortunate piece of timing meant that the League of Empire Loyalists received a message from Elizabeth, thanking them for their support, on the same day that Burbridge was being fined at Bow Street Magistrates' Court. Altrincham was prepared to give Elizabeth the benefit of the doubt over whether she had known of the assault.

Among the courtiers, Sir Edward Ford probably speaks for

many of his former colleagues when he dismisses Altrincham's central charge as irrelevant. 'He complained that she was surrounded by tweedy people from a single stratum of society, Well, most of the positions in this country *were* held by people who had a certain background and education. In a way, it was easier for both them and the Queen, if her staff were more or less the same kind.'

Ford's colleague in the Private Office, Martin Charteris, disagreed. Years later, in a debate at Eton College, he told Altrincham that he had rendered the monarchy a great service. According to Charteris, the controversy had forced the household to realise the need to open up the institution – even if that meant attracting still more criticism.

It was nevertheless a delayed reaction. The problem for courtiers like Charteris, who was tweedy (Eton and Sandhurst) but hardly stuffy (he liked rock-and-roll), was firstly that they were still in a minority within the household. Furthermore, Philip's office – the real focus for reform – operated virtually as an autonomous unit.

'You've got to remember that the court as a whole was not one amorphous mass of people doing the same thing,' says a former member of Philip's staff who joined in 1960. 'There was the Queen's household, there was Prince Philip's household, and so on. To a certain extent they were isolated. The concentration of thought and effort and interest was almost tunnel-vision on the royal you were working for. That could create a feeling that you weren't interested in other people's problems.'

Secondly, the evidence for popular disenchantment with the monarchy was insubstantial – even if reliance was placed on opinion polls, which, as has been seen, scarcely began to penetrate the complexity of attitudes to royalty.

Altrincham claimed on the basis of a poll in the *Daily Mail* about his article that 'most British people' supported him: '35 per cent of the whole population, and 40 per cent of men, agreed with me *entirely*, 13 per cent being undecided. In the age group 16 to 34 a clear majority agreed with me *entirely* (47 per cent against 39 per cent, with 14 per cent undecided). On the specific criticisms of the Court there was what could fairly be called a landslide. 55 per cent of the whole population supported me, as against 21 per cent, with 24 per cent undecided.'

And yet in 1964, seven years after Altrincham's piece, Mass Observation conducted its most ambitious study of public attitudes to royalty, based on two separate opinion polls. Published as a book with the provocative title *Long to reign over us?*, the answer to this question seems to have been 'yes'.

The pollsters reported that sixty per cent of those asked were 'entirely favourable' towards royalty, with only ten per cent 'entirely unfavourable'; seventy-eight per cent favoured a monarchy rather than a republic, with only sixteen per cent in the opposing camp.

Who were these republicans? There were at least twice as many men as women; at least three times as many in the sixteen-to-twenty-four age group as among the over-sixty-fives; nearly twice as many among working-class groups as in any upper- or middle-class group; nearly four times as many among Labour party sympathisers as among Conservative party sympathisers (the Liberals hedged their bets); and at least twice as many among non-churchgoers as among churchgoers. Most significant, though, was that there were not very many of them; and those who did own up to republicanism seemed curiously half-hearted.

'It's worth a try, anyway,' a painter's wife said. 'The USA are a few years ahead of us in every way. We might catch up with them.' A teacher said: 'A President and republic is more in line with the modern world. We must seem old-fashioned to other countries. Not that I've anything against royalty. It's just the idea that we should be more democratic.' A gas-fitter struck a rare note of exasperation. 'If we had a President we'd have someone doing something useful. What does the Queen do? I feel it's a waste of money.'

Mass Observation, once branded a subversive organisation and now a limited company, concluded that '. . . In the 1960s, there is widespread support in this country for the royal and monarchical system. Secondly, and perhaps more important, the royal idea appears as vital and compelling in the sense that it provides strong psychological securities. Its existence means safety, stability and continued national prestige; it is the "above party" focus for group identification; it implies unbroken leadership and a sense of final wisdom and authority; it means gaiety, excitement and the satisfactions of ceremonial pageantry; it is an important, and perhaps an increasingly important, symbol of national prestige.'

The fact that Mass Observation felt there was a market for such research illustrates how the monarchy had become a live issue in the 1960s, for the first time since Victoria retreated into mourning a century before. But in scale and intensity, there is no comparison between the republican controversy of the 1860s and the debate about royalty triggered by Altrincham's piece.

On the question of scale, criticism of the court in the 1960s was largely a pastime for the chattering classes. The *Daily Mirror*, which led the charge against toffee-nosed courtiers in the 1950s, had adjusted its position sufficiently by April 1965 to publish on its front page a full-scale picture of the royal family in the grounds of Windsor.

'April in England,' the caption read. 'Daffodil time. A time for a family to walk in a garden, laughing as they go. Sister Anne plants a flower on Edward's head. Mother laughs. Father watches. Brother Andrew looks impish. The happiest royal picture I've taken, says *Mirror* cameraman Freddie Reed.'

It was left to upmarket journalists to sound a discordant note, but their complaints about royalty seem frivolous compared with the serious republican case put by Victorian radicals like Sir Charles Dilke. In the Swinging Sixties, the central charge was that the Windsors had become a trifle dull. Margaret was more-or-less safely married to Snowdon, and the generation gap meant there was no other member of the family on the verge of a night-club phase.

'The English are getting bored with their monarchy,' Malcolm Muggeridge told Jack Parr on American television in 1964. '. . . The story goes on and on and the public realise it's been over-exposed. I think it's coming to an end.' Three years later the *Sunday Telegraph* claimed to detect 'a marked change in the public's attitude towards the Crown. Most people care much less than they did – particularly the young, many of whom regard the Queen as the arch-square. They are not *against* in the sense of being *for* a republic. They are quite simply indifferent.'

The significance of such criticism was not that it was especially accurate; the *Daily Mirror*, with a mainly working-class readership, certainly did not think so. Instead, it provided a context for the growing insecurity of the household in the 1960s, which ensured that Charteris and like-minded courtiers would eventually win the argument about reform.

Since the death of Edward VII in 1910, the Windsors had been an incurably anxious dynasty. Too many misfortunes had occurred, from the collapse of the international royal club to David's abdication, for them ever to regard the happy image reflected in Freddie Reed's camera lens as a true reflection of their inner selves. But in the 1960s several developments within the household brought their anxieties into sharper focus.

One of these was Philip's nagging sense that perhaps the critics were right after all; the royal family was becoming irrelevant. In February 1964 he gave what was, even by his standards, a tetchy performance at the Foreign Press Association in London (hailed the next day by the *Daily Mirror* as 'a splendidly frank speech').

Asked whether the monarchy had 'found its proper place in the Sixties', he snapped, 'Here we are in the Sixties. What am I supposed to say? Perhaps you would enlarge on the question.' The questioner went on: 'One sometimes hears criticism in the Press that the monarchy has not found its place, although it is, of course, playing a useful role in the country' – did the journalist perhaps think otherwise? – 'but has still not found the right approach to the problems of Britain today.'

'What you are implying is that we are rather old-fashioned,'

Philip replied. 'Well, it may easily be true: I do not know. One of the things about the monarchy and its place – and one of its great weaknesses in a sense – is that it has to be all things to all people. Of course it cannot do this when it comes to being all things to all people who are traditionalists and all things to all people who are iconoclasts. We therefore find ourselves in a position of compromise, and we might be kicked by both sides.'

If Philip betrayed a siege mentality, it was shared by a significant minority within the royal household. Not since the First World War, when George feared the red flag would be hoisted over Buckingham Palace, had there been so much concern about the threat to the monarchy from society. And as in 1917, the fear was disproportionate to the menace.

A courtier who joined the household in the early 1960s, after a successful career in the armed services, recalls being astonished by the social isolation of the court. 'There was this environment you went into, like going into a soap bubble; and a great unawareness of what was going on in the outside world.' His solution to the soap-bubble syndrome was to decline a grace-and-favour residence and rejoin reality in his own home at the end of each day.

Among such courtiers an atmosphere of near-panic developed, fed by the dire warnings of newspapers like the *Sunday Telegraph*, which predicted in 1967 that the monarchy could disappear in a 'vast collective yawn.' 'We had to change because we were getting so boring,' says one of Elizabeth's senior advisers from the period. 'We only did it just in time, though. I don't think we'd have survived if we hadn't done it.'

The alarm was increased by a belief that the monarchy was facing a financial crisis. 'We go into the red next year,' Philip told an American television audience in 1969. 'If nothing happens we may have to move into smaller premises . . . We had a small yacht which we had to sell, and I shall probably have to give up polo fairly soon – things like that.'

In the light of what is now known about the royal family's fabulous wealth – principally through the research of Philip Hall* –

it is worth asking how Elizabeth's husband arrived at this incredible conclusion. Firstly, he could believe what he said because, perhaps as an expression of their own insecurity, the royal family genuinely believed they were hard up.

Sir Edward Peacock, the Canadian banker who advised George, Bertie and Elizabeth on their investments, is credited by Elizabeth with having saved the family fortune. 'Otherwise we would have lost it all,' she is reported to have remarked melodramatically. 'She's mean,' observes one former courtier, when asked to name Elizabeth's faults; and even with her racehorses, her most conspicuous personal extravagance, she is known to make waspish comments to her trainers about spending 'my' money.

Secondly, there was a distinction between the royal family's private wealth and the allocation for the monarchy's public duties from the civil list. It was an unclear distinction, especially in the mind of the beneficiaries, as Philip's breezy reference to yachts and polo ponies illustrates. But strictly in relation to the civil list, it was true that by the late 1960s the royal budget was being eroded by inflation.

Worried about their 'irrelevance', preparing to renegotiate the civil list, the court wished to demonstrate that the monarchy was offering value for money: which is why Commander Colville's retirement from the press office in February 1968 was so important. Two years before, Philip had signalled his rejection of Colville's methods when he dispensed with the Press Secretary's services during a tour of the United States in 1966, in favour of an American PR man, Henry Rogers (whose other clients included Rita Hayworth and Brigitte Bardot).

Now, with Colville's departure, Philip already had his successor groomed. He was William Heseltine, a thirty-four-year-old Australian who had joined the press office as Colville's deputy in 1966 – or, rather, been imposed on the cantankerous Commander.

For someone who denied he was in the business of public relations, Heseltine was extremely knowledgeable about the subject. In the late 1950s he had worked as Private Secretary to the Australian Prime Minister (and sycophantic royalist) Sir Robert

Menzies, where he first came to Philip's attention while handling press relations for a royal tour. From 1962 to 1964 Heseltine was a national organiser for the Australian Liberal Party, a job which demanded constant liaison with the country's media organisations. He was, in short, both 'an absolutely brilliant press officer', in the words of an admiring former colleague, and a rather more sophisticated operator than Colville.

The question remains: were Philip, Heseltine and the reform party at court preparing the monarchy for what, in sales jargon, would be called a relaunch? 'The royal family – or at any rate their advisers – had not been very clever at evaluating the market place,' a former courtier says of this period: by his account, they seized the opportunity created by Colville's departure to do some market research. Another courtier, more attuned to the language of Bagehot, claims that 'as a deliberate policy, we decided to let light in on the mystery.'

Courtiers today resist such a glib description – and it is probably true that the 'relaunch' of the monarchy at the end of the 1960s owed more to contingency than it appeared in retrospect. One event in particular concentrated the courtiers' minds: the fact that in 1969 Charles would celebrate his twenty-first birthday.

Ten years before, to Charles's acute embarrassment, Elizabeth had declared to an audience at Cardiff Arms Park that she was creating her eldest son Prince of Wales, and that, 'when he is grown up, I will present him to you at Caernarvon'. It was scheduled to be the first investiture of a Prince of Wales since David's ordeal in 1911; and by 1969 the dreaded moment (for Charles at least), could be postponed no longer.

If the monarchy was not about to be relaunched, there is no doubt that Charles was in for some serious packaging. His household at this time was effectively a one-man show, run by his equerry (and later private secretary) David Checketts. A former RAF officer, Checketts had been seconded to Charles from Philip's staff in 1966 to look after Charles during a school exchange in Australia. There, Checketts displayed a sophisticated grasp of how to deal with the press, as might be expected of someone who was also a non-executive director of the PR firm Neilson, McCarthy. In the build-up to the investiture, Checketts was not prepared to let the diffident Charles hide his light under a bushel.

On his initiative, Charles was interviewed in March 1969 by the radio broadcaster (and fellow Neilson, McCarthy director) Jack de Manio. Charles's answers to the prearranged questions were not exactly hard-hitting. Referring to the threatened protests against his investiture by Welsh nationalists, he said: 'As long as I don't get covered too much in egg and tomato I'll be all right.' But as a public relations exercise, this early venture could not be faulted.

From Philip and Heseltine's point of view, supported by reform-minded courtiers like Charteris, Charles's investiture was a golden opportunity to dispel the atmosphere of dullness and irrelevance which had enveloped the royal family. They would show that the monarchy could still mount a spectacular pageant. Despite criticism of the investiture's expense, they would also demonstrate that the royal family gave value for money – whatever that meant.

Elizabeth's opinion on the subject of reform was, as ever, opaque. One of her senior courtiers in the Sixties describes her as possessing 'very good negative judgement', in the sense that she could tell if something was wrong. As an example, he tells the story of a message the Private Office received the morning after Elizabeth had been enjoying one of her favourite programmes, *The Black and White Minstrel Show*.

'"Why could you hear the dancers clicking their fingers when they were all wearing gloves?" she wanted to know. So a letter was sent to the BBC and the producer was happy to explain to her the complexities of pre-recorded sound.'

She was less good at taking the initiative. The same courtier cites another example, the Aberfan disaster of 1966, in which more than a hundred people, most of them children, were killed when a slag heap collapsed. Elizabeth needed to be prodded by her advisers to visit the scene – not because she was callous, the courtier explains, but because she lacked imagination.

On the other hand, she was less inclined by the late 1960s to treat as gospel the word of older courtiers like Sir Michael Adeane, who had served her father. After fifteen years on the throne, she felt she knew the ropes; and unlike the 1950s, when Philip's advice was sometimes overruled, she was more inclined to listen to her husband – especially as Philip seemed so sure of what he was trying to achieve.

Heseltine's account of the project which formed in Philip's head, and perhaps less distinctly in Elizabeth's, was provided in an article he wrote for the *Listener* in 1986, by which date he had become the Queen's Private Secretary. He said that when the news of Charles's impending investiture was first released in 1968, the Buckingham Palace press office received 'an unsolicited rush of requests from the media for facilities to prepare features about the young Prince.

'. . . The Queen and Prince Philip decided that a biography of such a young man, who had not even completed his formal education, was not likely to be a very interesting one. They also felt that an enterprise initiated by themselves was likely to be a more fruitful one than uncoordinated responses to the various suggestions coming from the media.

'So the idea took shape,' Heseltine said, 'of a television film designed to show something of the role for which the heir to the Throne was being educated and prepared – shown ultimately to a surprised audience of unprecedented millions as *Royal Family.*'

It sounded so straightforward. But in choosing to take control of their public image through the uniquely powerful medium of television, the royal family were entering uncharted waters. A quarter of a century later, they have yet to reach a safe harbour.

17

Royal Family, The Film of the Myth

Television had traditionally been kind to the Windsors. Until *Royal Family*, it had also presented them in an utterly traditional fashion.

The first live broadcast of a royal pageant was Elizabeth's coronation in June 1953. There were the usual objections from the clergy about people watching the service with their hats on, probably in pubs, and the Duke of Norfolk as Earl Marshal initially banned the television cameras from the ceremony. He was soon overruled after a public outcry and a face-saving statement by the BBC that they had not explained to the Duke – who probably did not own a television – just how discreet the cameras would be.

The broadcast was a triumph: for the television retail trade, which sold over a million new sets before the service; for the BBC, which estimated that over half the population watched the coronation; and above all for Richard Dimbleby, who confirmed his status as the supreme royal commentator of the post-war era.

Dimbleby is widely credited with bringing royalty closer to the people, but this was only true in a technological sense. Rhetorically, he did more than anyone to emphasis the remoteness of royalty, starting with the coronation. 'The Queen now wears a robe that may well be descended from the cloaks of the Byzantine emperors,' he informed viewers in hushed tones as Elizabeth processed through Westminster Abbey. Soon she would be donning the 'bracelets of sincerity and wisdom' which had been kindly presented to her by the Commonwealth.

As a house style, Dimbleby's commentary was well adapted in a deferential age to such pageants as Margaret's wedding to Snowdon in 1960 (a pity that the groom was merely a photographer) and the wedding of Princess Alexandra to Angus Ogilvy three years later. But it was completely unsuited to the royal family's purpose in 1969, which was to humanise themselves through the medium of television.

For Dimbleby's sake it was perhaps a blessing that he died of cancer in 1965. He remained unknighted for his considerable services to the monarchy. Instead, Elizabeth sent some bottles of champagne to his hospital death-bed.

In theory, the main event in 1969 was Charles's investiture in July; and in its own right the investiture marked a major landmark in the staging of royal pageantry for television. Until then, the demands of television had been subordinate to the dictates of all those time-hallowed rituals, many of which had been invented by Lord Esher and his colleagues at the turn of the century. Lord Snowdon, who as Constable of Caernarvon Castle devised the ceremony, reversed the relationship.

'I was designing the investiture for television, because we had an audience of 500 million,' he says. 'If you look at the 1911 investiture [of David] it was designed for the elite few, and it was in a tent, and nobody could see anything. Because I'm a photographer, I was designing it for cameras.'

To this end, Snowdon was locked in combat with the Garter King of Arms, Sir Anthony Wagner, who wanted to smother the castle with obscure heraldic banners and whose name – or something very similar – was often taken in vain by the castle Constable.

Snowdon also resorted to what he calls 'legitimate romantic cheating' to create the illusion of a majestic pageant. 'There was an area on the south side of the castle which was going to be filled with cars on the day of the investiture. So I asked the BBC if they could film it early one morning and cut the sequence into the live broadcast.'

The result was a spectacle which seemed quite different to television viewers than to the live audience. In Caernarvon, the investiture was a slightly dispiriting and occasionally alarming affair. After bomb threats from Welsh nationalists, who wanted to sabotage the ceremony, the crowds there were far smaller than had been expected. One reporter described them as only being of 'third division football club' proportions.

On television, by contrast, millions of viewers around the world were transfixed by the spectacle Snowdon and his team had created. According to the television critic Milton Shulman, 'in the recognition of the medium as something that has to be catered for with special verve, imagination and concern, [the investiture] has set a precedent which is bound to change the shape and atmosphere of all state occasions that are transmitted on TV in future.'

Unfortunately for Snowdon, his production was overshadowed in the public mind by Richard Cawston's film *Royal Family*, broadcast just before the investiture. Twenty-two million people watched the first broadcast on the BBC; a further fifteen million watched the repeat the following week on ITV; approximately a hundred and fifty television companies around the world bought the transmission rights. *Royal Family* was a sensation. It was not, however, quite the film it seemed to be.

In the first place, Richard Cawston did not receive as much help as he might have wished from the royal family. Cawston was an experienced documentary film-maker, who had never worked on royal broadcasts before. From the royal family's point of view that was an advantage, because of the project's unusual nature. Less advantageous from Cawston's point of view was their initial unwillingness to let him film them.

In their own minds, the royal family and the courtiers were quite clear what the film was supposed to achieve. 'To a certain extent that film was a PR exercise,' says a former member of the household who appeared in *Royal Family*. 'We were saying, "Hey fellers, this is the Queen. This is a year in the life of the Queen. And it isn't all gilt coaches and Rolls Royces, balls and banquets and champagne. It's bloody hard work, and this film reveals what sort of hard work it is."'

When it came to letting Cawston fulfil his brief, they were rather less clear-sighted. 'Get away from the Queen with your bloody cameras!' Philip is supposed to have shouted at Cawston, during the justly famous Balmoral barbecue scene.

Cawston's sometimes fractious relationship with the 'cast' during the first few months of filming did not help when he tried to draft a shooting script. His original plan was to produce a thematic film essay, taking different aspects of Elizabeth's work in turn; but it soon became clear that this rather worthy scheme was unfeasible, mainly because of the arbitrary nature of the royal schedule.

Instead, on the advice of his friend Antony Jay, who later wrote the commentary, Cawston changed tack after about three months and decided to film a simple, chronological diary of the royal family's year. There was some hurried filming in the Buckingham Palace gardens to signify 'summer' – it was now early autumn – and the production at last acquired a sense of direction.

The magisterial quality of *Royal Family* was the result of Cawston's skill in the cutting room and Jay's complementary skill as a scriptwriter: in other words, as a 'live' documentary it was essentially improvised. There is a moment when Elizabeth and a head of state are being ferried by carriage into Windsor Castle which typified their approach.

'This is not the panoply of power,' the commentary (read by Michael Flanders) declares: 'but while the Queen occupies the highest office of state, no one else can. While she is head of the law, no politician can take over the courts. While she is head of state, no generals can take over the government . . . Monarchy does not lie in the power it gives to the sovereign, but in the power it denies to anyone else.'

The passage appears to have been lifted from the pages of Bagehot. In fact, it was rewritten by Jay from an original conversation with Roger Carey, a member of the BBC's administrative staff, who had once heard his historian father say something similar. Such is the evolution of British constitutional theory.

In any case, the millions who watched the film were not interested in constitutional theory; they were interested in seeing Elizabeth and her family, live, close-up and for as long as possible. At this level, Cawston did not disappoint them.

The film contains many classic moments of royal television history. There is the scene where the incoming American ambassador Walter Annenberg is shown presenting his credentials to Elizabeth, and becoming completely tongue-tied in the presence of majesty. Have you moved into your residence? she asks him, by way of small talk (it was being redecorated). 'We're in the embassy residence, subject of course to some of the discomfiture as the result of a need for elements of refurbishing rehabilitation,' he replies. Elizabeth draws on years of experience to keep a straight face.

There is the scene where Elizabeth and Philip discuss 'world problems' with Annenberg's boss, President Nixon. 'The world problems are so complex, aren't they now,' Elizabeth tells him. 'You know, I was thinking how really much more complex they are than when we last met in 1957,' Nixon says. 'Oh yes, you can hardly recognise you're in the same place,' Philip chips in.

There is Charles accidentally snapping a cello string into Edward's face (a moment Philip originally wanted to censor). There is Philip sharing a polo joke with a Chilean general. There is Anne learning French at a West End language school (a 'craft skill for royalty').

But if there is a defining scene in the film, it is the barbecue in the grounds of Balmoral. The servants have been banished, perhaps to return afterwards to wash the dishes, and the royal family have been left, as it were, *en famille*.

'An absolute, total, guaranteed failure,' Anne predicts, looking at the steaks her father is cooking. 'Oily,' Elizabeth says with a grimace, dipping her finger into Charles's salad dressing. 'The salad is ready,' she says to Philip, who is in charge of the cooking. 'Good,' says Philip, staring at a half-cooked steak. 'This, as you see, isn't.'

The barbecue is subliminally important because it introduces the film's main subject: not Elizabeth, but as the title suggests, the royal family. Neither the script nor the pictures attempts to distinguish between the private life of the Windsors and their public functions. Instead, the distinction is consciously blurred.

'Some monarchs are remembered, some – a few – are best forgotten,' the commentary says over shots of Charles fishing in the River Dee. 'But at least he will have one thousand years of family experience to call on.'

At Christmas, the extended dynasty gathers at Windsor: we see the Ogilvies and the Kents arrive at the private entrance, to be greeted by a courtier (Patrick Plunket) in household uniform. It is 'a family reunion . . . but it also serves as an office party. Throughout the year all branches of the family in their different ways have been working at the family business. By the sort of accident that happens in families, they're different enough in age and inclination to reflect a wider variety of interest than a single person ever could. They come from different generations, they move in different worlds.'

So, the commentary explains, the Duke of Kent is a professional soldier, his wife takes an interest in her native Yorkshire, Princess Alexandra is involved with nursing, Angus Ogilvy is in business, and the Snowdons . . . the Snowdons are the 'artistic' ones in the family.

In a business, of course, it helps if the core partners get along; and the film works very hard to present an image of Elizabeth and Philip's ménage as an idyllic and 'typical' family. Immediately after Christmas, the Windsors move to Sandringham – 'the most private of all the royal family's homes'. Philip paints, Edward throws snowballs, and Elizabeth drives

Anne, Edward and Andrew in her Land Rover (at a breakneck speed) to see the puppies in her kennels. In the evening they settle down with the Queen Mother to watch television around the fireplace (over which hangs, unseen by the camera, the elder Bertie's tapestry of the Emperor Constantine).

In his same *Evening Standard* column Milton Shulman remarked of Cawston's film that 'it is fortunate that at this moment of time we have a royal family that fits in so splendidly with a public relations man's dream.'

Yet even in 1969 the dream royal family was a myth, sharply at variance with reality. The person who did more than anyone to foster the myth was seen in Cawston's film as she would have wished; joining her grandchildren round the Sandringham hearth for a cosy evening of telly and chat. She was Elizabeth's mother.

'As I crossed the lawn, I remember there came over me an eerie feeling that someone was watching me. It made me look up towards the house. Then it was I saw a face at the window, and for the first time I met that long, cool stare I was later to come to know so well.'

The face at the window was the elder Elizabeth's and the occasion was Crawfie's interview in 1932 at the Scottish home of Lord and Lady Elgin for the position of governess to the little princesses.

During the past decade, Elizabeth had made several calculations of her own about her place in the royal family. The first was that, on balance, it was worth marrying Bertie; but the balance had indeed been finely calculated.

When Bertie fell in love with Elizabeth, on 20 May 1920 at a ball held by Lord and Lady Farquhar in Grosvenor Square, she was the youngest daughter of the Earl of Strathmore, handsome, clever and rich, with the pick of the eligible men-about-town at her feet.

Bertie, on the other hand, was at this period prone to 'extreme moodiness' and 'disconcertingly nervous', according to one of Queen Mary's biographers, Anne Edwards. '. . . He had a serious speech impediment and numerous twitches, sometimes blinking his eyes with too much frequency and unable to control the muscles around his mouth. In addition, his drinking problem, though thought to be kept secret, had grown worse.'

Over the next two years Bertie proposed to Elizabeth on several occasions; each time she refused him.

In August 1921 Bertie's mother descended on the Strathmore family seat of Glamis Castle for one of her tours of inspection, which included on this occasion an inspection of the 'Strathmore girl'. Elizabeth was 'the one girl who could make Bertie happy,' Mary told Lady Airlie. 'I shall say nothing to either of them. Mothers should never meddle in their children's love affairs.'

She did not mean it. Shortly after this encounter Bertie's Equerry, Major James Stuart – who, it seems, also had a crush on Elizabeth – abruptly resigned his appointment to seek his fortune in the oil fields of Oklahoma. The coast was clear for Bertie.

Still Elizabeth resisted. In July 1922, almost a year after Mary had given her seal of approval, Bertie sought out the advice of an older man, the Conservative MP J.C.C. Davidson. According to Davidson, who scarcely knew Bertie (the interview was arranged by Bertie's Equerry Louis Greig), 'He [Bertie] seemed to have reached a crisis in his life, and wanted someone to whom he could unburden himself without reserve . . . Then out it came. He declared that he was desperately in love, but that he was in despair for it seemed quite certain that he had lost the only woman he would ever marry.'

Davidson gave Bertie some avuncular advice, along the lines of pulling himself together and having another shot. He also suggested Bertie might think about proposing in person. Up to this point, Bertie confessed, he had been using an emissary to pop the question, on the grounds that it was beneath the dignity of a prince to be rejected.

Elizabeth, too, was seeking advice a few months later from Lady Airlie. What was she to do? she asked the older woman in some distress, having repelled Bertie's most recent (direct) advances. Lady Airlie, knowing how badly George and Mary wished to see Bertie married to the girl, told Elizabeth about her own marriage. At first it had been miserable, 'resulting from the

clash of undisciplined personalities'; but in time she and David
Airlie had fallen deeply in love with each other – a love cut short
by his death in the Boer War.

Shortly after this meeting with Lady Airlie, Bertie made one
last, desperate proposal to Elizabeth in the garden of the
Strathmore country home in Hertfordshire. To his relief and perhaps astonishment, she accepted him.

'I was so startled and almost fell out of bed when I read the
Court Circular,' 'Chips' Channon wrote in his diary. In common
with many society gossips, he assumed Elizabeth had been destined for Bertie's elder brother David. 'He [Bertie] is the luckiest
of men, and there's not a man in England today who doesn't
envy him. The clubs are in gloom.'

Having at last joined the royal family, Elizabeth's next decision
was to make something of her new role as Duchess of York. Her
own natural vivacity, her ease in public situations – so different
from Bertie – would in any case have marked her out as a royal
star in the 1920s. But what added to her royal distinction was the
fact that her and Bertie's marriage was ultimately a happy one, as
Lady Airlie had predicted.

None of Bertie's siblings in the 1920s had achieved this bliss-
ful state, if David's illicit liaison with Mrs Dudley Ward is
discounted. Apart from David and Bertie, there were three other
boys and a girl produced by George and Mary. The youngest
boy, John, born in 1905, was an epileptic who lived with his
nurse at Wood Farm on the Sandringham estate, and was never
seen in public. He died suddenly in 1919 after a convulsive fit.
That left Bertie's surviving younger brothers Harry and George,
and his younger sister Mary.

Harry, created Duke of Gloucester in 1928, was a sad case;
even within the royal family he was known as 'poor Harry', on
account of his squeaky voice, his 'tiresome, nervous habit' of burst-
ing into tears, and his unerring instinct for the *faux pas*. 'Well, if
she's really dead, we can all go home,' he once exclaimed at a performance of *Tosca*, as Maria Callas plunged over the battlements.

A simple soldier, Harry lacked imagination in his pursuit of women. On safari in Kenya with David in 1928, he followed his elder brother's example of the previous night and jumped into bed with their host's wife, Mrs Mansfield Markham. Harry, unlike David, must have promised Beryl Markham more than he could deliver, because for the rest of her life she received an annuity from the royal family.

Harry was eventually taken in hand by the sensible Alice Montagu-Douglas-Scott, daughter of the Duke of Buccleuch, but he never really grew up. In his dotage, a favourite recreation was watching children's television programmes. He once kept his cousin King Olav of Norway waiting in the hall while he finished an episode of *Popeye*.

The younger George, who later married Marina of Greece, was much the most intelligent of George and Mary's children, and his mother's favourite; but in the late 1920s and early 1930s, he was playing very fast and loose. On one occasion he was arrested by police at the Nut House night-club in the company of a known homosexual, and kept in the cells until his identity was discovered. There were also rumours circulated by Randolph Churchill – not the most reliable witness – that George had written letters to a young man in Paris, and that David had paid a large sum on his brother's behalf for their recovery.*

David's other worry was George's cocaine addiction. In 1929 he was incarcerated at Fort Belvedere for several months under David and Freda Dudley Ward's scrutiny, while he attempted to kick the habit – successfully, it seems.* Incredibly, neither the elder George nor Mary had any inkling of the problem.

The younger Mary seemed destined to be the saddest of all George and Mary's children. By the end of the First World War, when she was twenty-two, she had been cast for the role of spinster companion to her parents. 'I don't feel that she is happy but she never complains,' David told Lady Airlie in 1919. 'The trouble is that she is far too unselfish and conscientious.' Once, she refused to make up a tennis foursome with Bertie and his equerries, on the grounds that she would not have time to change out of her plimsolls in time for tea with her parents.

In 1921, to everyone's surprise, she was engaged to marry Viscount Lascelles, who was fifteen years her senior, extremely rich, and heir to the earldom of Harewood and a magnificent stately home in Yorkshire. Opinion about whether the marriage was happy is divided. There were two children, and the elder Mary certainly enjoyed the company of her new son-in-law, whose house offered a convenient base for her raids on the antique shops of Harrogate. But there were rumours that Harewood mistreated his wife; and after Harewood's death in 1947 Chips Channon was among those who felt the countess blossomed as a widow.

The contrast with Bertie and Elizabeth's idyllic ménage could hardly have been more stark – especially after Lilibet arrived in 1926, to be followed four years later by Margaret Rose (as she was christened). It was here that Elizabeth made her second most important career decision, the first having been to marry Bertie.

If she and Bertie were to set an example of domestic bliss among their royal peers, Elizabeth reasoned, they should at least do the job properly. So it was that over the next quarter of a century, through a series of picture books and privileged biographies, Elizabeth nurtured the myth of a perfect family; until the point when Cawston's cameras transferred the myth to the far more powerful medium of television.

The story begins with *The Story of Princess Elizabeth, told with the sanction of her parents* written by Anne Ring, a former member of the Duchess of York's staff. Published in 1930, it was an instant bestseller with a public which had been starved of such material since the appearance of Victoria's Balmoral diary half a century before.

At three months old, Miss Ring revealed, 'already Princess Elizabeth was filled with a sense of comfort and well-being and serene courage – she was going forward'. Four months later, after a visit to her Strathmore grandparents, 'she has returned, there is no doubt about it – a Princess. She was sitting up by herself in the middle of the huge Chesterfield, like a white fluff of thistle-down, with her dainty Columbine skirts arranged around her – a queen upon her throne.'

'Some stories of Princess Margaret' were added by Miss Ring for a new edition in 1933 – and what a little scamp *she* was. '"Come and say good-night," says her Mother, and Princess Margaret comes running, running, and, in the generous way she has, lays the whole of a soft arm in the hand of a visitor – but it rests there hardly a second, for she is off again, running, running, and as she runs she falls, and Princess Elizabeth flies to pick her up and protect her, but Margaret doesn't cry; for her Life is real, Life is earnest, and far too full for tears.'

Meanwhile Lady Cynthia Asquith had been concocting *The Married Life of the Duchess of York, written and published with the personal approval of Her Royal Highness*; regularly updated, it mutated into *The Family Life of Queen Elizabeth*, etc, etc.

'How much the Duchess must delight in having a pretty daughter [Lilibet] to dress,' Lady Cynthia enthused; 'and what loving care goes to choosing the petalled frocks of palest pink, primrose yellow and speedwell blue.' In fact the task of dressing the little princesses was delegated to their nurse, 'Lala', previously responsible for the care of the epileptic Prince John.

In 1940, 'by authority of Her Majesty the Queen', the photographer Lisa Sheridan captured *Our Princesses at Home* – even though their residence at Windsor was supposed to be a military secret. 'What a good sister Princess Elizabeth is! When the princesses are playing a floor-game, the older sister consults the younger as to which hassock she would prefer. For she knows that to her more childish mind such matters are still of paramount importance.'

Our Princesses in 1942 and *Princess Elizabeth at Home* (1944) were to follow from 'Studio Lisa'; and then in 1954 we skip a generation for *Playtime at Royal Lodge*, published 'by permission of Her Majesty Queen Elizabeth the Queen Mother'.

'Prince Charles is seated in the same wheelbarrow with which I photographed Princess Margaret when she was also five years old,' Miss Sheridan notes in the text. Soon it is time for Charles and Anne to have an afternoon nap. 'The Queen Mother gathers her grandchildren beside her on one of the large chairs on the terrace. Before she tucks them down Prince Charles asks: "Tell us a story, Granny, about how Mummy and Margot played in this garden when they were little girls." "It was just over there . . ." the Queen Mother begins, and she tells the story that the children are never tired of hearing. The Queen Mother tells the children how their mother used to rest – just in that same place and just in the same way.'

With *Playtime at Royal Lodge*, the elder Elizabeth's work as a mythmaker was almost complete. Other royal writers, taking their cue from these 'authorised' versions, invented their own stories about the idyllic Windsor nest. Charles is 'a real little boy,' Dorothy Laird proclaimed in 1955 (she was later to write an approved biography of the Queen Mother). 'Charles loves knockabout games, running races and 'boxing' matches with his father . . . He is always ready for a good old rough and tumble.'

Anne, on the other hand, was 'becoming more doll-minded . . . Anne is very much a little girl, and greatly approves of pretty clothes and small pieces of jewellery she is allowed to wear on special occasions.'

Studio Lisa was invited back for an encore in 1962 when, 'with the authority of Her Majesty the Queen', she booked *A Day with Prince Andrew* – then two years old. 'You will see the boyish figure in one fascinating position after another,' Miss Sheridan announced in the introduction: 'his small shape delightfully poised and self-assured. One may judge from such a multitude of easy attitudes how the mind exercising this sturdy control is equally harmonious.'

The royal family, inspired by the Queen Mother, had thus played a significant part in creating their own myth for television – a myth already undermined by the Townsend affair and the rumours that surrounded Elizabeth and Philip's marriage in the early 1950s. But in the years that followed *Royal Family*, it was not television that destroyed the myth, for in general, television remained kind to the Windsors.

This was firstly because no film-maker since Cawston – despite his initial difficulties – has ever since been granted such privileged access to royalty. Several television programmes have been sold as intimate documentaries, notably ITN's 1985 portrait of Charles and Diana; but none has come as close as Cawston to the underdone barbecue steaks.

'I don't think any of us thought, "Let's update this by the month or by the year,"' says one courtier involved in *Royal Family*. 'The film wasn't creating something that the monarchy had to live by. It wasn't a soap opera, we weren't having to write the series for next week. It was a factual documentary of what was happening, not what was going to happen, or what should happen.'

The official sequel to Cawston's film was *Elizabeth R*, commissioned from the BBC to mark the fortieth anniversary of the reign in 1992. As the title suggests, however, the family scarcely feature in this later project, which was perhaps fortunate given the misery they were poised to inflict on each other and Elizabeth.

Meanwhile, in covering the pageants of Windsor monarchy during the 1970s and 1980s, television reverted to the tradition established by Richard Dimbleby. The actor Tom Fleming succeeded Dimbleby as the BBC's chief television commentator at these occasions, and he remained faithful to Dimbleby's spirit.

At the wedding of Charles and Diana, Fleming recalls in *The BBC Book of Royal Memories*, he treasured 'the medieval cheers that came from the crowds outside as the Archbishop pronounced them man and wife . . . the solicitous glances of The Queen Mother as the granddaughter of one of her closest friends knelt, veiled, beside her own grandson; the curtsy to Her Majesty The Queen, as the bride passed her Sovereign for the first time as Her Royal Highness The Princess of Wales.'

Fleming's counterpart on ITV, Alastair Burnet, took pride in covering the same event as a news story. But it was to Burnet and the cameras of ITN that Charles and Diana turned in 1985 for a privileged interview when they wished to dispel the rumours – accurate, it later transpired – that their marriage was in trouble.

The hostage to fortune presented by *Royal Family* was not the medium of television, but the message of the film. Cawston was not simply building on the myth of an ideal family, which would have been dangerous enough from the Windsors' point of view. He was also taking one stage further the misconception that, deep down, these people were just like us.

In the past, the perception had depended on almost complete ignorance of how the Windsors really lived, an ignorance paradoxically reinforced by the semi-fictional authorised glimpses of writers like Anne Ring and Lady Cynthia Asquith. In *Royal Family*, the Windsors appeared for the first time as people in their own right. Decorating the Christmas tree (Anne was bossy with Edward), telling jokes across the dinner table (Elizabeth told a good one about a gorilla), they behaved like ordinary, or at least archetypal people. Within a few years, however, having exposed themselves to such scrutiny, it became apparent that their normality was only a surface veneer. Underneath, they were emphatically not like us.

Several months after the broadcast, Philip appeared on the American television programme *Meet the Press*. Asked whether *Royal Family* had not stripped away too much of the monarchy's mystery, Philip replied: 'I think it's quite wrong that there should be a sense of remoteness, or majesty. I mean, this is in the minds of the spectator . . . I think if people see whatever head of state as individuals, as people, I think it makes it much easier for them to accept the system, or feel part of the system.'

It is easy with hindsight to accuse the royal family of lowering the drawbridge through which charged a new breed of predatory royal reporter, known collectively as the ratpack. The truth, however, is more complex. In 1969 Philip's remarks referred to the relatively benign medium of television. The threat to the royal family's hitherto impregnable sanctuary came from Fleet Street, as it had done during the 1950s when popular newspapers like the *Daily Mirror* tired of the stuffy 'new Elizabethan' courtiers. But it was almost a decade after Cawston's film before the Fleet Street ratpack became significant figures in the royal cavalcade.

If the origins of the ratpack are more obscure than at first appears, so too was the way in which they were perceived. To the royal family, they came to seem a permanent enemy — rough beasts slouching towards the gates of Balmoral and Sandringham. The ratpack's self-image was understandably more favourable; they saw themselves, sincerely in some cases, as the monarchy's most loyal supporters. And in the gulf between these two perceptions lay tears, tantrums and several thousand royal 'exclusives'.

18

Enter the Ratpack

The ratpack's predecessors were the old-style court correspondents, whose heyday was the 1950s. 'Relations with the press at that time were remarkably smooth,' Sir Edward Ford remembers. 'We had Mutt and Jeff, as we used to call them. One represented the Press Association and one represented Reuters. They used to come in every morning and see the Press Secretary and be told what was going on and what the Queen was going to wear if she was doing a visit. And they'd go off and make their notes and then they'd be there when the Queen arrived.'

A former colleague of Commander Colville recalls 'a tremendous two-way arrangement' with the court correspondents. 'We helped them absolutely as much as we could, and they in turn were reliable and helpful on their side.'

This happy state of affairs only began to change very gradually in the aftermath of *Royal Family*. During the early 1970s, the same courtier says, 'We felt it was better to offer the press something, rather than have the royal family snooped on and chased when they didn't want to be. I think the hopeful idea was that if a certain amount of leeway was given when the royal family didn't mind it, then they'd be left in peace when they really wanted to be alone – and for a very long time this happened.

Even the tabloids accepted that places like Balmoral and Sandringham were out of bounds.'

The journalist James Whitaker, who regards himself as the original rat in the ratpack, agreed with this judgement in a 1988 interview. Looking back on this period, he told *Majesty* magazine that 'there were weeks on end at Balmoral, in the summer and autumn, and Sandringham, after Christmas, when there would be no press around at all and the Queen and her family enjoyed a well-earned rest. But in those early days there were few pressures from newspaper editors to produce a story "come what may".'

The pressures arose during the 1970s partly because of a simple demographic fact. Charles, Anne and latterly Andrew all reached maturity, and for the first time since Margaret's well-concealed romance with Tony Armstrong-Jones in the late 1950s there were members of the royal family with interesting love lives.

Anne's marriage to Mark Phillips in November 1973 was poised, in terms of newspaper coverage, between the age of the court correspondents and that of the ratpack. The wedding itself, held in Westminster Abbey, was described with becoming deference and gravity. The honeymoon, on the other hand, presented journalists with irresistible copy due to Captain Phillips's various misfortunes.

Pursued by the world's press corps, Anne and Mark's holiday started badly in Ecuador when a tear-gas grenade exploded near the royal car. Ecuadorean officials explained reassuringly that it had been 'accidentally dropped' by one of the soldiers assigned to protect them from local terrorists. Shortly afterwards, suffering either from culture shock or the effects of Ecuadorean cuisine, Mark succumbed to a violent stomach upset. Anne spent the next day enjoying her honeymoon alone, as best she could.

Mark was back on his feet just in time for the next leg of the tour, Jamaica. Swimming off the coast of Montserrat, he was 'momentarily dazed' when he was struck on the forehead by a piece of floating timber. At a garden party later that day in the royal couple's honour, guests could not help noticing 'a pronounced lump' on his head, though Mark swore he was fit and well.

It was with some relief that the newlyweds returned to London where, because of the national energy crisis, the customary Rolls Royce was not waiting to collect them at Heathrow. Instead, they had to make do with a humble Austin, which immediately got stuck in a traffic jam of morning commuters heading for the capital.

On the basis of this experience and its coverage in the press, Mark decided that while he loved his wife, he did not enjoy being a member of the royal family. As he faded, temporarily, from the Windsor pageant, another dashing figure came into view: for Andrew, last seen playing football at his prep school in Cawston's film, was embarking on an enjoyable and protracted adolescence.

In 1976, when he was sixteen, he spent two terms at Lakefield College in Canada on a school exchange from Gordonstoun. What Andrew learned from the exchange was enough for the Canadian press to dub him 'the Robert Redford of royalty'. 'His escapades with pretty girls have earned him quite a reputation,' the Press Association court correspondent Grania Forbes reported.

One 'escapade' which journalists covered in depth involved Sandi Jones, who met Andrew at the 1976 Montreal Olympics. Andrew and Sandi went sailing, Andrew bought Sandi to an official reception, and when Andrew returned to Lakefield, he invited Sandi to a disco where they held hands 'for all to see'. As a sideline, Andrew enjoyed telling Sandi jokes 'of a slightly blue variety'.

But the running story in the 1970s was Charles's love life. Charles's choice of a wife was deemed to have constitutional significance, because he was heir to the throne; or that at least was the ratpack's defence, as they pursued Charles and his latest consort around the polo fields and stately homes of England.

It was generally assumed that Charles had lost his virginity while a student at Cambridge in the late 1960s. One story held that the Master of Trinity College, Lord Butler, put his lodge at Charles's disposal while he and Lady Butler spent the weekend at their house in Suffolk. An early girlfriend from this period was Lucia Santa-Cruz, the daughter of the Chilean ambassador, who seems to have found her royal date a trifle wearing. 'He can drive you crazy with all this Goon Show chat,' she told reporters – adding loyally, 'but he is marvellous company.'

The first of Charles's girlfriends to receive the full press treatment as a potential future queen was Jane Wellesley, the daughter of the Duke of Wellington. Shortly before Anne and Mark's wedding in 1973, she and Charles enjoyed a holiday of their own in that ill-fated royal destination, the Caribbean. Over a hundred reporters and photographers decided to keep them company.

Buckingham Palace denied that the couple were about to announce their engagement, a statement which for incompetence matched anything Colville had produced. 'It was an entirely private visit,' the statement declared – as if the press had assumed anything else. The Duchess of Wellington, an old friend of Elizabeth, said her daughter was 'absolutely horrified by the rumours'.

Fever pitch was reached at Sandringham in January 1974 when Jane Wellesley joined the royal family's New Year party. An estimated ten thousand people travelled to Norfolk on the Sunday to see her arriving at the little church adjoining the Sandringham gardens, confidently expecting an engagement to be announced after the service.

'I've had a lovely time,' was Jane Wellesley's mildly implausible remark as she left church. No announcement was forthcoming and shortly afterwards she departed the royal scene to pursue a career as a successful independent film producer.

The hordes of journalists who gathered at this media non-event rather bely James Whitaker's claim that he was to blame 'to a large extent' for the change in royalty's relations with the press, which he dates from 1976. 'I suggested to my editor (I worked on the *Sun* at the time) that together with a photographer, Arthur Edwards, I form a team to go everywhere with HRH,' Whitaker told *Majesty*. 'He agreed, and for the next two years we got away with murder, producing scoop after scoop . . .'

Other tabloid journalists did not perhaps need Whitaker's advice as badly as he imagined in order to spot a royal love story.

After Jane Wellesley, Charles was seen with a string of girlfriends, all of whom made good copy – and not only for the *Sun*'s dynamic duo.

There was Davina Sheffield, the daughter of the ICI tycoon Lord McGowan. She liked riding and hunting, which was promising; Charles's mother and grandmother liked her, which was even better; but unfortunately for Davina, in the future queen stakes she fell at the first hurdle, having had previous boyfriends. Although Charles was supposed to be 'deeply in love' she had to go – or so the tabloids claimed.

Then there was Fiona Watson, whom Charles met in 1977 at a house party in Lincolnshire. Charles was keen to 'develop the friendship' until he discovered she had posed for *Penthouse* magazine. Jane Ward forged another 'friendship' with Charles when he accidentally struck her on the leg during a game of polo at the Guards Club in Windsor. According to one nameless 'royal watcher', 'the filly had to be ousted' after Jane talked to the newspapers. 'Wildly social' Sabrina Guinness appeared in 1979, having formerly been 'romantically linked' with Jack Nicholson and Mick Jagger. Not a future queen, James Whitaker and his colleagues concluded.

Whitaker is on more reliable ground when he dates 1978 as the year when the rats began hunting on a permanent basis, rather than descending on their prey for periodic feeding frenzies. If there was a catalyst, it was not the ever-interesting story of Charles's girlfriends, but his aunt's quite spectacular mid-life crisis.

Margaret's *annus horribilis* was unquestionably 1978. In February Peter Townsend published his autobiography *Time and Chance*. Partly to escape the furore, and partly because it was that time of year, Margaret left England for her Caribbean retreat on the island of Mustique, accompanied by a landscape gardener about half her age called Roddy Llewellyn. The hacks and paparazzi followed on the next available plane.

No sooner had Margaret and Roddy arrived at Les Jolis Eaux, her house on Mustique, than he fell seriously ill with an internal haemorrhage and had to be flown to a hospital on a neighbouring island. While Margaret stayed at Roddy's side, outside the hospital the ratpack exchanged notes about the latest telephoto technology. In London, meanwhile, questions were being asked in Parliament about Margaret's leisure activities, allegedly at the taxpayer's expense. Distantly echoing Sir Charles Dilke's attack on royal corruption a century before, some members called for her civil list allowance to be cut.

Margaret was not surprisingly under the weather when she and Roddy finally returned to England. Almost immediately she was struck down by flu, and had to miss her daughter Sarah's confirmation. In May she was admitted to hospital with suspected gastro-enteritis. She was also suffering from lung and liver problems, caused by decades of heavy smoking and drinking, and for a time her life was in danger. To add insult to injury, while in hospital and as previously arranged, her divorce from Snowdon was announced.

Margaret's agony was recorded in exhaustive detail by journalists prepared to sleep in hospital car parks on both sides of the Atlantic. The rats in the pack were now fully grown beasts.

The emergence of the ratpack was obviously related to the fact that by the early 1970s, ten thousand people were prepared to disrupt their weekend, ignore government warnings about wasting petrol in an energy crisis, and create the worst traffic jam in Norfolk's history, on the off-chance that the heir to the throne would announce his engagement. Even at the height of the Townsend affair in 1955, no comparable crowds besieged the Berkshire home of Mr and Mrs John Lycett Wills, as Margaret and her lover bunkered down to discuss their future.

It was easy for the ratpack, pointing at Cawston's film, to claim that it was the royal family who had created a market for gossip about their private lives; but that failed to explain the time lag between the film's appearance and the collapse of traditional court reporting. It was just as easy for the royal family to accuse the ratpack of creating the same market; but that too begged the same question of how far the family had contributed to the process.

Both arguments ignored the underlying ambivalence of Elizabeth's subjects towards the royal family. Despite the criticisms of Lord Altrincham and others, the 1950s had remained a deferential decade in relation to the monarchy. The post-Cawston era, in contrast, promised to be an age of prurience; but it soon became clear to the ratpack that their readers could be both deferential *and* prurient regarding royalty; and that the trick, in marketing terms, was to exploit both attitudes.

It suited the ratpack's self-image to present themselves as a breed apart from the old-fashioned court correspondents. 'If you want to pay me £35,000 a year, plus £20,000 in expenses, I'll write it your way,' one of their number once bellowed at Michael Shea, Press Secretary from 1978 to 1987. 'You don't, so I'll write it the way my editor wants it written.' Shea's idea had been to offer leading members of the ratpack the privileges of court correspondents, such as guaranteed access to royal events. In return, they would have had to play by the rules, including a respect for the royal family's privacy.

But in reality, the ratpack were not so different from the court correspondents, for they were fundamentally supplying the same royalist market. The evidence can be found in the glossy pages of *Majesty* magazine, one of the publishing successes of the 1980s, which was launched shortly before Charles's marriage to Diana.

In spirit, *Majesty* was the direct descendant of earlier publications which tapped this market, such as *Royalty Annual*, produced in the 1950s by the BBC court correspondents Godfrey Talbot and Wynford Vaughan-Thomas. *Majesty* knew its readers – overwhelmingly female, working class and provincial – and until the débâcle of the early 1990s, not a breath of criticism was allowed to sully the royal image. A typical *Majesty* article had a title like 'Happy 21st, Ma'am', written by Valerie Anderson to mark Diana's birthday in 1982; or in the same year, 'Royals into Battle', by Dennis Bardens, as Andrew sailed off to the Falklands.

Mr Bardens was anxious to remind *Majesty* readers that 'the ranks held by our Princes in the armed forces are in no respects honorary'. Prince Charles, especially, in his 'Draconian preparation for the throne', had turned himself into a royal killing-machine. 'He can fly a plane, drop by parachute, drive a tank, steer a ship, engage in sub-aqua exploration, and manage any sort of firearm.'

Not surprisingly, *Majesty* was on the side of Michael Shea and his colleagues in their battle with the ratpack. 'Nobody can deny that journalists have a job to do,' Christopher Warwick wrote in a 1983 '*Majesty* viewpoint', after another ratpack atrocity (Andrew's Caribbean love tryst with 'soft-porn actress' Koo Stark): 'Nor, indeed, would one want to see censure [*sic*] of the press, far from it. But when common decency isn't seen to prevail, more positive steps are called for to rectify the situation.'

Opposite Mr Warwick's think-piece, *Majesty* readers were soothed by a picture of Diana, whose 'radiant smile has been much in evidence recently, and her relaxed manner dispels the absurd rumours of her predicted "nervous breakdown".'

Yet the same magazine could interview James Whitaker a few years later about his 'twenty years of royal watching'. Furthermore, Whitaker was an occasional contributer, writing either under his own name or pseudonymously, alongside court correspondents like Grania Forbes who were also moonlighting.

In July 1987, for instance, Whitaker appeared under his own byline with a piece of royal puff about the woman he described as 'Fergie' for his newspaper readers, but in this context referred to as 'Sarah, Duchess of York'. 'Thursday May 7 will forever remain a red-letter day for Sarah, Duchess of York,' Whitaker began. 'It was the day she flew high over Lincolnshire, carving out a great big loop-the-loop in an azure sky. And it was the day she dressed in the colour of her favourite Chris de Burgh song "Lady in Red". The occasion was her official visit to see the Red Arrows formation team at their Lincolnshire headquarters of RAF Scampton.'

Another, more junior member of the ratpack was also follow-ing the fortunes of 'Sarah, Duchess of York' for the benefit of *Majesty* readers – *Daily Star* reporter and future biographer of Diana, Andrew Morton. A month before Whitaker's piece, Morton described the Yorks' visit to the Channel Islands. *Majesty* readers were told how Sarah had to borrow a raincoat to prevent her silk dress from blowing in the stiff sea breeze.

'The Queen and other royal ladies weight the hems of their dresses to stop any embarrassing scenes,' Morton noted. But, '. . . while Sarah still has many details to learn about handling clothes and timing, she displayed a confidence and *savoir faire* that will hold her in good stead in the coming months.'

Many of *Majesty*'s readers would, of course, already have been familiar with Morton and Whitaker's journalism, since they overwhelmingly fell into the tabloid newspaper market; and it was hardly the ratpack's fault if the same members of the public who required their magazine's royal coverage to be drenched in deference also enjoyed the salacious gossip which landed on their breakfast table each morning, courtesy of the *Sun*, the *Mirror*, and others. Hypocrisy was no bar to membership of the ratpack – or indeed, to the production of magazines like *Majesty*.

But the whiff of double standards was also evident among younger members of the royal family. In the wake of Cawston's film, Elizabeth and Philip had no desire to behave like celebrities. Despite hundreds of requests, buoyed by the expectations raised by *Royal Family*, Elizabeth resolutely refused to give press interviews. Her husband was rather more keen to have his say, both in the newspapers and on television; but he too knew where to draw the line. 'I'm not a pop star,' was Philip's withering remark to his host at a luncheon, when he was asked to autograph the menu.

When they were under siege, Philip's children shared his contempt for the ratpack. In 1985 Andrew tried to define for listeners of BBC's *Woman's Hour* the limits of press intrusion on the royal family. 'I think there are three areas,' he told Sue MacGregor. 'There's the area of the public engagement, there's the area of the private engagement, and then there's home life; and I think that of those three areas, one is to a large degree fair game, the private area is all right if you're found, and the third area – completely private at home – is a no-go area for anybody': – except, Andrew should have added five years later, when the photographers are from *Hello!* magazine, you have two beau-

Shooting: Bertie (Edward VII, *centre right*) hosts a shooting party at Sandringham, 1909. 'He was somewhat *journalier* in his shooting,' Lord Walsingham recalled, 'but naturally shot better when keenly interested than when his thoughts appeared to be distracted by other, and doubtless more weighty matters.' Those matters included approving a gargantuan menu for the evening's banquet and (away from Sandringham) deciding which of the ladies would share his bed.

Shooting: George bags a rhinoceros during a visit to Nepal, 1911. Six hundred elephants and 14,000 beaters were enlisted by the local Maharajah to provide George with some sport. At home, the carnage continued. 'Seven guns in four days at Sandringham killed 10,000 head,' Lord Lincolnshire noted in December 1912. 'The King one day fired 1700 cartridges and killed 1000 pheasants. Can this terrific slaughter possibly last much longer?'

Collecting: Mary leaves an antique shop in Edinburgh, 1924. If Mary had pocketed an item, a lady-in-waiting would stay behind and explain to the shop owner that payment would be forthcoming on receipt of an invoice at Buckingham Palace. Descending unannounced on stately homes, Mary adopted less underhand methods. 'I am caressing it with my eyes,' she would tell her hosts, looking pointedly at a particularly desirable object. They usually took the hint, and another 'gift' would be added to the Royal Collection.

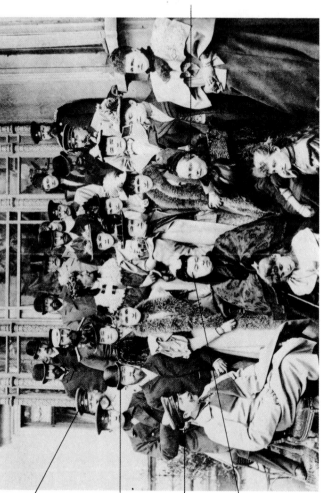

Empress Frederick (Victoria's eldest daughter)

Prince of Wales, later Edward VII

The Tsarevich, later Tsar Nicholas II

Kaiser Wilhelm II

Queen Victoria

Some of Victoria's extended family at Coburg, 1894. Already her grandson Willy (the German Kaiser) was the family black sheep. 'Willy is a bully, and most bullies, when tackled, are cowards,' said Bertie (the Prince of Wales). Willy's favourite pastime was to beat Bertie's yacht in the annual Cowes regatta. In 1914 he and his admirals moved up several classes to take on the British Navy in the First World War. 'No man can dominate the world, it has been tried before,' was George's verdict when Willy abdicated in 1918; 'now he has utterly ruined his country and himself.'

Nicky (Tsar Nicholas II, *left*) and his cousin George at Cowes in 1909. Their friendship should have been for life but in 1917, fearing the spread of revolution to Britain, George blocked his government's proposed offer of asylum to Nicky. His part in Nicky's death was easily forgotten. In July 1918 he and Queen Mary attended a memorial service for the former Tsar in London. 'It was a foul murder,' George wrote in his diary. 'I was devoted to Nicky, who was the kindest of men and a thorough gentleman: loved his country and people.'

Bertie (later George VI, *far right*) and Elizabeth at the christening in Belgrade of the future King Peter of Yugoslavia, October 1923. Also in the picture (*from left*): King Alexander and Queen Marie of Yugoslavia (the baby's parents), and King Ferdinand and Queen Marie of Romania (the baby's grandparents). It was an ill-starred gathering. Bertie thought the British Foreign Secretary should have been 'drowned' for making him attend; the baby nearly did drown when the Serbian Patriarch dropped him in the font (Bertie scooped him out); King Alexander was assassinated by a terrorist in 1934; King Peter was forced into exile in 1941 and died an alcoholic.

Bertie, Elizabeth, Lilibet and Margaret - 'us four', as Bertie called his exceptionally happy family. Additions to the quartet were regarded by Bertie with apprehension. 'I can see that you are sublimely happy with Philip which is right,' he wrote to Lilibet on her wedding day, 'but don't forget us is the wish of, Your ever loving & devoted PAPA.'

Philip and his Private Secretary Michael Parker crocodile-shooting in the Gambia during Philip's world tour, February 1957. 'Gambians are mostly Moslem, happy, hardworking and loyal,' the official tour brochure noted. Philip is fresh from judging the tour's 'great beard-growing contest'. Commander Parker is about to be sued by his wife for divorce, bringing the tour to an unhappy conclusion.

It's a Royal Knockout, Alton Towers, June 1987. Andrew leads his team into the jousting arena, where Knockout veteran Stuart Hall is waiting to greet them. The team includes John Travolta, Nigel Mansell and 'former James Bond' George Lazenby. Andrew and Sarah (*below, left*) were already in festive mood the evening before, when they staged an impromptu food fight at a nearby hotel. Edward (*below, right*), the show's impresario, ended the biggest day of his life on a low note, haranguing journalists for their lack of enthusiasm.

Here comes trouble. Charles and Diana arrive for a Remembrance Day ceremony in South Korea, November 1992, a month before their official separation. By now, journalists were speculating about whether the couple had shared the biggest hotel bed in Seoul, and a royal aide had admitted the marriage was in difficulty.

SCENES FROM THE COURT CIRCULAR

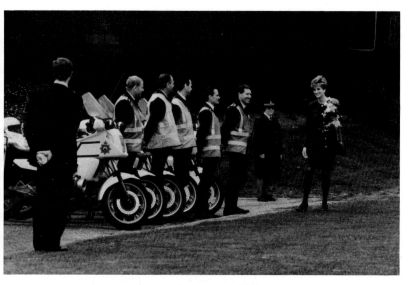

Diana inspects a motorcycle guard of honour, Sudbury, Suffolk, 27 July 1993, the last of the day's royal duties. She has just officially opened two Injector Manufacturing Cells at Lucas Diesel Systems. Her equerry is waiting in the helicopter, but there is still time for a last wave to the Lucas workforce before flying back to Kensington Palace.

Charles onstage at the Haven All-Action Holiday Centre, Caister, Norfolk, 2 April 1993, bringing the Prince's Trust Work, Sport and Leisure Week for unemployed young people to a climax. 'C'mon Charlie!' the audience shouted, as he took the microphone from rock star and Prince's Trust volunteer Phil Collins. The previous year Charles played the drums; in 1993 the drums stood idle as the Prince of Wales delivered a pep talk.

Elizabeth in Hull, 19 May 1993, Francis Askew Primary School. Mr Brian Leaman (*third from right*), the city's Senior Beadle, has donned a cap of maintenance made of Russian sable fur in order to surrender Hull's sword of state to the Queen. Mr Peter Nendick, Junior Beadle (*fourth from right*), holds his mace in the reverse position, signifying that Elizabeth is in no physical danger. While the ceremony is performed, an arrangement of Beethoven's 'Ode to Joy' is played by the North Humberside and Northern Lights Girls Brigade Band.

Forty-five minutes later, Elizabeth inspects the Parents and Toddlers Group in the main hall of the Francis Askew Primary School. During her visit, the Humberside Dance Agency has performed a pageant and older children have taken part in Hull City FC's 'Football in the Community Scheme'. Her next engagement is at the British Red Cross Centre, where she is scheduled to unveil a plaque, spend six minutes with the Elderly Persons' Pop-In Club and meet sixty representatives of the creche, youth section and trustees.

tiful daughters and a dream home in Berkshire, and your wife has negotiated a substantial fee for the pictures.

During the 1980s and early 1990s, the younger royals frequently echoed Andrew's Garboesque plea to be left alone. The reason the press failed to take heed was not simply because there was an unquenchable demand for royal gossip. It was also because, in the minds of Andrew, his siblings and his cousins, the distinction between public, private and home life altered and even merged according to the circumstances.

Sometimes they liked to be private; sometimes they liked to be private in a public sort of way; but wherever they were, unlike their parents, they seemed to enjoy their fame, just as they enjoyed the company of celebrities. In the area of the public engagement, and even in the area of the private engagement, they wanted their share of the limelight. And who were the ratpack to deny them?

19

The Advent of Fergie

In the early autumn of 1983, 'The Mark Phillips Horse Trials' were held for the first time at Gatcombe Park in Gloucestershire. Princess Anne stood at the gate, collecting tickets from the paying customers. Her husband, meanwhile, fielded questions from journalists.

'I wanted to put something back into a sport I have got so much from,' he told reporters. Why, in that case, was his wife taking money from the customers? 'We're just like any married couple with a mortgage,' he explained in another interview that year. 'The pot is only so big.' This cannot have been a reference to the house, which was bought for Anne by her mother in 1976 for an undisclosed six-figure sum. Perhaps Mark was referring to the surrounding fifteen-hundred-acre estate, which was indeed mortgaged.

The twenty thousand customers – 'a nice crowd', in Mark's opinion – were not complaining; they had been given value for money. Croft, the sherry firm, sponsored the three-day event, and as a bonus, there was a 'Celebrity Land Rover Race' featuring newscaster Angela Rippon and actor Anthony Andrews, both friends of Anne and Mark.

In several ways 'The Mark Phillips Horse Trials' were an

emblematic royal event for the 1980s. There was, for instance, the faint suspicion that a peripheral member of the royal family was exploiting his status for personal gain. Officially Mark was not even royal, having opted out of public duties soon after his ill-starred honeymoon. He was simply married, as a matter of fact, to the daughter of the Queen. For this reason, there was nothing wrong with his appearance in New Zealand in a series of commercials for a brand of tea. Everyone knew he was Mark Phillips, famous equestrian, not Mark Phillips, husband of Princess Anne.

Another member of the dynasty who was quite emphatic about having forsaken his royal identity was the furniture-maker David Linley, the son of Snowdon and Margaret. It was hardly David's fault if the fame of his birth pursued him up and down London's King's Road, where he opened his retail outlet.

Sometimes he put that fame to good use. In December 1984, for instance, he organised the Raj Ball at the London Lyceum, which raised £35,000 for charity. Everyone had to wear imperial costume from the days of the Raj, and many of the young royals were there – including Edward, who entered the ballroom via the back door, protected by police officers with dogs (there was an IRA scare), a metal helmet on his head and a Raj-style coat of gold braid over his shoulders.

At other times, David's behaviour was more perplexing. In October 1993, when he married Serena Stanhope, it was not immediately clear why he felt the need to issue an official wedding photograph taken in the Throne Room of St James's Palace, beneath a red canopy bearing Victoria's insignia, a lion and a unicorn, and the royal mottos *Honi soit qui mal y pense* and *Dieu et mon droit*. Perhaps Elizabeth insisted that her nephew and his bride should bear the stamp of royalty.

At the opposite extreme was Princess Michael of Kent, once described by David Linley as the Christmas present he would give to his worst enemy. No one stands on her royal dignity more zealously than the former Mrs Tom Troubridge. Soon after her marriage to Prince Michael in 1978, two girls were hired to redecorate the newlyweds' grace-and-favour apartment in Kensington Palace. Entering the room unannounced, Princess Michael was reported to have insisted that the girls climb down from a stepladder and curtsy in her presence. Posterity does not record whether the girls were wearing dungarees.

Such is the deference due to royalty; and as she has said, Princess Michael and her husband take their royal obligations 'very seriously'. Their disadvantage is to have no private fortune, and in the days of the civil list, to receive no allocation from public funds: so, as Princess Michael told *Majesty* magazine in November 1986, they have had to 'pay their own way' as royals.

Princess Michael, known to her husband as Marie-Christine, became an author. Her first book, *Crowned in a Far Country*, an account of foreign princesses who were crowned in a far country, was not entirely her own work. Accused of plagiarism, she confessed she had been a trifle careless with her references.

She also became a grateful recipient of the kind of gifts which are laid at royalty's feet. Prince and Princess Michael's Georgian home in Gloucestershire does not fall into this category, as they were able to pay the asking price of about £300,000 without any difficulty. On the other hand, the American breeder John Galbreath offered a token of his friendship in the form of a race-horse valued at £115,000. From another friend, the tycoon Peter de Savary, came a plot of land on Antigua valued at £150,000.

But it is Princess Michael's remark that she would 'go anywhere for a meal' which has attracted most interest. In 1989 she and Michael could be found singing for their supper in (among other exotic locations) the newly opened exhibition centre in Hong Kong, converted into a replica of the Vienna Opera House for a gala ball. Money was to be raised for a local orchestra, and for this important cause the royal couple flew halfway round the world to be guests of honour. The rest of their stay in Hong Kong was spent on a private island which had been put at their disposal.

In the autumn of 1993 Prince and Princess Michael returned to the Far East as guests of honour on the Asian version of the

Orient Express. The social diarists of Malaysia and Thailand were gathered in force to record the royal couple chugging in imperial splendour – along with a host of fellow celebrity passengers – between the countries' respective capitals.

Royalty's infatuation with showbusiness, illustrated by that train ride as much as by the Celebrity Land Rover Race between Angela Rippon and Anthony Andrews, can be traced at least to the moment two centuries before when the Prince of Wales lost his virginity to a Drury Lane actress. More decorously, there was a long tradition of theatre and music stars staging private performances for the royal family. In the spring of 1973, for instance, the violinist Yehudi Menuhin and the comedian Joyce Grenfell (plus pianist) staged an evening of music and entertainment after dinner at Windsor. Some of these favourites – Noël Coward is the most conspicuous example – also regarded themselves as 'friends' of royalty (in his case, the Queen Mother).

But in the 1980s, among the younger generation of royalty, the relationship was coarsened, until it was impossible to tell whose infatuation was the greater: the royals or the celebrities who swarmed around them, like flies to a honeypot. What to make, in this respect, of the occasion in the early 1980s when Margaret and the Queen Mother arrived at Elton John's home near Windsor to admire the bed which David Linley had made for the rock star?

The relationship was brought to one of its many climaxes by Charles's fortieth birthday party at Buckingham Palace in November 1988. While Elizabeth danced to 'La Bamba', clutching her handbag, Barry Humphries, Billy Connolly and Elton John mixed with royal playboy King Juan Carlos of Spain and the extremely staid (and possibly bemused) King Olav of Norway. At the end of the evening Phil Collins joined Elizabeth in a rousing chorus of 'Happy Birthday'. 'It was the best party I've ever been to,' said Jimmy Savile, who had spun the discs.

These famous friends and their fawning ways provided a milieu in which the younger royals could deceive themselves that they possessed talents which deserved a wider audience. Since Victoria published some 'leaves' from her Balmoral journal in 1867, to be followed by 'more leaves' in 1884, no member of the British dynasty had fallen for this delusion. Margaret's theatrical début in the 1950s and her later appearance – as herself – on *The Archers* were minor exceptions; but these ventures were essentially a form of distraction therapy, to while away the *longueurs* of an empty life.

On the other hand, no royal generation before Elizabeth and Philip's children had ever been told so emphatically that they had to prove themselves as people, as well as representative figures. The 'chaff' which George directed at his sons throughout their lives expressed a fear that they would not make the grade as princes. As for their abilities as mortals, he was happy to believe they had none.

Unlike her brothers, Anne had a talent which did merit recognition, independently of her royal status. It is possible to argue that as a little girl who was more horse- than doll-minded (contrary to Dorothy Laird's claim), she had unusual opportunities to develop her equestrian skills. But the skills were real enough, as her selection for the 1976 Montreal Olympics demonstrated.

It is thus interesting that alone among her siblings, Anne has produced (on her own) a book that is worth reading. *Riding Through My Life*, published in 1991, is a thinly disguised autobiography, since it rapidly becomes apparent that horses have loomed larger in the author's career than people. The book, she explains in the introduction, 'was entirely written by the Princess Royal': and within its covers are a competent first-hand account of her fall in the cross-country stage of the Montreal Olympics, and a thoughtful chapter on riding and the disabled (one of her charities).

Anne's brothers have backed more diffidently into the royal book market, perhaps aware that their talents shine less brightly. Introducing his 1991 book of paintings, Charles confesses that 'no one could have been more surprised than me to discover that a courageous (or perhaps foolhardy!) publisher wished to compile a book of my watercolour sketches. When I first started dabbling in watercolours, over twenty years ago, any thought of such an eventuality would have seemed utterly ludicrous.'

The few who bought this coffee-table book might have been inclined to agree. 'This, I fear, is another very rapid sketch,' Charles says of a semi-abstract blur, which is disclosed in the caption as Wensleydale, North Yorkshire. And yet: 'I would also point out that as a result of this sketch being reproduced in an article in a British Sunday newspaper colour supplement, an art publishing company liked it so much that they asked if it could be made into a limited edition of lithographs.' The royal desire to be appreciated is palpable.

Andrew, like his distant ancestor King Victor Emmanuel of Italy, preferred photography. In the introduction to his 1985 book of photographs, called *Photographs* and conceived as the sequel to his Ilford calendar, Andrew takes pride in his incompetence.

'This book is a compilation of photographs,' he begins, in case the title had unintentionally misled his readers. '. . . It is intended, above all, for the enthusiast and for the person who wants to "have a go". It is because I took my courage in both hands and "had a go" that I have found such enjoyment in taking pictures . . . Nothing would please me more should this book persuade more people to "have a go".'

More poignantly, Andrew summarises the perennial dilemma of the royal who 'has a go': the fear of being misunderstood. 'I would ask you, if you would, to see this as a book by me, tyro-photographer, rather than by me, member of the Royal Family. I am the first to grant that some people would see this book as being published because of who I am.'

But: 'All the proceeds from the sale of this book will go to deserving causes and charities.' Furthermore: 'I have regarded it as a responsibility to see that the book is, in the widest possible sense, as entertaining and interesting as possible.'

If Andrew was having a go, his wife Sarah – in the manner of the blockbuster heroines she resembled so closely – was having it all. No other member of the royal family in the 1980s embodied so comprehensively the triple impulses towards fame, money, and recognition for talents either real or imagined. By day she was the

Duchess of York, member of the royal family; by night, she was Sarah Ferguson, career girl – or was it the other way round?

Majesty magazine, clucking like a maiden aunt, doubted whether she could balance her life so perilously between royalty and commerce. When she married Andrew in July 1986, Sarah announced she would continue her career with a fine art publishing company. *Majesty* warned that 'she has now to prove to everybody that she can be a wife, a princess, a career woman and a homemaker all in one, *and* retain that famous "Fergie sparkle" for the cameras.'

Undaunted by such advice, Sarah took flight in the competitive world of children's literature with *Budgie the Little Helicopter*. Discerning readers found a remarkable similarity between the Budgie concept and a children's story book in the 1960s. But unlike Princess Michael, Sarah seems to have had no references to mislay, and the first serial rights were sold in 1989 for £60,000.

Answering criticism that only part of the proceeds for *Budgie* went to charity, Sarah pointed out that she and Andrew – a mere naval officer – were 'not rich' by royal standards. 'Luckily Sarah is not materialistic,' her 'friend' the *Majesty* editor Ingrid Seward reported, 'so lack of substantial funds does not worry her unduly.'

Sarah's idea of poverty was revealed in December 1989, when she returned to Heathrow after a shopping trip in New York, carrying fifty-one pieces of excess luggage. In the cases were six pairs of shoes at £562, handbags to the value of £3,125, six Italian sweaters worth £625 each, and a £515 teddy bear.

Americans liked Sarah, and not only for her personal contribution to the Reagan consumer boom. 'She's been a breath of fresh air,' her friend Cornelia Guest, America's 'Deb of the Decade', told the press. 'She's a straight shooter. She's the best thing in the royal family, full of *joie de vivre.* It is great to see someone having fun, especially in that family.'

Sarah, in return, liked America. Among her many transatlantic trips, the one which still glows in the memory was her visit to New York in the summer of 1990. After a Friday-night flight on Concorde, base camp was established at the Plaza Hotel on

Fifth Avenue. The weekend was spent in Connecticut with her mother and stepfather, who was seriously ill with cancer.

Back in Manhattan by Monday, Sarah got down to business — or rather, shopping. At the studios of the artist Julian Schnabel she looked for pictures to adorn hers and Andrew's dream home at Sunninghill Park, near Ascot — which, despite Philip's veto on hiring the expensive American designers Parish-Hedley, would soon be ready to grace the pages of *Hello!* magazine. Next stop was Ralph Lauren, where Sarah stocked up on some more shoes.

By now she had been joined by Andrew, and together they plunged briefly into the arena of the public engagement. Across the Hudson River in New Jersey, the Jaguar company was waiting to have its new headquarters opened. As she clambered into a sports car, Andrew worried whether his wife was showing photographers a little too much leg, even knicker.

But in truth, he had no time to worry: for it was back to Manhattan in time for lunch and an afternoon visit to Barney's, the menswear store, where Sarah and Andrew shopped for some more bargains. In the evening, they were off to a dinner party in Greenwich Village hosted by New York socialites Bobby and Jean Fomon. During the meal, Sarah blew another breath of fresh air through the cobwebs of royal protocol when she 'knighted' the Fomons' pet dog with a kitchen knife.

It is perhaps unfair to single out Sarah, since she was only taking her lead from the example set by her in-laws. Less than a year after her marriage to Andrew, she learned all she needed to know about fresh air and straight shooting from Andrew's younger brother Edward. The location was Alton Towers, a theme park set in the grounds of a ruined castle; the occasion was *It's a Royal Knockout.*

Edward's production has been seen, retrospectively, as a unique occasion in royal history. This was not so. In the same year Ascot racecourse played host to *Three Quarters of a Royal Knockout*, the clumsy title explained by Andrew's absence on naval duties. While Edward, Anne, and Sarah, joined by the inevitable

Princess Michael and the improbable Rosie, Marchioness of Northampton, raised money for charity in a showjumping event, 'Rolling Stone' Bill Wyman and *Dempsey and Makepeace* star Michael Brandon staged their own stock-car race. It was fun, but not as good as the total knockout experience.

The evening before the Alton Towers extravaganza, the participants assembled for dinner at the Isaac Walton Hotel in nearby Dovedale, where the famous Fergie sparkle was in evidence as she pelted Andrew with after-dinner mints. In the morning, before a live audience of four thousand and a television audience of millions more, the teams assembled in their kitsch medieval costumes. From the middle range of the pop music spectrum, Cliff Richard, Tom Jones and Sheena Easton lined up for Anne and the Save the Children Fund. Sarah's self-styled 'Big Bad Blues' team contained a host of celebrities: Michael Brandon (again), royal friend and comic Pamela Stephenson, transatlantic rock star Meat Loaf (game for anything), and the mini-series actress Jane Seymour, like Sarah a favourite with *Hello!* magazine readers.

Still they came, pouring through the ancient battlements of Alton Towers in their tights and jerkins: 'former James Bond' George Lazenby, John Cleese, Fiona Fullerton, Nigel Mansell, Barry McGuigan, 'Superman' Christopher Reeve, and the great West Indian cricketer Vivian Richards, looking acutely embarrassed in such unstately company.

Royal protocol dictated that the team leaders – Anne, Edward, Andrew and Sarah – had to remain on the sidelines. It was too much for Andrew who, forgetting his naval training, ignited a cannon so close to the compère, *It's a Knockout* veteran Stuart Hall, that the explosion singed the television personality's eyebrows.

The only people who refused to join in the fun were the reporters, who spent most of the day sheltering from the rain-swept arena and complaining about the facilities. At the end of the day Edward's patience snapped and he gave the hacks a right royal dressing-down. Instead of behaving like a bunch of moaning minnies, he shouted at them, why didn't they pull their fingers out and be a bit more appreciative?

It was not for reporters to point out that the event was ridiculous and the performance demeaning to royalty (though they did, over acres of newsprint, the next day). That conclusion had already been reached by Edward's mother, watching in horror as the disaster unfolded on television. Never again, Elizabeth resolved; but the damage had already been done.

20

Diana's Dilemma

Elizabeth was not the only member of the royal family watching the knockabout fun at home. Diana had originally been game for a laugh when Edward asked her to participate, but Charles had vetoed the idea as unsuitable for the wife of the heir to the throne. One of Charles's better decisions, Diana must have thought, as she watched Sarah cheering on the 'Big Bad Blues' team.

Diana's ability to rise above the morass into which her royal peers had sunk owed something to luck. She, too, was intrigued by her own celebrity, and in the early years of her marriage collected press cuttings about herself. Her stage fever peaked at Covent Garden in November 1986, when she and Wayne Sleep danced a specially rehearsed number to the tune of Billy Joel's 'Uptown Girl' as a birthday surprise for Charles. The birthday prince ungratefully cringed with embarrassment in the royal box.

'She has rhythm, she can do high kicks and has a real feel for jazz dancing,' was Wayne Sleep's verdict on his partner. 'She could easily have become a jazz dancer.'

'A good dancer,' John Travolta had agreed the year before, following a turn with Diana at a White House ball hosted by President and Mrs Reagan. Reporters asked him what had been his best moment with the Princess of Wales. 'When I put my arm around her waist,' Travolta confided. 'She's so tiny.'

Diana was possibly less happy with the effect she had on politicians of a certain age. When she visited Canada with Charles in the summer of 1983, the country's leaders were certainly appreciative. 'Why do you ask such negative questions?' the federal Prime Minister Pierre Trudeau scolded reporters when asked whether he minded playing second fiddle to his royal guests. 'Why don't you ask me about the Princess's beautiful blue eyes?'

'The music of that smile, was made by Lady Di,' the bandleader crooned at a reception for Charles and Diana in New Brunswick. Then it was the turn of the province's premier, Richard Hatfield, to sing Diana's praises in a speech described by one royal correspondent as 'obscure gush'. The audience wondered if the premier was not in fact drunk. Yes, he had been, Mr Hatfield confirmed the next day – 'totally drunk on her charm'.

Mr Hatfield's counterpart in Newfoundland, Brian Peckford, also found Diana irresistible. When Diana told him, as a way of making conversation: 'I am doing my job better than I previously did,' she was nonplussed by his response. 'I guess I am just falling in love,' he told her.

In the early 1980s, it seemed the whole world was falling in love with Diana. 'Is this lovely young woman ever going to stop delighting us?' Sheena More wrote to *Royalty Monthly* from Scotland in June 1984. 'You're wondering who I'm talking about? No, of course not – I'm sure that you, along with myself and many others, are overjoyed that the Princess of Wales is expecting another child.'

So wide was Diana's appeal – ranging from Hollywood film stars to provincial housewives – that it was easy to overlook the fact that it depended on her marriage to the heir to the throne. At first, even Charles made jokes about how Diana was stealing his limelight. 'I'm sorry, I haven't yet found a way to split my wife in half,' he told a disappointed crowd in New Zealand in 1983, while Diana conducted her own walkabout on the other side of the road.

Yet, on the eve of her formal engagement in February 1981, when Diana drove the short distance from her flat in Kensington to Buckingham Palace, she had forfeited her independence. It was not simply that she was marrying the Prince of Wales. She had also been assigned her place in the unfolding myth of the perfect royal family, a myth only marginally dented by Margaret's divorce from Snowdon in 1978.

'Here is the stuff of which fairy stories are made,' the Archbishop of Canterbury told his congregation in St Paul's Cathedral and a global television audience of about seven hundred and fifty million at the start of the wedding service. And though Diana and Charles fumbled their marriage vows, she at least gave early proof that she intended to live up to the myth. By the autumn she was pregnant with William, who was followed two years later – to the delight of Sheena More and countless others – by Harry.

As for the seemingly happy parents, it was still possible as late as 1985 for many to agree with Alastair Burnet's judgement, delivered after an interview 'in person' with the Prince and Princess of Wales. 'Theirs is a partnership, and it works,' Burnet wrote. 'They are busy, very much in love, and trying to do their job, pleasing people, working for people, day by day.'

Even Diana's visible distress, especially during her first pregnancy, could be incorporated into the myth. 'I watched helplessly as her face whitened during one crowded walkabout,' Valerie Anderson told *Majesty* readers, recalling an incident in December 1981. 'As she made for a public loo . . . women in the crowd clucked sympathetically. Eventually a halt was called to the busy schedule planned. A concerned Prince Charles, backed by doctors, made her drop the walkabout. But she insisted on carrying on with engagements involving children. "I'm simply not going to disappoint them," she said.'

It was only a decade later, when Andrew Morton published his quasi-authorised biography* of Diana, that the full story became known. Diana had not been suffering from morning sickness, but from the symptoms of bulimia. Far from being sympathetic,

Charles was exasperated by his wife's condition; and in her despair, Diana was to make what were described by her friends as several 'suicide attempts' (though as told by Morton, they seem more like cries for help).

Morton's book played a critical part in Diana's life, helping to precipitate the formal separation from Charles in December 1992. His achievement, relying principally on the evidence of Diana's friends James Gilbey and Carolyn Bartholomew, and her younger brother Viscount Althorp, was to prove that from the beginning the marriage was based on a lie. Furthermore, the deception originated with Charles, however spitefully Diana behaved towards her husband during their later years together.

With hindsight, Charles all but revealed his hand in the television interview he and Diana gave on the eve of their wedding. Asked whether they were in love, Charles replied cautiously that they were – 'whatever love means'. It was left to Diana to confirm that 'of course' they were both in love, which at the time she probably believed.

According to Charles, he first consciously set eyes on Diana during a shooting weekend at the Spencer family seat in Northamptonshire in November 1977. One of Charles's former girlfriends was in fact Diana's elder sister Sarah, who had eventually fallen out with Charles by giving an interview to a women's magazine about dating the Prince of Wales. 'I wouldn't marry anyone I didn't love,' she concluded tactlessly, 'whether it was the dustman or the King of England. If he [Charles] asked me, I would turn him down.'

Charles has always implied that from his initial encounter with Diana in a muddy field, acquaintance became friendship, which gradually blossomed into love. The transition was neither so smooth nor so complete. In the first place, Diana was quite different from Charles's previous girlfriends – including Sarah – who had tended to be experienced women with lives of their own to lead. Diana, by contrast, was only sixteen when Charles set eyes on her, and barely twenty when she married him. Until her engagement, she was also almost certainly a virgin.

Charles had had several other girlfriends between Sarah and Diana. One of them, Anna Wallace, earned a footnote in royal history in 1980, when she stormed out of Windsor Castle during a birthday party for the Queen Mother. She complained that Charles had neglected her throughout the evening. 'No one treats me like that, not even you,' she was reported to have said, before turning on her heels. Shortly after this débâcle, Charles began his courtship of Diana.

In various interviews during the 1970s he had already given notice that his eventual choice of a bride would involve a degree of princely calculation. 'You have to remember that when you marry in my position, you're going to marry someone who, perhaps, is one day going to be Queen,' he told one reporter. 'You've got to choose somebody very carefully, I think, who could fulfil this particular role, and it has got to be somebody pretty unusual.' What made Diana unusual, compared with Charles's previous girlfriends, was that she seemed to be spotless in the medieval sense, and possessed of a compliant nature.

Charles gave another hostage to fortune in the same interview. He declared that 'my marriage has to be forever. It's sad, in a way, that some people should feel that there is every opportunity to just break it off when you feel like it. I mean, the whole point about the marriage contract was that it was for life.'

At that time, he may well have been sincere. The most damning revelation in Andrew Morton's 1992 book was that even after the royal engagement, Diana was competing for Charles's affection with the woman who has joined Mrs Simpson in the pantheon of Windsor mistresses: Camilla Parker Bowles. Two years after Morton's book, Jonathan Dimbleby's authorised biography of the Prince of Wales sought to put the most favourable gloss on Charles's relationship with Camilla. By Charles's own admission, he had fallen in love with Camilla in the autumn of 1972, only to lose her in marriage to Andrew Parker Bowles. In the years that followed, their relationship rekindled to the point where, according to Dimbleby, it 'could properly be described as "love"'.

When Charles became engaged to Diana in February 1981 he told his bride-to-be that his intimate friendship with Camilla was over. From that day, Charles and his former lover had 'virtually no contact' until Charles concluded that his marriage had irretrievably collapsed. Although Dimbleby's chronology is obscure, Charles's relationship with Camilla appears to have resumed by the end of 1986. 'In Camilla Parker Bowles,' Dimbleby wrote, 'the Prince found the warmth, the understanding and the steadiness for which he had always longed and had never been able to find with any other person.'

The drawn-out saga of Charles's romance with Camilla had understandably reduced Diana, even before the marriage, to a state of volatile depression. By the late 1980s, Diana's solution to her deepening marital crisis was to seek a separate identity from Charles, both in her private life and her public career. Superficially, her quest often degenerated into a feud which was manifested by a determination to upstage her husband.

A trip by Charles and Diana to Australia in January 1988 provided two notorious examples. At Geelong in Victoria, where Charles had spent two terms on a school exchange from Gordonstoun in the mid-1960s, he was confronted by a media set-up. A cello stood in the middle of the music room, which Charles was expected to play. Dutifully he sat down and picked up the bow – only for Diana to stride to the piano in the corner and start playing the first few bars of a Rachmaninov concerto. All cameras turned to the Princess of Wales. In Sydney, Diana pulled the same trick. While Charles obliged the press by donning an Australian slouch hat, she caught the eye of a photographer and surreptitiously raised the hem of her dress. According to the photographer, Diana revealed 'precisely an inch more thigh than we'd ever seen before' as she sat next to Charles, seemingly entranced by her husband's performance. In the following morning's newspapers, the hat was forgotten; the thighs, on the other hand, were front-page news.

But Diana's search for independence had a more serious side, which eventually took shape in her image as the 'caring princess'. Princess Anne may have been less than happy about how Diana appropriated the image, given her own dedicated patronage of the Save the Children Fund over two decades. There were times, as well, when Diana's compassion seemed unnecessarily melodramatic. In January 1992 she flew to a hospital in Rome where Mother Teresa of Calcutta was gravely ill, knowing her mission would be splashed across the papers. Charles, meanwhile, sent flowers.

But Diana's charitable work was not always for the cameras. In such areas as Aids, leprosy, drug abuse and the hospice movement for the terminally ill, she has been consistent in her support. Aids, especially, has been a cause close to her heart, following the death from the syndrome of her friend the arts administrator Adrian Ward-Jackson. 'From the beginning she has wanted to find out more about this terrible virus,' says Les Rudd of the National Aids Trust. 'At charity events, she will seek out the experts in the field and ask them questions. It's much more than a token interest.' He adds that Diana has tried to break down taboos about the disease; in her case, by showing it is possible to touch and hug the victims without being infected. Her example makes a favourable contrast with another, older member of the royal family, who once wondered aloud whether people who were HIV positive should not be castrated.

When John Major told a stunned House of Commons on 9 December 1992 that the Prince and Princess of Wales were to separate, he was at pains to add that the split had no 'constitutional significance'. Diana, he assured his audience, would one day be Queen; her rights as Princess of Wales were not impaired; the royal pageant would continue its stately course.

Events had moved swiftly since the publication of Morton's book in the summer. In November, after the couple's disastrous tour of the Far East, Charles made the decisive move. The trigger was Diana's refusal to join Charles for a traditional autumn weekend at Sandringham, or to let their children join him. A meeting was arranged at Kensington Palace on 25 November, when Charles told Diana that a separation was unavoidable. She agreed.

In symbolic terms, it was the most severe blow to the British dynasty since the abdication crisis; and because – unlike the Duke and Duchess of Windsor – Diana showed no sign of disappearing from the royal scene, its aftershock would be felt for decades to come. The unpredictability of the situation was compounded by Diana's reluctance to indicate her plans for the future, beyond stating that she wished to continue her royal duties.

Charles and the rest of the royal family appear to have hoped that Diana would gradually retreat into the background, only materialising for grander state occasions. The stage would thus be left clear for Charles to re-establish his credentials as monarch-in-waiting. Here lay the roots of the conspiracy theory current in 1993, which held that Diana was being forcibly excluded from royal engagements by a malevolent court eager to be rid of her. If she would not disappear of her own accord, they would write her out of the script. The theory seemed to acquire substance in April 1993, when Diana was prevented by Buckingham Palace from attending the memorial service for two IRA bomb victims in Warrington. Instead, Philip represented the royal family, while Diana had to be content with telephone calls to the parents of the victims. Reporting the story, the *Daily Mail* said that 'extensive inquiries . . . confirmed that the Palace's decision to send Prince Philip to the service was the latest gambit in a sustained campaign to rehabilitate Prince Charles by "marginalising" his wife.'

The conspiracy theory, however, had a flaw. From the point of view of the rest of the royal family, including Charles, marginalising Diana would only have made a bad situation worse. As a royal outcast, sniping from beyond the palace walls, Diana would have possessed immense potential to undermine the monarchy. Strategically, it was far more sensible to keep Diana inside the royal circle, lending credence to Mr Major's comforting illusion that, beyond personal unhappiness, the separation had no wider implications for the monarchy. The Warrington episode can perhaps be explained by the fact that the only member of the royal family known to demur from this argument was Philip, who thought Diana's ambiguous position was untenable. Either she was in the royal family or she was not, Philip was reported to have said with typical forthrightness: but his was not the majority view.

If a campaign to exclude Diana ever existed, it had surely collapsed by the autumn of 1993, judging from her official diary. During the first two weeks of November, for instance, Diana could be found with the rest of the royal family at a memorial service in the Guards Chapel (2 November); at the Welsh Festival of Remembrance in Cardiff (6 November); at the state banquet for the King of Malaysia (9 November); at the return banquet hosted by the Malaysians (11 November); at the main Festival of Remembrance in the Albert Hall (13 November); and the following morning, representing the monarchy, at an Armistice Day ceremony in Northern Ireland.

The main problem was not the royal family's attitude to Diana, but the doubts which existed in her own mind about her novel status as a semi-detached princess. In relation to her official diary, Diana proved remarkably successful at organising her itinerary in 1993. Her first overseas visit was to Nepal in March, where among other engagements she visited a leprosy unit. The trip was made in the company of the Minister for Overseas Development, Baroness Chalker, with whom she became good friends. With the support of Lady Chalker, Diana became an effective lobbyist on her own behalf in Whitehall; rather more effective, it seems, than Charles, who complained in the autumn about how his efforts to promote British trade received no official backing.

For instance, when Diana proposed a visit to Zimbabwe in the summer of 1993, it became mired in red tape and Foreign Office inertia. The Foreign Office was reluctant to give the trip government backing, perhaps fearing that the palace would disapprove (civil servants can also believe conspiracy theories). Diana requested a meeting with the Foreign Secretary, Douglas Hurd, and the tour went ahead with full official support. When she arrived in Harare, her first call was on President Mugabe. 'She brings a little light into your life,' Mr Mugabe told reporters afterwards, showing that Diana still knew how to charm senior statesmen. 'Naturally you feel elated, you feel good.'

Yet, despite Diana's friends in high places, her situation bore uncomfortable parallels with that of another royal whose marriage collapsed in 1992: the Duchess of York. Sarah was left friendless after the débâcle of her holiday with her 'financial adviser' John Bryan, when she was photographed cavorting topless by the pool with only Bryan, two detectives and a plastic inflatable duck for company (the children had left before the royal bikini top was removed). In the manner of the Duchess of Windsor, Sarah was no longer entitled to style herself 'Royal Highness', a formal sign that she had been excluded from the Windsor hearth.

Diana was never in danger of experiencing Sarah's total eclipse as a royal personage because her image was damaged far less badly than Charles's by the separation. The so-called 'Squidgygate' tape, allegedly an intercepted phone conversation between Diana and James Gilbey, was swiftly overwhelmed in the public mind by the seamier revelations of the 'Camillagate' tape, first published by an Australian magazine in January 1993. When the Prince of Wales was allegedly exposed arranging a rendezvous with a woman presumed to be Camilla Parker Bowles, as well as indulging in a bizarre sexual joke about tampons, Diana could not help appearing as the aggrieved party.

Similarly, in the autumn of 1994 Diana escaped censure when allegations of an affair with a Guards officer called James Hewitt were published in a book by the journalist Anna Pasternak. Although Ms Pasternak defended her source, there was a strong suspicion that Hewitt had agreed to talk because he needed the money. More important, the publication the following month of Dimbleby's biography confirmed – despite the author's sympathy for his subject – that if Diana had sought solace with other men, Charles's betrayal of the marriage had been far worse.

Diana was nonetheless left with a dilemma as a result of the separation. 'To be a symbol, and an effective symbol, you must be vividly and often seen', the much-quoted Walter Bagehot wrote

of royalty in 1874, with critical reference to the reclusive
Victoria. As Charles's consort, that had posed no difficulty for
Diana, who had become the most vividly seen princess in history.
But separated from the heir to the throne – even one whose star
had fallen – Diana found it more difficult to fulfil Bagehot's
prescription.

In 1993, for the first time in her career Diana had to earn her
credentials as a princess by making her presence felt in the small
print of the Court Circular. Only by answering the tedious call of
duty – a call the palace was quite ready to issue on her behalf –
could she invest her image as a caring celebrity with the allure of
royalty.

So it was that in the late summer of 1993 Diana descended on
Suffolk for a day of public engagements. Her itinerary on 27
July reflected both her own interests and those of the monarchy.
In the morning she was to open the St Nicholas' Hospice in Bury
St Edmunds and attend the conference of a housing society at the
local Athenaeum. Afterwards, she was due to conduct a walk-
about in the town's main square. Her sternest test would come
last: a visit to Lucas Diesel Systems in the neighbouring town of
Sudbury, where Diana would express – it was hoped – a close
interest in local manufacturing and industry.

The hospice for the sick and dying stands in the grounds of the
town's hospital. At 10.30 a.m., ten minutes before Diana's
arrival, it is raining steadily. In the hospice forecourt the welcoming party huddle beneath their umbrellas. They include the
local mayor, Councillor Ted Spooner, the chief executive of the
borough council, Mr Richard Toft, and the high sheriff for the
county of Suffolk, Mr Carol Gurney, together with their respective wives. The men wear their chains of office, the women a
variety of hats. This is, after all, a royal visit.

Inside the brand-new building, designed in a synthetically
cheerful Scandinavian style, a room has been set aside for the
press, who are gathered in force: about twenty photographers
and reporters in total. 'She does leprosy, Aids and Red Cross

youth,' the correspondent from a national tabloid explains to a local reporter, 'but not so much Aids any more.'

The press are briefed by a woman from the Central Office of Information, signifying that Diana's visit is a fully fledged royal occasion. There are the usual severe admonitions. 'Any questions to the Princess of Wales will result in the forfeiture of your pass,' she tells the hacks. The man from Fleet Street, who has heard it all before, continues his parallel lecture. 'Diana's dressing down dramatically these days,' he informs the local reporter. 'She always wears business clothes.'

Her business suit this morning is a bright turquoise skirt and matching jacket with gold buttons. By her side is Lady Miriam Hubbard, who has secured Diana's presence at the event using her personal contacts at Kensington Palace. Lady Miriam freely admits later that she traded on the fact that a niece had once been Diana's lady-in-waiting.

A second welcoming party, composed of nurses, doctors and administrators, is waiting to greet Diana in the front lobby. Diana looks relaxed in Lady Miriam's company, and has a word for everyone she meets. A mother, clutching her baby, just manages to curtsy without dropping the infant. As Diana moves away, the mother turns to exchange reactions with her neighbour in the line. Both women glow from their first royal encounter.

To the frustration of the press, Diana has ordained that her tour of the wards is off-limits. These scenes with bed-ridden patients will only be witnessed by a privileged few: Lady Miriam; the Lord Lieutenant of Suffolk, Sir Joshua Rowley, in full regalia; the hospice's general manager; doctors, nurses and administrators; two detectives from the Royalty and Diplomatic Protection Squad; the local chief constable; and Diana's faithful equerry, Captain Edward Musto RM, a dashing figure even in a dark grey suit. In all, the royal entourage numbers about twenty-five.

However Diana performs in this intimate setting, her conduct when she returns to public view is undeniably impressive. Emerging through the swing doors that lead to the wards, she is confronted by pandemonium. At least a hundred worthies, many with their wives and children, are jostling for a better view of Diana, whose reappearance they greet with applause. In the mêlée, the photographers struggle to seize the picture opportunity, while over the hospice tannoy can be heard the sound of James Galway's *Greatest Hits*, which someone has decided to use as soothing background music.

As 'Shenandoah' fades to make way for 'Annie's Song', Diana moves to a sunken area in a corner of the lounge, where a dozen terminally ill patients, propped up in armchairs, are waiting to meet her. Like the audience in a classical amphitheatre, the crowd gathers around the pit to observe the spectacle.

Moving from one patient to the next, Diana ignores the background clamour and dispenses royal comfort with dignity, charm and tact. An old woman, clearly very sick, shows her a locket which Diana examines with unfeigned interest. In an adjacent armchair, tended by a nurse, a younger man is painting. 'Well, it's very nice to see you,' Diana says, and makes a joke about her own lack of skill as an artist. After she has moved on, the patients murmur their approval. 'I can't believe it's happened,' a middle-aged woman says to a visiting friend. 'She's better at the job than all the others,' the friend replies.

Lady Miriam confirms that Diana evoked the same response during her progress round the hospice wards. 'She talked to all the patients, and they all said "it's magic." At one point I said to her, "You know you're running late," and she just said, "I don't care."'

A mile away, in the main square of Bury St Edmunds, is further evidence of Diana's enduring appeal. Bury St Edmunds is a small market town, but perhaps three thousand people (the police are unsure) have gathered in a horseshoe around the square for Diana's scheduled walkabout, now nearly forty-five minutes late. To hem in the crowd, the police have erected crush barriers. More spectators crane their necks out of every available window: from the eighteenth-century Angel Hotel, which stands on one side of the square; from the Bury Kebab House and the Bury Hearing Aid Centre opposite; and from the upper floors of the

Athenaeum, another elegant Georgian building, where Diana has at last arrived for the housing society's conference.

The walkabout, when it begins, evokes a response from the crowd that balances uneasily between acclaim for a superstar and the deference due to royalty. As Diana emerges from the Athenaeum, there are loud cheers and a few wolf-whistles; but first she inspects the Suffolk Red Cross Cadets, neatly dressed in their uniforms, who have been positioned at the start of the walkabout route.

Diana begins her progress around the horseshoe. She is visibly enjoying herself, joking, chatting, laughing, handing the many flowers which are thrust towards her to an increasingly harassed local policewoman. In fact, Diana is having such fun that she does not want the walkabout to finish. As she reaches the end of the horseshoe, she notices that the crowd continues into a side street, unprotected by crush barriers. Oblivious to the frantic signals from the police, who call for reinforcements from their colleagues across the square, Diana continues to walk down the line, shaking hands, smiling, finding everything and everyone a delight.

Captain Musto, meanwhile, motions anxiously to Diana's chauffeur, whose official Rover is parked in the middle of the square. The chauffeur starts the car and cruises slowly towards Diana, now disappearing in the general direction of Sudbury, her next port of call. The car catches up with her, the rear passenger door is opened by Captain Musto, and he all but bundles Diana inside. She is still waving and smiling as the car drives away; behind her, the crowd cheers and a few lads give her a final wolf-whistle.

It is in Sudbury, at the Lucas Diesel Systems plant, that Diana faces her most severe test of the day. The test, unlike her hospice visit, does not involve drawing on reserves of tact and sympathy; instead, it requires an ability to show interest and concern where none, surely, exists.

Here they are, the factory manager, the factory accountant, the quality manager, the injector unit manager, the nozzle unit manager, and the filter and delivery valve unit manager, waiting to welcome Diana in the Lucas forecourt. And here she is, at her last engagement of the day, still smiling and graciously accepting yet another posy from yet another schoolgirl.

In her bachelor days, when she was driving her Metro around Kensington and Knightsbridge, it is a safe assumption that Diana never peered inside the bonnet of a car. Not to worry: a red Ford Escort has been parked in the front reception, its bonnet raised, so that the manager can identify for Diana's benefit the diesel components that are made by Lucas. She looks interested, even concerned, asking the manager to explain in more detail the workings of this particular internal combustion engine.

Inside the Lucas plant, a huge workshop built before the Second World War, Diana is escorted first to a display stand which outlines the company's links with local schools. 'The whole emphasis of our discussion with the Princess of Wales was how the national curriculum helps bring industry and schools together,' the acting personnel officer at Lucas explains to the press after Diana has moved to the next stand. Here she learns about LIFE – or 'Little Improvements For Everyone' – the company's vocational training programme. Diana takes note of 'some of the successful examples of implemented improvements from our "LIFE" initiative'. The improvements include 'quality world-class labels to enhance the departmental communications board'. Behind her, hovering in a rather crumpled fashion, Captain Musto looks tired.

On she goes, past the Nozzle Functioning Demonstration, the Filter Product Display, the Delivery Valve Unit Process Improvement Team Project Display and the Process Improvement Team Display. Her attention never wavers as the mysteries of diesel engineering are at last revealed to her. She arrives eventually at the Injector Manufacturing Cells, where she is to unveil a plaque.

A group of about twenty workers, dressed in dirty overalls and a range of Heavy Metal tee-shirts, is waiting to greet her. As she approaches, their cigarettes are extinguished and silence descends. She pulls the rope and grins at the lads, who break into applause.

Outside the factory, along one side of the building, a crowd of Lucas employees and their families have assembled to greet Diana. Inevitably she is required to go walkabout, and though she is flagging a little, she still has the energy to sign a couple of autographs – another reminder, along with the wolf-whistles, of the fine line between royalty and celebrity. It is the police, not Diana, who call a halt to the walkabout as she reaches the field at the back of the factory

And here, in the middle of the field, stands Diana's reward for doing her royal duty: a giant red Wessex helicopter of the Queen's Flight, its engine already turning over, waiting to transport her back to Kensington Palace. Diana and Captain Musto head for the helicopter, but on the edge of the field she spots an honour guard of police motorcyclists and, for some reason, a vintage fire engine from the local brigade. Captain Musto continues to march purposefully towards the helicopter; she feels bound to walk across to the honour guard to perform her last royal inspection of the day.

Behind a chicken-wire fence on the factory side of the field, the lads have gathered to bid Diana farewell. Crossing towards the helicopter, she waves at them and they wave back. She waves again as she climbs the steps into the helicopter. Already its giant propellors are whirring, and within a few seconds the helicopter has taken off. The lads continue to wave, and through the window of the helicopter Diana waves back for the last time. At an elevation of several hundred feet and rising, she seems to be enjoying herself.

As an experience which is endlessly repeated over a lifetime, however, a royal 'awayday' is not a lot of fun. Diana's visit to Lucas Diesel Systems was an almost impeccable royal performance; but even as she observed the Nozzle Functioning Demonstration, she may have asked herself whether she wished to walk this treadmill indefinitely. Along with the helicopters, the cheers and the wolf-whistles come the gallery of district council officers, borough architects, mayors, mayoresses, local MPs and rotarians, who are the supporting cast for any royal visit. At the heart of this dilemma is Diana's manifest confusion about her royal identity. While Elizabeth brings to the business of unveiling, launching and tree-planting an absolute inner conviction of her symbolic role, Diana is visibly unsure of what, exactly, she is supposed to symbolise.

In December 1993, she featured in a vignette which spoke volumes about her ambiguous public role. The occasion was the Concert of Hope at London's Wembley Arena to mark World Aids Day, organised under Diana's official patronage. Shortly before the concert was due to begin, an eclectic gathering of the famous and not-so-famous assembled to welcome Diana in the arena's hospitality suite. At one end of the line were rock stars George Michael and Mick Hucknall, who would be performing in the concert, together with the master of ceremonies David Bowie. At the other end stood the junior government and opposition health ministers, John Bowis and Dawn Primarolo. In between were a swathe of Aids researchers and charity fundraisers, including the film producer David Puttnam.

Just as curious as the mixture of people was their behaviour when Diana entered the room. No-one, it appeared, could agree whether they were in the presence of royalty or mere celebrity. Neither did Diana seem to know. She had brought the usual entourage for a royal engagement: a detective who looked ill at ease next to David Bowie's spectacularly unbuttoned wife, the Somalian model Iman, and a lady-in-waiting, billed in advance as Anne Beckford-Smith, but in fact her sister Sarah.

Some of the line-up felt they ought to bow or curtsy (Ms Primarolo, wrestling with her socialist principles, merely inclined her head). Diana treated them with regal grace. Others, including David Puttnam, preferred a democratic handshake, with no value-added obeisance. Diana took them in her stride. But with those she knew well, her royal guard dropped entirely. 'Snap!' she giggled, pointing at Les Rudd of the National Aids Trust, whose cream-coloured suit matched her own. It was not a remark her mother-in-law has ever made in similar circumstances.

Only two days later, Diana surprised everyone with her sudden announcement of a temporary retreat from public engagements. The speech all but admitted her confusion and unhappiness. Although she had been contemplating such a move for several months, the final decision was triggered by the *Sunday Mirror's* publication in November of photographs which had been secretly taken while she was exercising at a West London health club. Having blamed the press for her predicament, she told her audience that 'over the next few months I will be seeking a more suitable way of combining a meaningful public role with, hopefully, a more private life . . . I hope you can find it in your hearts to understand and to give me the time and space that has been lacking in recent years.'

The statement was interpreted at the time as virtually an abdication. It was no such thing. During 1994 Diana did scale down the number of representative functions she performed on behalf of the monarchy; there were no more visits to diesel manufacturing plants. But she displayed every intention of wishing to remain a princess rather than a semi-reclusive celebrity. Despite withdrawing her active patronage from a range of charities, she kept up a steady round of nominally private visits to hospitals, refuges for battered women and hostels for the homeless. In November 1994, wishing to learn more about high-security jails, she was escorted around Broadmoor.

Her 'relaunch' on the public stage was imminent. Throughout her eleven-month sabbatical, Diana had continued to discuss with political allies including Lady Chalker, and trusted courtiers such as her private secretary Patrick Jephson, the question of a suitable role for a solo princess. They persuaded her to become a patron of the British Red Cross for its 125th anniversary celebrations. The move must have been approved by the Queen, who is the charity's president.

Yet Diana's relaunch, like her abdication a year before, failed to resolve the questions about her future. Another royal 'event' in November was the publication of Andrew Morton's sequel to his original biography, *Diana: Her New Life*. Even Morton concluded that the direction of Diana's new life remained uncertain. As ever the uncertainties began with Diana, whose need for advice and reassurance remained insatiable. Beyond mainstream figures like Lady Chalker and Jephson, her counsellors in 1994 included the astrologer Debbie Frank, the psychotherapist Susie Orbach and, most bizarrely, the American 'business motivation guru' Anthony Robbins. Robbins, Morton wrote, 'has the ability to cheer up Diana when she is feeling down'.

Diana's emotional state cannot have been helped by her experience of relationships with other men. Her friendship with James Gilbey was broadcast to the world in the 'Squidgygate' tape; Hewitt betrayed her with his kiss-and-tell interviews; and in the autumn of 1994 came further embarrassment for Diana when circumstantial evidence suggested she had been making nuisance phone calls to an older married man, the art dealer Oliver Hoare. These entanglements were generally seen by a sympathetic public as further signs of her unhappiness. The allegations did not dent her consistently high ratings in the opinion polls. But they did bode ill for Diana's chances of forming trusting and stable relationships in the future.

Both in her public and private roles, Diana has yet to come to terms with her situation. It is conceivable that she will eventually find fulfilment in a solo royal career. Equally, she may attempt to retreat altogether into a private life. But it is just as likely that she will be unable to find a balance between her conflicting impulses, and thus be caught in an endless cycle of 'abdications' and 'relaunches'. For Diana, that would be a recipe for perpetual misery. It would not, however, inflict fatal damage on the monarchy.

The seeming threat posed by Diana to the monarchy looms large because her situation is unique: there are no immediate historical parallels. A century ago, another Princess of Wales, Alexandra, learned to suffer her husband's infidelity in silence. Alexandra was so steeped in Victorian values that when Bertie died in 1910, she ushered his last mistress Mrs Alice Keppel (the great-grandmother of Camilla Parker Bowles) into the royal bedroom for a final look at the royal corpse. One has to go back to the early nineteenth century to find a Princess of Wales, Caroline of Brunswick, openly in conflict with her husband, the future George IV. Their battle reached a spectacular climax in 1820 when Caroline was barred from entering Westminster Abbey to attend George's coronation.

In practice, since her separation from Charles, Diana has not done anything wilfully to undermine the monarchy's survival. This is partly a matter of personal belief. In her public statements, including the 1993 'abdication' speech, she has always emphasised her respect for the institution, and more personally, her respect for the Queen. As the daughter of an earl who served as the Queen's equerry, and whose family have been courtiers for centuries, she is likely to be sincere in such professions of loyalty. As the mother of the second and third in line to the throne, Diana also has a personal stake in the monarchy's future.

At issue is not her loyalty to the throne, but her place in the royal pageant. Mr Major's image of a dual coronation for Charles and Diana is implausible. Yet even if she is never crowned Queen, Diana will always retain an unbreakable bond to the throne through her sons. When she announced her temporary retreat from public duties, she told her audience that 'my first priority will continue to be our children, William and Harry, who deserve as much love, care and attention as I am able to give . . .' Already, Diana is keenly aware of her role as a future Queen Mother, taking a close interest in William's training for kingship. In early 1994, for example, she and William were escorted by Cardinal Basil Hume around a hostel for down-and-outs in central London. The visit was supposed to be private, but naturally reached the attention of the press. Her message was clear: whatever Charles and Elizabeth might wish for William, she would impose her own stamp on his princely upbringing.

Because Diana's strongest claim to a royal future is through her sons, rather than her husband, the question of divorce has relatively little bearing on her prospects. If, eventually, she decides to remarry, her image as a princess would no doubt alter. But even if she ceased to be an active, royal symbol, 'vividly and often seen' according to Bagehot's definition, her blood ties to William and Harry would ensure that she never lost the fundamental attributes of royalty. Her proximity to the throne, in contrast to the Duchess of York, guarantees that she cannot be written out of the Windsor script.

In the long term, the speculation surrounding Diana's royal future is secondary to the question of Charles's fitness for kingship. For Diana, divorce, possible remarriage and the style of her future royal career are essentially matters of personal choice. For Charles, the same issues have a direct bearing on the survival of the crown he hopes to inherit.

21

The Long March of the
Prince of Wales

In middle age, Prince Charles continues to add to his portfolio of nervous mannerisms. He twists the signet ring on his left little finger; he tugs at his shirt cuffs, as if to check the shirt is still there; he thrusts his hand into his jacket pocket, only to remove it as the next civic dignitary is ushered towards him. The mere act of talking appears to cause him pain; at regular intervals, he drops his jaw with a grimace, a minor speech defect he acquired in childhood.

To those unfamiliar with these tics and twitches, he does not seem a prince at ease with his station in life. Yet Charles's aides insist that despite the collapse of his marriage, the exposure of his relationship with Camilla Parker Bowles, and the attendant nightmare of the 'Camillagate' tapes – in short, despite the worst humiliation experienced by any heir to the throne in modern times – he is utterly confident that he will one day become King.

Since the separation from Diana, Charles and his advisers have struggled valiantly to focus the public's mind on his endeavours as Prince of Wales. In May 1993, during a visit by Charles to Poland, a member of his entourage explained how the separation from Diana had liberated Charles to concentrate on more serious issues. 'Almost every aspect of these [overseas] visits now represents personal interests,' the courtier pointedly told journalists. 'Unlike the old days with the Princess when he went on handshaking trips, his self-confidence in his role on the world stage is growing.'

It was a pity that not everyone was willing to pay attention. On a trade promotion tour to the Middle East in the autumn of 1993, Charles was dismayed by the lack of interest shown by Whitehall and the press. 'The idea I am searching to redefine my job is rot,' he told the *Financial Times*, one of the few publications apart from *Hello!* magazine to cover the trip. 'It is just that, since the day I got married, people have chosen to ignore the things I continue to do day in, day out.'

By December 1993, the public relations strategy was on the point of collapse. Diana's decision to quit the royal scene in a blaze of publicity was against Charles's wishes; he had wanted her to withdraw quietly. As he feared, her temporary 'abdication' encouraged speculation that she was the victim of a conspiracy, masterminded by him. Once again, their marriage was seen as the pivotal issue in the debate over his suitability for kingship. The debate was reignited by the Archdeacon of York, in a BBC interview. Asked if he thought Charles was still assured of becoming King in the light of the separation, the Archdeacon replied: 'My view would be that Charles made solemn vows before God in church about his marriage, and it seems – if the rumours are true about Camilla – that he began to break them almost immediately. He has broken his trust and vows to God on one thing. How can he then go into Westminster Abbey and take the coronation vows? Are we to believe that he will keep those? I think it brings into question the whole attitude of Charles to vows, trust and so on.'

The Archdeacon's remarks provoked a furious response among Charles's advisers and friends, not to mention Cabinet ministers. Their evident alarm belied the message they were trying to convey, that Charles would in due course succeed his mother as sovereign. 'The Prince will become King, and nothing and nobody will stand in his way,' a member of Charles's staff briefed journalists a few hours after the broadcast. Next day, Charles's close friend and former equerry Nicholas Soames, now a junior government minister, accosted journalists in the parliamentary lobby. 'What the Archdeacon has said was a disgrace,' he told them, in an outburst which was certainly cleared beforehand with St James's Palace. 'It's wounding and hurtful. He [Charles] will inherit the throne. That is the end of the matter.'

By the weekend, Cabinet ministers were riding to Charles's rescue in the form of Lord Wakeham and William Waldegrave. Lord Wakeham wrote in the *Mail on Sunday*: 'When the time comes for him to ascend the throne he will be as fully prepared as any individual can be for the unique and immense responsibilities he will inherit.' More revealing was William Waldegrave's eulogy to Charles in the *Sunday Telegraph*: 'He will be our King. He has prepared himself for the role perhaps more conscientiously than any in the long line of his predecessors.' Mr Waldegrave's sister, Lady Susan Hussey, is one of Elizabeth's senior ladies-in-waiting and the *Sunday Telegraph* article must have been sanctioned by the Queen.

From Charles's point of view, the best that could be said for 1993 was that it was not as bad as 1992. And 1994 offered cause for hope. It was the twenty-fifth anniversary of his investiture at Caernarvon Castle, and to mark the occasion his office announced a rolling programme of events highlighting Charles's interest in the principality. Over the previous quarter of a century, the Welsh could have been forgiven for failing to note this particular interest, and when a mere fourteen people turned up to greet him outside a school in Cardiff, it seemed likely that Charles's celebrations would fall flat. In the end, Charles's anniversary became the pretext for two far more significant, connected events: the broadcast in June of a television film about the heir to the throne, and the publication in November of Charles's authorised biography, both produced by the journalist Jonathan Dimbleby.

The rationale which led to these projects was disclosed by Charles in a letter to Elizabeth's Private Secretary, Sir Robert

Fellowes, reproduced by Dimbleby in his book. Writing in the autumn of 1992, at the lowest point of the *annus horribilis*, Charles proposed various reforms of the Palace press office. In particular, he argued that 'we need a relatively narrow definition of "private lives" and that there are many cases where things which we would prefer to keep private must, nevertheless, be commented upon because they have been brought (whether we like it or not) into the public domain'. Charles continued: '. . . Any hint of defensiveness will only encourage a negative story . . . I do hope that every serious question or proposal for an article, film, etc., can be seen as an opportunity rather than a threat . . . I do hope we can make as much use as possible of television. As the medium which carries the greatest weight of authority with the public, it should be a real asset in countering tabloid excesses.'

Yet the letter scarcely hinted at just how far Charles was prepared to venture. No member of the royal family had ever before offered a writer the free run of his private letters and diaries, the cooperation of his closest friends, and an undertaking not to exercise any editorial censorship. Charles's predecessors as Princes of Wales had generally been more concerned with obliterating their past than exposing their most intimate secrets to the nation. As Dimbleby wrote in the preface: 'I had no expectation that he [Charles] would offer me the unprecedented and unfettered access to the original and entirely untapped sources on which this biography is based.'

The television documentary was broadcast in June 1994 shortly before the anniversary date. While the next day's newspapers almost uniformly derided Charles's performance in the two-and-a-half hour film – 'Prince of Whines' was one headline – it seems that most of the estimated 14 million viewers saw a completely different person. Judging from opinion polls and the anecdotal evidence of radio and television phone-in shows, they found the Prince to be an altogether more appealing figure than they had imagined. Eighteen months after the separation, it was Charles's first, authentic public relations coup.

For Charles, the most dangerous moment in the film was also the most predictable, as Dimbleby was bound to ask Charles about his alleged affair with Camilla Parker Bowles. On this question, Charles declined to give a straight answer. 'All I can say is that, I mean, there is no truth in so much of this speculation,' he told Dimbleby, before adding: 'And Mrs Parker Bowles is a great friend of mine and I have a large number of friends.' Dimbleby then pressed his point: 'Were you, did you try to be, faithful and honourable to your wife when you took on the vow of marriage?' he asked. 'Yes, absolutely,' Charles replied. 'And you were?', Dimbleby continued. 'Yes', Charles said, pausing to reflect: '– until it became irretrievably broken down, us both having tried.'

It was the film's one moment of genuine drama, yet Charles's confession of adultery did not have the catastrophic effect on his public standing many royal watchers had predicted. It appeared that Charles's future subjects, in contrast to tabloid journalists and conservative clerics like the Archdeacon of York, were more forgiving of his sins. In the short term, Charles and his advisers felt vindicated in adopting a policy of courage and openness about his private life.

The real danger, however, lay in the long term. There had been many heirs to the throne who had committed adultery, but none who had felt obliged to admit the fact on peak-time television. By answering Dimbleby's questions, Charles tacitly accepted that the line of enquiry was legitimate. He was, in effect, inviting the people to judge him firstly as a man, and only secondly as a prince. By doing so, he dispelled the last vestiges of the royal aura which had allowed his predecessors as Prince of Wales to conceal the details of their human frailties from public view. Charles appeared to welcome this transition. If his highly-strung manner suggested that he lacked assurance as heir to the throne, his unprecedented cooperation with Dimbleby told a very different story. With a confidence bordering on recklessness, Charles was convinced that once the people had all the facts at their disposal, they would judge him a worthy future king.

Dimbleby's book, published in November, was far more extensive and detailed than the television programme. The author was anxious to distinguish himself from the royal ratpack, whose prurience he repeatedly condemned in the biography. He agonised most on the question of Charles and Diana's marriage. 'I have had to decide how much of what I have learned about the miseries of this marriage should be made public,' he declared in the preface, 'when the couple themselves have already endured so much torment and when their children would have to live with the consequences of what I might write. In seeking to reconcile what has become a matter of public interest with their right to privacy, I have written just enough of what I believe to be the truth about the breakdown of their marriage to establish what a more detailed and intrusive account of the facts as I know them would merely confirm . . .'

He had also written 'just enough' for the *Sunday Times* to buy the serial rights and reproduce the relevant sections under the headlines 'The Prince's Agony – "How could I have got it all so wrong?"'; 'Camilla – "The most intimate friendship of his life"'; and 'Stern father who drove him to tears'. Unlike the television programme, the book gave chapter and verse on Charles's three affairs with Camilla, and confirmed the Prince still loved her at the time of his engagement to Diana. The diaries and letters Charles made available to Dimbleby also recounted his distant relationship with his parents.

Charles let it be known that he had 'no regrets' about the book, though he was irritated by the selective serialisation in the *Sunday Times*. Dimbleby had concluded: '. . . It is not perhaps too fanciful to suppose that future generations will judge that in the latter half of the twentieth century Britain was blessed to have as heir to the throne an individual of singular distinction and virtue.' The current judgement was rather different. While the public had responded favourably to the television film, the book provoked genuine shock. Many of Charles's future subjects felt that here, contrary to Dimbleby's verdict, was a Prince whose flaws had been laid bare for posterity. The effect of the book was to question whether, as king-in-waiting, Charles could rebuild the respect and affection he had once enjoyed.

In 1969, a few months before his investiture, Charles told the radio broadcaster Jack de Manio how he felt when he realised he was heir to the throne. 'I think it's something that dawns on you with the most ghastly inexorable sense,' he said. 'I didn't suddenly wake up in my pram one day and say "Yippee!" . . . I think it just dawns on you, you know, slowly, that people are interested in one . . . and slowly you get the idea that you have a certain duty and responsibility, and I think it's better that way.'

In theory, no Prince of Wales had been better prepared for his destiny. 'Who should educate the Prince of Wales?' an anonymous pamphleteer had asked in 1841, after the birth of Charles's great-great grandfather, the future Edward VII. The answer in the elder Bertie's case was a series of private tutors, who followed a draconian programme of instruction laid down by his father Prince Albert. 'The Plan', as it was ominously described, merely succeeded in reducing Bertie to tantrums, and left him with a lifelong resistance to any form of cerebral activity.

Elizabeth and Philip also had a plan for their eldest son. At the time, it seemed well designed for a Prince of Wales growing up in the second half of the twentieth century. Charles was the first heir to the throne to be educated almost entirely at school rather than privately.* Superficially, his academic career followed the pattern of other upper-class boys of his age, including attendance at his father's old schools. After two terms as a part-time day boy at Hill House School in Knightsbridge, Charles spent five years from 1957 to 1962 at Cheam preparatory school, where Philip had been sent in the late 1920s. A further five years were spent at Philip's alma mater, Gordonstoun, before Charles went up to Cambridge to read archaeology and anthropology (subsequently switching to history). After his graduation in 1971, Charles's training for his responsibilities was completed by five years in the Navy.

His education, however, was far more disjointed than this

seamless résumé suggests. Charles's studies were constantly inter-rupted, not only because his attendance was required for royal functions, but also because of decisions made by his parents. The disruption began on his first day at Hill House. Rather than reg-istering at the start of the academic year, Charles was enrolled for the second term. It was further decreed that he would continue to spend the mornings at Buckingham Palace receiving private tuition, and would only join the classmates he barely knew for their afternoon lessons and recreation.

In 1966 there was a happier interlude when he spent two terms away from Gordonstoun at Timbertop in Australia, the outward bound section of Geelong School. He was far less happy three years later when he was dragged away from Cambridge to spend a term at University College, Aberystwyth learning ele-mentary Welsh, prior to his investiture. Charles's naval service, conceived as the final stage of his princely training, was also truncated. Less than a year after achieving command of his first boat, the coastal mine-hunter HMS *Bronington*, his career came to a halt. Henceforth, he was expected to be a full-time Prince of Wales – whatever that meant.

In his undemonstrative fashion, Charles was almost as miser-able during his formative years as the elder Bertie had been. He was homesick at Cheam, and loathed Gordonstoun even more, as Dimbleby was able to confirm from Charles's letters home. 'It's such hell here especially at night,' he wrote from Gordonstoun in February 1964. 'I don't get any sleep practically at all nowa-days . . . The people in my dormitory are foul. Goodness they are horrid, I don't know how anyone could be so foul. They throw slippers all night long or hit me with pillows or rush across the room and hit me as hard as they can, then beetle back again as fast as they can, waking up everyone else in the dormitory at the same time. Last night was hell, literal hell . . . I still wish I could come home. It's such a HOLE this place!'

His parents and interested courtiers, reflecting the prejudices of the English upper classes about boarding school education, assumed the experience was character building. 'I think had he gone to Eton he may well have found that more comfortable, but it wouldn't have done him any good,' said one courtier who knew Charles at this time. 'I think one of the things about Gordonstoun is that whether or not he liked it is almost immaterial. It certainly developed an awful lot of character in him. It taught him that sometimes, whether or not you like it, there are certain things you've got to do.'

By 1974 Charles had also convinced himself that Gordonstoun had been good for him. 'I'm glad I went to Gordonstoun,' he told the *Observer*. 'It helped me to discipline myself, and I think that discipline, not in the sense of making you bath in cold water, but in the Latin sense – giving shape and form and tidiness to your life – is the most important thing your education can do.' But it is doubtful whether the character shaped by Gordonstoun was mature enough to cope with the burden of being heir to the throne, both in defining his public career and conducting his private life.

Looking back on Charles's investiture in 1969, a former member of his staff says: 'I'm absolutely sure that at that stage he had no idea what he would eventually be doing. What I think he was developing then were areas of interest. By nature, he is a romantic, he's a caring, sensitive person – but not entirely sure what he should care for or be sensitive about. Because at that stage he was still very inexperienced and unworldly – naive, almost.'

Charles's difficulties as a newly launched Prince of Wales were compounded by the absence of any guidelines about his role. 'There was no set pattern, no programme,' the same courtier recalls. 'In the past, the Prince of Wales did a few public visits, and the rest of the time he was meant to keep employed to the best of his abilities.' With no helpful precedents, a makeshift strategy was adopted. At this early stage in Charles's public career, the courtier says, 'we accepted invitations which were firstly enjoyable, where he could learn something and perhaps experience something new, and with a view to relieving the public pressure to see him'.

But the same adviser became disillusioned with Charles's lack of direction during the 1970s. 'I didn't feel he had mapped it out.

You have to understand the nature of the individual. There are some of us who get totally absorbed and involved in things, and others who don't – who like instead to be part of lots of things but not deeply immersed in them. It depends how you see your role. By playing the part of an ombudsman, you can be a lot of things to a lot of people. But you can only do that if you don't become totally immersed in a few things.'

Among members of the Queen's household, there have been other misgivings. 'There's no self-discipline with him,' says a former senior adviser to Elizabeth. 'Look at the way he runs through his Private Secretaries.' Charles's first Private Secretary was David (now Sir David) Checketts, a former RAF officer who joined the royal household in the early Sixties as an equerry to Philip. When Charles went on his school exchange to Australia in 1966, Checketts was assigned to act *in loco parentis*, a task he performed with some panache from the farm which he rented 120 miles from Timbertop. For the next thirteen years Checketts ran the Prince's household, but by 1979 Charles had tired of the older man's avuncular presence. Checketts resigned with a knighthood, to pursue a successful business career away from court.

His successor, Edward Adeane, was the son of Lord Adeane, Elizabeth's Private Secretary in the Fifties and Sixties, and the grandson of the legendary Stamfordham, George's long-serving Private Secretary. With such a background, it seemed nothing could go wrong, but at the beginning of 1985 Adeane resigned to resume his career at the Bar. At the time it was rumoured that Adeane had been pushed out by Diana, who was anxious to rid Kensington Palace of Charles's cronies from his bachelor days. The real dispute was over Charles's growing taste for public controversy, which Adeane felt was inappropriate for a Prince of Wales. Adeane was replaced by Sir John Riddell, a successful City businessman with no previous court connections. He, too, left prematurely in 1990, having failed to bring administrative order to Charles's headquarters at St James's Palace, but having succeeded – unlike his predecessors – in remaining on good terms with the Prince of Wales.

That was not the case with Charles's next Private Secretary, Sir Christopher Airy, who resigned in May 1991 at the age of fifty-seven after only a year in the job. 'Sir Christopher's age was a factor,' a palace spokesman told reporters, 'but not the key one. One cannot go into details about personal factors or into personalities. Anyone appointed to the royal household has an escape route if things do not work out, so that they are able to leave the job.' In Sir Christopher's case, the 'personal factor' was Charles's fury at his Private Secretary's inability to prevent Diana's public engagements clashing with his own. Sir Christopher's resignation was precipitated when a broadside by Charles about declining standards in English was overshadowed in the next day's newspapers by coverage of a speech by Diana about Aids.

It reveals something of Charles's idiosyncratic approach to management that, according to Dimbleby, among those he had canvassed before appointing Sir Christopher was the veteran disc jockey Sir Jimmy Savile. It says even more about his truly royal attitude to personnel matters that when the time came to sack Sir Christopher, the task was left to a member of the inappropriately named Prince of Wales Coordinating Committee. Charles, meanwhile, went for a walk in the garden.

Older courtiers suggest that Charles has a general tendency to walk away from some of the drearier royal duties. 'I'm sure the Queen works a jolly sight harder at the papers than Charles would want to,' a former adviser says. 'He's not a paper man. He doesn't like paper – he's had no staff training, you see. He's an action man.'

To understand how Charles sees his public role, there is no better place to start than the Haven All-Action Holiday Centre at Caister, a few miles north of Great Yarmouth on the Norfolk coast. In late March, before the tourist season begins, the Prince's Trust takes over the camp for its annual 'work, sport and leisure course'. From all corners of Charles's future kingdom come four hundred 'unemployed but employable' young people for a week of training in social and work skills which, it is hoped, will improve their self-esteem and their job prospects. And on the last day of the week, Charles descends on Caister to inspect his creation.

At 10.30 a.m. on Friday 2 April 1993, twenty minutes before Charles is due to arrive, a party of about thirty hacks are gathered outside Jumbo's Bar, a bleak wooden hut close to the Norfolk beach which serves as the Trust's makeshift hospitality suite. The royal correspondent from *The Times* is here, as is a reporter from the *New York Times* who is preparing a feature on the monarchy in the wake of the *annus horribilis*.

In the distance, Charles's helicopter can be seen landing in a field opposite the main entrance to the All-Action Holiday Centre. A convoy of four motorcycle outriders, two marked police cars and three official Rovers is waiting to escort him the short distance to Jumbo's Bar – a larger fleet than the one put at Diana's disposal in Suffolk. But then Charles, unlike Diana, is heir to the throne.

When he arrives, Charles characteristically refuses to turn his face to the bank of cameras which point at him from the designated press position. It is the first of several photo opportunities he will ignore, for Charles's mind is on the business in hand. He strides into an adjacent wooden hut, where a group of eleven young people are waiting to tell him about their experiences during the week. They sit nervously in a circle, staring at the vacant chair which has been provided for Charles.

Sitting down, Charles skilfully starts a conversation with people who are dumbstruck by his presence. He has heard there have been rave parties this year at Caister, and wants to learn more. 'Have any of you been to them? What sort of music is it?' A girl from Birmingham offers to take him to one. 'You'd protect me, would you?' he says with a smile. Everyone laughs and the ice is broken.

Another girl offers him a badge she has made in her art workshop, showing a grotesque cartoon head of Charles with enormous ears. It bears the legend 'Rave on Charlie'. Charles takes the badge, winces at the sight of himself, and declines her suggestion that he should wear it; and then, realising she might be offended, says, 'Well, perhaps I'll wear it for a bit.' With a dubious glance at his cartoon head, he attaches the badge to his immaculately hand-tailored pinstripe suit.

Outside in a muddy field, a group of physical training instructors from the RAF are supervising press-ups, bench-sits and other fitness exercises for about thirty flabby youths. Like the guest of honour at a school prize day, Charles tours the field, hands behind his back, dutifully inspecting the lads, offering words of encouragement. Behind him one of his Private Secretaries and his press officer hover self-importantly.

On he moves, pursued by the press, to a room above the All-Action cafeteria, where another collection of Prince's Trust clients are arranged in a circle. They are supposed to be practising job interview skills with the help of a video recording, but as Charles enters and walks briskly towards the designated royal chair, they break into nervous applause. Silence returns as the heir to the throne sits down.

A mock interview is replayed on the video, and for two minutes the instructor from the regional Training and Education Council – who is as nervous as her charges – asks the group to comment on the recording. They repeat the answers they gave before Charles arrived and then, on cue, she turns to Charles and requests a royal opinion.

'I was just looking at all the things you're supposed not to do. Hands, for instance,' he says, looking quizzically at his own. 'The most important thing, I think, is making a good impression.' He turns to the girl next to him, who is nodding in vigorous agreement. Her hair is dyed purple and three rings pierce her nose.

Charles turns to the rest of the group and starts peppering them with questions. 'How did you all find school? Did you get bored? Would it have helped to have things like this? Are you mechanically minded?' In another life, it is easy to imagine that Charles would have made a successful careers officer. The woman from the TEC regards his performance with approval.

In a few minutes Charles has completed this part of the programme, and to further applause he and his entourage proceed to

Neptune's Palace, the All-Action Holiday Centre's entertainment theatre. Here, all four hundred course members are gathering for the week's finale, a concert for the Prince of Wales. The show's compere is the rock star Phil Collins, a trustee of the charity, who has spent three days in Caister supervising the music workshop.

There is a commotion at one end of Neptune's Palace as Charles and his suite arrive. 'Let's have a resounding welcome for His Royal Highness the Prince of Wales, please,' Collins asks the audience. They respond with whoops, cheers, and one or two shouts from the rear of 'Good old Charlie!' Charles smiles self-consciously and makes his way to the front row, where a dozen seats have been reserved for himself, his suite, and senior figures from the Prince's Trust.

The drama workshop begins the show with a sketch called 'Dear Diary', about an imaginary week in Caister. There is a running joke about a royal visit, featuring another cartoon of Charles, which this time is life-size. He grimaces, not enjoying the joke at all, and turns away to talk to the Prince's Trust executive sitting next to him. He flinches again when the dance workshop performs a mime to the rock song 'My first name is Prince'. The music workshop is more to his taste, singing their own version of Monty Python's 'Always Look on the Bright Side of Life', specially adapted to a week in Caister. Charles applauds enthusiastically as the song reaches its climax.

Phil Collins, wearing a red Prince's Trust tee-shirt and jeans, takes the microphone again to give a general vote of thanks to Charles from everyone at Caister. Then it is time for Charles's speech. As he rises to his feet and takes the microphone from Collins, the audience starts to cheer again. 'C'mon Charlie!' someone shouts, a remark which Charles pretends not to hear. Only the press are disappointed. Last year Charles joined Collins on stage and played the drums, and the photographers had been hoping the duo would pull the same stunt. But today Charles resists the lure of the drum set. The press start to grumble that there is no story.

Charles's speech, delivered without notes, is extremely good.

He neither condescends to his audience, nor pretends he is anyone other than the Prince of Wales. 'I want to tell you that I'm very, very impressed with what I've seen here at Caister,' he begins. He thanks Collins, who looks bashful. 'I've heard he could have gone to Beverly Hills this week to discuss a film, but instead he chose Caister.' Everyone applauds Phil's devotion to duty. Charles also thanks the RAF instructors, 'who have been valiantly trying to get rid of all those beer paunches I've seen this morning.'

'You might ask,' he concludes, 'what do I get out of all this? I get a lot of encouragement from seeing all this activity and energy, and believe me, that makes me feel really good.' He means what he says; no press secretary has drafted these remarks.

'There are more cheers, more shouts of 'Good old Charlie', but the heir to the throne is already on his way to the official Rover which is waiting for him outside Neptune's Palace and takes him across the road to the red Wessex helicopter of the Queen's Flight: the same one, perhaps, that Diana will use four months later in Suffolk. As the helicopter disappears westward over the horizon, Charles's press officer is happy to confirm to a journalist that, yes, 'the boys' – that is to say, William and Harry – will be spending the weekend at Sandringham with their father.

Twenty-five years before this visit to Caister, there had been no Prince's Trust, no Prince's Youth Business Trust, no Prince's Trust Volunteers, no Prince of Wales' Community Venture, no Prince of Wales's Institute of Architecture. In practice there had been no role for Charles, beyond filling the time until his mother died with the traditional round of representative duties.

Few would argue that in pursuing his own agenda as heir to the throne, Charles has displayed far more energy than any of his predecessors. The doubts concern whether the energy is misdirected, actually undermining the institution he hopes to inherit. Flitting by helicopter from one engagement to the next, Charles is vulnerable to the charge that he has a 'scattergun' approach to public duties. His advisers disagree: they insist that as heir to the throne, he is obliged to take an interest in every aspect of his future kingdom. Nor do they agree that Charles has a limited attention span. 'He isn't good like a cabinet minister, churning through three hours of boxes every evening,' says a senior figure at the Prince's Trust. 'He just isn't. On the other hand, I might get a twenty-page letter handwritten late one evening, because he's been thinking about a particular problem to do with our work.'

The advisers deny the charge made by some older courtiers that Charles has become too 'political' by meddling in areas which are not his business, such as unemployment, the environment and architecture. 'There's a line about him not being involved in politics,' says the Prince's Trust executive. 'It's a very fine line, and of course he is involved in politics really. He's making political speeches, but in that self-deprecating way he's developed, which makes it possible for him to do so as the Prince of Wales.'

His staff distinguish between politics, which is acceptable, and party politics, which is not. As an example of the former, they cite a private visit by Charles to Germany in March 1993, during which he paid a courtesy call on Chancellor Kohl. The Chancellor asked Charles to explain the growth of anti-German feeling in Britain, and on his return to England Charles sent Downing Street a report of the conversation. Mr Major was duly grateful for Charles's briefing.

But beyond politics and party politics there is straightforward polemic. No modern Prince of Wales has been as outspoken as Charles, and over the past decade he has made many enemies. At the top of the list are modernist architects, whom he castigated in his 1989 book *A Vision of Britain*. 'The further I delve into the shadowy world of architecture, planning and property development,' Charles wrote, 'the more I become aware of the powerful influence of various interest groups, hence the frequently violent and vitriolic reactions to the points I have been making.'

By 1993, when he published his book on the gardens and farm estate at Highgrove, Charles had widened his attack to include a still more shadowy group called the avant garde. 'Suddenly the avant garde became the establishment,' he wrote of the post-war era. 'The worlds of art, music, literature, architecture, [and] education all fell under the spell of this revolutionary and, to many of its proponents, exciting philosophy of the future. Everything was carried before it and anyone who had serious doubts about the wisdom of adopting such a radical approach to life itself was instantly labelled a reactionary or worse.'

At St James's Palace, his aides maintain that when Charles becomes King, 'the trapdoor shuts'. Overnight, his controversial activities as Prince of Wales will cease and Charles III will assume the strict impartiality of a constitutional monarch. Charles's subjects, accustomed to his tirades about the state of the world, may find such a transition less plausible. One potential Cabinet minister has already sounded a warning. Interviewed in December 1994 by the BBC Panorama programme, the Shadow Home Secretary Jack Straw remarked: 'He [Charles] needs to take account of the kind of role he has marked out for himself as Prince of Wales. He needs to think whether or not that is an appropriate role for a monarch.' Mr Straw added pointedly that 'if a monarch is too closely following an agenda of his or her own, people are going to say, "What is the point of having this monarchy? Why don't we go to the Irish system where you have a republic?"'

The debate about the monarchy's future inevitably focuses on Charles, as Mr Straw implied. Most immediate is the question of whether a prince whose marriage has failed so publicly is a credible heir to the throne. More generally, his personality and career as Prince of Wales may prove ill-suited to preserving the monarchy's popular appeal.

Constitutionally, Charles's supporters have a strong case that the marriage break-up has no bearing on his succession rights. The British branch of the Hanoverian dynasty was founded in 1714 by a divorcée, George I, who renounced his wife Sophia Dorothy because of her adultery with an adventurer called Konigsmarck. For her sins, Sophia Dorothy was locked in a castle until her death over thirty years later. Nor would divorce bar Charles from becoming the next Supreme Head of the Church of

England. The Anglican church owes its sixteenth-century origins to Henry VIII's determination to divorce Katharine of Aragon. This led to the break with Rome and Henry's new job as head of the English church. For good measure, the first Supreme Head went on to marry five more wives.

In a more secular age, however, it is public opinion that counts, not constitutional niceties. At the start of Elizabeth's reign, even innocent parties in a divorce case were banned from the royal enclosure at Ascot, for fear of tainting the monarch with their presence. Today, after the break-up of three of her children's marriages, those rules seem laughable. The collapse of the royal family myth may have made Charles's life easier, for public expectations of the Windsors' ability to embrace traditional family values are now somewhat diminished. In the short term, it is inconceivable that Charles could marry Camilla – who divorced her husband in January 1995 – and retain his credibility as a future king. In the longer term, however, the narrow legal issue of whether Charles is separated, divorced or remarried will probably matter less than whether he can shake off the impression created by his first marriage of callousness and hypocrisy.

Concerning the wider doubts about his temperament and public agenda, Charles is bound to be judged against the example set by his mother. After more than four decades on the throne, Elizabeth more powerfully embodies the royal myth than any sovereign since Victoria. The shortcomings of her children have scarcely affected her standing with her subjects.

How much of Elizabeth's aura can Charles inherit? Charles's staff point out that he could become King tomorrow, next year, in a decade, or perhaps never, given the propensity of the Windsor women to outlive the men. As the memory of the *annus horribilis* fades, so Charles's supporters must hope he appears an increasingly worthy future monarch.

At times, these uncertainties may even trouble Elizabeth's unspeculative nature. For the most part, though, she is far too busy being the Queen to worry about such abstract matters.

22

Elizabeth, Still Getting On With It

'She never bloody lets you down,' a former courtier says of Elizabeth. 'She's available every single morning, she'll call you in the afternoon if there's a problem, she'll even call you at home in the evening if something is worrying her.'

For someone who takes pride in continuity and tradition, Elizabeth's approach to state duties is strikingly different from her predecessors. Victoria shared her appetite for politics, while driving Sir Henry Ponsonby to distraction with her whims. The elder Bertie tried to accommodate political business in between his lengthy holidays, but more pressing social duties frequently intervened. George and the younger Bertie retired to the grouse moors and pheasant drives of Balmoral and Sandringham, there to escape the ceaseless flow of state papers. As for David, he was so careless with the red boxes during his brief reign that cabinet minutes were returned from Fort Belvedere bearing wine and food stains.

Only Elizabeth, it appears, combines a serene temperament with steady application to official business. As she ploughs through the red boxes, corgis at her feet, she is the very image of a constitutional monarch.

Yet no less than her predecessors, it is a mistake to see her as a figure above politics. Her political reflexes are those of an instinctive one-nation Tory, and these are the people with whom she feels most comfortable. Much is made of her excellent relations with the Labour Prime Ministers Harold Wilson and James Callaghan, both ardent royalists. Even the would-be republican Richard Crossman, a cabinet minister throughout the Wilson years from 1964 to 1970, gradually softened his stance, as Sir Edward Ford remembers. 'Dick Crossman was a really naturally hostile person towards the royal family and thought the Privy Council was absolute mumbo jumbo. But he came round entirely in the end, and wanted to bring his family to his last Privy Council.'

Elizabeth's tolerance for socialists still has its limits. They may be welcome as guests at Sandringham and Balmoral, but they are not her preferred company. Her four Women of the Bedchamber in 1993 illustrate the point. On a rota basis, they were in constant attendance on Elizabeth, and all four have close family connections with the patrician wing of the Conservative party.

Lady Susan Hussey, the wife of the chairman of the BBC governors, is also the sister of the Tory cabinet minister and Old Etonian William Waldegrave. Lady Elton is the wife of another patrician Tory, who served as a minister of state at the Home Office and the Department of the Environment in the 1980s. Mrs John Dugdale is the daughter of the late Oliver Stanley, a Conservative MP in the 1930s and 1940s, and a minister in Neville Chamberlain's pre-war cabinet. Stanley in turn was the son of George V's lifelong friend Lord Derby.

The Hon. Mary Morrison is unusual only because she has ties to both the patrician and Thatcherite wings of the Tory party. One brother, Sir Charles Morrison, was Conservative MP for Devizes until 1992 and an unreconstructed one-nation Tory. The other, Sir Peter Morrison, was Mrs Thatcher's Private Secretary at the time of her downfall.

Nor is it the case that Elizabeth keeps her political opinions to herself, in alleged contrast to Charles. If her dealings with the government of the day remain scrupulously correct, her own speeches are saturated with the traditional Tory values of loyalty, service and nation. The self-perception of one-nation Tories is that these values are also above politics, having nothing in common with the ritual trading of slogans that occurs in the House of Commons. But in the sense that she has a dominant ideology, Elizabeth is a thoroughly political Queen.

Her *annus horribilis* speech at London's Guildhall in November 1992 was a pure expression of that ideology. The audience included the Prime Minister and the Leader of the Opposition; and she told them emphatically that 'no institution . . . should expect to be free from the scrutiny of those who give it their loyalty and support, not to mention those who don't. But we are all part of the same fabric of our national society and that scrutiny, by one part of another, can be just as effective if it is made with a touch of gentleness, good humour and understanding.'

The speech was also a reminder that Elizabeth has a specific political goal of her own: to ensure the survival of the monarchy. Over the years, Philip has made off-the-cuff remarks about how, if the moment comes, they will go quietly – a feat his own Greek royal family has achieved twice this century. For her part, Elizabeth has tended increasingly to emphasise how she reigns by the consent of her people. In 1993, that was the message she sent via a press spokesman to her distant Australian subjects, who face a referendum on whether to opt for a republic.

The image evoked is of passive resignation; yet it is just as misleading as the idea that she operates above politics. At Balmoral in September 1993, the Australian Prime Minister Paul Keating, who hopes to lead his country to a republic, experienced the full force of Elizabeth's displeasure. In public, she was indeed resigned to his decision to hold a referendum. In private he had to endure an audience with Elizabeth that was so frosty as to be almost glacial. It was followed by a barbecue on the Balmoral lawn where Mr Keating was reportedly ostracised by his hosts.

More generally, the fact that she rules by consent implies – in political terms – that there is a royalist constituency to be nursed. In this respect, Elizabeth has been a model to any aspiring MP

with a marginal seat. Her judgement, as will be seen, has sometimes been lacking; her application to the task of maintaining her
support can hardly be faulted.

For reasons beyond her control, the constituency has shrunk dramatically during her reign, with the loss of empire and the
progressive demise of the Commonwealth. In 1993, despite Mr
Keating's initiative, Elizabeth was still Queen of seventeen of
the fifty Commonwealth member states; but at the biennial
Commonwealth conference in October, she pointedly remarked
that she would 'certainly not be betting' on how many of these
countries would be monarchies in forty years time.

As head of the Commonwealth, she remains fervently attached
to the organisation – far more so, it appears, than either her
advisers or the British government. 'Britain is what matters to
the monarchy, whatever she feels,' says a former courtier. 'This is
where the seed is planted. The Commonwealth is just a constitutional arrangement. In the 1950s Lord Altrincham suggested
she should live three months in one Commonwealth country,
three months in another, but the whole idea was mad. She
couldn't be away from Britain for more than a few months without endangering it.'

Elizabeth has nevertheless worked hard to nourish what she
calls the 'Commonwealth idea'. Where Philip's 'sacrifices' for the
idea have been a happy mixture of business and pleasure – such as
in the spring of 1993, when he and *Britannia* enjoyed an island-
hopping tour of the Caribbean – Elizabeth's Commonwealth
tours have included a fair amount of tribulation.

Her trip with Philip to New Zealand and the South Pacific in
February 1974 was especially stressful. In Wellington, 'while
chatting to the 5000 strong crowd near the harbour' – a feat
only royalty could achieve – a group of Maori demonstrators,
'some in hippie-style dress', tried to hand her a letter protesting
about their racial oppression. At Waitingi, where the Maoris
pledged allegiance to Elizabeth's great-great-grandmother in
1841, a petrol bomb was thrown at her as she was ferried ashore

from *Britannia.* Fortunately, 'she only saw a puff of smoke'.

A few days later she arrived in the New Hebrides. Demonstrators at the welcoming ceremony brandished placards with the slogan 'It's not a Condominium so much as a Pandemonium' – a reference to the local parliament. Before Elizabeth could find a Private Secretary to decipher the message, she was confronted on the quayside by a painted warrior with a spear. 'Who are you, what do you want!' he shouted at her. It was a traditional New Hebridean greeting, the warrior (otherwise an electrician) explained afterwards. He told reporters that in the past, his forbears would have attacked first and asked questions later.

On Pentecost Island, real tragedy occurred during a local fertility rite. To signify their manhood, warriors dived head first from seventy-foot-high towers, with only a rope of vine leaves to arrest their fall. One of the ropes snapped and a diver plummeted to earth a few yards from Elizabeth. He was rushed unconscious to hospital, where he died.

With such experiences in mind, Elizabeth was able to tell the Commonwealth conference in Cyprus that after forty years as head of the organisation, 'my capacity for being surprised has lessened'. She was nevertheless reported to be 'upset' on her return to London a few days later, when the Foreign Office decided to cut its subsidy to the Commonwealth Institute in London. Douglas Hurd justified the decision 'in view of the fall in visitor numbers over the last ten years and the need to look afresh at ways to promote the Commonwealth within Britain.'

The Institute, in Kensington High Street, is a monument to the decay of the Commonwealth 'idea'. By 1993, thirty-one years after it was opened, the building was already in urgent need of repair. A particular danger was the roof, whose copper tiles, donated by African member states, were falling off the structure. According to one Foreign Office source, as much as £8 million would be required to refurbish the Institute – 'and that's just to stop it becoming a public menace'.

Inside, the exhibits from different member states were equally dispiriting. Visitors could admire, for instance, the central display from New Zealand: a model of 'a typical farmland in Taranaki Province, North Island, the world's largest exporter of cheese'. It was somehow fitting that Elizabeth's most embarrassing moment as head of the Commonwealth should have occurred at the Institute. A few months before the Foreign Office announcement, she attended a reception there. The time came to deliver a speech, Elizabeth fished in her handbag for her glasses, only to discover she had left them at the palace. Philip, much amused, read the speech on her behalf.

Elizabeth's inheritance has also been threatened closer to home. During the 1970s, when the IRA launched its campaign of terror on the mainland, she worried that her kingdom was poised to disintegrate. 'We may hold different points of view,' she declared in the aftermath of the 1974 pub bombings in Guildford and Birmingham, 'but it is in times of stress and difficulty that we most need to remember that we have much more in common than there is dividing us.'

Neither an Irish nationalist nor an Ulster unionist would have agreed with her sentiments. But because of the tribal divisions in Northern Ireland, the position of the crown is relatively straightforward. On pain of death, the citizens of Ulster are either royalists or republicans.

The situation in Wales and Scotland is rather more complicated, and there is little sign that Elizabeth appreciates the historical subtleties of Celtic nationalism. Her most conspicuous intervention in the devolution controversy occurred in May 1977, in her reply to the loyal addresses of the Lords and Commons which marked her Silver Jubilee. After initial resistance from the Labour Prime Minister James Callaghan, whose party was deeply split on the issue, she was allowed to include a ringing defence of her inheritance.

'I number Kings and Queens of England and of Scotland and Princes of Wales among my ancestors,' she told her audience in Westminster Hall, 'and so I can readily understand these aspirations [towards devolution]. But I cannot forget that I was crowned Queen of the United Kingdom of Great Britain and Northern Ireland. Perhaps the Jubilee is a time to remind ourselves of the benefits which union has conferred, at home and in our international dealings, on the inhabitants of all parts of this United Kingdom.'

In terms of her royal ancestry, Elizabeth was in fact especially ill-qualified to understand Scottish and Welsh nationalism. The title of Prince of Wales had been created in 1301 for the future Edward II to consolidate the English monarchy's subjugation of the native Welsh dynasty of Gwynedd. To a twentieth-century Welsh nationalist this was no mere historical detail, as Charles had discovered during the turbulent prelude to his investiture.

The ignorance of the Windsors regarding their Welsh principality was well illustrated by Charles's 1969 description of some nationalist demonstrators he encountered as 'a sort of modern, ghastly phenomenon'. He at least had the courage to confront them, but it was not a meeting of minds. In a radio interview with Jack de Manio in March 1969, Charles explained how 'I asked one chap, who was holding a placard, what it was, what it meant, because it was in Welsh, and I'm afraid I haven't learnt it properly yet. So I asked him but he just hurled abuse at me, "Go home, Charlie", or something like that. So after I'd asked him more questions, I gave up. There was no point.'

Much to the disappointment of Charles's language tutor at Aberystwyth, Edward Milward, his Welsh has not improved over the years. Nor has he shown any special interest in his principality, concentrating instead on his Duchy of Cornwall estates, which are mainly located in the south-west of England.

Elizabeth's response to potential Celtic rebellion has been to disarm the Welsh by regular royal visits. In October 1993, for instance, she could be found in Cardiff, naming the Butetown Tunnel Link 'Queen's Gate', meeting local worthies at South Glamorgan County Hall, holding an investiture at the city's castle, and inspecting a guard of honour at the National Museum of Wales. So far, she appears to have the principality under control.

As the owner of a Highland holiday home, her visits to Scotland are a fixture in the royal calendar. Late summer always finds Elizabeth at Balmoral, where she likes to remain for at least six weeks. Yet like her predecessors, she has often seemed oblivious to the undercurrents of Scottish nationalism.

Ever since Prince Albert bought Balmoral in 1852 the royal family has acted out the fantasy of its own, largely fictitious, Scottishness. 'I always give her five poond,' Victoria told a lady-in-waiting, after visiting a humble cottager near Balmoral. '*Un costume un peu écossais demain*,' the elder Bertie would tell his Swiss valet as the royal yacht approached Scotland; and the following day he might appear in a tartan waistcoat. By the time he reached Balmoral, Bertie was ready for what one historian has called 'the full exuberance of kilt, sporran and skean-dhu'.

Elizabeth, who can at least claim a Scottish mother, revels in these kitsch traditions. Philip and the royal princes still wear the Balmoral tartan, specially designed by that well-known Caledonian, Albert of Saxe-Coburg. Kilts, according to the royal rule, must not be worn below the line of Perth (except, it seems, for Christmas at Sandringham); north of the line, Scottish costume is obligatory. Each year, drenched in tartan, the royal family pays its annual visit to the Highland Games at Braemar, where cabers are tossed, jigs are reeled, and drams of whisky are drunk.

Some of Elizabeth's Scottish subjects find royalty's periodic bouts of tartan fever rather appealing. But if there are nationalists who happen to be royalists, there is also a tradition of left-wing republicanism which persisted long after it was extinguished in England.

During the 1936 abdication crisis, for instance, the Scottish MPs George Buchanan and James Maxton were the only members to call openly for the monarchy's abolition. 'I have listened to more cant and humbug than I have ever listened to in my life,' Buchanan said in the abdication debate, sickened by the sight of his English colleagues queuing up to praise David's virtues, even while they rejoiced at his departure.

Against such a complex background, Elizabeth ought to have taken particular care in cultivating her royalist constituency in

Scotland. Instead, her reign began with what seemed to be a calculated snub to Scottish national pride. There was no calculation, however, for Elizabeth and her advisers were completely unaware of the offence they had committed until it was too late.

As befits a separate kingdom, Scotland has its own royal household whose titles, if possible, are even more arcane than their English equivalents. Clutching the national banner of Scotland are the Scrymgeour-Wedderburn family, Hereditary Banner Bearers since time immemorial. The Maitlands hold the honour of Hereditary Bearers of Scotland's national flag, after a legal battle with the Scrymgeour-Wedderburns which was finally settled in 1901. A Hereditary Carver cuts the royal meat, and in the person of the Hereditary Lord High Constable, Scotland has its own version of Gold Stick, responsible with his gold truncheon for the sovereign's security once she crosses the border.

In June 1953 the household, together with the flower of Scottish nobility, prepared to welcome Elizabeth as she embarked on a 'coronation tour' of her northern kingdom. The highlight was a service in St Giles' Cathedral, Edinburgh, where she was due to receive the honours of Scotland.

'The honours of Scotland,' Sir Thomas Innes of Learney marvelled in the official souvenir of the tour: 'for centuries an almost magic name and still a loved and familiar one to Scottish folk of town and countryside. The "honours thrie" of song and story: the Scottish Crown, fashioned in part from gold which, legend has it, adorned the brow of our patriot King, Robert the Bruce, the Sceptre, and the Sword of State.'

Sir Thomas was too modest to mention that as Lord Lyon King of Arms, it was he who placed the hallowed crown on the sovereign's head – a privilege denied him by Elizabeth's unaccountable decision to hold only one coronation, in her southern capital of London. And he was far too polite to note that on the day in question, while he and the rest of the royal household wore their full regalia – kilts, feathers, daggers, berets and batons, with lashing of tartan – Elizabeth appeared in a plain blue dress and matching handbag.

The official artist who commemorated the scene could scarcely bear to record her faux pas. In the painting which now hangs in Holyroodhouse, the offending handbag is discreetly obscured from view; the dress itself is all too visible. Sir Alan Lascelles, shortly to retire as Private Secretary, took the blame for failing to advise Elizabeth to wear her Scottish state robes.

The blame really lay with Elizabeth. She may have numbered Queens of Scotland among her ancestors, but it seems she would have been hard pressed to name them. In a further outrage to Scottish patriots, she originally styled herself 'Elizabeth the Second' north of the border. The Scots threatened legal action, and she discovered that to her northern subjects, she was in fact only 'Elizabeth the First'. Her sixteenth-century namesake Elizabeth Tudor claimed no sovereignty over Scotland, because her reign pre-dated the union of the crowns in 1603. The mistake was acknowledged, and post-boxes in Scotland still bear the distinctive insignia 'E.R.'.

England is Elizabeth's heartland, however many leeks and thistles adorn her coins. Bagehot's masterwork, which she read as an adolescent under the Vice-Provost of Eton's tutelage, is called *The English Constitution*; and it is as an English Queen – though with Scottish and German ancestry – that Elizabeth has sought to fulfil Bagehot's brief.

In the fifth decade of her reign, she performs her duties as head of state with total self-assurance. 'I have had quite a lot of Prime Ministers', she remarked in the 1992 film *Elizabeth R*, over footage of the ninth, John Major, being shown round the gardens at Balmoral. She needs no instruction from such novices. From the signing of army commissions to the approval of orders in council, Elizabeth knows the ropes.

She also knows how to stand on her constitutional dignity, as Mr Major discovered in the autumn of 1993. Such was the backlog of business from the previous session that the government was unable to give Elizabeth a firm date for the annual state opening of Parliament. Exasperated by the disruption to her schedule, she insisted a date must be fixed; otherwise, the palace implied, she might discover there were more pressing engagements that required her attention. A chastened Downing Street rapidly sorted out its own plans, and humbly requested her presence at Westminster on Thursday 18 November. Meanwhile, the government whips were mobilised to meet the royal deadline.

Yet Elizabeth's rebuke was essentially symbolic, and posed no threat to the wheels of government. If she had failed to appear for the state opening of Parliament, the government could simply have published the Queen's Speech it had written for her, and political business would have continued. For much of Victoria's reign that is exactly what happened, because the Queen found the state opening too nerve-shattering and preferred to remain at Windsor.

Nor would the state collapse if Elizabeth declined to receive the credentials of foreign ambassadors – the ceremony immortalised in *Royal Family* by the bumbling American envoy, Walter Annenberg. The ambassadors' letters would instead be delivered direct to the government, and the Marshal of the Diplomatic Corps, who collects the diplomats in a carriage from the royal mews, would be out of a job.

If Elizabeth failed to read the legendary red boxes, the 'Queen's business' would continue to be transacted, as it was quite successfully under her less conscientious predecessors. And if future prime ministers were no longer welcome for the weekly audience at Buckingham Palace, they might miss the benefit of Elizabeth's advice. They would still, however, be Prime Minister.

Even in the case of a hung parliament, Elizabeth's role in the appointment of a prime minister is less important than is sometimes supposed. Republicans tend to exaggerate this aspect of her 'political' power. As a symbol of the continuity of the state, she plays a pivotal part in orchestrating the constitutional drama which ensues. But she has little personal influence over the outcome. No decision is made that requires her independent initiative and judgement, for the procedures are laid down by precedent. Drawing on the guidance of nameless constitutional advisers (the historian Lord Blake is one of the few to have been identified), her task is to ensure the drama is resolved according to an unwritten rule book.

In reality the rites of constitutional monarchy matter far more to the monarchy than they do to the running of the country. Despite her irritation over the question of dates, it is inconceivable that Elizabeth would have refused to attend the state opening of Parliament. For if she had, a question would have floated in the air: why was her presence required at all?

To the small but growing number of die-hard republicans in Britain, the answer is simple: the monarch is an unwelcome and unnecessary fixture at the heart of the state. Because the Queen has not been elected, she undermines a political system that is democratic. Far better, they say, to replace her with a president holding no allegiance to any political party, but elected by the people. The symbols of the state would thus reflect the popular will.

Republicans are correct that the business of drafting a new constitution would be relatively straightforward, for there are models going back to the ancient Greeks. The real difficulty in making the transition from monarchy to republic is political. No government would risk splitting the nation by holding a referendum on the monarchy unless there had been a massive shift in public opinion in favour of a republic. Even if many voters wanted to end the monarchy, they would have to represent an overwhelming majority before Downing Street would dare go to the people on such a divisive issue.

The shift in public attitudes and political will has instead been more modest, and was described by the Shadow Home Secretary Jack Straw in December 1994. 'What we [the Labour party] are observing is in tune with what the public are thinking, that the monarchy will inevitably have a role which will mean its survival but its redefinition,' he told BBC radio. In response to this mood, Labour had assembled a package of constitutional reforms which would form part of its manifesto at the next election. It promised to scrap the Royal Prerogative, the constitutional device by which the government could, for example, declare war in the Crown's name without reference to Parliament. Labour also said it would remove the right of hereditary peers to sit and vote in the House of Lords, and halve the size of the official royal family from about forty to twenty. In another interview, Mr Straw said reform of the Lords would make a 'big difference' to the way people saw the monarchy. 'I think it will hasten the process towards a more Scandinavian monarchy, a monarchy symbolising a much more classless society, someone [sic] who's above the political battle.'

Labour's package provoked an immediate storm of Tory protests. The President of the Board of Trade, Michael Heseltine, declared that the opposition was 'undermining the very fabric of our political constitution'. The Home Secretary, Michael Howard, said Labour had a 'sinister hidden agenda' which would 'break up the Britain we know'. Yet as members of the shadow cabinet insisted, Labour's plans were hardly revolutionary. On the question of the Royal Prerogative, for instance, Labour's plans struck at the power of ministers rather than the crown. The term is a misnomer, since the Queen can only exercise her 'prerogative' by following ministerial 'advice' – another euphemism which disguises the real relationship between Buckingham Palace and Downing Street.

The Labour leadership was at pains to emphasise that it had not adopted the republican banner. 'We are not suggesting getting rid of the monarchy or drastically descaling it and Jack Straw hasn't departed from party policy', a member of Tony Blair's office said. Mr Straw claimed an unlikely ally for his cause, remarking that the Prince of Wales was 'way ahead of Conservative ministers' on the question of reforming the monarchy. Given the Shadow Home Secretary's other, more critical observations about Charles's future role, it is doubtful whether the Prince appreciated this remark. But in December 1992, writing to his Private Secretary, Charles had made proposals for slimming down the royal family which were not dissimilar to Labour's. 'Is not part of the problem with the media', Charles asked, 'that it is considered in the country at large that there are too many members of the family and too much public money being spent on them? Would it not be better to sit down and examine how many members of the family you actually _need?_'

Within the parliamentary Labour party, the package may have seemed too modest to the increasing number of MPs who now admitted their preference for a republic. In October 1994, a survey by the _Independent on Sunday_ newspaper found that out of a sample of 92 Labour backbenchers (a third of the parliamentary party), 40 said they wanted to end the monarchy. Yet as one, anonymous republican put it, the question of abolition 'depends on public opinion. It is not for politicians to decide.' Despite the royal scandals of the early 1990s, opinion polls continued to show majorities of between 70 and 75 per cent in favour of keeping the monarchy, compared with between 85 and 90 per cent a decade before. The sea change in popular attitudes to the monarchy had scarcely begun.

If anyone within the royal family is given credit for shoring up the monarchy, it is Elizabeth. Like Victoria, a far more erratic sovereign, this is partly a question of longevity. Over more than forty years, the perception has grown of a monarch who, in sharp contrast to her children, seems to personify the imagined values of an earlier age: decency, dedication and service.

In an off-camera interview for the 1992 film _Elizabeth R_, she summed up her own view of her role. 'If you live this sort of life, which people don't very much, you live very much by tradition and by continuity. I find that's one of the sad things – that people don't take on jobs for life. They try different things all the time. I mean, as far as I'm concerned, you know what you're going to do two months hence. And I'm even beginning to know about next year. And I think this is what the younger members find difficult, the regimented side of it.'

The regimentation begins with the reading of the legendary red boxes, the 'pricking' of sheriff's lists, the ministerial audiences, the Privy Council meetings and the rest of Elizabeth's daily constitutional business. These duties, however, barely interest the mass of her subjects. Nor are the stage props which embellish her constitutional dignity central to Elizabeth's appeal. If the ceremonial of British monarchy is widely seen as its hallmark, pageantry is far less important to sustaining the royal mystique than many monarchists assume. Silver Stick could retire to barracks, the Lord Chamberlain could walk forwards, the State Coach could be melted down, and Elizabeth would still be unmistakeably a queen, for the roots of her popularity are found away from the synthetic pomp of Windsor and Buckingham Palace.

Loyalty to Elizabeth is principally inspired by her presence as head of the nation, a position unrecognised by constitutional textbooks. At the Cenotaph, laying a wreath, or on the Normandy beaches, honouring D-Day veterans, she is a uniquely powerful focus for feeling of national sorrow and remembrance. In a quieter way, the royal mystique pervades the countless visits to schools, hospitals, community centres, old people's homes, factories and fire stations which are recorded with monotonous regularity in the court circular.

'I think the possibility of meeting more people is important,' Elizabeth remarked in the 1992 film, on her way to unveil several more plaques. It is important to many people; it is also important to her: for in this communion lies the key to the monarchy's survival. The fawning, the puffed-up civic pride and the manipulation of flag-waving children which accompany these events can also seem ludicrous. But as Elizabeth moves among her people, brightly dressed (for she must be visible), serene and stately, few would deny that hers is a highly professional performance.

23

Elizabeth's People

Elizabeth's core constituency materialises each year at the Festival of Remembrance in the Albert Hall. It includes the world war veterans who come to honour the fallen, and repledge their allegiance to Queen and Country. It also includes the myriad volunteers who, when they are not selling poppies for the British Legion, can be found in the church halls, women's institutes and community centres of England, and who share Elizabeth's values of family, service and duty. These people are the patriotic nation; and as they turn to the royal box to sing the anthem (both verses, off by heart, fervently), they stand guard against the march of republicanism.

St David's Home for Disabled Ex-Servicemen in Ealing, west London, is a fragment of the patriotic nation. The home was once the residence of Elizabeth's great-great-great grandfather, the Duke of Kent, father of Victoria, and since its foundation at the end of the First World War, St David's has been favoured with several royal visits. Elizabeth's mother came in November 1953, when she accepted the gift of a rug from Paddy Delaney, one of the residents, and a pair of children's chairs for Charles and Anne. In 1960 Princess Marina met a former naval shipmate of her late husband, in 1976 the present Duchess of Kent was presented with a bouquet of white roses, and in 1988 Diana took the royal road to St David's.

Now, on 30 March 1993, after months of correspondence between the home and her Private Office, Elizabeth is at last visiting St David's to mark the seventy-fifth anniversary of its foundation. No trouble has been spared by Buckingham Palace to ensure the visit is a success. The itinerary has been settled, questions of protocol have been answered, and on the morning of the big day, the royal chauffeur has driven to St David's from Buckingham Palace to check where he should park the car in the forecourt.

The welcoming party will stand here, the chauffeur is told by the nursing manager Tom Connell, directly behind the front gates; and the press will be here, to the side of the main entrance. Satisfied he can deliver Elizabeth at the correct distance and alignment from these people, the chauffeur returns to Buckingham Palace, about ten miles away.

Within the royalist bastion of St David's, however, echoes from the *annus horribilis* can be heard. Not all the residents are as unswervingly loyal as they once were. 'I wish the Queen wasn't so rich,' says Michael, a former doctor with the Royal Army Medical Corps. 'I also wish she wasn't head of the church, primarily for practicality, but also because the only head should be the archbishop.'

He weighs his words, and then delivers a short speech. 'The Queen Mother has had one daughter who's divorced, one granddaughter the same, two grandsons in the same boat – and that is a terrible thing: for marriage in general, which I'm very much in favour of (I am married), and for the respect of the monarchy as a whole, that's the most important point. I think any country looks to its head of state for an example, particularly when it's a hereditary concern – in other words a monarchy.'

Michael speaks from the heart of the patriotic nation. He is the brother-in-law of the late Sir Leonard Cheshire, whose charitable work Elizabeth praised in her 1992 Christmas broadcast; and the brother of Cheshire's widow, Baroness Ryder, whose own charitable homes are patronised by Elizabeth.

Patrick is a former head teacher who, like many other men at St David's, qualified for residence because of National Service during the war. He, too, has thought much about the royal family's self-inflicted wounds. 'I was a profound royalist at one point, but recent events have rather shaken me,' he says.

Yet in his view, the damage to the monarchy has to be seen in a historical perspective. 'Victoria wasn't all she was cracked up to be, you know,' he says. He tells the story of Flora Hastings, an unmarried lady-in-waiting whom Victoria falsely accused of being pregnant, and who died of a tumour in 1839. 'I used to live quite close to where she once lived, at Loudoun Castle, just outside Ayr; and the people round there had no time for Victoria, because she put it round that Flora was pregnant. And the poor girl wasn't. And she never retracted that. The local people were adamant that Victoria was an evil, scheming woman.'

If history, for these old men, offers a scale to measure the monarchy's present disgrace, it is also a reservoir for their own royal memories. 'I once had a wave, a personal wave, from the Queen Mother,' Patrick recalls. 'It was just after the war. She was in residence at Windsor Castle and I was a student at a training college. And I was pushing my bicycle up Priest Hill, a very steep hill, and all of a sudden there was a police escort coming up to my level. And sure enough the car came alongside and there was the Queen Mother; and I sort of acknowledged her and she gave me a royal wave.'

'I did a similar thing when I was sixteen,' Patrick's friend Eric says (this would have been in the 1920s). 'It was Queen Mary. I'd just started working in the City and came out of the office in Threadneedle Street, and they were all stopping the traffic. So I thought, hello, something's going to happen. Queen Mary had been down to a hospital in the East End, and was on her way back. And I was standing absolutely on my own. So I politely doffed my bowler and got a personal wave back.'

For all their misgivings about the recent past, Patrick, Eric and

Michael are still deeply royalist. 'I should hate them to do away with the monarchy,' Patrick says. As for Elizabeth's visit: 'It's nice to keep these traditions going. It's a bit formal and artificial, I mean, everywhere's tidied up – but still, it's good, it *should* be like that.'

A few hours later, Elizabeth's Rolls Royce glides through the front gates and stops at its designated position in the St David's forecourt. Behind her are several police cars, four police motor cycles, and a second Rolls Royce. Ahead of her lie eighty minutes which represent a particular kind of royal challenge.

In theory, Elizabeth is the guest at St David's, being entertained by her hosts; in practice, it is she who must provide a performance for her audience. Having spent most of her life opening, planting, launching and unveiling, it would be easy to act as if she were just going through the motions. Her task is to turn a routine royal visit – indistinguishable from thousands she has made over the past four decades – into a memorable occasion for St David's. Her mere presence is not enough. She must make her hosts feel that they, of all people, have been specially graced.

What allows her to be spontaneous is the knowledge that her hosts will be programmed. No detail has been left to chance, and furthermore, Elizabeth knows that people always behave the same way in the presence of royalty. Their greetings are rehearsed, their small talk is negligible, and more often than not they are lost for words. Against such an unchanging background, even Elizabeth can afford to improvise a little, suggesting hidden depths of humanity. But it will not be easy. For the next eighty minutes, while conveying the opposite impression, Elizabeth will be at full stretch.

'You have to work out in your own mind the hard work, and then what you enjoy in retrospect,' she said in *Elizabeth R.* '[There are] the people you've met like the soldier I was giving a gallantry award to; and I said, "That was a very brave thing to do," and he said, "Och, it was just the training." And I have the feeling that in the end the training is the answer to a great many things. You can do a lot if you're properly trained – and I hope I have been.'

As the Rolls Royce slows to a halt, her detective jumps out of the front passenger seat and runs round the back of the car, in time to open the door for Elizabeth. She steps out into a wet March day, glowing in a bright scarlet mohair coat and hat, with a warm smile to match. The first smile of the afternoon is turned on the welcoming party, who are standing in the rain to greet her (umbrellas were felt to be disrespectful).

St David's is a Catholic foundation (though run on non-denominational lines) and here is its president, Cardinal Hume, at the head of the queue. Next to him is the Mayor of Ealing, Mrs Joan Ansell, who has been fretting that the rain will tarnish her chain of office. And at the end of the line is seven-year-old Hayley Cozens, in her best party frock, who is presenting Elizabeth with a posy.

Hayley's moment arrives. She drops a curtsy, and gives Elizabeth a rather sodden bouquet. Elizabeth gives Hayley a wonderful smile (the cliché that it lights up her face is true), and puts the posy in her left hand, where it stays for the rest of the visit. On her left wrist she suspends her black handbag, leaving her right hand free to shake hands and sign the visitors' book.

Behind Elizabeth, her suite is introduced. Lady Susan Hussey has accompanied Elizabeth in the first Rolls Royce as the duty Woman of the Bedchamber. She is much taller than her mistress, and is deliberately dressed in less striking colours – a cream hat, for instance, rather than the royal scarlet.

From a second Rolls Royce emerge Sir Kenneth Scott and Major James Patrick. Sir Kenneth is Elizabeth's Deputy Private Secretary and a former ambassador to Yugoslavia. His high-powered credentials and his slightly crumpled appearance are proof that not all courtiers are figures from the pages of P.G. Wodehouse. Major Patrick is only twenty-seven, and the very picture of a dashing equerry. Unlike his counterpart in Diana's household, Captain Musto, he is dressed in the equerry's uniform, complete with the aiguillettes on his shoulder. Elizabeth likes to do things properly: after all, it is a compliment to her hosts.

Elizabeth walks serenely past a group of about fifteen reporters and photographers (this is not, by her standards, a major event), who are standing, as instructed, by the main entrance. Inside, in the main dining room of St David's, she is scheduled to meet a dozen residents of the home, deployed around two tables. At each table there is the familiar vacant seat for Elizabeth to sit on, if she so decides.

There is a problem with John, one of the residents, who is nearest the door where Elizabeth will appear, and is thus the person she is most likely to meet first. He keeps falling asleep, and the nurses have to shout to wake him up. Eventually one of them stands behind John's chair, nudging him every few seconds to keep him awake.

Elizabeth enters the room, trailing her own particular problem: the welcoming party who met her in the forecourt, the welcoming party who met her in the front hall, her detective and the rest of the royal entourage – a total of about twenty people, who will follow her wherever she goes and are far more intrusive than the press.

Yet as the officials fan out behind her, she behaves for the next three minutes as if these very old men are just the people she has been looking forward to meeting. 'Well, it's lovely to see you all. I hear everyone comes from a long way away.' (She has been briefed by the ward matron about the men's backgrounds.) They tell her where they were born and the names of their regiments. Encouraged by her sincere interest, some of them produce old regimental photographs for her to see. She looks at each in turn, going round the table, making sure everyone has their say. Even so, at this early stage in the performance she is still warming up.

In another ward, a depressing room with sickly cream hospital paint on the walls, more residents wait for Elizabeth. They sit glumly around their tables, touching their medals nervously, not talking to each other. A nun pops her head round the door to announce that the Queen is on her way. 'Now, don't be slack in saying something,' she tells the men – which makes them still more anxious.

Elizabeth arrives. She smiles at everyone, and sits down at the nearest table. Now she has hit her stride she is in total command of a tricky situation. 'Oh, you were in the Irish Guards? And where do you come from?' In a playful way she is quite bossy, pointing to each of them, provoking them to start a conversation.

She has a closer look at a tie one of the men is wearing. 'Oh, you must be a Grenadier. Yes, I know, they changed the tie. Very confusing!' She laughs at her joke and the ice is broken. Once again she starts a conversational circuit, only this time – more confident – she varies it with little asides to the men on the other side of the table. 'Now what were you doing between while? The Stock Exchange!' – as if this is a big surprise. To another man, hearing he is Scottish: 'You're not a pipeman, I hope.' She laughs again, and they all join in.

On she goes to the next table. 'Hello, good afternoon.' She sits down, giving them her warmest smile. 'My goodness,' she says, amazed at the coincidence, 'two of you in the RAF and another one there.' Someone from the side of the ward, feeling bold, makes his own joke. She turns, smiling, really enjoying herself now. 'Now that's most unkind,' she says – but her eyes are sparkling. Everyone in the room is beaming with delight: Elizabeth, the men, and the nurses and the nuns, who think (wrongly) that it is the men who are staging a bravura performance.

In the St David's day room, a brighter area which resembles a primary school assembly hall, about thirty staff have gathered for their royal moment. Here is the cook, her assistant, the members of the occupational therapy unit and the head of the local contract catering firm. Less important in the royal schedule than the residents, they are allotted proportionately less of Elizabeth's time. But even during an encounter lasting seconds, she does enough to ensure they have a memory to cherish.

Linda, in charge of the occupational therapy unit, presents Elizabeth with a bird-table on behalf of the home. The idea is that she can put the table in the gardens of Buckingham Palace, which some of the residents visit each summer for a party held by the Not Forgotten Association (after the royal family have decamped to Balmoral). Elizabeth asks if the men have made the bird-table, as part of their therapy. Linda confesses it has been bought in a local shop.

In the St George's Lounge, an annexe to the day centre, a further group of about fifty await Elizabeth. The lounge is the only remnant of the original building, and the poshest room in the home. One hundred and eighty years ago, Elizabeth's great-great-great grandfather used to take breakfast here. Today it holds local dignitaries, trustees and fundraisers for St David's: important people in the hierarchy of the home, but for Elizabeth (though neither she nor her scrupulously polite courtiers would ever say so), not the object of her visit. Royal duty beckons, and for the scheduled ten minutes Elizabeth circulates among the suits, the frocks and the habits – for there is a sprinkling of abbots and priests.

On a table by the entrance to the annexe is the home's seventy-fifth-anniversary cake. By the table in his wheelchair is Freddie, who is to cut the first slice. Freddie is only in his forties, but after a motorcycle accident as a young man, he is St David's longest-serving resident. He is severely disabled and has great difficulty talking.

Elizabeth avoids condescending to Freddie by the simple act of sitting next to him. Tremulously, he tries to cut the cake, but is unable to break the icing. 'You do realise it's made of stone,' she says in a mock whisper to Freddie, and everyone laughs – Elizabeth, Freddie, the VIPs gathered behind him, and the audience in front. A fundraiser for St David's steps forward and gives Freddie a hand. Elizabeth rises to her feet, and before she leaves allows Freddie to play the *galant*, holding out her own gloved hand for him to kiss. Everyone applauds this act of fealty.

It is time for the walkabout. In the garden at the rear of St David's it is pouring with rain. For the past half-hour, about four hundred children from local schools have been waiting to meet

Elizabeth. They are drenched, excited that she is about to appear, but thoroughly bored with the long wait. One little boy is trying to see if his plastic Union Jack – provided by St David's – will fly if he throws it. The flag drops on the rush matting, which traces the route Elizabeth will follow around the garden.

Her technique with the children, perfected from years of experience, is to stop every ten yards and chat for twenty seconds. 'So what school do you come from? Oh, I see, I thought you were different because you're wearing a different uniform from the ones back there.'

'You must be very wet,' she tells a bedraggled group further down the route. 'She asked me what school I went to, 'cos I think she'd forgotten,' a little girl tells reporters. Her mother adds 'Two hours in the rain, I mean it's great for them' – pointing at the children – 'but I'm not sure it's really worth it.'

For a few minutes, the Supreme Governor of the Church of England disappears from public view for a private tour of the Catholic chapel. Re-emerging through a covered walkway which adjoins the chapel, she sits at a table to sign the visitors' book. 'Elizabeth R,' she writes, carefully and legibly. An official photograph of herself in state robes is produced by the secretary of the home, Joyce Valvona. 'Elizabeth R,' Elizabeth signs again, and then – for the record – '1993'.

Her visit is over. For the last time that afternoon, Elizabeth walks past the press party as if they were invisible, and returns to the forecourt, where her Rolls Royce is now pointing in the direction of Buckingham Palace. The welcoming party mutates into a farewell party, she shakes hands with everyone, and almost before they have time to wave, her Rolls Royce glides through the front gates and begins the journey home.

Her family may be a disappointment; Elizabeth is never so. Among the residents, all doubts about the monarchy have been banished by her presence. 'She asked me about my sister Sue, Sue Ryder, you see,' says Michael, the memory still vivid. 'She said, "A hard worker," and I enlarged on that and said, "An incredibly hard worker, and has been so for many years."'

'Oh, she was charming, absolutely charming,' says Patrick. 'I was sitting on my own, because I can't get near a table you see, because of my legs. And I was sitting there with my sister, and introduced my sister to her, and she asked me how I was looked after – she was just charming.'

How long did she stay? 'Well, I wouldn't say a long time but she seemed interested in what I was doing. I told her I was in the Highland Light Infantry and her eyes brightened up, you know, and I said: "Of course, that was the Harry Lauder Light Infantry," and she really laughed at that. I mean, the impression you got that she was a fuddy duddy – she *wasn't*, she was very with it and charming . . . yes, charming.'

'She's very easy to talk to,' says Eric. 'Nothing at all awe-inspiring. A very charming person. I had a friend visiting me, an old lady of ninety-two, and she spoke to her too. My friend was over the moon.' What did she say? 'Well, she asked me about my service and I told her. Mentioned I was in the 14th Army, and told her it was the Forgotten Army, and she said, "Oh, not all that forgotten." Then she asked me, did I do well here, and I was able to reassure her on that . . . It's nice to know that she's really human, because I saw a majestic figure before.'

Inside the front door of St David's, the photograph signed by Elizabeth has already been framed and hung in the place of honour. As her Rolls Royce delivers her to Buckingham Palace in time for a late tea, Elizabeth's visit to Ealing has already been enshrined in the history of her reign.

It was, nevertheless, a very small piece of royal history, of little interest to the other residents of Ealing. Half an hour before Elizabeth was due to arrive at St David's, no more than twenty-five people had gathered outside the front gates to witness her arrival. They included two Australian girls who were tourists, a French au pair and her best friend, and a mother with a little boy who wanted to see 'the cars' – the police cars, not the Queen's. Perhaps another thirty had appeared by the time the royal convoy arrived.

In the surrounding houses, people were either ignorant of Elizabeth's visit, or apathetic. 'Oh, no, I can't hang around for that,' said a woman in her sixties, who was looking after her daughter's small children. 'You see, I've got to get home, otherwise the traffic's too bad, what with all the schoolkids coming out.'

Next door, a retired man had no idea Elizabeth was coming. Would he watch her? 'I don't know. It depends what we're doing, I suppose. But thanks for telling us.'

Only one local resident seemed excited by the royal visit. 'Well, actually, I didn't know until a friend phoned half an hour ago,' a middle-aged woman said. 'Of course I'm going to watch – you've just caught me washing my hair so I can look my best.' She was an immigrant from eastern Europe who had been starved of royalty in her communist youth.

Two months later, during her springtime visit to Hull, the fervour of those honoured by Elizabeth's visit scarcely extended across the street. 'I'm a bit surprised it's so low-key,' said the owner of a shoe-repair shop opposite the Red Cross centre, a few hours before the royal arrival. 'None of the schools are doing anything.' He added that he does not feel strongly 'one way or the other' about royalty. 'I don't like the way people go on about their private lives. They should just be left in peace.'

'I've no interest in them,' said the woman in the next-door grocery store, 'so I'm certainly not going to watch. Let them get on with their lives, that's what I say, and I'll get on with mine.'

As with almost any statement about royalty, these remarks cannot be taken at face value. A newsagent said he would ignore Elizabeth because he, too, had 'no interest in that kind of thing'. But his wife would look out for her, because she was a 'royalist'; and in the evening, he was planning to see the ceremony for Elizabeth as *Britannia* left port, because 'I like a good parade.'

Numerical support matters less to Elizabeth than it does to ordinary politicians; or rather, it matters in a different way. It is reassuring if her people turn out in force, and when they reached Hull her entourage were ecstatic about the reception she had been given in Hartlepool (the previous port of call). But unqualified royalism is a rare commodity, as the residents of St David's attested. More important is that Elizabeth should register in the public mind as an active presence: and to hear people expounding freely and at length about how little interest they have in the subject is to hear people who, notwithstanding their feigned indifference, she holds in thrall.

When Elizabeth pays a visit, she taps deep historical memories a mere politician could never evoke. Where Patrick, the former head teacher, spoke of the Flora Hastings affair, in Hull a grocer's wife spoke of the Tranby Croft scandal in 1890, another 'local' event, when the elder Bertie witnessed a partner cheating at baccarat. She argued, like Patrick, that the current disgrace of royalty has to be seen in a long-term perspective.

Across the decades, Elizabeth herself has added a whole volume to the historical store. Some memories are personal, like Patrick's account of the special wave he received from the Queen Mother in Windsor. 'I was that close to her I could have touched her,' said one woman shopper across the road from the Red Cross centre in Hull, remembering Elizabeth's first visit to the city at the start of the reign. 'She patted my little boy on the head – that's how close she was.'

But Elizabeth is also enveloped in the collective memory of her reign. After the unveilings, the launches, the tree-plantings, the speeches, the handshaking, the presentations, the investitures, the openings, the commemorations, the ribbon-cuttings, the audiences, the receptions, the banquets, the dedications, and the garden parties – after all that, year in, year out, it seems incredible that she can single out a little boy to pat his head: even though, observing Elizabeth at close range, it becomes apparent how much care she takes with these small gestures.

The key to Elizabeth's appeal is repetition. Since the 1950s the pattern of her public engagements has altered little. There may be fewer visits to public schools, and rather more to state comprehensives. These days there will be walkabouts – though older courtiers like Sir Edward Ford claim walkabouts occurred long before the term was coined. But as she descends on the Red Cross centre in Hull, Elizabeth is fundamentally doing what she has always done.

At first, the monotony of Elizabeth's round drove critics as different as Lord Altrincham and the *Daily Mirror* to distraction. Forty years into the reign, the same commitment to utter tedium – interspersed, it is true, by generous holidays – seems impressive. The fact that so many of these duties appear futile and wearisome only enhances the perception of selfless dedication.

Her subjects fondly believe she would much prefer to stay at home with her corgis, a box of chocolates close to hand (Bendick's bittermints are supposed to be her favourites), watching the detective series and soap operas which are her preferred television viewing. In fact she would much rather be out and about, for the call of royal duty is what gives Elizabeth's life meaning.

Her subjects also like to speculate about whether she will ever stop. It is reassuring to imagine that that is her most fervent wish; and equally reassuring to know that she will keep on going, just as her mother has done, so long as she is mistress of her faculties. Abdication is inconceivable to Elizabeth, not simply because of the awful precedent set by David in 1936, and her conviction that she has been anointed by God. To resign would undermine a record of devoted service acquired over four decades. Posterity, which matters greatly to Elizabeth, would never forgive her.

In the meantime, her myth radiates to corners of her kingdom even she has never seen. Three weeks before she went to Ealing, Elizabeth was due to visit Manchester. The pretext was to open the new terminal at Manchester airport, part of the city's doomed bid to stage the Olympics; but in her thorough fashion, Elizabeth also agreed to inspect two rather less glamorous projects.

One was a sheltered housing scheme in Salford run by the Church Urban Fund, a charity she patronises; and in nearby Irlam, she planned to see a family centre administered by another of her charities, the National Children's Homes. But the day before the visit a doleful message arrived from Buckingham

Palace: Elizabeth had flu, and Philip was coming instead. Elizabeth is rarely ill – she does not like disappointing people – and in Irlam especially there was general dismay.

It is a dismal suburb to the west of Manchester, next to an old trunk road that heads towards Liverpool. Beside the road, in the middle of a huge, underused car park, stands a tatty shopping mall, long since overtaken by the superstores nearby. In the mall's cafeteria, three users of the family centre – Dave, an unemployed man in his thirties, Linda, his wife, and Sylvia, a friend – talked about the Queen they would not now see.

All thought Elizabeth should pay more tax, and (until told) were unaware of the new arrangements which had recently been announced. But their real concerns were closer to home: the abduction and murder of James Bulger in nearby Liverpool a month before and the unemployment problem in Irlam. For Dave at least, Elizabeth had a definite role to play in these local issues.

'I think she should do more for her country, and help out and all this. Try and help stop all these rapes and things like little Jamie Bulger, you know, try and help out on things like this. And help out with all the people who's on the dole. Forget the rich, that's what I say, forget the rich and help the poor, the poor need her more than the rich.'

Sylvia disagreed with Dave. 'Unemployment's not the Queen's fault, it's the government's,' she said.

'Yeah, I know it's the government's fault,' Dave replied, 'but the Queen should help out more.'

'Well, she's agreed to pay her income tax, what more can she do?'

'Yeah, I agree with all that, but she should sit down and talk it all out.'

'Who with?'

'Other countries, get together with them.'

'But she can't do that, because she's ruled by the government, by our government.'

'So what you're saying is, if Margaret Thatcher wants her head, or John Major wants her head, they got it, is that it?'

'No, no, not like that, no – they tell her what speeches you can make, what she can do, what she can't do.'

Linda now returned to the original subject, the murder of James Bulger. 'There are all these children getting killed and all that. I think we should make somebody deal with them to stop them.'

Dave enlarged on his wife's point, but perhaps not in the way she meant. 'What we're trying to say is, the Queen should help out to try and make the world a better place for the kiddies – because now you can't go to the shops, leave the buggy outside, without your kiddy getting kidnapped.' He turned to Sylvia: 'Do you agree with that?'

'I agree that this place, England, should be made safer,' Sylvia said, 'but I don't see there's any way the Queen can do it. I mean, what can the Queen do about these murders, there's nothing she can do. Only try to make the government put more money into centres like ours. It's not her job.'

Constitutionally, Sylvia's case was impeccable: there is nothing Elizabeth can do in these areas, because she must appear to remain above politics. But if Dave's understanding of her power was exaggerated, he was imaginatively far closer to Elizabeth's own idea of how she serves the nation. 'I want to show that the Crown is not merely an abstract symbol of our unity, but a personal and living bond between you and me,' she told her subjects in her 1953 Christmas broadcast.

Sylvia and Linda left to take their children back to the family centre. Like the staff at the centre, they were uninspired by the prospect of meeting Philip. Sylvia thought a professional wrestler would be more exciting as someone to open the centre.

Dave lingered behind; there was something more he wanted to say about Elizabeth. 'I've seen the Queen before, so it's nothing new to me. When I was in the Territorials, we were all lined up like that, stood at attention, and she walked round, took one glance at you, and then walked away to the left. I spoke words to her but – it's private, so I can't really say.'

At the time, he was obeying his sergeant's orders; but Dave believed the injunction must always be honoured. 'Say she were coming tomorrow, if she speaks to you, whatever she says to you, you can't reveal to anybody else because it's private, it's confidential. She's royalty, she's got to have her secret kept.'

He paused to reflect on his own and Elizabeth's contrasting predicaments. 'I don't travel around in jet planes and have a nice big juicy palace and have all her money. I mean, that's my biggest dream, to have money like that, but I'll never even win the pools or even win the bingo. So, you know, that's all right, she's made the money but – can she keep her head above water, can she keep going, can she last out for a few more years?' Dave had answered his own question. No monarch who occupies such a dominant place in popular consciousness is in danger of abolition. The throne is Elizabeth's for as long as she lives.

Republicans hope that Elizabeth's death will mark the imminent demise of the British monarchy. They assume that the scandals which have engulfed the dynasty over the past decade must eventually prove too much for rational people to endure.

In May 1993, a conference on the monarchy organised by *The Times* and the constitutional reform group Charter 88 offered a platform for republicans to claim that the tide of opinion had finally turned in their favour. Royalists such as the patrician Lord Rees-Mogg and the populist Tory MP Teresa Gorman were heckled from the floor of the Queen Elizabeth II conference centre, which stands in the heart of Westminster. At the end of the day, an impassioned speech by the republican playwright David Hare received a standing ovation.

None of the delegates, however, was prepared to argue that the monarchy would collapse before the end of the present reign. Their optimism was grounded in a belief that Charles, as Elizabeth's most likely successor, could never command the loyalty enjoyed by his mother. At first sight, the opinion polls seemed to support this view. By late 1994, two years after the *annus horribilis*, between 35 and 50 per cent of those canvassed did not believe the monarchy would exist in fifty years time. But fifty years is a long time in the history of the monarchy: long enough for Charles to live out his reign and leave the throne intact for his successors.

Several factors can help Charles achieve this outcome. His private and public image is too tarnished for him to inherit the aura of royalty which surrounds his mother. But her death will inevitably provoke sincere, national grief, and some of this sympathy will redound to Charles. He can hope that at the start of his reign, his subjects will give him the benefit of the doubt.

The doubts will return if Charles approaches kingship with the same lack of self-restraint which has marked his career as a free-range Prince of Wales. The 'trapdoor' analogy used by his advisers is implausible, but there will be other forces acting as a straitjacket on the new king. Most immediately, a wary government can invoke the concept of ministerial 'advice' to restrict Charles's room for political manoeuvre. Failure to follow this advice, Charles will know from his own reading of Bagehot, risks toppling the entire edifice of constitutional monarchy.

Most powerfully, Charles's stewardship of the monarchy will be protected by deep historical taboos. Apart from Oliver Cromwell's brief interregnum in the seventeenth century, the English monarchy has survived continuously for over a thousand years. This ancient lineage carries its own message: that for a monarch to destroy his inheritance would require a correspondingly spectacular act of folly or wickedness. In this context, Charles's failings seem pitiable rather than monstrous.

Charles's great-uncle David was the last sovereign to display an outstanding talent for self-destruction, and even he passed the throne to his brother in surprisingly good order. As individuals, the other Windsor kings have had their share of vices. The elder Bertie was a glutton and a lecher, George was a bully, and the younger Bertie could be mean and short-tempered. But these generally modest shortcomings, which suited their uniformly mediocre abilities, did not prove lethal to their standing as constitutional monarchs. They were saved by a combination of luck, the sagacity of a few courtiers, and the tolerance of politicians who had their own stake in the monarchy's survival.

For the monarchy to be destroyed from without, future politicians would have to decide that raising the spectre of abolition was to their advantage. That would depend on a radical shift in public attitudes to royalty. Despite the scandals which led to Elizabeth's *annus horribilis*, there is no convincing evidence that such a shift is imminent.

At some future date, the British may change the habit of centuries and abolish the monarchy. But if the Windsors really wish to destroy themselves, their behaviour needs to deteriorate on an epic scale. So far, they have not behaved badly enough, while lacking the imagination to behave any worse.

Envoi: Hull

19 May 1993

At the Red Cross centre in Hull, Elizabeth has met the Elderly Persons' Pop-In Club and is now circulating among a group of sixty volunteers and their children in the garden at the rear. To one side, a forty-strong choir sings 'Love is Everything' from the Lloyd Webber musical *Aspects of Love*.

Elizabeth's host, David Whincup, suggested the choir. 'I thought it would be nice to have a little bit of music in the background, so that when she does speak to someone they don't think everyone's stood there, waiting for their reply.'

After nine minutes in the garden, it is time for Elizabeth to leave. As the choir sings 'Rose of England', she shakes hands with Mr Whincup and the other Red Cross officials and steps into her Rolls Royce. A brief wave to the crowd that has gathered across the street, and she is away.

Fifteen minutes later, at 5.30 p.m., she arrives at the King George dock in Hull, where the crew of *Britannia* are preparing for an evening reception. After the reception, the band of the Royal Marines will beat the retreat, watched by a crowd already assembling behind crush barriers along the dockside. As

Elizabeth steps out of the car, her police outriders salute. She walks up the gangway and then, almost as an afterthought – for this is not in the schedule – she turns and waves to the crowds. They wave back, and she disappears into *Britannia* to change for the reception.

The Rolls Royce is dismantled for the day. Off comes the transparent roof, designed for maximum visibility, to be replaced by a conventional cover. Out come the flowers, which during the day have been stacked behind the rear window. And after a brief conference between Elizabeth's chauffeur, her faithful Equerry Major Patrick, and a policeman, the car is driven to one end of the dock, away from public view.

At the other end of the dock, the guests are beginning to arrive for the reception. Elizabeth has asked, as she always does, to meet representative leaders of the local community – and here they are in force. From corporation limousines, their chains of office glinting in the evening sun, emerge mayors and mayoresses from Beverley, Boothferry and other small towns in the Humberside area. About two hundred people have been invited, including teachers, doctors, local MPs, rotarians, trades union officials and the president of the Hull University students' union. They are Humberside's finest.

They are also early. To pass the time until 6.30 p.m., when the reception is due to begin, they have their photographs taken for the local press beside the *Britannia* 'crucifix' (lifebelt holder). Bryan and Shirley Pearson (Beverley), Ken and Marian Sills (Glanford), and Stan and Sheila Burch (East Yorkshire) stand proudly to attention as their royal moment is recorded for posterity.

Opposite the gangway, the crowd has steadily increased to over a thousand. Even so, some of the spectators are disappointed with the turn-out. 'Me and my wife came seventeen years ago when she was here, and there were a lot more people then,' says one man. Like others, he blames poor publicity: it was only mentioned on the local radio this morning, and none of the papers carried advance notices – or so he claims.

The *annus horribilis* is in the front of people's minds. 'I think what it was,' a woman says, 'years ago, everyone wanted to see more and more of the Queen – so she opened herself up, she started walkabouts, and the result is, people know far too much of what's going on in the family. Whereas before, it probably still went on, but no one knew about it, and I think that was far better. Because let's face it, everybody's private lives are private.'

Another woman, keeping a firm hold on two excited toddlers, echoes this view. 'I think we're all a bit fed up with the hoohah they keep writing about Charles and Diana. We're not terribly interested. We've all got lives to lead, haven't we?'

A man in his sixties, standing behind her, bristles with patriotism. 'I served under two monarchs, that's my opinion,' he says emphatically. And what of Charles as King? 'Then we'd have flower power,' is his contemptuous verdict.

Asked why she is here, his wife speaks for all the spectators. 'I love a parade. I love pageantry. Nobody can match this sort of thing. You don't get this anywhere else in the world, do you?' Her neighbours nod vigorously in agreement.

At the foot of the gangway, Commander Nick Wright, press officer for *Britannia*, is briefing journalists about the ship. They learn that it is extremely slow, taking three weeks to cross the Atlantic, and extremely useful: involved not only in royal tours, but as a base for business seminars and trade promotions. Only a few weeks before, Commander Wright explains, *Britannia* played host to a Scotch whisky sales conference off the coast of Florida. At an annual cost to the taxpayer of about £8 million, he feels it is money well spent. The journalists are sceptical.

At 6.30 p.m., the VIPs begin the long march up the gangway, along the deck, and into the main reception area where Elizabeth is waiting to meet them. With two hundred local worthies (plus wives and husbands) to be processed in an hour, she is working at about medium pace: slower than for a walkabout, but faster than at the Elderly Persons' Pop-In Club, where twenty-four people were granted her attention for eleven minutes.

After their brief encounter, the guests are ushered towards the upper deck from where, clutching their wine glasses, they survey the crowd below and the band of the Royal Marines, now ready to beat the retreat. Punctually at 7.30 p.m., the royal party appears on the flag deck, directly above the band: Philip, who has arrived from a separate engagement, his Private Secretary Brigadier Hunt-Davis, John Haslam from the press office, Sir Kenneth Scott from the private office, Major Patrick, and the Duchess of Grafton, Elizabeth's Mistress of the Robes. They leave a space in the centre of the deck for Elizabeth, who emerges last of all.

She is wearing a blue dress, and for the first time in the day is hatless. The crowd cheer as she appears, and she waves at them. At this point, a huge North Sea ferry passes the adjacent dock behind the spectators, dwarfing *Britannia*. The ferry passengers are unsure what is happening beneath them, but for good measure Elizabeth waves at them as well. Suddenly the passengers realise who she is, and wave frantically. Almost as quickly, the ferry disappears from view. Elizabeth looks down at the band, and they start to beat the retreat.

They march up and down the dockside, running through the patriotic repertoire: 'Men of Harlech', 'Rule Britannia', and 'Land of Hope and Glory' all feature, warmly appreciated by the crowd. The highspot is a bugle duet performed before Elizabeth, who applauds. There is more marching, further melodies, and then the moment comes to lower the colours. Slowly, the ensign is pulled down from the flagpole which stands to one side of the gangway, about thirty yards from Elizabeth. She watches intently.

It is time for the national anthem. The band march into position beneath Elizabeth, wait for silence, and begin to play. The policemen supervising the crowd salute, and at the end of the anthem, everyone applauds: everyone, that is, except Elizabeth, who maintains a severe expression while the applause lasts, and then waves to the crowd.

For another minute she continues to wave and then – with no question of an encore – she disappears inside. Her day is over; and quickly, her guests return to the flag deck by a separate route, so avoiding a second, unplanned brush with majesty. They descend the gangway and make for their cars, content that civic duty has been fulfilled. The crowd lingers, hoping to watch *Britannia* leave the harbour.

Two tugs, the *Lady Elizabeth* and the *Lady Catherine*, begin to tow *Britannia* out of the port to the Humber estuary. On board, the band is entertaining the royal party with a selection of popular classics. 'Raindrops keep falling on my head' wafts across the evening air, while the tugs pull *Britannia* gently into the distance.

As she enjoys the music, who can tell what Elizabeth is doing? Perhaps she has a well-earned drink in her hand; perhaps she is discussing the next day's engagements in Great Yarmouth. But whatever she is doing, she has already done before – even this journey on *Britannia*, which now takes her eastwards out to sea, away from the setting sun.

Select Bibliography

Books

Mabell, Countess of Airlie (ed. Jennifer Ellis), *Thatched with Gold* (Hutchinson, 1962)

Queen Alexandra of Yugoslavia, *For a King's Love* (Odhams, 1956)

Prince Andrew, *Photographs* (Hamish Hamilton, 1985)

Princess Anne (with Ivor Herbert), *Riding through My Life* (Pelham Books, 1991)

Asquith, Lady Cynthia, *The Married Life of the Duchess of York* (Hutchinson, 1933)

Asquith, H.H. (ed. Michael and Eleanor Brock), *Letters to Venetia Stanley* (OUP, 1982)

Bagehot, Walter (ed. Norman St John Stevas), *Political Essays, Vol. V* (The Economist, 1974)

Batchelor, Vivian, *The Princess Margaret Gift Book* (Pitkin, 1952)

Battiscombe, Georgina, *Queen Alexandra* (Constable, 1969)

Belloc-Lowndes, Marie, *His Most Gracious Majesty King Edward VII* (Grant Richards, 1901)

Benson, A.C., and Weaver, Sir Lawrence, *The Book of the Queen's Dolls' House* (Methuen, 1924)

Bloch, Michael, *The Duke of Windsor's War* (Weidenfeld and Nicolson, 1982)

Boothroyd, Basil, *Philip* (Longmans, 1971)

Bradford, Sarah, *King George VI* (Weidenfeld and Nicolson, 1989)

Bradlaugh, Charles, *The Impeachment of the House of Brunswick* (Freethought Publishing Company, 7th ed., 1880)

Broadhurst, Henry, *From a Stonemason's Bench to the Treasury Bench* (Hutchinson, 1901)

Brook-Shepherd, Gordon, *The Last Habsburg* (Weidenfeld and Nicolson, 1968)

Brook-Shepherd, Gordon, *Victims at Sarajevo* (Harvill, 1984)

Bruce Lockhart, Sir Robert, *Diaries 1915–38* (ed. Kenneth Young) (Macmillan, 1973)

Burgoyne, Elizabeth, *Carmen Sylva* (Eyre and Spottiswoode, 1941)

Burnet, Alastair, *In Person, the Prince and Princess of Wales* (Michael O'Mara Books, 1985)

Buxton, Aubrey, *The King in his Country* (Longmans, Green, 1955)

Cameron, James, *The Best of Cameron* (New English Library, 1981)

Cannadine, David, 'The British Monarchy and the Invention of Tradition' in *The Invention of Tradition* (ed. Eric Hobsbawm and Terence Ranger) (CUP, 1983)

Cannadine, David, *The Decline and Fall of the British Aristocracy* (Yale University Press, 1990)

Cassels, Lavender, *The Archduke and the Assassin* (Muller, 1984)

Channon, Sir Henry, *Chips: The Diaries of Sir Henry Channon* (ed. Robert Rhodes James) (Weidenfeld and Nicolson, 1967)

Prince Charles and Charles Clover, *Highgrove, Portrait of an Estate* (Chapmans, 1993)

Prince Charles, *In His Own Words* (ed. Rosemary York) (W.H. Allen, 1981)

Prince Charles, *The Old Man of Lochnagar* (Hamish Hamilton, 1983)

Prince Charles, *A Vision of Britain* (Doubleday, 1989)

Prince Charles, *Watercolours* (Little, Brown, 1991)

Prince Christopher of Greece, *Memoirs* (Hurst and Blackett, 1938)

Clark, Kenneth, *Another Part of the Wood* (Murray, 1974)

Clark, Ronald W., *Balmoral, Queen Victoria's Highland Home* (Thames and Hudson, 1981)

Clark, Brigadier Stanley, *Palace Diary* (Harrap, 1958)

Colville, Lady Cynthia, *Crowded Life* (Evans Brothers, 1963)

Constant, Stephen, *Foxy Ferdinand* (Sidgwick and Jackson, 1979)

Cooper, Diana, *The Light of Common Day* (Hart-Davis, 1969)

Cooper, Duff, *Old Men Forget* (Hart-Davis, 1953)

Corbitt, F.J., *Fit for a King* (Odhams, 1956)

Coster, Ian, *The Princess Margaret Gift Book* (Pitkin, 1953)

Coward, Noël, *Diaries* (ed. Graham Payn and Sheridan Morley) (Weidenfeld and Nicolson, 1982)

Cowles, Virginia, *Edward VII and his Circle* (Hamish Hamilton, 1956)

Crawford, Marion, *The Little Princesses* (Cassell, 1950)

Marchioness Curzon of Kedleston, *Reminiscences* (Hutchinson, 1955)

Cust, Sir Lionel, *King Edward VII and his Court* (Murray, 1930)

Davidson, J.C.C., *Memoirs of a Conservative* (ed. Robert Rhodes James) (Weidenfeld and Nicolson, 1969)

Dean, John, *HRH Prince Philip, Duke of Edinburgh* (Robert Hale, 1955)

Dimbleby, Jonathan, *The Prince of Wales* (Little, Brown, 1994)

Donaldson, Frances, *Edward VIII* (Weidenfeld and Nicolson, 1974)

Dress and Insignia Worn at Court (Lord Chamberlain's Office, 1937)

Elliott, Caroline (ed.), *The BBC Book of Royal Memories* (BBC Books, 1991)

Emden, Paul H., *Behind the Throne* (Hodder and Stoughton, 1934)

Fawcett, Frank Burlington (ed.), *Court Ceremonial and the Book of the Court* (Gale and Polden, 1937)

Fischer, Bernd J., *King Zog and the Struggle for Stability in Albania* (Columbia University Press, 1984)

Fleming, Tom, *Voices out of the Air: The Royal Christmas Broadcasts 1932–1981* (Heinemann, 1981)

Forbes, Rosita, *These Men I Knew* (Hutchinson, 1940)

Queen Frederica of the Hellenes, *A Measure of Understanding* (Macmillan, 1971)

Fry, C.B., *Keybook of the League of Nations, with a chapter on the Disarmament Question by HH Prince Ranjitsinhji* (Hodder and Stoughton, 1923)

Fry, C.B., *Life Worth Living* (Eyre and Spottiswoode, 1939)

Gaitskell, Hugh (ed. Philip M. Williams), *Diary of Hugh Gaitskell 1945–1956* (Cape, 1983)

Gardiner, Leslie, *Curtain Calls* (Duckworth, 1976)

A German Agent, *The Near East from Within* (Cassell, 1915)

Gilbert, Martin, *Winston S. Churchill, Vol. VI, 1939–1941, Finest Hour* (Heinemann, 1983)

Gilbert, Martin, *Winston S. Churchill, Vol. VII, 1941–45, Road to Victory* (Heinemann, 1986)

Gore, John, *King George V: A Personal Memoir* (Murray, 1941)

Greville, Charles, *Leaves from the Greville Diary* (ed. Philip Morrell) (E. Nash and Grayson, 1929)

Gunther, John, *Inside Europe* (revised ed., Hamish Hamilton, 1936)

Hall, Phillip, *Royal Fortune: Tax, Money and the Monarchy* (Bloomsbury, 1992)

Hamilton, Gerald, *Blood Royal* (Anthony Gibbs and Phillips, 1964)

Hardinge, Helen, *Loyal to Three Kings* (Kimber, 1967)

Harris, Leonard M., *Long to Reign Over Us?* (Kimber, 1966)

Harrisson, Tom, *Britain Revisited* (Gollancz, 1961)

Hartnell, Norman, *Silver and Gold* (Evans Bros., 1955)

Haslip, Joan, *The Lonely Empress* (Weidenfeld and Nicolson, 1965)

Hoggart, Richard, *The Uses of Literacy* (Chatto and Windus, 1957)

Holden, Anthony, *Charles* (Weidenfeld and Nicolson, 1988)

Holden, Anthony, *The Tarnished Crown* (Bantam Press, 1993)

Hyde, Robert R., *The Camp Book* (Ernest Benn, 1930)

Sir Thomas Innes of Learney, *The Queen's Coronation Visit to Scotland* (Official Souvenir, 1953)

Jenkins, Roy, *Sir Charles Dilke: A Victorian Tragedy* (revised ed., Collins, 1965)

Jennings, Humphrey, and Madge, Charles, *May 12th 1937: Mass Observation Day Survey* (Faber, 1987)

Jones, L.E., *An Edwardian Youth* (Macmillan, 1956)

Judd, Denis, *King George VI* (Michael Joseph, 1982)

Judd, Denis, *Prince Philip* (Sphere, 1991)

Junor, Penny, *Charles* (Sidgwick and Jackson, 1987)

Killearn, Lord, *The Killearn Diaries* (ed. Trefor Evans) (Sidgwick and Jackson, 1972)

Laird, Dorothy, *Fourth Golden Gift Book of Prince Charles and Princess Anne* (Pitkin, 1955)

Laird, Dorothy, *Fifth Golden Gift Book of Prince Charles and Princess Anne* (Pitkin, 1956)

Lascelles, Sir Alan, *Diaries and Letters, Vol. II, In Royal Service 1920–1936* (ed. Duff Hart-Davis) (Hamish Hamilton, 1988)

Lees-Milne, James, *The Enigmatic Edwardian: The Life of Reginald, 2nd Viscount Esher* (Sidgwick and Jackson, 1986)

Lloyd George, David, *Family Letters 1885–1936* (ed. Kenneth O. Morgan) (University of Wales Press and OUP, 1973)

Longford, Elizabeth, *Victoria RI* (Weidenfeld and Nicolson, 1964)

Longford, Lord, *Born to Believe* (Cape, 1953)

Lytton, Lady, *Lady Lytton's Court Diary* (ed. Mary Lutyens) (Hart Davis, 1961)

Macmillan, Harold, *War Diaries 1943–1945* (Macmillan, 1984)

Magnus, Philip, *King Edward the Seventh* (Murray, 1964)

Princess Marie Louise, *My Memories of Six Reigns* (Evans Bros., 1956)

Queen Marie of Romania, *The Country That I Love* (Duckworth, 1925)

Mallet, Marie, *Letters from Court: Life with Queen Victoria* (ed. Victor Mallet) (Murray, 1968)

Marquand, David, *Ramsay Macdonald* (Cape, 1977)

Mortimer, Penelope, *Queen Elizabeth: A Life of the Queen Mother* (Viking, 1986)

Morton, Andrew, *Diana: Her New Life* (Michael O'Mara Books, 1994)

Morton, Andrew, *Diana: Her True Story* (Michael O'Mara Books, 1992)

Nairn, Tom, *The Enchanted Glass* (Radius, 1988)

Nickolls, L.A., *Our Sovereign Lady* (Macdonald, 1955)

Nickolls, L.A., *The Queen's Year* (Macdonald, 1954, 1956, 1957)

Nicolson, Harold, *Diaries and Letters, Vol. I, 1930–1939; Vol. II, 1939–1945; Vol. III, 1945–1962* (Collins, 1966, 1967, 1968)

Nicolson, Harold, *King George V: His Life and Reign* (Constable, 1952)

Ormathwaite, Lord, *When I Was at Court* (Hutchinson, 1937)

Pakula, Hannah, *The Last Romantic* (Weidenfeld and Nicolson, 1985)

Paoli, Xavier, *My Royal Clients* (Hodder and Stoughton, 1911)

Pearson, John, *Edward the Rake* (Weidenfeld and Nicolson, 1975)

Pearson, John, *The Ultimate Family* (Michael Joseph, 1986)

King Peter of Yugoslavia, *A King's Heritage* (Cassell, 1955)

Prince Philip, *The Duke of Edinburgh's World Tour 1956–1957, based on the diaries of Viscount Cilcennin and Michael Parker* (Official Souvenir, 1957)

Prince Philip, *A Question of Balance* (Sphere, 1982)

Prince Philip, *Selected Speeches 1948–1955* (OUP, 1957)

Prince Philip, *Selected Speeches 1956–1959* (ed. Richard Ollard) (Collins, 1960)

Pollo, Steffanaq, and Puto, Arben, *The History of Albania* (Routledge and Kegan Paul, 1981)

Ponsonby, Arthur, *Henry Ponsonby: His Life from his Letters* (Macmillan, 1942)

Ponsonby, Sir Frederick, *Recollections of Three Reigns* (Eyre and Spottiswoode, 1951)

Pope-Hennessy, James, *A Lonely Business* (ed. Peter Quennell) (Weidenfeld and Nicolson, 1981)

Pope-Hennessy, James, *Queen Mary* (George Allen and Unwin, 1959)

Power, L.J., *Royal Ladies of the Netherlands* (Stanley Paul, 1939)

Rhodes James, Robert, *Victor Cazalet* (Hamish Hamilton, 1976)

Ring, Anne, *The Story of Princess Elizabeth* (2nd ed., Murray, 1932)

Robyns, Gwen, *Queen Geraldine of the Albanians* (Muller, Blond and White, 1987)

Roosevelt, Eleanor, *The Autobiography of Eleanor Roosevelt* (Hutchinson, 1962)

Rose, Kenneth, *King George V* (Weidenfeld and Nicolson, 1983)

Rowland, Peter, *Lloyd George* (Barrie and Jenkins, 1975)

Ruffer, Jonathan, *The Big Shots: Edwardian Shooting Parties* (Quiller Press, 1989)

Russell, Peter, *Butler Royal* (Hutchinson, 1982)

St Aubyn, Giles, *Edward VII: Prince and King* (Collins, 1979)

Sheridan, Lisa, *Our Princesses at Home* (Murray, 1940)

Sheridan, Lisa, *Our Princesses in 1942* (Murray, 1942)

Sheridan, Lisa, *Princess Elizabeth at Home* (Murray, 1944)

Sheridan, Lisa, *Playtime at Royal Lodge* (Murray, 1954)

Sheridan, Lisa, *A Day with Prince Andrew* (Murray, 1962)

Schmidt, Paul, *Hitler's Interpreter* (ed. R.H.C. Steed) (Heinemann, 1951)

Shirer, William L., *The Rise and Fall of the Third Reich* (Secker and Warburg, 1960)

Sitwell, Osbert, *Queen Mary and Others* (Michael Joseph, 1964)

Stevenson, Frances, *Lloyd George: A Diary* (ed. A.J.P. Taylor) (Hutchinson, 1971)

Taylor, A.J.P., *English History 1914–1945* (OUP, 1965)

Taylor, A.J.P., *The Struggle for Mastery in Europe 1848–1918* (OUP, 1954)

Temple, Solomon, *What Does She Do with It?* (A. Boot, 1871)

Thackeray, William Makepeace, *The Four Georges* (Falcon Press, 1948)

Thomas, J.H., *My Story* (Hutchinson, 1937)

Townsend, Peter, *Time and Chance* (Collins, 1978)

Queen Victoria, *Leaves from the Journal of Our Life in the Highlands from 1848 to 1861* (ed. Arthur Helps) (London, 1868)

Queen Victoria, *More Leaves from the Journal of a Life in the Highlands from 1862 to 1882* (Smith, Elder and Co., 1884)

Queen Victoria, *Queen Victoria in her Letters and Journals* (ed. Christopher Hibbert) (Murray, 1984)

Watson, Alfred E.T., *King Edward as a Sportsman* (Longmans, Green, 1911)

Watson, Francis, *Dawson of Penn* (Chatto and Windus, 1950)

Webb, Beatrice, *Diaries, Vol. II, 1924–32* (ed. Margaret Cole) (Longmans, Green, 1956)

Day, J. Wentworth, *King George V as a Sportsman* (Cassell, 1935)

Day, J. Wentworth, *Princess Marina, Duchess of Kent* (2nd ed., Robert Hale, 1969)

Wheeler-Bennett, John W., *King George VI: His Life and Reign* (Macmillan, 1958)

Kaiser Wilhelm II, *My Early Life* (Methuen, 1926)

HRH Wilhemina, Princess of the Netherlands, *Lonely But Not Alone* (Hutchinson, 1960)

Wilson, Sir John, *The Royal Philatelic Collection* (Dropmore Press, 1952)

The Duchess of Windsor, *The Heart Has its Reasons* (Michael Joseph, 1956)

The Duke of Windsor, *A Family Album* (Cassell, 1960)

The Duke of Windsor, *A King's Story* (Cassell, 1951)

Zedlitz-Trutschler, Count Robert, *Twelve Years at the Imperial German Court* (Nisbet and Co., 1924)

Ziegler, Philip, *Crown and People* (Collins, 1978)

Ziegler, Philip, *King Edward VIII: The Official Biography* (Collins, 1990)

Articles

Altrincham, Lord, 'The Monarchy Today' in *The National and English Review* (August 1957)

Harris, Kenneth, Interview with Prince Charles in the *Observer* (9 and 16 June 1974)

Laski, Harold, 'The King's Secretary' in *Fortnightly Review* (December 1942)

Muggeridge, Malcolm, 'The Queen and I' in *Encounter* (July 1961)

Osborne, John, 'This Scepter'd Isle' in *Encounter* (October 1957)
Trevelyan, G.M., Introduction to *The Times* Souvenir of the Royal
   Wedding (20 November 1947)

Periodicals and Newspapers
Daily Mirror 1956, 1964–1965
Majesty 1981–1994
Royalty Annual 1952–1956
Royalty Monthly 1981–1987
The Royal Year 1973–1981
The Times 1936, 1947, 1955

Manuscripts
Mass Observation File Reports 1940–1944
Lord Snowdon, Investiture Scrapbook (Personal Collection)
Viscount Templewood, Papers (Cambridge University Library)

References

The page and line numbers refer to the place in the text where the catchphrase appears. The catchphrase is taken from the end of the passage quoted. The citation uses the author's name only, followed by the page number in the relevant work. For the full title, see the bibliography.

Where more than one book by the same author is listed in the bibliography, an abbreviated title of the relevant work appears after the author's name: for example, Nicolson, *Diaries, Vol. II*, p. 359 or Nicolson, *George V*, p. 257.

Periodicals are described by their full titles, with the relevant date.

Introduction: Elizabeth in Hull

p. 2	l.27	waist like a waiter. *Royalty Annual*, 1952, p. 18
p. 4	l.2	not a security threat. *Yorkshire Post*, 20 July 1981
p. 10	l.12	an ordinary sort of fellow. Bradford, p. 144

Chapter One: Bertie's Club

| p. 15 | l.6 | fourteen Monarchies. Christopher, p. 15 |
| p. 16 | l.14 | never really forgave him. Ibid., p. 38 |

p. 16	l.30	flowers might not be lonely. Constant, p. 193
p. 17	l.5	generous picnic hamper. Ibid., pp. 187–188
p. 17	l.12	Wait for him. Paoli, p. 279
p. 17	l.22	spare skirt. Ibid., p. 9
p. 17	l.30	pink ribbon. German Agent, p. 140
p. 17	l.33	fond of her. Burgoyne, p. 155
p. 18	l.2	spiritualist seance. Gardiner, p. 87
p. 18	l.17	exactly the same time. For more on Bertie's annual routine, see Magnus, pp. 274–275
p. 18	l.30	*à la Souvaroff*. Magnus, p. 268
p. 20	l.3	the Paris Sûreté. Paoli, pp. 214–216
p. 20	l.27	Paris in future. Ibid., p. 221
p. 20	l.32	mannerisms were all wrong. Ibid., p. 222
p. 21	l.3	King's day. Ibid., p. 223
p. 22	l.3	Willy is a bully. Magnus, p. 214
p. 22	l.5	handicaps are perfectly appalling. Ibid., p. 263
p. 22	l.15	seriously to be deprecated. E. Longford, p. 366
p. 22	l.19	*Bertie was not directly accused of adultery by Sir Charles, who cited instead two of Bertie's friends, Lord Cole and Sir Frederick Johnstone. When a counter-petition was filed, alleging that Lady Mordaunt was mad, Bertie was called as a witness by her counsel. Although he had written several letters to Lady Mordaunt, Bertie replied with a resounding 'No!' when asked in court if their relations had been improper. Sir Charles's counsel declined to cross-examine the Prince of Wales. Victoria (for once) gave her eldest son the benefit of the doubt, and soon afterwards Lady Mordaunt was admitted to a lunatic asylum.
p. 22	l.31	colonel of the Prussian Hussars. Magnus, p. 228
p. 23	l.2	can be afflicted with. Ibid., p. 231
p. 23	l.20	bore him to death. Belloc-Lowndes, p. 253
p. 23	l.28	terrified of him. F. Ponsonby, p. 275
p. 23	l.33	out of date. Ibid., p. 244

p. 25 1.15 spirit of France. Magnus, p. 312
p. 25 1.27 favoured the *Entente Cordiale*. Magnus, p. 313
p. 25 1.32 suite of the American ambassador. Ibid., p. 364
p. 26 1.10 stick by his promises. Ibid., p. 341
p. 26 1.24 this is the greatest. Ibid., p. 400
p. 26 1.29 duty towards Humanity. Ibid., p. 321

Chapter Two: The Siege

p. 28 1.7   no harm done. Magnus, p. 265
p. 28 1.17 straight at us. Nicolson, *George V*, p. 59
p. 29 1.8   Aunty and Cousins. Magnus, p. 265
p. 29 1.25 were all madmen. E. Longford, p. 446
p. 30 1.8   that horrible man. Haslip, p. 439
p. 30 1.13 spared nothing. Ibid., p. 440
p. 30 1.32 member of my profession. Cowles, p. 273
p. 31 1.20 officers and soldiers. Gore, p. 212
p. 31 1.34 lucky people here. Ibid., p. 212
p. 32 1.4   threw the bomb. Ibid., p. 213
p. 32 1.20 height of the Troubles. Taylor, *Struggle for Mastery in Europe*, p. 520n
p. 32 1.25 could jump at me. Brook-Shepherd, *Victims at Sarajevo*, p. 235
p. 33 1.7   choke violently. Cassels, p. 179
p. 33 1.22 soda siphons. Christopher, p. 101
p. 34 1.1   Wied is a void. Pollo and Puto, p. 158
p. 34 1.14 loved his country and his people. Gore, p. 307
p. 34 1.22 ruined his country and himself. Ibid., p. 308
p. 34 1.28 rules of cricket. Wilhelm, p. 209
p. 35 1.9   *le Colonel Summerhayes*. Brook-Shepherd, *The Last Habsburg*, p. 224
p. 35 1.28 dear Gerald, the last. Hamilton, p. 26
p. 36 1.17 *Apart from Brown's, the role of other London hotels in the history of Balkan monarchy is not to be underestimated. It was at Claridge's in 1934 that the future Duke of Kent was introduced to Princess Marina of Greece, whom

he married at the end of the year. The exiled
Albanian court occupied an entire floor of the
Ritz in Piccadilly from 1940 to 1941. And in
1945 Claridge's once again featured in the
Balkan royal pageant, when a suite of rooms
was used for the birth of Crown Prince
Alexander of Yugoslavia (the suite was
designated Yugoslav territory for the day by
the British government).

p. 37   l.21   *C.B. Fry, *Life Worth Living*, pp. 296–300.
According to Fry, the Albanians were looking
for 'an English country gentleman with ten
thousand a year'. When an Albanian delegation
arrived in Geneva, where Fry was working for
the League of Nations, Fry's friend and former
Test match batting partner Prince Ranjitisinhji
arranged a meeting. Somewhat to his chagrin,
Fry heard no more from the Albanians.

p. 37   l.24   League of Nations. See bibliography

p. 39   l.2   *very* modern days. Pope-Hennessy, p. 408

Chapter Three: The Great Escape

p. 40   l.11   a nice distinction. H. Asquith, p. 285

p. 40   l.16   blue-eyed German. H. Asquith, p. 287

p. 40   l.21   my usefulness. Rose, p. 171

p. 41   l.13   St George's at Windsor. Ibid., p. 173

p. 41   l.25   living in it. Nicolson, *George V*, p. 38

p. 41   l.36   stick in stamps. Nicolson, *Diaries*, Vol. III, 17
August 1949, p. 174

p. 42   l.2   else in the world. Nicolson, *George V*, p. 51

p. 42   l.12   to say to me. Stevenson, p. 25

p. 42   l.17   alien and uninspiring Court. *The Times*, 21
April 1917

p. 42   l.19   if I'm alien. Nicolson, *George V*, p. 308

p. 42   l.20   started and grew pale. Ibid., p. 309

p. 42   l.29   Wipper or Wettin. Ibid., p. 309

p. 43   l.19   admire and envy you. Ibid., p. 310n

p. 43   l.24   House and Family of Windsor. Ibid., p. 310

p. 43   l.27   *Saxe-Coburg-Gotha*. Rose, p. 174

p. 44   l.4   about Arrr-r-rangement. Cust, p. 34

p. 44   l.18   on every subject. Nicolson, *George V*, p. 57

p. 44   l.22   the image of him. Lytton, p. 73

p. 44   l.33   in the past. Nicolson, *George V*, p. 299

p. 45   l.14   not to be refused. Rose, p. 211

p. 45   l.17   time of year. Ibid., p. 211

p. 45   l.27   residence in this country. Nicolson, *George V*, p. 301

p. 46   l.14   their Imperial Majesties? Rose, p. 212

p. 47   l.18   lovable figure. Taylor, *English History 1914–1945*, p. 142n

p. 47   l.24   accomplished in Russia. Nicolson, *George V*, p. 308

p. 47   l.28   and a snob. Webb, p. 65

p. 47   l.35   to Balmoral tomorrow. *The Times*, 5 September 1930

p. 48   l.5   lost his head. Nicolson, *George V*, p. 385

p. 48   l.8   common people like themselves. Nairn, p. 341

p. 48   l.22   future of the Empire!! Duke of Windsor, *A King's Story*, p. 123–124

p. 48   l.31   no Derby today. Airlie, p. 144

p. 49   l.3   no grandstand, enclosures, luncheons. H. Asquith, p. 487

p. 49   l.8   settle down. Nicolson, *George V*, p. 340

p. 49   l.13   never saw any. Nicolson, *George V*, p. 341

Chapter Four: Bertie in the Balkans

p. 50   l.18   gift from God! Bradford, p. 2

p. 51   l.2   get used to it. Ibid., p. 30

p. 51   l.7   or in naughtiness. Airlie, p. 113

p. 51   l.22   quite well again. Nicolson, *George V*, p. 278

p. 51   l.28   this little attack. Bradford, p. 70

p. 52   l.16   pushing like Hell! Hyde, p. 40

p. 53	l.4	a precious possession. Marie, p. 12
p. 53	l.8	once in a century. Pakula, p. 267
p. 53	l.23	awfully pleased. Wheeler-Bennett, p. 146
p. 54	l.3	richness of our land. Pakula, p. 319
p. 54	l.7	So very picturesque. Ibid., p. 319
p. 54	l.13	many flattering observations. Wheeler-Bennett, p. 146
p. 54	l.21	things are different now. Ibid., p. 192
p. 54	l.27	no hot water!! Ibid., p. 193
p. 54	l.32	the service altogether. Ibid., pp. 193–194
p. 55	l.7	next visit to London. Channon, 27 August 1937, p. 136
p. 55	l.17	better pleased I am. Forbes, p. 123
p. 55	l.29	palace gardens. Gunther, p. 418
p. 55	l.33	refound my mother. Forbes, p. 113
p. 56	l.4	utmost good friendship. Wentworth Day. *Princess Marina*, p. 94
p. 56	l.33	looked ridiculous. Channon, 28 January 1937, p. 57
p. 57	l.34	'M' – for Majesty. *Daily Herald*, 10 January 1938. Interview with Carol by A. L. Easterman
p. 58	l.13	autographs and stamps. *Nottingham Guardian*, 19 November 1938
p. 58	l.20	leaked to the newspapers. Hartnell, p. 94

Chapter Five: Ourselves Alone

p. 59	l.17	to remember me. Wheeler-Bennett, p. 422
p. 60	l.11	*Simeon eventually settled in Spain, where he has pursued a successful career in business. Married to a Spanish aristocrat, he has nonetheless sought to maintain his credentials as a plausible royal exile. In several interviews since the collapse of the communist Zhivkov regime in 1989, Simeon has indicated that he is willing to serve his former subjects, if they should choose to restore the monarchy.

p. 60	1.21	critical in this time. Ibid., p. 493
p. 60	1.28	the right decision. Ibid., p. 497
p. 60	1.36	weak and unfortunate prince. Channon, 9 April 1941, p. 299
p. 61	1.8	treated me very kindly. Peter, p. 91
p. 61	1.15	damned sloppy! Wheeler-Bennett, p. 737
p. 61	1.22	big washbowls. Peter, p. 125
p. 61	1.29	to Aunt Elizabeth. Ibid., p. 142
p. 62	1.28	can build a state. Fischer, p. 142
p. 62	1.34	Lloyd's Bank in London. Robyns, p. 104. The estimate was made by Sir Andrew Ryan, the British minister in Durres, Albania
p. 63	1.10	The acquaintance was Auberon Herbert, brother-in-law of Evelyn Waugh.
p. 63	1.18	*Leka's career as an exiled king has been colourful even by the standards of Balkan royalty. He has been arrested in Thailand for arms smuggling, and while living in Spain in the 1970s his fortress-like retreat was guarded by Shan tribesman from the hills of Burma. Since their expulsion from Spain as undesirable aliens, Leka and his consort Queen Susan – the daughter of a wealthy Australian sheep rancher – have made their home in South Africa. In 1993 Leka was refused entry to post-communist Albania for passport irregularities (his passport described him as King of the Albanians, a title no longer recognised in Tirana).
p. 63	1.29	far worse things too. Wheeler-Bennett, p. 450
p. 63	1.36	privacy and solitude. Power, p. 174
p. 64	1.23	no clothes with her. Wheeler-Bennett, p. 451
p. 64	1.27	hat for me. Crawford, p. 68
p. 65	1.8	looking for Germans. Wheeler-Bennett, p. 464
p. 65	1.17	'mixed up' his duties. Ibid., p. 455
p. 65	1.36	popularity of the King. *The Monarchy in Sweden* (The Swedish Institute), 1986, p. 14

p. 66   1.22   *Now in his seventies, Michael has not given up hope of returning permanently to Bucharest. There is a significant royalist movement in Romania, especially in the countryside, and the charitable activities of his eldest daughter Princess Margarita have raised the royal family's profile in the aftermath of the Ceausescu regime. In 1993, after persistent obstruction from the present authorities, Michael was allowed to visit his former kingdom. The odds against a restoration of the monarchy remain very long; but compared with his fellow Balkan exiles, Michael's prospects do not appear totally hopeless.

p. 66   1.35   on your other side! Frederica, p. 142

p. 67   1.5   after Palo's accession. Frederica devotes a whole chapter to her friendship with Marshall. See Frederica, pp. 113–128

p. 67   1.12   *is the Power Unseen.* Ibid., p. 145

p. 67   1.22   drinking too much. Private information

p. 67   1.25   shot themselves. Rose, p. 366

p. 68   1.12   partner in discussion. *The Monarchy in Sweden,* p. 15

p. 68   1.22   champion among Queens. Royal Danish Ministry of Foreign Affairs Factsheet (1990) p. 1

p. 68   1.30   stronger than before. *The Times* Royal Wedding Souvenir, 20 November 1947

p. 69   1.9   in South Africa, 1900. Official list of wedding gifts

p. 69   1.29   *Zog claimed to have fallen in love with the adolescent Alexandra on the basis of seeing her photograph. An emissary was sent to Venice, where Alexandra was living with her mother, with the purpose of luring the princess to Tirana. Alexandra's mother told the emissary

her daughter was too young for romance, and
soon afterwards Zog married a half-American
Hungarian countess, known to posterity as
Queen Geraldine of the Albanians.

p. 69	l.36	have a drink. Alexandra, p. 162
p. 70	l.7	at suitable moments!! Wheeler-Bennett, pp. 754–755
p. 70	l.27	but very much so. Bradford, p. 431

Chapter Six: David's Disgrace

p. 73	l.2	published his memoirs. *A King's Story*. See bibliography
p. 73	l.21	he ever said. Duke of Windsor, *A King's Story*, p. 57
p. 74	l.6	Royalty who displeased. Ibid., p. 60
p. 74	l.11	looked so nice. Nicolson, *George V*, p. 148
p. 74	l.23	seem a little silly. Duke of Windsor, *A King's Story*, p. 79
p. 74	l.27	person requiring homage. Ibid., p. 79
p. 74	l.33	against my position. Ibid., p. 133
p. 75	l.5	born and bred. Donaldson, p. 62
p. 75	l.13	satisfy the impulse. Duke of Windsor, *A King's Story*, p. 155
p. 75	l.27	on a pedestal. Ibid., p. 136
p. 75	l.36	break his neck. Lascelles, p. 50
p. 76	l.6	end of his nose. Lascelles, p. 65
p. 76	l.17	next morning. Lascelles, p. 109
p. 76	l.35	put you through. Donaldson, p. 159
p. 77	l.9	launch her socially. Channon, 5 April 1935, p. 30
p. 77	l.24	Horrible to see. Bradford, p. 147
p. 77	l.29	*morphia and cocaine. Watson, p. 28. It was because he administered this lethal potion that Dawson was able to state with such confidence, in a famous bulletin from the Sandringham deathbed, that 'the King's life is moving peacefully to its close'.

p. 78   l.14   its prestige. Duke of Windsor, *A King's Story*, p. 386

p. 78   l.19   concept of kingship. Ibid., p. 334

p. 78   l.29   refused a lesser sacrifice. Pope-Hennessy, *Queen Mary*, p. 575

p. 78   l.32   upon that sofa. Nicolson, *Diaries*, Vol. III, 21 March 1949, p. 167

p. 79   l.17   blue-and-white singlet. Diana Cooper, p. 175

p. 80   l.8   The storm breaks. Nicolson, *Diaries*, Vol. I, 3 December 1936, p. 281

p. 80   l.25   on the telephone. Channon, 9 December 1936, p. 98

p. 81   l.36   full of Cantuar! Donaldson, p. 298

Chapter Seven: David and the Germans

p. 83   l.12   one side of his head. Duke of Windsor, *A King's Story*, p. 97

p. 83   l.19   came from Alsace. Pope-Hennessy, *A Lonely Business*, p. 213

p. 84   l.5   no longer conceivable. Donaldson, p. 194

p. 84   l.11   the Great War. Ibid., p. 194

p. 84   l.21   seldom exposed. Ibid., p. 197

p. 84   l.31   Tell him that, please. Ibid., p. 199

p. 85   l.18   done it this time. Duff Cooper, p. 202

p. 85   l.24   an English king. Channon, 22 November 1936, p. 84

p. 86   l.27   a good Queen. Schmidt, p. 75

p. 87   l.22   so is *he*! Donaldson, p. 347

p. 87   l.31   the front line. Ibid., p. 351

p. 88   l.8   *Prince de Galles!* Duchess of Windsor, p. 335

p. 88   l.28   contact with him. Donaldson, p. 364

p. 89   l.5   came from Germany. Ibid., p. 364

p. 89   l.11   unless he does. Templewood to Halifax, 26 June 1940. Templewood Papers, Box XIII:20

p. 89   l.24   wishes of Government. Gilbert, Vol. VI, p. 698

p. 89	l.34	his brother will. Bradford, p. 435
p. 90	l.6	their stay here. Templewood to Halifax, 30 June 1940, 1 July 1940. Templewood Papers, Box XIII:20
p. 91	l.3	*Royal Librarian. The note illustrates the secretive attitude of the royal family towards their own recent (and not so recent) past, which has led to the periodic destruction of historical material by members of the family and loyal courtiers. When Victoria died in 1901, for example, many of her letters and journals were burnt by her youngest daughter and effective literary executor, Princess Beatrice. Almost all Edward VII's personal papers were destroyed when he died in 1910; and when Alexandra died in 1925, her lady-in-waiting Charlotte Knollys spent several days at Sandringham burning her mistress's letters.

The royal family has also been highly selective in granting access to the vast range of material which has survived this 'weeding' process and is housed in the royal archives at Windsor. Their preferred method has been to commission authors to produce 'official' biographies. Some of these works, like James Pope-Hennessy's 1959 biography of Queen Mary, have stood the test of time; others, like Sir John Wheeler-Bennett's 1958 biography of George VI (a stupendously tedious book) have not: but in all cases, the credibility of these 'official' biographies is undermined by the manner in which they were commissioned.

Harold Nicolson, whose own 1952 biography of George V is deeply flawed, experienced at first-hand the problems of being an official royal historian. In the summer of 1948 he was approached by the then Private Secretary, Sir Alan ('Tommy') Lascelles with the commission. 'I . . . said that in principle I did not like writing biographies when I could not tell the whole truth', Nicolson wrote to his wife after the meeting. 'Tommy said (well, I thought), "But it is not meant to be an ordinary biography. It is something quite different. You will be writing a book about a very ancient national institution, and you need not descend to personalities." He said that I should not be expected to write one word that was not true. I should not be expected to improvise or exaggerate. But I must omit things and incidents which were discreditable. I could say this in the preface if it would ease my mind.' [Nicolson, *Diaries* Vol III pp. 142–143].

Nicolson accepted the commission on these terms, and claimed to be favourably surprised by the lack of censorship exercised by Lascelles. In the light of Kenneth Rose's magnificent 1983 biography of George V (which used much material Nicolson had discarded) it is tempting to assume Lascelles' task was made easier by Nicolson's self-restraint.

Like other historians, this writer asked for permission to consult the royal archives at Windsor and received the usual courteous response. The archives were not open for general research, he was told; instead, the Deputy Keeper of the Archives invited him to consult the various official biographies and only then, if he still had queries, to submit a limited number of specific requests for material. In the absence of a published catalogue for the archives, this advice is virtually useless, and

until the archives are opened to the public, the
royal family's frequent complaints about ill-
informed authors will ring hollow.

p. 91	l.12	recalled to the throne. Ziegler, *Edward VIII*, p. 425
p. 91	l.22	dangerous adventures. Donaldson, p. 364
p. 91	l.28	event of peace. Ibid., p. 364
p. 92	l.17	propaganda for peace. Ziegler, p.425
p. 93	l.5	ready for peace. Huene to Ribbentrop, 11 July 1940. Templewood Papers, Box XIII:20
p. 93	l.14	readiness for further developments. Donaldson, p. 365
p. 93	l.36	return to Spain. Shirer, p. 788
p. 94	l.14	very pensive. Ibid., p. 788
p. 94	l.36	on that account. Donaldson, p. 375
p. 95	l.5	answer be made? Ibid., p. 375
p. 95	l.26	contempt it deserved. Shirer, p. 792
p. 95	l.32	the traitor's part. Ziegler, p. 435
p. 96	l.21	French Resistance. Donaldson, p. 377
p. 97	l.9	attack on London. Ziegler, p. 434

Chapter Eight: Bertie's War

p. 98	l.11	war canteens. Roosevelt, pp. 185–186
p. 98	l.20	champagne as usual. Templewood Papers: RFI. Notes on visit to Sandringham, 11–13 January 1945
p. 99	l.7	last for years. Corbitt, p. 67
p. 99	l.19	too expensive. Corbitt, p. 73
p. 99	l.31	sympathetic note possible. Hartnell, pp. 101–102
p. 99	l.35	*East End in the face. Wheeler-Bennett, p. 470. Like many of the elder Elizabeth's reported remarks, the quote has no direct attribution. Wheeler-Bennett cites a biography of Elizabeth by Betty Spencer Shew, whose source is anyone's guess.

p. 100 l.12   nobody is immune. Wheeler-Bennett, pp. 469–470

p. 100 l.20   very wonderful. Bradford, p. 325

p. 100 l.29   a phenomenon? Nicolson, *Diaries*, Vol. II, p. 128. Nicolson to Vita Sackville-West, 20 November 1940

p. 100 l.32   since Cleopatra. Nicolson, *Diaries*, Vol. I, p. 405. Nicolson to Vita Sackville-West, 23 June 1939

p. 101 l.5   their six houses. Mortimer, p. 179

p. 101 l.21   may be helpful. Bradford, p. 303

p. 101 l.36   bluff had been called. Killearn, p. 107

p. 102 l.10   at this moment. Bradford, pp. 310–311

p. 102 l.16   have him as PM. Ibid., pp. 312–313

p. 102 l.28   hard times of war. Gilbert, Vol. VII, p. 251

p. 102 l.31   what you have done. Wheeler-Bennett, p. 553

p. 103 l.1   ought to send. Bradford, p. 340. Cazalet unpublished diary, 3 June 1942

p. 103 l.5   Who will tell him? Ibid., p. 340. Cazalet unpublished diary, 19 August 1942

p. 103 l.16   remain at home and wait. Wheeler-Bennett, p. 603

p. 103 l.19   care about the future. Bradford, p. 359

p. 103 l.25   liked to do myself? Wheeler-Bennett, p. 605

p. 103 l.29   indeed commands. Ibid., p. 606

p. 104 l.2   and Winston wouldn't. Private information.

p. 104 l.12   undertake it at all. Macmillan, p. 120

p. 104 l.23   you've got to. Bradford, p. 327

p. 104 l.35   behaving well. Bradford, p. 354

p. 105 l.2   spoke in good French. Macmillan, p. 122

p. 105 l.8   distant part of the USA. Ibid., p. 123

p. 105 l.18   interested in them. Mass Observation File Report No. 247, 4 July 1940

p. 106 l.2   use they ever had. Mass Observation File Report No. 219OD, 4 December 1944

p. 106 l.23   beauty of the whole. Nicolson, *Diaries*, Vol. II, p. 462. Letter to Nigel Nicolson, 17 May 1945

Chapter Nine: The Royal Learning Curve

p. 108 l.1   ruler with brains? Stevenson, p. 25

p. 108 l.6   not much in his head. Lloyd George, p. 153

p. 108 l.9   I would be an idiot. Rhodes James, p. 255

p. 108 l.16   mental powers. Rose, p. 8

p. 109 l.2   *to read*. Ibid., p. 21

p. 109 l.4   grammatical construction. Ibid., p. 21

p. 109 l.22   country squire. Gore, p. 375

p. 109 l.28   power in him. Nicolson, p. 8

p. 109 l.35   Harriet Beecher Stowe. Gore, pp. 447–450

p. 110 l.2   furniture, furniture. Rose, p. 288

p. 110 l.4   Turner was *mad*. K. Clark, p. 236

p. 110 l.7   something to make you laugh. Rose, p. 317

p. 110 l.12   It shall be done. Jones, p. 113

p. 110 l.19   Canon C.C. Dobson. Bradford, p. 113

p. 110 l.27   obvious sincerity. Mortimer, p. 179

p. 110 l.31   bewildering rapidity. Wheeler-Bennett, p. 735

p. 111 l.2   verbal webs. Rose, p. xiv

p. 111 l.8   things in general. Ibid., p. 182

p. 111 l.11   millions of shells. Lloyd George, p. 153

p. 111 l.17   race horses etc. Rose, p. 183

p. 111 l.19   *George inherited the crisis from his father Edward VII. It was provoked by Lloyd George's 'People's Budget' of 1909, which proposed some modest social welfare measures, to be financed in part by a series of land taxes. The budget was assured passage through the Commons, where the governing Liberals had an overwhelming majority; but in the Lords, the Tories had an inbuilt majority of recalcitrant peers who, fearing for their estates and the advent of 'socialism', repeatedly blocked the finance bill. At issue was whether unelected

aristocrats could overturn the 'democratic' will
of the people, represented by the Liberal
majority in the Commons. The crisis was
finally resolved in August 1911 when the Lords
passed the Parliament Bill by a slender
majority, denying themselves the ultimate right
of veto over measures passed in the lower house.

p. 111	l.32	low-down trick. Rose, p. 125
p. 112	l.2	So is the Queen. Lloyd George, pp. 158–159
p. 112	l.12	resented this. Bradford, p. 385
p. 112	l.20	treated fairly. Nicolson, *George V*, p. 389
p. 112	l.27	like his views. Bradford, p. 385
p. 113	l.5	be the end? Gaitskell, p. 244, pp. 250–251
p. 113	l.11	an automaton. Webb, p. 2. 19 January 1924
p. 113	l.12	join them? Lord Longford, p. 159
p. 113	l.20	of the expense. Nicolson, *George V*, p. 391
p. 113	l.28	on simple ground. Thomas, p. 158
p. 113	l.34	your crockery. Bradford, p. 387
p. 114	l.10	*Uncle Fred in the Springtime*. Crawford, p. 51
p. 114	l.17	useful limited monarchs. Bagehot, p. 258
p. 114	l.22	an adequate force. *The Economist*, 15 April 1871
p. 114	l.30	with the Crown. Nicolson, *George V*, p. 62
p. 115	l.14	a common good. Rose, p. 376
p. 115	l.36	painless illness. A. Ponsonby, p. 406
p. 116	l.7	too much crape. Ibid., p. 390
p. 116	l.13	space of time. Ibid., p. 37
p. 116	l.20	democratic monarchy. Victoria, *Letters and Journals*, p. 266. Victoria to W.E. Forster, 25 December 1880
p. 116	l.26	eighty-two and a half. E. Longford, p. 518
p. 116	l.33	sing your praises. A. Ponsonby, p. 150
p. 117	l.8	the other papers. Ibid., p. 48
p. 117	l.17	in my confidence. Nicolson, *George V*, p. 65
p. 117	l.19	be a King. Ibid., p. 452
p. 117	l.24	low, rich, poor. A. Ponsonby, pp. 402–403

p.117 1.34   cast out fear. *Dictionary of National Biography*
                     1931–1940, p. 77

p. 118 1.7   a public nature. Knollys to Asquith, 16
                     February 1913. Copy in Crewe Papers,
                     Cambridge University Library, C58.

p. 118 1.19   with the Crown. Rose, p. 141

p. 118 1.24   own reward. Ibid., p. 141

p. 118 1.35   officer at Aldershot. Ibid., p. 145

p. 119 1.2   understand things. Ibid., p. 370

p. 119 1.10   light under a bushel. Ibid., p. 226

p. 119 1.10   smile on duty. Gore, p. 148

p. 119 1.16   the Labour forwards. Rose, p. 371

p. 119 1.24   sign of fatigue. Gore, p. 409. Wigram to
                     Archbishop Lang, 27 August 1931

p. 120 1.14   leaving party. Private information

p. 121 1.1   distributions of power. *The Times*, 20 November
                     1947

Chapter Ten: At Home with George and Bertie

p. 122 1.18   Royal Academy pictures. Nicolson, *Diaries*,
                     Vol. III, p. 175. 4 October 1949

p. 123 1.12   hideous and gloomy. Pope-Hennessy, *A Lonely
                     Business*, p. 226

p. 124 1.4   all over the country. R. Clark, p. 46

p. 124 1.12   which they don't. Ibid., p. 56

p. 124 1.15   one at Balmoral. Ibid., p. 56

p. 124 1.30   singularly fatuous exercise. Rose, p. 286

p. 125 1.6   without being luxurious. Benson, p. 11

p. 125 1.11   contemporary authors. Ibid., p. 11

p. 125 1.18   at Surbiton. Nicolson, *Diaries*, Vol. III, p. 175.
                     4 October 1949

p. 125 1.35   settled in well. Sitwell, p. 34

p. 126 1.21   rest of her life. Airlie, p. 158

p. 127 1.14   charming in it. Curzon, p. 111

p. 127 1.29   for the guns. Buxton, pp. 93–94

p. 128 1.4   last much longer? Rose, p. 100

p. 128	l.11	too far today. Duke of Windsor, *A King's Story*, pp. 86–87
p. 128	l.24	pulled the trigger. Rose p. 360
p. 129	l.26	the damned fool. Wilson, p. 41
p. 130	l.11	could not acquire. Ibid., p. 40
p. 130	l.20	all we want. K. Clark, p. 238
p. 130	l.33	National Portrait Gallery. Ibid., p. 236
p. 131	l.10	excellent factory inspector. Pope-Hennessy, p. 472
p. 131	l.18	dear little cabinet. Rose, p. 284
p. 131	l.33	*ought* to know. Bradford, p. 408
p. 132	l.25	duller than the King. Rose, p. 96
p. 133	l.24	played during dinner. Duke of Windsor, *A King's Story*, p. 184
p. 133	l.26	high-hat business. Bradford, p. 299
p. 133	l.36	men were swimming. Roosevelt, pp. 159–160
p. 134	l.6	a stop-watch. Ibid. p. 156

Chapter Eleven: Keeping Up Appearances

p. 135	l.2	complete privacy. Channon diary, 14 June 1923, in Rose, p. 299
p. 135	l.12	take your hat off. Bradford, p. 125
p. 135	l.22	to be taken. Ibid., p. 124
p. 136	l.5	red kilt. Duke of Windsor, *A Family Album*, p. 24
p. 136	l.18	was very smart. Ibid., p. 184
p. 136	l.23	Army in India. Ibid., p. 185
p. 137	l.1	at the Fort. Ibid., p. 34
p. 137	l.11	with his game. Ibid., p. 30
p. 137	l.17	this outfit home! Ibid., p. 41
p. 137	l.23	upside down. Ruffer, p. 65
p. 138	l.24	herself did so. Hardinge, p. 30
p. 139	l.4	temper leads you. Thackeray, p. 21
p. 139	l.13	neglected nothing. Victoria, *Letters and Journals*, p. 297. Victoria to Ponsonby, 26 February 1886

_p. 139_ l.18   damned if she would. A. Ponsonby, p. 64

_p. 139_ l.32   passed before her. Airlie, p. 40

_p. 140_ l.4   mass of MPs. F. Ponsonby, p. 33

_p. 140_ l.21   *Edwardian court. The full story is told by
                   David Cannadine in his brilliant 1983 essay on
                   the British monarchy and the invention of
                   tradition. See bibliography.

_p. 141_ l.2   know is wonderful. Esher, 22 January 1901

_p. 141_ l.13   very fine. Ibid., 20 October 1901

_p. 141_ l.20   _Basta!_ Ibid., 18 November 1901

_p. 144_ l.27   full evening dresses. Airlie, p. 161

_p. 144_ l.36   in a taxi. Nicolson, _Diaries_, Vol. I, 17 March
                   1937, p. 296

_p. 145_ l.19   head kept up. _Court Ceremonial_, p. 38

_p. 145_ l.24   dislocated her knee. Corbitt, p. 26

_p. 146_ l.18   this kind of thing now. Gaitskell, p. 78

_p. 147_ l.9   more interesting. Airlie, p. 239

Chapter Twelve: The Royal Variety Show

_p. 148_ l.6   with real joy. Victoria, _Letters and Journals_, 22
                   June 1897, p. 335

_p. 149_ l.4   whole world. Nicolson, _George V_, p. 526

_p. 149_ l.23   his prejudices. Cannadine, _The British Monarchy_,
                   p. 109

_p. 149_ l.31   manner and behaviour. Greville, p. 312

_p. 150_ l.20   under every trial. Victoria, _Letters and Journals_, 8
                   December 1864, p. 186

_p. 150_ l.23   *Since the late 1980s, republicanism has
                   experienced a revival in Britain. But to date
                   (1994), no contemporary mainstream politician
                   of the stature of Sir Charles Dilke has raised
                   the republican standard – notwithstanding
                   Tony Benn's commitment to the cause. In
                   February 1993 the Labour front-bench
                   spokesman Jack Straw called for reform of the
                   monarchy along bicycle-riding continental

lines, but fell short of demanding the institution's abolition.

p. 151 l.8   let it come. Jenkins, p. 70

p. 151 l.27   they were wrong. Ibid., p. 86

p. 152 l.11   with his hat off. Victoria, *Letters and Journals*, 27 February 1872, p. 216

p. 153 l.34   back to my room. E. Longford, p. 501

p. 155 l.12   and a Queen. *Daily Mail*, 23 June 1897

p. 155 l.21   countries of the world. *Vanity Fair*, 23 June 1897

p. 156 l.15   The survey. Mass Observation Day Survey, 12 May 1937. See bibliography

p. 157 l.10   our King. Jennings, p. 116

p. 157 l.18   ancient seal. Ibid., p. 121

p. 157 l.25   could be taken. Wheeler-Bennett, p. 312

p. 157 l.34   nearly fell down. Ibid., p. 313

p. 158 l.6   against their will. Jennings, p. 116

p. 158 l.11   her granddaughters. Ibid., p. 131

p. 158 l.14   What a coach! Ibid., p. 134

p. 158 l.23   a nap. Ibid., p. 271

p. 158 l.28   had been judged. Ibid., p. 255

p. 159 l.1   to move off. Ibid., p. 197

p. 159 l.8   shortest time. Ibid., p. 32

p. 159 l.18   crowning ceremony. Ibid., p. 245

p. 160 l.2   just it. Bradford p. 144

p. 160 l.10   by Fabergé. Windsor, p. 183

p. 160 l.16   middle class of her subjects. E. Longford, p. 567

p. 160 l.26   man in the tube. Asquith to Venetia Stanley, 18 March 1915

p. 160 l.34   Minister of Labour. Bradford, p. 331

p. 161 l.3   for the night. Private information

p. 161 l.12   an astonishing memory. *The Times*, 11 December 1936

p. 161 l.26   *The sequence has been broken on four occasions: in 1936, due to David's abdication earlier that month; in 1938, when Bertie refused to broadcast; in 1964, when Elizabeth was preoccupied by the birth of Prince Edward (she delivered a short pre-recorded greeting instead); and in 1969, when she and Philip feared over-exposure so soon after the BBC film 'Royal Family.'

p. 162 1.18 broken in half. Pope-Hennessy, *Queen Mary*, p. 594

p. 162 1.34 did not fear. Churchill radio broadcast, 7 February 1952

p. 163 1.10 for a long time. *Sunday Pictorial*, 9 September 1951

p. 164 1.3 Please try. Cameron, p. 328

p. 164 1.9 full of beans. Ibid., p. 328

p. 164 1.25 showed a shadow. Bradford, p. 452

p. 165 1.12 dignity, patience and courage. Cameron, pp. 41–43. *Illustrated London News*, 23 February 1952

p. 165 1.19 employed to do. Cameron, p. 41

Chapter Thirteen: Margaret, Getting Down To It

p. 169 1.4 something about it. Coster, *Princess Margaret Gift Book* Vol. II, 1953, unnumbered.

p. 170 1.10 Peter Townsend. Batchelor, *Princess Margaret Gift Book* Vol. I, 1952, unnumbered

p. 170 1.29 become one. Ibid.

p. 172 1.10 brilliance and distinction. Crawford, p. 93

p. 172 1.15 small ornaments. Ibid., p. 97

p. 172 1.18 a good time. Ibid., p. 120

p. 172 1.28 a joke. Ibid., p. 120

p. 173 1.27 his autobiography. *Time and Chance*. See bibliography

p. 174 1.3 sorely troubled us. Townsend, p. 195

p. 174 1.12 half-embrace. Judd, *Philip*, p. 232

p. 175 1.31 my dreams. Townsend, p. 189

p. 176 1.18 capital N. *Royalty Annual*, 1955

p. 176 l.35   politely and left. Coward, 6 June 1954

p. 177 l.9   works of the Brontës. *Royalty Annual*, 1956

p. 177 l.24   to criticise. Nickolls, *The Queen's Year, 1956*, 6 February 1956

p. 178 l.5   Prince of Prussia. Victoria, *Leaves*, 29 September 1855, p. 107

p. 178 l.27   of the country. *The Times*, 1 November 1955

p. 179 l.29   has ever been. Pearson, p. 119

Chapter Fourteen: Elizabeth, Getting On With It

p. 180 l.3   left hook. Crawford, p. 33

p. 180 l.9   curls blue. Ibid., p. 21

p. 181 l.2   justice with mercy. Ibid., p. 85

p. 181 l.18   happy marriages. Ibid., p. 20

p. 181 l.24   me personally. Ibid., p. 28

p. 182 l.12   night with them. Ibid., p. 84

p. 182 l.35   even talk about it. Judd, *Philip*, p. 131

p. 183 l.13   in our Navy. Channon, 21 January 1941, p. 287

p. 183 l.17   what I mean? Judd, *Philip*, p. 110

p. 184 l.16   quarterdeck language. Judd, p. 167

p. 185 l.12   I will be good. E. Longford, p. 32

p. 185 l.23   give me your opinion? Roosevelt, p. 230

p. 185 l.34   pompous platitudes? *BBC Book of Royal Memories* p. 33

p. 187 l.21   knee breeches. Dean, p. 161

p. 188 l.29   on 3 March. References from Nickolls, *Our Sovereign Lady*.

p. 190 l.1   but she can't. For similar views, see Richard Hoggart's study of working-class attitudes to royalty in *The Uses of Literacy*, p. 92

Chapter Fifteen: Philip, Getting Stuck In

p. 191 l.5   in my life. Judd, *Philip*, p. 183

p. 191 l.9   to happen now. Ibid., p. 185

p. 191 l.17   very considerably. Boothroyd, p. 49

p. 192 l.12   don't exist. Judd, *Philip*, p. 192

p. 192 l.32   come to me. Boothroyd, p. 50

p. 193 l.13   twentieth century. Philip, *Speeches, 1956–1959*,
                     p. 14

p. 193 l.17   let up. Boothroyd, p. 226

p. 194 l.12   fifteen mattresses. Philip, *Speeches, 1948–1955*,
                     p. 35

p. 194 l.14   High Productivity. Ibid., 15 October 1953,
                     p. 72

p. 194 l.22   an editorial. Nickolls, *The Queen's Year, 1954*,
                     1 December 1954

p. 195 l.9   national value? Boothroyd, p. 223

p. 195 l.22   in the community. S. Clark, p. 191

p. 196 l.31   serious decline. Pearson p. 172

p. 198 l.22   just a grand conception. Nickolls, *The Queen's
                     Year, 1957*, 26 February 1957

p. 198 l.29   quite unique. Philip, *World Tour 1956–1957*.
                     Unnumbered.

p. 200 l.23   lean years and famine. Nickolls, *The Queen's
                     Year, 1957*, 26 February 1957

Chapter Sixteen: The Royal Boredom Threshold

p. 202 l.14   no doubt. *National and English Review*,
                     September 1957

p. 204 l.4   24 per cent undecided. Ibid.

p. 204 l.14   opposing camp. Harris, p. 77

p. 204 l.22   among churchgoers. Ibid., p. 78

p. 204 l.33   waste of money. Ibid., p. 79

p. 205 l.9   national prestige. Ibid., p. 137

p. 205 l.28   Freddie Reed. *Daily Mirror*, 21 April 1965

p. 206 l.9   simply indifferent. Pearson, p. 168

p. 207 l.7   kicked by both sides. *Daily Mirror*, 26 February
                     1964

p. 207 l.36   *Hall, *Royal Fortune*. See bibliography. Hall's
                     book is by far the most detailed analysis of the
                     royal family's and the monarchy's finances – and
                     the confusion between the two.

p. 208 1.8   lost it all. Private information

 p. 211 1.25   as *Royal Family. Listener*, 9 October 1986

Chapter Seventeen: Royal Family, The Film of the Myth

p. 214 1.19   TV in future. Pearson, p. 199

p. 218 1.9   public relations man's dream. *Evening Standard*, 25 June 1969

p. 218 1.20   know so well. Crawford, p. 9

p. 219 1.2   had grown worse. Anne Edwards, *Matriarch* (1984), p. 292

p. 219 1.10   children's love affairs. Airlie, p. 167

p. 219 1.24   would ever marry. Davidson, p. 109

p. 220 1.13   clubs are in gloom. Channon unpublished diary, 16 January 1923, quoted in Rose, p. 312

p. 221 1.12   episode of *Popeye*. Russell, p. 176

p. 221 1.22   *their recovery. Bruce Lockhart, 28 April 1932 p. 215. Both Lockhart and Churchill, however, were notoriously unreliable witnesses.

p. 221 1.26   *successfully, it seems. Prince George appears to have been introduced to cocaine by an American girl called Kiki Whitney Preston. This murky story, and the rumours about his homosexual affairs, is perhaps why – apart from the epileptic Prince John – he is the only one of George V's six children yet to be accorded an official biography.

p. 221 1.33   unselfish and conscientious. Bradford, p. 94

p. 222 1.10   blossomed as a widow. Private information

p. 222 1.31   going forward. Ring, p. 16

p. 222 1.36   upon her throne. Ibid., p. 20

p. 223 1.9   full for tears. Ibid., p. 126

p. 223 1.17   speedwell blue. C. Asquith, p. 81

p. 223 1.27   paramount importance. Sheridan, *Our Princesses at Home*. Unnumbered

p. 224 1.7   in the same way. Sheridan, *Playtime at Royal Lodge,* p. 18

p. 224 1.27   equally harmonious. Sheridan, *A Day with
                      Prince Andrew*. Unnumbered.
p. 225 1.31   Princess of Wales. *BBC Book of Royal Memories*,
                      p. 176

Chapter Eighteen: Enter the Ratpack
p. 229 1.10   come what may. *Majesty*, November 1988
p. 230 1.17   quite a reputation. *Royal Year Book*, 1978
p. 231 1.34   scoop after scoop. *Majesty*, November 1988
p. 234 1.14   editor wants written. *Majesty*, February 1986
p. 235 1.11   rectify the situation. *Majesty*, March 1983
p. 236 1.24   not a pop star. Boothroyd, p. 38

Chapter Nineteen: The Advent of Fergie
p. 238 1.10   only so big. *Majesty*, October 1983
p. 240 1.24   valued at £150,000. Pearson, p. 260
p. 241 1.33   ever been to. *Majesty*, January 1989
p. 242 1.36   utterly ludicrous. Charles, *Watercolours*, p. 12
p. 243 1.20   have a go. Andrew, p. 7
p. 243 1.30   interesting as possible. Ibid., p. 14
p. 244 1.10   for the cameras. *Majesty*, November 1986
p. 244 1.21   worry her unduly. *Majesty*, August 1988
p. 244 1.26   teddy bear. *Guardian*, 29 December 1989
p. 244 1.32   in that family. *Majesty*, August 1988
p. 245 1.24   a kitchen knife. *Majesty*, July 1990

Chapter Twenty: Diana's Dilemma
p. 250 1.22   day by day. Burnet, p. 7
p. 250 1.34   *quasi-authorised biography. Whether or not
                      Diana formally authorised Morton's biography,
                      there is no doubt that she knew and approved
                      of the project.
p. 252 1.16   pretty unusual. Charles, *In His Own Words*, p. 85
p. 252 1.23   for life. Ibid., pp. 85–86.
p. 252 1.36   described as love. Dimbleby, p. 278
p. 253 1.4   virtually no contact. Ibid, p. 395

p. 253 1.10   any other person. Ibid, p. 395
p. 253 1.31   ever seen before. Holden, *Charles*, p. 259
p. 255 1.25   marginalising his wife. *Daily Mail*, 8 April
                    1993
p. 257 1.36   vividly and often seen. *The Economist*,
                    10 October 1874
p. 266 1.18   is feeling down. *Sunday Times*, 13 November
                    1994

Chapter Twenty-One: The Long March of the Prince of Wales

p. 271 1.14   he will inherit. *Mail on Sunday*, 12 December
                    1993
p. 271 1.17   his predecessors. *Sunday Telegraph*, 12 December
                    1993
p. 272 1.15   tabloid excesses. Dimbleby, p. 501
p. 272 1.26   biography is based. Dimbleby, pp. xvii–xviii
p. 274 1.15   would merely confirm. Dimbleby, p. xix
p. 274 1.32   distinction and virtue. Dimbleby, p. 566
p. 275 1.25   *rather than privately. Although the future
                    Edward VIII did receive the skeleton of a
                    'normal' upper-class education at Osborne,
                    Dartmouth and Magdalen College, Oxford.
p. 276 1.33   hole this place! Dimbleby, p. 65
p. 277 1.13   education can do. *Observer*, 9 June 1974
p. 284 1.32   have been making. Charles, *Vision*, p. 19
p. 285 1.6   reactionary or worse. Charles, *Highgrove*, p. 13

Chapter Twenty-Two: Elizabeth, Still Getting On With It

p. 291 1.1   puff of smoke. *Royal Year, 1974*
p. 291 1.12   questions later. Ibid.
p. 291 1.18   where he died. Ibid.
p. 291 1.36   a public menace. *The Independent*, 22 September
                    1993
p. 292 1.19   dividing us. Christmas broadcast, 1974
p. 294 1.8   five poond. Lytton, p. 36

p. 294	1.10	*écossais demain*. F. Ponsonby, p. 150
p. 294	1.14	sporran and skean-dhu. Rose, p. 91
p. 294	1.31	in my life. Buchanan, House of Commons debates, 10 December 1936
p. 295	1.27	Sword of State. Innes. Unnumbered.
p. 300	1.4	you actually need? Dimbleby, p. 503
p. 300	1.10	end the monarchy. *Independent on Sunday*, 23 October 1994

No references for Chapter Twenty-Three and Envoi.

Acknowledgements

The idea for this book came from an article I wrote for the *Independent on Sunday Review* in December 1991 about the British royal family and their continental relatives. I am very grateful to Liz Jobey and Richard Williams for encouraging me to write the piece, and for the interest they have shown in the book ever since.

I would also like to thank Ian Jack, Peter Wilby and Brian Cathcart at the *Independent on Sunday*, who commissioned me to write further pieces on the monarchy, which helped me to clarify my thoughts during research for the book; and Fiammetta Rocco, who wrote a magisterial article on Prince Philip for the *Independent on Sunday* in December 1992, and has been extremely generous in sharing her ideas with me. The staff of the *Independent*'s library have, as ever, answered all my journalistic requests with speed and efficiency. I am grateful to all of them.

During research, I have met and interviewed various past and present members of the royal household. I regret that most of these interviewees wished to remain anonymous, but would like to thank them collectively for agreeing to see me. On many occasions their first-hand knowledge of post-war royal history shed new light on the subject, especially regarding the family they were called to serve.

One courtier who did agree to talk on the record was Sir Edward Ford, Assistant Private Secretary to George VI and the present Queen from 1946 to 1967. He has been unfailingly helpful in answering my questions about the court since the Second World War, even though, like his former colleagues, he may not agree with my conclusions. I am most grateful for his time and patience.

Throughout my research, the Buckingham Palace press office has been an invaluable source of information and advice on the monarchy (again, with no foreknowledge of my eventual conclusions). I would also like to thank the staff of the Cambridge University Library, where I did the academic research for the book.

At Little, Brown, Alan Samson commissioned the book and has been generous with his time and support throughout the project. I am very grateful indeed to Helga Houghton for her advice and help during editing, and to Linda Silverman for her picture research.

My stepfather, Humphry Crum Ewing, has been an endless source of information about the monarchy and the constitution, as well as keeping me up to date with events in Parliament concerning the royal family. Mark Redhead, whose ITV television series on the monarchy remains the best documentary about the Windsors, prevented me on several occasions from losing my way in the royal thickets.

In Cambridge, Amanda and Kevin Jones put me up (and put up with the monarchy) for weeks on end while I was working in the University Library. I am extremely grateful to both of them.

This book would never have been written without my agent, Jane Turnbull, who has been tireless on my behalf over the past two years. From the original proposal to eventual publication, she has kept the project (and sometimes the author) on the rails. I thank her again for all her help.

Above all, I wish to thank Tess for her constant encouragement, for her advice at every stage of research, and for her skill and patience in editing the various drafts of the book. I can never thank her enough, and it is to her that the book is dedicated.

Picture Credits

The author and publisher are grateful to the sources listed below for pictures reproduced in the book, as follows:

Section I

12 Buckingham Palace garden party *(copyright HM The Queen, courtesy of Royal Archives, Windsor Castle)*

13 Edward VII *(Illustrated London News Picture Library)*

14 George V's children at Balmoral *(Topham)*

15 George V at Windsor *(copyright HM The Queen, courtesy of Royal Archives, Windsor Castle)*

Section II

16 Edward VII at Sandringham *(Popperfoto)*

17 George V in Nepal *(Illustrated London News Picture Library)*

18 Queen Mary in Edinburgh *(copyright HM The Queen, courtesy of Royal Archives, Windsor Castle)*

19 Queen Victoria's family at Coburg *(Illustrated London News Picture Library)*

20 Tsar Nicholas II and his cousin George *(copyright HM The Queen, courtesy of Royal Archives, Windsor Castle)*

21 The christening of the future King Peter of Yugoslavia *(Popperfoto)*

22 Bertie, Elizabeth, Lilibet and Margaret *(Syndication International)*

23 Prince Philip and Michael Parker *(Popperfoto)*

24 It's a Royal Knockout *(all pictures: Photographers International)*

25 Charles and Diana in South Korea *(Press Association/Topham)*

26 Princess Diana in Sudbury *(East Anglian Daily Times)*

27 Prince Charles in Caister *(Prince's Trust/Stuart Colwill Photography)*

28 & 29
Queen Elizabeth in Hull *(Hull Daily Mail Publications)*

Pages xii–xvi
Camera Press; Royal Archives, Windsor Castle; Popperfoto; Syndication International; Richard Gillard; Tim Graham; Anwar Hussein.

Index